PIT BOSS WOOD PELLET GRILL & SMOKER COOKBOOK

The Most Complete Guide to Be a Top Pitmaster. 600+ Easy and

Tasty Recipes. Includes Exclusive Tips & Tricks for Perfect

Smoking

Danny Carpenter

Table of Contents

Introduction

Occasionally, many people ask about a grill that can also be used as a smoker. These are usually gas grills with a smart technology of converting the fuel to wood pellets in order to fire up the grill and use it as an outdoor smoker. The term "pellet smoker" is often used interchangeably with "wood pellet grill".

We will introduce you to the wood pellet smokers and barbecue grills available on the market today. We will also show how easy they are to operate and maintain, what types of food they can prepare for you, as well as their durability and performance ratings.

When it comes to smoking your meat, pellet smokers are always in the running. They offer a ton of versatility with their ability to cook different types of food. What's more, they're some of the most affordable smokers available today. But among all those benefits, does pellet smoking really live up to its hype? Let's take a look at this question and find out more about how this type of smoker has developed over time!

It's hard to believe that, before the late 1940s, smokers were typically heated with coal or wood. It was only when World War II ravaged Europe's forests that we transitioned from coal to wood. This didn't go without problem. And so began the search for an alternative fuel source: one that could be produced cheaply and in volume and wouldn't spoil as easily as traditional woods like hickory and mesquite. That new fuel turned out to be sawdust or wood pellets (hence their nicknames: sawdust smokers and pellet grills).

Wood pellets, which are all-natural compressed wood chips (and sometimes sawdust), came into vogue when sawmills were clamoring for an alternative fuel source to provide the millions of tons of biomass they were producing each year. But the Japanese government made wood pellets too expensive for many Americans to afford and caused sawmilling companies in the States to close their doors – including most notably our nation's largest pellet producer, Oregon-based Pacific Northwest Pile Products.

Nowadays, however, wood pellet grills are a popular choice among homeowners and smokers alike. Their small size is perfect for a compact family, but their portability and fuel-efficient design means they're useful in the field. And they work on every kind of fuel, which means you can use them to fire up almost any sort of grill – from charcoal to gas grills – or even to light up those hard-to-get-rid-of campfires.

Wood Pellets of Old

Because wood pellets did not exist until after World War II, the technology to make and use them wasn't around at the time. And so during that war, US soldiers used sawdust mixed with sawdust, and they didn't get the quality of smoke that we're used to from these days. However, sawdust isn't necessarily a bad choice for the big outdoor family gathering – its great for adding flavor to foods like hamburgers and steaks – but it doesn't put off nearly as much smoke as wood pellets can. In fact, some experts believe that old-fashioned campfire cooking with wood and charcoal is better suited for your health than cooking any other way – including with wood pellets.

It all started around 1950s when members of an American Society for Outdoor cookery were looking for an alternative fuel source that would be easier on nature. They eventually discovered that wood pellets could be used instead of charcoal to support the flavors of the meat.

The first pellet smoker was built in 1975 by Frank and John Mayer. It was called the "Trail Boss" and it was made from a 55-gallon drum with a garden auger inside to feed the pellets. More improvements were made in 1981 when two brothers Jim and Bob Hickman built their own modified version. This particular smoker would later be rebranded as "Smokey Mountain Cooker" by Steve Latham, owner of Camp Chef Inc until 1988. In 2001, Camp Chef released Smokey Mountain Cooker II which featured improved thermodynamics and design tweaks to make it more user friendly.

Several years later, other brands started incorporating their own version of the smoker as well. It was during this time that smokers like Dyna-Glo became popular choices for outdoor cooking enthusiasts with its affordable price range and incredible performance.

The word "smoker" has been shortened from "smokehouse". Smokehouses/smokers did two things, they produced smoke and were used to preserve foods. Smokehouses were generally large so that they could contain several large fires. Besides smoking, today some of them are also used as a place to dry out products such as sausage and jerky until they are ready for storage, or smoked fish for example. However, from the late 19th century onwards smokehouses became increasingly less common on the American landscape as people ceased smoking (at least indoors) in favor of kerosene lighting, coal stoves and other modern heating methods.

Many of the smokers can also be used as grills, which is why I have given them a separate section for their description.

The best way to cook food is in a way that brings out the natural flavors of the ingredients. There are many different types of smokers on the market, and they each have their own unique features. One example would be a pellet smoker. When it comes to these types of smokers, wood pellets make quick work of cooking your food because they heat up very fast, unlike charcoal or firewood that you would need to spend hours upon hours preparing before cooking begins.

Even with the benefits of wood pellets, there are many other types of smokers on the market.

When you grill a lot, you will probably notice that your pellet grill gets very hot.

The best part about having an excellent pellet smoker is that there are so many different options to choose from. If you are new to the market, the selection can appear a bit daunting at first glance. Not every model is meant for beginners, and some may even require a little more skill than others.

After taking a look at some of the best smokers that are currently on the market, it is now time to list down some of the things that you should be looking for in a smoker. The first thing that you need to do is consider your needs and budget before jumping off into a head first frenzy. If you are planning on being able to use your smoker on a regular basis, then you may need something larger than someone who only uses it for special occasions.

Things to Consider

When purchasing a smoker, there are several things that you should keep in mind. For starters, decide whether you want an electric model or a more traditional charcoal or propane model. We recommend that you stay away from the electric models as they do not perform to the same level as charcoal and propane models.

Replacing your smoker is not cheap, and neither is rebuilding it once it has worn out.

1- Consider A Warranty

While most smokers are designed in such a way that they are very reliable and durable, there are some models that may not hold up over time. A warranty is a great way to ensure that you purchase something that will work out for you over the long run.

There are reputable manufacturers who never leave out this important step in their product, and buying from companies such as them will put an extra level of trust in your purchase.

2- Choose A Quality Brand

Nowadays, there a lot of brands that produce excellent smokers on the market. You need to get a smoker that you can afford and that will last for many years. While there are some less expensive models, if you do not purchase something from a reputable manufacturer, it is quite likely that you will end up with a low quality product that may not last.

In addition to this, you need to choose a model that has the right balance of quality and affordability.

3- Know Your Needs

When you are just starting out, you will not need something that is made for larger amounts of food. If you have a small family, consider getting one that has room for four people and not six. Once you have a family, the size of your smoker will also be an important factor to consider because it will help determine how much food your smoker can hold.

It is also important to know what types of foods you plan on cooking so that you can pick a model that has all the right features and options. If you plan on smoking salmon, then you need to make sure that your smoker has a smoker rack.

If you are planning on smoking beef and pork regularly, you need get a model that is designed exclusively for these types of foods. Once you know exactly what you want in your smoker, it should be easy to find the model that will work for you.

4- Reduce Space

Another factor to consider when buying a new pellet smoker is the amount of room available in your house. If space is limited, a smaller model might be preferable because it is more portable and simpler to use than larger models. However, if you have plenty of room in your garage or on your outdoor patio for a larger smoker, then you should get one that can hold more food.

5- Prep Work

In addition to the size and capacity of your new smoker,

you also need to think about how much prep work is required before you start smoking. Generally speaking, electric smokers are going to require the least amount of prep time while charcoal and wood pellet smokers will take some time to get going. If you are not someone who enjoys this aspect of smoking meat, then you will want to stick with an electric model as they are the easiest to use without putting a lot of work into it.

6- Set It Up

Most electric smokers come with a manual that will guide you through the whole process. However, if you do not have one or if you have never used one before, then it is important to get someone to walk you through the steps of the installation process. Most smokers are fairly easy to assemble, but it does help to get someone who has experience with these types of products to do this for you.

7- Season It Right

If possible, make sure that your new smoker is prepped and ready to go before you even purchase it so that nothing will be wasted when unpacking it and setting up your new grill. As with most products, it is important to season your smoker properly before you use it. Seasoning is a long process and consists of using a brine, oil or spray that comes with the smoker.

8- Seal It Up

After you have been smoking for some time, the flavors from your food will start to permeate through the wood in your smoker. In order to keep those great flavors in and out of your food, you need to get a good seal on all openings within your new smoker. A good seal will help keep smoke from escaping and moisture from getting inside the wood.

9- Start Smelling It

For most smokers, it is best to get started as soon as possible. However, with some electric models you can start smoking right away. With other models, it will take some time before you see any smoke coming from the smoking chamber.

A lot of people love to cook, whether it is just for themselves or they do it as a hobby. When you do cook, it is always important to use the right equipment in order to get the best results. That is why when you are choosing dishes to cook, you should always think about which ones have the best quality ingredients.

I am sure that you definitely love to cook and if that is the case, then you certainly need to invest in a good set of kitchen utensils. The only thing that makes a big difference when it comes to cooking is the quality of the ingredients you use. One of those items that every chef will tell you about are knives, since they really help when it comes to cutting food into pieces.

As you can see, the quality of your kitchen utensils will make a big difference in the end, and that is why it is very important that you buy some good ones.

In addition to getting good quality knives, you also need to invest in a good set of kitchen utensils and that will include things such as pans and bowls. If you want to have a nice meal for yourself or your family members then you need to have some dishes around that will be able to cook great food for them.

As soon as I started shopping for new kitchen utensils, I noticed that there were so many different models available out there. That is why I decided to put together a list of different kitchen utensils that will help you when it comes to preparing and cooking your food.

In addition to this, I have also listed down some things you need to know about these utensils, especially if you plan on buying some for your kitchen.

Chapter 1:   Pit Boss Wood Pellet Smoker and Grill

1. What is Pit Boss Wood Pellet Smoker and Grill?

A wood pellet smoker and grill can be used as an alternative to traditional barbecue grills. These smokers use water instead of gas or charcoal for fuel, which prevents flare-ups that can cause burns or fires. Most wood pellets smoke meats like pork butt or brisket very well with even low temperatures of around 250 degrees Fahrenheit (F).

While pellet smokers and grills are somewhat similar in that they both involve cooking meat using internal heat and a little smoke, other differences include:

Pellet smokers use a water pan to slow down the burning process. The water absorbs the heat allowing the meat to finish cooking. This mimics real wood pellet smoking where you add liquids to your food as it cooks; for instance, you would usually add beer to barbecue. The benefit of adding a water pan is that it always stays liquid, even when barbecuing at temperatures above 250 degrees Fahrenheit (F). This means the meat will never scorch or dry out in your smoker, leaving you with more tender meat instead of tough jerky or dried out steaks.

Pellet smokers also usually have an internal thermostat. The thermostat can be adjusted to the desired temperature that is best for the type of meat you are cooking. The smoker will remain at this temperature no matter how long you cook or what other variables change, until you reach the specified time or temperature for your meat.

A wood pellet smoker and grill is designed to use a separate pan for catching any grease or drippings that drip from a meat during barbecuing or grilling. Most of these smokers also have a hinged grate on the side, which allows you to easily empty out the excess grease after cooking is complete without dripping onto your coals and causing flare-ups. The Grate-Style Wood pellet smoker and grilling Panel can be used with any traditional or electronic wood pellet smoker and grill that has an interior thermostat for maintaining your desired cooking temperature.

Wood pellet smokers are quite efficient because they have a lower energy consumption than gas or charcoal grills, use water as their main combustion source, and burn smaller amounts of food at once. It's a great idea to plan on having enough cord to allow you to plug all your meat smokers in at once by typing in your cord length in terms of feet on uprotoborg.com.

The wood pellet smoker is a device that every suburban or rural housewife needs. It helps you smoke meats and fish without using any other fuels so much. You can do this in your backyard or on your terrace. Some of these products are bigger than the normal pellet smokers and grills so they require more room in the yard, but they all serve the same purpose. Due to the fact that it has been around for almost thirty years, there are plenty of testimonies out there about how great these products are. When you are looking up for one of these, make sure to check out the choices which are available. The wood pellet smoker helps you find the best pellet smoker that suits your needs and your budget.

A wood pellet smoker and grill is an innovative product that has been recently developed to produce high quality charcoal barbecue. This new technology provides a smokey flavor with the health benefits of clean burning and closed combustion, thereby reducing the amount of harmful substances that are released into the air.

Wood pellet smokers also provide a rich source of food for your family or your company, especially if you have a large house. They can even be installed outdoors on patios or decks because they can heat up to up to 550 degrees Fahrenheit at low cost. In short, this product is not only eco-friendly but is also highly energy efficient and versatile in its use.

The good thing about wood pellet smoker is its versatility. Its design allows it to be used in different ways and with different materials. You can use it for grilling and smoking meat, fish, vegetables, and even drinks or desserts. It comes in several sizes that allow you to fit the smoker wherever you want to install it - on your kitchen counterbursts, around your living room or outdoors while entertaining guests. Coincidentally, all these devices are powered by electricity.

For those who love using wood pellet smokers as outdoor grills, you can even buy them with wheels so you don't have to lift them up to move them from place to place.

If you don't have enough space for your unit on your countertop or kitchen table, then it is advisable to get one that has wheels.

It would also be advantageous if the product was

durable and not prone to rust. The best wood pellet smokers are even painted with stainless steel, ceramic or quartz to make them resistant to corrosion.

The material quality is also important, particularly if you plan to use the device outside. This ensures your safety because cheaply-made materials may be flammable or may emit toxic gases when heated up. When buying wood pellet smokers, you should select a device that has a thick, sturdy construction since they are durable.

It is also important to choose the right wood pellets for your pellet smoker and grill. There are different options on the market, including butane-propane and natural gas - each of which has its own benefits. You will find that some pellets provide more smoke or even more taste than others. If you have a choice between different types of wood pellets, consider what type of smoke flavor you prefer for your favorite food items most.

If you enjoy using wood pellet smokers and grills outdoors, then get a product that has a dial thermometer so you can monitor the temperature of the device with ease. It would also be advisable to install a water pan to catch drippings that may build up inside the device.

A basic wood pellet smoker and grill should have its own storage space so you can keep your wood pellets fresh and dry. You can choose from different designs with wire shelves, as well as those that have several hanging rods at various levels for your convenience.

2. How Do They Work?

If you've never used a wood pellet smoker or grill before, it can be difficult to know where to start. You may think that they require a lot of fuss and special equipment. But in reality, these types of cookers are actually pretty simple — once you understand how they work!

You see, a wood pellet smoker or grill isn't actually that different from your commercial kitchen oven.

A wood pellet smoker and grill is a cooking appliance that features multiple cooking functions. It can simultaneously smoke, grill, bake, roast, and barbecue foods to produce a wide variety of flavors.

Wood pellets are fed through the fire pot from the top of the cooking cabinet where they are lit by an electric igniter and then slowly smoldered over natural hardwood charcoal. This process heats up the wood pellets to produce smoke which is captured in order to infuse food with flavor. The smoking temperature can be regulated by adjusting vents on the fire pot or opening or closing dampers in order to maintain optimum temperature for providing consistent heat throughout

food level ranges including cold smoking for longer periods of time needed for curing meats like cheese or fish.

The wood smoker and grill cooks food by using indirect heat. This allows the wood to be heated slowly and to cook foods evenly at a low temperature. The indirect heat source also prevents food from burning once it is cooked. Smaller foods like vegetables are generally treated at a lower temperature than bigger foods like roasts or steaks.

If you have been wondering how wood pellet smoker and grill works, the truth is that it does not actually burn wood. It uses a cylinder-shaped chamber to provide heat for cooking. It is placed in the base of the unit and surrounded by charcoal briquettes like normal stovetops. These briquettes are lit, which provides a source of heat that is radiated through the entire chamber on both sides of the device. This produces an effective means to cook food without using fire, since it doesn't require gas or electricity.

You will notice that the chamber is shaped like a cylinder. This is to ensure that the heat distributed evenly from both sides, so that no food would be cooked unevenly and cause problems. It also guarantees that the food is cooked evenly on both sides and retain natural juices. The precise temperature of the grill may be adjusted by regulating the amount of briquettes lit in it to suit your needs.

When it comes to using wood pellet smoker and grill, it is a slower process than using other types of stovetops due to its design, but this only helps in producing better quality food.

A wood pellet smoker works by using electricity to turn the firebox on and off so that the pellets burn evenly and slowly. When the pellets are lit by the flame of a gas burner, they burn very slowly. The fire stays inside a sealed box so that smoke and ash do not escape into the room.

The wood pellet smoker should be placed at least fifteen feet away from any living quarters. It is placed outside, where it can be used safely without having to worry about its effect on people indoors. A lot of backyard cooking is done with these smokers so that family and friends can gather around for outdoor fun.

Once you have selected your food, you need to leave the wood pellet smoker and grill on.

You would need to spend some time researching in order to determine what type of wood pellets is best suited for your grill.

Pellets are formed by heating a viscous mixture of wood sawdust, clay minerals, and water to high temperatures using the indirect heat of burning natural gas. These pellets are then forced into a long cylindrical tube with an auger that pushes them through the tube and into a combustion chamber where they get burned. The smoke released from the pellet grill creates a convection oven heat that sears meat quickly while preserving juices.

The pellet grill's auger forces hot air to be pushed out in an even stream which generates more constant flames at lower temperature levels resulting in less flare-ups. More leaves the pellet grill with a consistent temperature throughout the cooking process and creates even heat distribution. This also means fewer refusals and a more consistent colour on the meat. (Source: Pellet Grills)

The question here is how do wood pellets differ from other forms of heat? Essentially burns wood refuse and produces smoke. Wood pellets burn hotter than any liquid fuel because they are burned at high temperatures in a closed system without oxygen, allowing for more efficient use of fuel and higher output.

In my opinion, all pellets are NOT created equal. Some pellets leave a grey ash, while others produce black or yellow ash.

Wood pellets are a subject of debate among pellet grill owners but, the combination of wood and charcoal burners create great flames to cook with. I personally think that all burners have their advantages and disadvantages; it all depends on what kind of grill you have. Wood burning pellet grills are my favorite because everything is cooked in a perfect heat without any smoke or flame, which I am not able to get with a gas burner grill.

Wood pellets are natural, renewable resources that fit in any environment. They do not require fuel, maintenance, or cleaning. Like some other kinds of pellets, wood pellets are made from organic materials such as tree bark and wood shavings. However, in these cases the bark is difficult to remove from the wood when burnt. Wood pellets, on the other hand, are made from sawdust and can be burned easily.

Because wood pellets are less expensive per unit compared to other types of pellet, they have become very popular among consumers. Wood pellets not only help to save money, but they also do not produce smoke pollution which is a major concern for many people. They also produce little ash and do not require any special storage facilities like plastic containers or tanks.

Wood pellets are easy to handle because they come in a variety of sizes and are light in weight.

The grill would run on electricity and therefore it needs to be plugged in for the sake of deriving power. The design is such that pellets have to be added to the hopper that in turn will funnel down owing to the presence of a rotating auger and a motor.

The auger aims to make sure that the pellets get pushed down to the fire pot at the pre-configured speed which is determined by the yard control panel showing the temperature. As soon as the pellets reach the fire pot, there is an ignition rod that creates a flame that in turn causes the production of smoke.

Also, a fan is present at the bottom which helps in pushing both the generated heat and smoke upwards on the grill and thereby allows for the convection style of even cooking.

This happens to be the basic mechanism of the working of a wood pellet smoker and grill.

However, before we venture further into the recipes, we are going to shift our focus on some important points about these grills. This is because the right knowledge is crucial to ensuring that you know what you are getting into.

3. Parts of Wood Pellet Smoker and Grill

Cooking Chamber

The cooking chamber is the outermost part of the grill. It contains an airtight fire box with a removable lid, and holds wood pellet fuel. The cooking chamber is made of welded steel, and can be made in many different shapes, sizes, or colors.

The cooking chamber is an enclosed, insulated box that contains a fire pit to heat food. There are three basic cooking chambers available: the solid plate, ceramic plate and the ceramic coated steel plate. All three have advantages and disadvantages and it is recommended to look into getting a stainless steel or ceramic coated cooking chamber for the best results.

The cooking chamber is positioned above the fire pit which burns through a gas or wood burning source. The pellets are then distributed evenly through openings in the grill's internal pan via monitoring systems which vary with each manufacturer. The air flow around the pellets helps warm them up for better cooking results and also prevents them from getting too hot before they hit your food. The cooking chamber also has multiple exhaust vents that help to keep the fire pit from getting too hot.

Auger

Augers are used in most wood pellet systems to feed the pellets into the heating element at a predetermined rate (approximately one per minute). The auger usually consists of a motorized screw shaft to spin the feeder at a precise rate, and a hermetically sealed screw auger housing to protect the auger during use. A good quality auger is important to limit jamming and ensure proper pellet flow.

Pellet grills use auger tubes to rotate food as they cook. Pellets are processed by grinding them into smaller pieces, which frees the wood pellets from any potential sawdust or other impurities, and then these chips are mixed with flavorings and then heated in a kind of "bakery" oven where the seasoning sets in. When they're ready, the pellets go into an auger that feeds them into your grill. All grills with auger tubes feature an ash pan that holds spent pellets or ash, preventing it from falling onto your cooking grate.

The auger is one of the most essential parts of your pellet grill. A bad auger can break or damage a lot of expensive parts like burners, grates, and even electronics. They can literally ruin what you have invested in your grill in just one use. That's why it's important to understand how this works so you don't damage your new pellet grill before you even get to use it.

The auger is essentially a long screw made out of metal that turns the wood chips into smaller pieces as it turns slowly by your side. It also mixes these smaller pieces with the flavorings and then feeds them into the firebox for cooking.

Hopper

Wood pellet smoker and grills produce both smoke and heat, but what makes them different from other grill cooking methods is that they use "smoke pellets"—a more substantial fuel than sawdust or coal. The hopper in a wood pellet smoker and grill is where the smoke pellets are stored for use (or reuse) during cooking. It typically has a capacity of one pound of smoke pellets, which can last through several hours of cooking time.

The hopper in a wood pellet smoker and grill can be opened and refilled through the top, just like an old-fashioned coffee canister. You open the lid and pour new smoke pellets into the bucket while it's hot or being used so that they can melt. It's a very simple process.

The hopper is located on the left side or in the bottom of the grill, depending on your model. It looks like a big canister with a lid on top, and it's right next to the firebox. The hopper holds about one pound of pellets, which is enough fuel for several hours of cooking time in most wood pellet smoker and grills.

The hopper is used to hold wood pellets as they are being fed into the heating chamber. Included with most wood pellet smoker and grills is an automatic feeder that meters out the correct amount of fuel for the cooking chamber based on the profile of each individual fire box, and automatically dispenses pellets into it as required.

Heat Element

The heating element is the part of the pellet cooker that uses the fire box to generate heat. It generates a convection flow of air around the pellets, which in turn produce the heat. This is an important point to understand for home grillers who want to use wood pellets as their fuel source. Since most wood pellets are manufactured from kiln dried lumber, they must first be burnt in a fire before they can be used as fuel. This typically takes three or four hours, but can vary with different models and manufacturers. The desired thickness of food required for cooking will determine the length of time it will take to burn wood pellets into energy. The amount of pellets needed for a meal will depend on the type of food being cooked and how many people are eating.

The heating element in the wood pellet smoker and grill is one of the fireboxes that does not use electricity to heat up. The cooking temperature is controlled by thermocouples, which deliver a steady supply of heat to the grill. This allows for even, low-temperature cooking and saves on gas or electricity costs. In more simple terms, the heating element in your wood pellet smoker and grill turns on and off with a series of spikes that pass through a transformer. The spikes make it possible for electricity from outside sources to flow into the system without interruption because they create high inductance at regular intervals. This means that you can control the temperature of your grill within a specific range.

A heating element in a wood pellet smoker and grill looks like an ordinary stove's heating element; it is essentially an electric coil used to heat up metal bars arranged near the top of the firebox. This type of heating is well suited for grilling, because there are fewer cold spots in the cooking area and no need to rotate food during cooking due to uneven distribution of heat. It also requires less fuel than solid fuel fireboxes, making it more environmentally friendly.

Control Panel

The Control Panel in the Wood pellet smoker and grill is a key component of the grill that allows users to adjust settings for different cooking modes. It's also where you would enter settings for pre-programmed cooking routines, such as "Smoking" or "Grilling". The control panel helps regulate temperature and time in order to achieve desired outcomes, while also preventing over-grilling or under-grilling meat.

Greater control over the heat and time necessary to cook your food is possible with this pellet grill's four temperature zones: upper, lower, smoke and direct heat. There's also a built in timer that can be used from up to 240 minutes.

As with most pellet grills, the Wood pellet smoker and grill has an automatic start-up and shut-down feature. This is helpful for those who are frequently forgetful or just have a busy schedule.

The control panel is used to adjust the temperature and time periods required for cooking. Usually, it is equipped with a digital read-out of the internal temperature, as well as the amount of time remaining until it reaches that temperature. It also contains an on/off switch, as well as other safety features such as off/on indicator lights, and power interrupt switches to prevent overheating in case of malfunction or interruption in power supply.

The control panel is the selection of electronic features and functions you can control, find out more about your grill's operations, and diagnose its problems. Some might include a meat probe, an adjustable temperature dial or timer, as well as a fan that pushes away smoke and heat. The control panel has been designed with features for both novice cooks as well as experienced grilling experts who wish to move beyond pre-programmed settings. Some will also offer an option for wireless remote control via Bluetooth technology or WiFi connectivity.

4. Wood Pellet and Smoker Functions

Grill-Searing

There are grills that can be used for roasting or baking foods like a conventional oven, but grilling remains the most common cooking method due to the high temperature that can be maintained in the grill. The temperature is controlled in the grill by turning a control valve to add or release pellets as needed. The ability to control not only temperature but also time and thickness allows for precise cooking which is vital in many gourmet dishes such as low temperature sous vide cooking.

Grilling is a wonderful pastime and there are many different methods to get the perfect charred, crispy, savory flavor on your beef, pork, or poultry. You can grill with Foil Packages which are easy to prepare and cook in a snap. You can grill on an outdoor gas grill, in your charcoal grill with wood pellets, or you can sear meat to get a wonderful crust on the outside and leave the inside of the meat nice and moist.

Searing is perfect for cooking steaks and other cuts of beef, lamb, and pork. It's also good for cooking poultry like turkey breasts and chicken breasts. The difference between grilling and searing is that grilling doesn't brown the meat or poultry before cooking it all the way through. Grilling always seals in all flavors so that when you cut open your steak, everything will be juicy and flavorful.

The method of searing creates a delicious bark on the outside of the meat and seals in all flavors, while leaving the inside nice and moist. Searing has many purposes but is most commonly used to cook poultry and pork. There are a few different ways to sear your meat. You can use your grill or you can use your grill pan with tight fitting lid.

How do you Sear Meat?

You want to heat up your meat until the internal temperature reaches 160 degrees Fahrenheit (70 degrees Celsius) for medium rare to 165 degrees Fahrenheit for well-done. Then you want to place the meat on a hot grill and let it get a nice brown color on all sides. You can also wait to add your seasonings until you sear your meat.

There are several advantages when it comes to searing. First, you'll get that flavorful crust and seal in all the juicy flavor of the interior of the meat. Next, searing the meat creates a layer between the meat and temperature fluctuations outside your grill so that when you're ready for serving, you won't have any cold spots.

When you're grilling with wood pellets on your smoker, you don't have to be concerned about having a charcoal fire going. However, when it comes to your gas grill or charcoal grill you will need to have a fire going. Make sure any flames are out before trying to move the meat around on the grill and always use long grilling tongs. If you're using high smoke wood pellets, then add a small amount of them right on the flames and they will start to smoke. Remember that this should be done when you're already preheating your grill so that you don't let the outside temperature fluctuate too much.

When you're ready to sear the meat, brush an oil that has a high smoke point over the top of your meat. We recommend that you use a vegetable oil like olive oil or coconut oil. Add some seasonings and spices as well if you like, such as garlic salt, black pepper, cumin and chili powder. It's important that you leave the lid closed so that when you flip your meat it won't get cold on the outside before cooking all the way through on bottom side.

After 5 minutes flip your meat over and allow it to cook for another 3 minutes until both sides are browned. Pull out your meat and place it in a warm, spot to rest. Let it sit for 5-10 minutes before cutting and serving. Now take a look at that beauty!

To give your food the perfect sear, make sure that your grill is very hot. Heat is what will give you an amazing crust on your food. You should heat up all sides of the grates as well as the lid so that everything is uniformly heated to allow even heating. If your food doesn't get seared, then it might not be cooked well enough on the inside either.

Smoking

Another increasingly popular use of wood pellet smoker and grills is in smoking. The heat generated by the grill reaches temperatures higher than what is required for cooking, which allows for the drying or curing of food. It can also be used to add flavor and texture to different types of meat such as beef and pork. The smoke itself can also be used to enhance the flavor of the food while it cooks, although most grills have a separate chamber for smoking meats.

According to Smoke-free.gov, "Smoking is the use of fire to transform some types of plant or animal material into inhalable smoke and thereby heat the end product".

In other words, smoking in a Wood pellet smoker and grill is when you add wood pellets to a heating area (usually below a water pan) that's usually used for cooking meat. As the heat from the flame reaches the wood pellets, they turn them into steam which then condenses and falls down onto your food. The end effect is typically that you can taste hardwood flavor mixed with smoke on your food which can sometimes leave an unpleasant burnt taste.

While smoking may not be the most effective way to add flavor, you can actually use wood pellets as an alternative fuel source when cooking with gas. This is because wood pellets produce fewer emissions which makes it more environmentally friendly than propane or charcoal (however you should still only use wood pellets that have been certified by the EPA). The main advantage of wood pellet smoker and grills is that when they cook food, the pellets convert the heat from the flames into usable energy which feeds your appliances.

Grill-Roasting

Similar to grill-searing, grill-roasting uses high heat from a wood pellet smoker and grill which causes foods to caramelize and cook quickly on the outside with a moist interior. It is typically done over a grill grate using direct heat, though some grills will include a pan that can be used to assist in heating the food.

Grill roasting in wood pellet smoker and grill is a cooking technique used to cook large pieces of meat for a long time. This technique can be done by adding the soaked pellets directly onto the grid, or by placing them on top and inserting them into an existing fire. After the desired browning time has been reached, it's suggested that you dump out and remove any remaining wood pellets from the frame before proceeding with your final cooking.

Grill roasting is a great way to cook various kinds of meat such as turkey, chicken, pork spareribs, or even beef brisket. It not only produces tender meat but also provides your meal with that smoky flavor from real wood. Most recipes out there suggest that you create a two-zone fire using medium-high heat on one side for searing the meat while using low heat on the other to slow cook or smoke it. Grill roasting lets you skip all those steps because it does both – quickly sears the outside of your meat while cooking it slowly at the same time.

Grill roasting means you're creating a direct heat fire that's burning at the same time, above, and below the food. This fire is then going to keep the meat hot for a very long time – up to 15 hours without running too low. With this prolonged low temperature cooking, you'll be able to get everything from crispy skin right down to juicy tenderness with just one switch of a knob on your griddle.

Grill-Sealing

A similar function as grill-roasting, grill sealing essentially places food into the fire where the internal temperature reaches a certain level of temperatures before returning to its original temperature. This is often referred to as grilling meat directly over coals and can be done by placing the food atop a grate, either directly over or around burning coals that are placed on top of bricks or other materials. Grilling sealing is obviously a low temperature cooking method, and it is sometimes done by substituting the coals if the original fuel source cannot provide much heat.

Grill sealing is the act of adding a layer of flavor to your food by cooking with smoke, just before you serve. This can be achieved by either adding liquid smoke or using hardwoods that produce a lot of smoke. Use this technique in conjunction with the 5-2-1 method to guarantee perfect results every time.

Grill sealing is a process in which flavor is added to the food by using smoke in the last few minutes of cooking. This is done before you serve your food, so if you are looking for those great grill marks, consider sealing your food. You want to make sure that you do not add too much smoke or it will overpower your meat and ruin the taste. Grill marks are made after sealing, when you remove the lid from the grill.

It is strongly recommended that you use hardwood chips or chunks when grilling over charcoal or gas; avoid using liquid smoke during this step because it will ruin other flavors in flavor. This is a process that should be done late in the cooking process, about 2-3 minutes from being finished. This should only be used on foods that are going to be served rare; if used on meats that are going to be well done, it will give you a bitter taste. This step can also be done on foods cooked on a stovetop to seal in flavor.

It is important to note that grill sealing will not make your food taste like smoked ham, or any other type of meat. It simply adds an extra layer of flavor to your meat; it does not change the basic properties of the food in any way. This is a process that you will want to do with foods such as hamburgers or marinated chicken.

So next time you are grilling, remember that the goal of sealing is to give your food an extra layer of flavor, not to grill marks. By adding a small amount of hardwood chips or chunks into your cooking chamber; ideally, do this at the end of cooking to avoid over-smoking. Seal in the flavors by using a bit of liquid smoke last 5-10 minutes before removing the lid from the grill.

5. **How to Pick the Best Wood Pellets**

Picking the best wood pellets for your needs can be a difficult decision. You want to find a quality pellet that will last and burn efficiently.

Why use pellet wood for cooking? The answer is very simple, they burn clean and hot, almost like real wood! Your pellets will retain their heat for a long time. Wood pellets have high BTU's and tons of great flavors. They are also very cost-effective way to fuel your pellet grill.

Why Pellets?

Wood pellets are a great option if you wish to use wood for cooking or heating purposes. Wood pellets are simply compressed sawdust and they burn at lower temperatures than real wood. They match up very well with gas/propane grills and smokers as they produce less ash than any other fuel.

They're a clean-burning fuel that is easy to use and store, but you won't get the authentic look that real wood provides as it won't develop a nice smoke ring on your meat or have the same texture as real wood. There are disadvantages with wood pellets too, notably the potential for higher levels of carbon monoxide. This has caused many wood pellet manufacturers to reduce the carbon level in their pellets. But as long as this is done at a reasonable rate you should be in good shape.

Wood Types

Hardwood: Common hardwood varieties are: oak, hickory, and mesquite (mahogany). They all have very unique flavors that make cooking more enjoyable. Some examples of hardwoods include apple, pear, hazelnut, cherry, and walnut. Hardwoods can become very bitter if not prepared properly so you will need to know how to use them properly when cooking with these types of woods.

Softwood: Softwoods are the major pellets used in pellet stoves. Common varieties of softwood include: alder, apple, ash, aspen, and maple. They produce very little smoke and have some of the best flavors of all the woods. Some examples of softwoods include pine, fir, spruce, and hemlock. Softwoods are very easy to use and they can be burned easily with no preparation needed.

All-Pellet Blends: For a long time most manufacturers would sell you wood pellets that were made with softwood only but now you can find blends that combine hardwood and softwood pellets to create a better flavor for your smoking experience. Some examples of blends are: Oak/Alder, Hardwood/Softwood, and Hickory/Maple.

Weight Level: The weight level refers to the amount by volume of pellets in a bag. As the wood is compressed into a pellet it loses moisture over time which affects the weight that you will be able to purchase and store. As you may notice I prefer pellets that are less than 1 pound per bag because I generally use them in my pellet smoker and they don't weigh down my food as much as some heavier ones can. Many people can't afford to buy a bag of pellets that weighs over 3 pounds but if you do you can burn about 5-10 lbs. of pellets and have plenty of dry material to use as long as you are careful with it. The trick is to not let the pellets get too hot or they will start to burn up and no longer be usable for your stove.

Types of Pellets
Wood Pellets: These are the most common type of wood pellet. They do come in different weights and grades, but typically the heavier ones will cost more and provide better smoke flavor. Hardwoods: These are wood pellets that have been compressed to a hardwood form. These types of pellets are much more difficult to find, but they provide great smoke flavor and won't weigh down your food as much.

Bamboo Pellets: Bamboo is an extremely sturdy grass that can be used for many different things including furniture and even clothing. Bamboo is high in silica which means it burns hotter than most other biofuels, but it also takes a long time to dry. Bamboo pellets will burn up to 3 times faster than wood pellets at the same heat setting, but they are not as long lasting.

We chose Bamboo pellet blends that have a lower percent of bamboo content for our stove because the firmer pellets we bought were able to burn hotter. If you are using a stove that is not very hot or has only a few burners, then you might want to consider purchasing a bag of bamboo pellets.

Hay Pellets: These can be made from many different sources including alfalfa, straw, or oat hay. They are generally much cheaper than wood pellets and they have a low heat output that would work great in a simple stove with few burners.

Any one of the products I mentioned should work great for most stove brands and should bring your pellet experience to the next level.

What makes a wood pellet smoker and grill unique is the very thing that fuels it -- wood pellets. Wood pellets are compressed sawdust, made from either pine wood, birch wood, fir wood, or crop stalks. Culinary-wise, wood pellets are used mostly as fuel for pellet smokers and grills, although they can also be used for household heating. What makes wood pellets for cooking special, though, is that they come in flavors.

Wood Pellet Types
There are two main categories of pellets: round wood pellets (RWP) and square wood pellets (SWP). As with other forms of heating, however, not all wood pellets are created equally.

RWP has more ash content than SWP, and is usually used for indoor heating. SWP is almost pure cellulose fiber and is great for outdoor use and in pellet stoves. As a bonus, it burns hotter than RWP.

Round Wood Pellets: RWP is a product of the lumber industry, usually sawdust left over after wood is milled into planks. The wood is ground up and then steam dried to remove chemicals, moisture, mold and other contaminants. After that it's formed into pellets for use as fuel.

Pellet stoves burn RWP more efficiently than forced air furnaces because they have more surface area per cubic foot, so they'll heat your home faster and more evenly. RWP also provides better indoor air quality than propane, natural gas or oil because it produces almost no byproducts when burned.

The main downside to using this type of pellet is the ash content, which can be up to 40 percent. On the plus side, RWP is great for landscaping and your yard's ambiance. It also conveniently burns hotter than other types of wood pellets, which means less ash is left behind at the end of the burn.

Square Wood Pellets: SWP comes from a different source than RWP and has much less ash content. Most often it is trees such as oak or hickory that have been cut down for lumber and then ground up into sawdust, which is then melted down into pellets for heating systems.

SWP burns hotter than other types of wood pellets, but also leaves ash behind more often. It's best used for outdoor heating and as a wood substitute in stoves.

Although it may be less expensive than RWP, SWP is still higher in price than other types of wood pellets.

Regardless of what type you choose, making sure you buy the right size pellet can be key to getting the most from your burner. When buying wood pellets for use in a stove, go for the largest pellet they offer that will fit your stove. Because the heat generated by burning pellets usually isn't enough to melt them, you'll get more cooking space with larger diameter pellets. If you want to save money, make sure your wood pellets are the same size as your stove's burner. If you're unsure of the size of your stove, or what size pellets you should be buying, consult an expert at a wood pellet company or fireplace shop.

Wood Pellet Flavors
Apple & Cherry Pellets: These pellets possess a smoky, mild, sweet flavor. They can enhance mild meat and are

usually the go-to flavor for cooking pork or poultry. Despite being able to produce great smoke, these pellets are very mild.

Alder Pellets: This type of pellet is mild and neutral, but with some sweetness in it. If you're looking for something that provides a good amount of smoke but won't overpower delicate meat like chicken and fish, this is the flavor to go to.

Hickory Pellets: Hickory pellets produce a rich, Smokey, and bacon-like flavor. These are the pellets that are widely used for barbecue. Since this type of pellet is rich and Smokey, it can tend to be overwhelming. If that is the case, consider mixing it with apple or oak pellets.

Maple Pellets: If you are looking for something that is mild and comes with a hint of sweetness, maple pellets are the best option for you. They are great to use on turkey or pork.

Mesquite Pellets: A favorite option for Texas BBQ, mesquite pellets are characterized by a strong, spicy, and tangy flavor.

Oak Pellets: Oak pellets come in between apple and hickory. They are a bit stronger than the former and a bit milder than the latter and are an excellent choice when you're cooking fish or vegetables.

Pecan Pellets: Pecan is an all-time favorite. It's very similar to Hickory, but with a touch of vanilla, nutty flavor. The perfect pellets for beef and chicken, pecan pellets are very palatable and suits all occasions.

6. Cooking Temperatures, Times, and Doneness

Most of us are aware that the right cooking time and temperature will make or break a recipe. This is no less true for wood pellet smoker and grilling. If you follow recommended times and temperatures, your food will taste amazing! But what does this actually mean? What cooking times and temperatures do I need to know to get great results with my grill?

The right temperature sets the stage for creating a perfectly done meal, whether you're cooking meat or fish, chicken or vegetables. The lowest temperature you should cook your food is 130 degrees Fahrenheit. This is the temperature at which 120 minutes of cooking time will create a perfect medium-rare (or medium on an internal thermometer). Cooking times and temperatures for other cooking methods are listed below.

Cooking temperature is critical for wood pellet smoker and grills because you want to maintain the right temperature, or doneness, of your food throughout the cooking process. The best grills are equipped with built-in probes that measure internal temperatures at various parts of the cooking surface. These probes flash an error message if it is too hot or too cold. There are also a lot of different user-created programs and "Twin Fan" controllers that can be accessed through smartphone apps. These programs will allow you to program the grill to maintain a specific temperature range and time.

If you're grilling your meat at the recommended temperatures, then you're doing a great job. But what if you're not, and what if even these lower temperatures aren't providing the results you want? The secret is in the fuel.

Cooking food until it reaches the desired doneness can take a lot of time and patience. Grilling food over an open flame — such as with a wood pellet smoker and grill — can be challenging because it requires juggling four demanding tasks: controlling the heat, cooking with fat, maintaining proper cooking temperature, and monitoring meat doneness.

When cooking meats, doneness is essentially the point at which they are ready to eat. Cooking meat for any amount of time beyond what it takes to cook it until it's ready to eat results in both a loss of flavor and texture. We've created this guide to help you understand how each setting on your grill impacts your food when cooking at various temperatures.

No matter what type of wood pellet smoker and grill you use, and no matter how well-equipped it may be, unless your grill is using wood pellets as its main fuel source, it will not be cooking food at temperatures high enough to maintain its best temperature.

7. Accessories Needed

You're off to a great start with your pellet grill, but there are a few other valuable tools that are well worthwhile to invest in. These tools appear throughout this cookbook – some are vital, and some simply elevate your repertoire.

The wood pellet smoker and grill is a very popular cooking appliance that people have been using for a long time because of its convenience and affordability. It is also a very good alternative to the more expensive grills. There are some accessories that you need to purchase for your unit to make it work properly, and taking care of them will prevent them from wearing out quickly. With these tips in mind, you'll never needlessly spend money on replacements again!

The Grate Holder
This accessory will make it easier to change the grate as well as keep food from falling through the gaps between

the bars. It also includes a little tool to help push the grate into place when it's time for a replacement.

The Grease Trap

The grease trap is a good idea if you do not filter your cooking fat before it enters your unit. Your heart will love you, and your neighbors will applaud you, for using this appliance! To keep all these wonderful flavors from being wasted, I recommend investing in a large one with at least 70 gallons' capacity. It's easy enough to clean by simply removing the old one and replacing it with the new one.

The Digital Thermometer

This is a very important accessory if you're going to do any smoking. It allows you to keep an eye on the temperature of your goods while they are on the grill. This helps to ensure safety and to maintain quality of the product. I recommend getting at least one digital thermometer, as well as a clock thermometer if possible. They don't need to be expensive, but they should be high quality.

The Tongs and Fork Set

This set consists of tongs and a fork to turn the food while it cooks on the grill. They will make your food more appealing and tasty, or you can use them as a bottle opener if that's what you're into.

The Cooking Thermometer for Wood pellet smoker and grills.

This thermometer is a very useful accessory for wood pellet smoker and grill owners because it allows you to know exactly how hot your cooking surface will get while using that particular appliance. It can be found at any major retail outlet.

Probe Meat Thermometer

If your grill doesn't have probe thermometers built-in, you 100% need to get one or two of them. They are crucial to almost any recipe, but especially for smoking recipes. Measuring your meat's internal temperature is the only way you can know when your food is safely cooked all the way through. It will also help you pull your food off of the cooker at your exact desired doneness.

The Side Tables and Storage Box

If you own multiple wood pellet smoker and grills, then the side tables and storage box are highly recommended. They help to organize your cooking equipment so that it's easy to find what you want. Furthermore, they are good for storing tools that you use during cooking. They can even be used as extra seating after a meal. These are available at almost any major retail outlet. They are also affordable, so you can pick more than one if necessary.

It also has a meat probe that helps you monitor the internal temperature of whatever it is you're cooking. This is an important accessory, as it can help you to cook your food to perfection without having to guess at what it should be.

The removable shelves or trays allow dishes and other items to be placed on them while in use.

A storage box and side table set are important accessories because they allow you to keep all the necessary cooking tools in one place. They can also be used to store food after it has been cooked. This helps to keep your kitchen clean and organized. If you purchase a unit with this item, you should check with the retailer for measurements and availability.

A detachable grease tray is very important for wood pellet smoker and grills because it traps grease and fat from your food before it enters your home or gets into the air. This keeps your grill clean, but also helps to preserve the natural flavors of whatever you're cooking on it.

BBQ Gloves

For your safety, it's best to have a pair of BBQ gloves just in case. Most of our recipes don't require BBQ gloves to safely handle your food, but some do. Plus, it never hurts to take extra caution when you're dealing with scorching hot temperatures.

Silicone Basting Brush

Many grill and smoker recipes utilize marinades that need to be brushed or basted onto your food. Basting brushes are quite affordable and a borderline necessity for any grilling toolbox.

8. How to Clean Your Grill

Just like every appliance, keeping your smoker clean is essential as well. If you neglect your appliance, it might slowly accumulate debris, oil, and drips, which might ultimately result in the appliance getting damaged.

The good idea is to keep a mixture of mild dish detergent and warm water handy as they are perfect when it comes to cleaning smokers. Alternatively, you may use non-abrasive cleaners as well should you choose.

A good tip is to clean your Smoker after every smoking

session to avoid having a massive clean-up session down the road.

Steps for cleaning the Smoker after every use:
1- If you have used Wood Chips, make sure first to empty your smoker box and discard any ash. Carefully wipe the side of the box with a damp rag;
2- Next, remove the cooking racks, water pan, drip tray pan and wash them with warm soapy water, rinse and dry them;
3- As an added to apply a gentle coat of vegetable oil over the racks before your next smoking session for mess-free Smoking;
4- Remove the meat probe and clean it with a damp cloth as well;
5- Allow your Smoker to dry up before using again completely.

Step to keeping the outside of your Smoker clean:
1- Gently wipe the control panel on the top of your Smoker using a damp cloth with warm water, wipe it dry.

Steps to cleaning the thermostats (If your device has it):
1- Carefully wipe the surface of the two thermostats located on the reading inside of the wall of your Smoker using a soft, damp cloth;
2- Make sure to dip the cloth in warm soapy water before wiping, let them dry once done.

Steps for cleaning the inside of your Smoker:
1- Make sure that your Smoker is wholly cooled off;
2- Take out the racks, water pan, drip tray, and smoker box;
3- Take a small brush/towel and brush any debris alongside the bottom and upper part of the Smoker;
4- Wipe any residue out of the chamber;
5- Use warm soapy water and carefully scrub the interior surfaces of the Smoker using a plastic bristle brush, wipe it dry once done.

9. **Safety Precautions for Wood Pellet Smoker and Grilling**

Safety precautions for wood pellet smoker and grilling are a bit more complicated than other, more traditional forms of cooking food. This is because outdoor grills can be extremely high in temperature. As such, it's important to take several steps before and during the cooking process to ensure you don't start a fire.

Before you begin, put away any flammable objects that are around the grill. Things like dry leaves and straw can be easily ignited by high temperature flames or sparks.

Grilling a hot dog over an open flame is one thing, but cooking food over open flames can be extremely dangerous. Also, because sparks from the fire could potentially set your food on fire or catch nearby buildings on fire, it's important to be cautious when cooking with wood pellets.

This is especially important when using a wood pellet smoker and grill, as you may not be able to see the flame from the grill itself.

If you have pets or small children nearby, make sure they are far enough away from the grill area that they cannot reach it and take something off of it. It's also important to keep any flammable materials away from the area in which you'll be grilling.

Use a long-handled grilling tool to turn over the food on your grill. Bottles, cans, and other sorts of containers can cause high temperatures and sparks to erupt from your food if they touch it while it's cooking.

If you plan on using a wood pellet smoker and grill for cooking, take the time to invest in some safety equipment such as a silicone glove. The best way to avoid burning yourself is to wear protective clothing, such as a long-sleeved shirt and pants, and gloves. These gloves are also extremely useful when handling hot charcoal or wood pellets on the grill.

When using the grill, never leave it unattended. A fire can start quickly due to high temperatures that easily reach thousands of degrees F and incinerate all the food inside it.

Avoid leaving food out for long periods of time without refilling your wood pellets supply tank or completely removing it from your smoker. Leaving food out on a grill can indirectly cause a fire by drawing heat from the burning pellets in the wood fire.

To wash your wood pellet smoker and grill, complete all preparations before going outside to clean it. Mop up all spilled food and liquids using a mop and sponge or, if available, an automatic dishwasher. Then, put on some gloves and work to scrub the area until all residue is removed from the surface of your grill. Afterward, wipe down any remaining stains with a rag that is soaked in soapy water.

Stains from spilled food should be removed immediately after removing it from your grill so they don't become permanent when exposed to high temperatures and direct sunlight.

To clean the interior parts of your smoker, use a damp rag to wipe down the surfaces. Be sure not to splash any water or liquid onto anything electrical.

Use a brush to remove any burnt residue from the inside of your smoker.

If you are looking for a simpler option, try using a rag soaked in vinegar or baking soda.

Wood pellet smoker and grills are designed to withstand high temperatures and relatively small flames.

It is natural for the inside of your grill to rust as a result of cooking. Just make sure that you keep up with a regular cleaning schedule so you can avoid any build-up of residue or grease within the body of your grill.

Try to perform your regular cleaning tasks while the grill is turned on as normal, so that you can ensure all aspects are clean during use. Be careful that you don't accidentally scratch or damage your wood pellet smoker and grill while cleaning it.

Wood pellets are available in many sizes and shapes, which is a good thing. When buying pellets online, be sure to buy from reputable stores with good return policies so you won't be stuck with unusable product.

Pellets are also available in different grades of wood. The wood used in the pellets you buy can determine whether your food will taste better or worse, based on the quality of the wood used.

Some pellet grills have an adjustable burn control setting to help you make precise, even temperature adjustments for different foods. For example, you could use a dial-type controller to set the temperature for cooking hamburgers and steaks.

Some wood pellet smoker and grills, however, use a gas grill with a lid. These models are not your best choice if you're looking for quality and consistent cooking results. If your temperature is too high, then you can turn down the heat to avoid burning your food.

A thermometer also allows you to monitor the temperature of your wood pellet smoker and grill in order to avoid overheating it and causing a fire. If temperatures are up too high, then you can make some adjustments to the controls or take steps to wait out the heat wave.

With a thermostat, you can take advantage of the temperature control settings that most wood pellet smoker and grills feature and make sure that you are not overcooking your food.

Some grills also have a fan so that the lid won't overheat and may explode if it gets too hot.

Some wood pellet smoker and grills come with a temperature gauge, thermometer, fan and or thermostat. Having one of these features can take the guesswork out of using your wood pellet smoker and grill.

Check the gauge of your grill's cooking grate to see if it is made from high heat grill material. This is the material that most grills are built with, regardless of their main fuel source.

A quality sealer and paint job can go a long way in enhancing the overall look of your grill and its performance.

The steel wool can cause scratches, chips or wear down the paint on the grill.

Another good tip is to avoid cleaning your wood pellet smoker and grill in direct sunlight. This will cause oxidation to occur, which can ruin the paint job or rust on the parts of your grill.

Wood pellets are fuel that is made from sawdust and wood chips. Wood pellets do not burn like propane or charcoal briquettes, so they aren't as hot as other options.

When using a pellet grill, you will want to make sure that the temperature gauge of your device is set between 325 and 350 degrees F. If your pellet grill is not accurate, you risk over- or under-cooking your food.

Grills with this material can withstand high temperatures, and you won't have to worry about them getting too hot.

Look for a grill that has a hopper at the bottom to catch the pellets once they are loaded into the grill. In some wood pellet smoker and grills, you have to slide the wood pellets into a hopper in order to start cooking. This was not always a problem, but it is more common for newer wood pellet smoker and grills than older ones.

10. Tips and Tricks to Master Your Wood Pellet Smoker and Grill

Wood pellet smoker and grills have some unique benefits that make them worth talking about. Here are some great tips and tricks for mastering your wood pellet smoker and grill!

1) Clean out your pellets after every use--don't leave them in the device all year round! This will prevent gunk buildup that can clog up the works with your unit's "brain", so to speak, preventing it from properly regulating temperature or controlling airflow.

2) To get the most out of your wood pellet smoker and grill, use a log lighter to start your fire. Don't just go tossing wood pellets into the device; you'll end up with

logs and debris instead of a nice, hot fire. Nobody wants to eat charred logs!

3) If your wood pellet smoker and grill produces too much smoke for your tastes, consider using an air purifier like this one. It'll remove smoke particles from the air in less than an hour. This is especially important if you are cooking in a small area with neighbors close by.

4) Use a chimney starter to get your fire going. If you don't have a chimney starter, you can use newspaper and wood chips to make a tidy little (ugh) fire. However, be sure that you don't have any "hot spots" on the bottom of your device that will cause the logs to burn.

5) Make sure that your device has sufficient airflow--this is key! You want your cooking area at least one foot away from the heat source or else it will cook too slowly and won't be worth it! Also, proper airflow means no smoke (or only minimal smoke). Keep an eye on temperatures as well--too much heat and you'll have food that isn't done properly.

6) Be sure that your wood pellets are stored in a dry place away from direct sunlight--this will also protect them from moisture.

7) Use your device at a lower temperature when cooking with wood pellets. You don't want to cook your food any faster than you need to! Also, be sure that you keep the temperature of the food below the heat source. Cooking too hot can cause charring which is not good for your food.

8) Use cheap and low-quality pellets as this will raise the cost of your fire. However, don't go overboard; these tend to burn out quickly and have no real effect on flavor or quality of taste.

9) Don't overfill your device with wood pellets. Also, wood is a very heavy substance--it doesn't take much to add that extra weight to your grill!

Tips in Grilling

Grilling can be a lot of fun: the slight crackle of cooking smoky meats, the inviting aroma wafting through outdoor living rooms, and a variety of different tasty dishes for your family and friends to enjoy. These tips include not only tips on temperature control but also how to prevent certain injuries.

1. Temperature Control

For the best results, start your grill on low heat and close it to prevent the temperature from rising rapidly. This will allow you to determine the temperature at which your meat is finished cooking without burning it. As for

the time frame, keep in mind that grilling takes longer than other cooking methods such as roasting or baking because of a lower heat environment that surrounds the food being grilled. For example, a thick steak will take longer to grill than a thin chicken breast or pork chop - depending on how tough or tender they are.

2. Preventing Cross-Contamination

Cross-contamination is the transfer of harmful bacteria from one food to another. It can be very dangerous if you choose to serve raw or undercooked meat and then cook a side dish of vegetables since the harmful bacteria could be transferred from one to another. To avoid this, always clean your grilling equipment after you cook meat or poultry on it and do not place these cooked foods on the same plate with uncooked foods without thoroughly cleaning it first. This will prevent any cross-contamination from occurring.

3. Preventing Fires

Be careful when using flammable materials to clean the grilling surface or lid. Always turn off your gas tank when you're not using it and do not leave it on. Also, always keep any open flames far away from any barbecue. Even small flames can quickly spread out of control if you are not careful. The safest way to prevent dangerous fires is to keep everything around your barbecue covered in case there are some mishaps. If any accidents are to occur, cover them up immediately with a lid - even if it's only a minor accident.

4. Prepping Your Grill

Always create a nice surface for your grill since that is the only thing you're going to use it for. If you don't have one, check out the various barbecue starter kits such as those from Weber or Char-Broil that are available in many different sizes and prices. These come with an extra grill grate, basting brush, tool set and other accessories that will allow you to start grilling right away. If you don't have room on your patio or deck to create a BBQ area there is plenty of grilling accessories available online including heavy duty floor mats, charcoal lighter blankets and much more so you can try out grilling on your deck or patio without having to purchase all new equipment.

5. Grilling Safety

While grilling is a great way to cook food at home, it can be dangerous too if you don't use the proper equipment. If you skimp on safety concerns when grilling, the risks increase dramatically. Always follow these tips whenever you grill:

Always use a grill cover or basting brush before cooking

to prevent any flare-ups caused by flare-ups which are often caused by fire in the area around your grill. Also, always extinguish any open flames with water as soon as they are extinguished so that they never start again while cooking. Check out these other helpful tips for grilling safety from Washington State University Extension.

6. Backyard Grill

A backyard grill can be an excellent addition to your home. The most common type of backyard barbecue is the gas grill, which is used in conjunction with a propane tank and the associated accessories. Wood burning grills are also becoming increasingly popular, especially for their rustic look, and are available in many different sizes. A charcoal grill may also serve as a backyard grill, or you may choose to use this as an outdoor kitchen or barbeque spot where you can set up an outdoor cooking area.

7. Sear Grilling

A good way to improve the flavor of your meal on the grill is through searing it before placing it on the rack on top of your heat source. Searing essentially seals in the juices of the meat and keeps it from drying out while it cooks. This gives you a tender, juicy piece of meat. To sear your meal, simply add a little oil to your grill and set your heat source to high. A few minutes later, place your meat on the heated surface and sear for about three minutes per side. Then, cover the grill again until it's done cooking.

8. Cleaning Your Grill

The best way to clean your grill is to use a wire brush or pad prior to starting a barbeque because this will prevent any harmful bacteria from building up on any leftover food particles that have hardened onto the grates from previous cooking dishes. If you don't have a grill brush available, a stiff wire brush will work well as long as you're extra careful because the metal bristles can easily damage the grates. However, if you accidentally damage your grates, they are rather inexpensive and it's easy to replace them too.

9. Grilling with Foil

If you want to keep your meal moist while it grills, try wrapping it with aluminum foil while grilling it. This works especially well with chicken breasts, fish fillets and other meats that are naturally prone to drying out as they cook. Another technique that works well is wrapping the food item in a paper towel and then wrapping it in aluminum foil. The combination of moisture from the paper towel and the aluminum foil will steam your food, keeping it nice and moist.

Chapter 2:   Meat Recipes

1. Bloody Mary Flank Steak

Preparation Time: 5 minutes
Cooking Time: 10-15 minutes
Servings: 3
Ingredients:

- 2 cups bloody Mary mix or V8 juice
- 1/2 cup vodka
- One whole lemon, juiced
- Three cloves' garlic, minced
- One tablespoon Worcestershire sauce
- One teaspoon ground black pepper
- One teaspoon celery salt
- 1/2 cup of vegetable oil
- 1 1/2-pound flank steak

Directions:

1. Place all ingredients, excluding the flank steak, in a bowl. Mix until well-combined.
2. Put the flank steak in a plastic bag and pour half of the marinade over.
3. Marinate for at least 24 hours in the fridge.
4. When ready to cook, fire your pellet grill to 500°F.
5. Closed the lid and preheat for 15 minutes.
6. Drain the flank steak and pat dry using a paper towel.
7. Place on the grill grate and cook for 7 minutes on each side.
8. Meanwhile, place the remaining marinade (unused) in a saucepan and heat until the sauce thickens.
9. Once the steak is cooked, removed it from the grill, and rest for 5 minutes before slicing.
10. Pour over the sauce.

Nutrition: Calories: 719 kCal, Carbs: 15.4 g, Protein: 51.9 g, Fat: 51 g

2. Pastrami

Preparation Time: 10 minutes
Cooking Time: 4-5 hours
Servings: 12
Ingredients:

- 1-gallon water, plus 1/2 cup
- 1/2 cup packed light brown sugar
- 1 (3- to 4-pound) point cut corned beef brisket with brine mix packet
- 2 tablespoons freshly ground black pepper
- 1/4 cup ground coriander

Directions:

1. Cover the beef and refrigerate overnight, changing the water as often as you remember to do so—ideally, every 3 hours while you're awake—to soak out some of the curing salt originally added.
2. Supply your smoker with wood pellets and follow the manufacturer's specific start-up procedure. Preheat, with the lid closed, to 275°F.
3. Merge the black pepper and ground coriander to form a rub.
4. Drain the meat, pat it dry, and generously coat it on all sides with the rub.
5. Place the corned beef directly on the grill, fat-side up, close the lid, and smoke for 3 hours and 30 minutes.
6. Add the corned beef, cover tightly with aluminum foil, and smoke on the grill with the lid closed for an additional 30 minutes to 1 hour.
7. Remove the meat.
8. Refrigerate.

Nutrition: Calories: 123 kCal, Carbs: 0.4 g, Protein: 12g, Fat: 4 g

3. Smoked Texas BBQ Brisket

Preparation Time: 30 minutes
Cooking Time: 5 hours
Servings: 4
Ingredients:

- 6 pounds whole packer brisket
- Commercial BBQ rub of your choice

Directions:

1. Trim the brisket from any membrane and lose fat.
2. Trim the fat side to 1/4 inch thick.
3. Season all edges of the brisket with the BBQ rub and allow resting for 30 minutes inside the fridge.
4. When ready to cook, fire your pellet grill to 275°F.

5. Use mesquite wood pellets when cooking.
6. Close the lid, and then preheat for 15 minutes.
7. Place the brisket fat side up on the grill grate and cook for 5 hours or until the internal temperature reaches 165°F (as read by a meat thermometer).
8. Once cooked, remove the brisket from the grill and allow to rest before slicing.

Nutrition: Calories: 703 kCal, Carbs: 0 g, Protein: 93.9 g Fat: 33.4 g

4. Braised Mediterranean Beef Brisket

Preparation Time: 30 minutes
Cooking Time: 5 hours
Servings: 16
Ingredients:
- Three tablespoons dried rosemary
- Two tablespoons cumin seeds, ground
- Two tablespoons dried coriander
- One tablespoon dried oregano
- Two teaspoons ground cinnamon
- 1/2 teaspoon salt
- 8 pounds beef brisket, sliced into chunks
- 1 cup beef stock

Directions:
1. Mix the rosemary, cumin, coriander, oregano, cinnamon, and salt in a bowl.
2. Massage the spice mix into the beef brisket and allow to rest in the fridge for 12 hours.
3. When ready to cook, fire your pellet grill to 180°F.
4. Close the lid, and then preheat for 15 minutes.
5. Place the brisket fat side down on the grill grate and cook for 4 hours.
6. After 4 hours, change the heat to 250°F.
7. Continue cooking the beef brisket until the internal temperature reaches 160°F.
8. Remove and place on a foil. Crimp the ends of the foil to make a sleeve.
9. Pour in the beef stock.
10. Return the brisket to the foil sleeve and continue cooking for another hour.

Nutrition: Calories: 453 kCal, Carbs: 1 g, Protein: 33.5 g, Fat: 34 g

5. Grill a Burger without Flipping Them

Preparation Time: 15 minutes
Cooking Time: 50 minutes
Servings: 6
Ingredients:
- 1 Ground Beef Patties
- Beef Rub
- Cheese
- Pretzel buns

Directions:
1. Start with cold but not frozen patties and sprinkle on the Beef Rub, and massage into both sides of the patty.
2. Preheat grill to 250 degrees F and cook for 45 minutes.
3. Add cheese and other topic varieties of your liking.
4. Close the grill back up and wait for another 10 minutes before removing it.

Nutrition: Calories: 696 kCal, Carbs: 11 g, Protein: 38 g, Fat: 54 g

6. Cheeseburger Hand Pies

Preparation Time: 35 minutes
Cooking Time: 10 minutes
Servings: 6
Ingredients:
- 1/2 pound lean ground beef
- One tablespoon minced onion
- One tablespoon steak seasoning
- 1 cup cheese
- Eight slices of white American cheese, divided
- 2 (14-ounce) refrigerated prepared pizza dough sheets, divided
- Two eggs
- 24 hamburger dill pickle chips
- Two tablespoons sesame seeds
- Six slices of tomato, for garnish
- Ketchup and mustard, for serving

Directions:
1. Supply your smoker thru wood pellets and follow the manufacturer's specific start-up.
2. Preheat, with the lid closed, to 325°F.
3. On your stovetop, in a medium sauté pan over medium-high heat, cooking the ground beef for 4 to 5 minutes.
4. Add the minced onion and steak seasoning.

5. Toss in the shredded cheese blend and two slices of American cheese and stir until melted and fully incorporated.
6. Remove the cheeseburger mixture from the heat and set it aside.
7. Make sure the dough is well chilled for easier handling.
8. Working quickly, rolls out one prepared pizza crust on parchment paper and brush with half of the egg wash.
9. Arrange the remaining six slices of American cheese on the dough to outline six hand pies.
10. Put the cheese burger mixture in the six pieces of extended dough, top with cheese and cover with another top of dough. Tidy the edges with a pizza cutter and press them together with a fork.
11. Bake for ten minutes. Eat while still warm.

Nutrition: Calories: 325 kCal, Carbs: 11 g, Protein: 23 g, Fat: 21 g

7. Pellet-Grilled New York Strip

Preparation Time: 5 minutes
Cooking Time: 15 minutes
Servings: 6
Ingredients:
1. 3 New York strips
2. Salt and pepper
3. Directions:
4. If the steak is in the fridge, remove it 30 minutes before cooking.
5. Preheat the pellet grill to 450°F.
6. Season the steak with salt and pepper.
7. Put it on the grill and let it cook for 5 minutes per side or until the internal temperature reaches 128°F.
8. Rest for 10 minutes.

Nutrition: Calories: 198 kCal, Carbs: 0 g, Protein: 17 g, Fat: 14 g

8. Grilled Butter Basted Porterhouse Steak

Preparation Time: 5 minutes
Cooking Time: 8 minutes
Servings: 4
Ingredients:
- Four tablespoons melted butter
- Two tablespoons Worcestershire sauce
- Two tablespoons Dijon mustard

- Prime rib rub, as needed
- Two porterhouse steaks, 1 1/2 inch thick

Directions:
1. Fire the pellet grill and preheat to 255°F. Use desired wood pellets and closes the lid and preheats for 15 minutes.
2. In a bowl, mix the butter, Worcestershire sauce, mustard, and Prime Rib Rub.
3. Massage all over the steak on all sides. Allow steak to rest for an hour before cooking.
4. When ready to cook, raise the temperature to 500°F.
5. Put the steaks on the grill grates and cook for 4 minutes on each side or until the internal temperature reads 130°F (as read by a meat temperature) for medium-rare steaks.
6. Take away from the grill and allow resting for 5 minutes before slicing.

Nutrition: Calories: 515 kCal, Carbs: 2.1 g, Protein: 65.3 g, Fat: 27.7 g

9. Brined Smoked Brisket

Preparation Time: 30 minutes
Cooking Time: 8 hours
Servings: 6
Ingredients:
- 1 cup brown sugar
- 1/2 cup of salt
- One flat cut brisket
- 1/4 cup beef rub

Directions:
1. Make the brine by melting the sugar and salt in 6 quarts of hot water.
2. Allow to cool at room temperature and place the brisket in the solution.
3. Put in the fridge and allow marinating for 12 hours.
4. Remove the brisket from the brine and pat dry with a paper towel.
5. Sprinkle with the beef rub mixture and massage until all surfaces are coated.
6. When ready to cook, fire your pellet grill to 250°F.
7. Close the lid and heat up for 15 minutes.
8. Place the brisket on the grill grate and cook for 4 hours.

9. After 3 hours, double wrap the brisket in foil; turn the temperature to 275°F and cook for another 3 hours.
10. Unwrap the brisket and grill for 30 minutes more.
11. Detach the brisket from the grill before slicing.

Nutrition: Calories: 364 kCal, Carbs: 16.6 g, Protein: 48.7 g, Fat: 11.6 g

10. BBQ Brisket with Coffee Rub

Preparation Time: 20 minutes
Cooking Time: 9 hours
Servings: 10
Ingredients:
- 5 pounds whole packer brisket
- Two tablespoons Coffee Rub
- 1 cup of water
- Two tablespoons salt

Directions:
1. Trim the brisket and remove any membrane.
2. Leave a 1/4" inch cap on the bottom.
3. In a bowl, combine the coffee rub, water, and salt until dissolved.
4. Season the brisket with the spice rub and allow to rest in the fridge for 3 hours.
5. When ready to cook, fire your pellet grill to 250°F.
6. Close the lid and heat up for 15 minutes.
7. Move the brisket on the grill grate and close the lid.
8. Cook for 6 hours or up until the brisket's internal temperature reaches 160°F (as read by a meat thermometer).
9. Wrap the brisket in aluminum foil and increase the temperature to 275°F.
10. Cook for another 3 hours.

Nutrition: Calories 352 kCal, Carbs: 0g, Protein: 47g, Fat: 16.7g

11. Pastrami Short Ribs

Preparation Time: 30 minutes
Cooking Time: 3 hours
Servings: 4
Ingredients:
- 2 quarts water
- 1/3 cup salt
- Two teaspoons pink salt

- 1/4 cup brown sugar
- Four garlic
- Four tablespoons coriander seeds
- Three tablespoons peppercorns
- Two teaspoons mustard seeds
- Two tablespoons extra virgin olive oil
- One large ginger ale
- 2 pounds beef short ribs

Directions:
1. Place all ingredients except for the oil, ginger ale, and short ribs in a large bowl.
2. Mix until well-combined. Add in the short ribs.
3. Marinate the short ribs in the fridge for at least 12 hours.
4. When ready to cook, fire your pellet grill to 300°F.
5. Close the lid and heat up for 15 minutes.
6. Place the short ribs on the grill grate and smoke for 2 hours. Drizzle with oil.
7. Transferred the ribs to a roasting pan and pour enough ginger ale all over the ribs.
8. Cover the pan with foil.
9. Place in the grill and increase the temperature to 350°F and cook for 1 1/2 hour.

Nutrition: Calories: 521 kCal, Carbs: 16.9 g, Protein: 46.7 g, Fat: 30.1 g

12. Meat Chuck Short Rib

Preparation Time: 20 minutes
Cooking Time: 5-6 hours
Servings: 2
Ingredients:
- English cut 4 bone slab beef chuck short rib
- 3-4 cups of mustard yellow mustard or extra virgin olive oil
- 3-5 tablespoons of Western Love

Directions:
1. Cut the fat cap off the rib bone, leaving 1/4 inch fat, and remove the silvery skin.
2. Remove the membrane from the bone and move the spoon handle below the membrane to lift the piece of meat and season the meat properly. Grab the membrane using a paper towel and pull it away from the bone.
3. Apply mustard or olive oil to all sides of the short rib slab. By rubbing it, you can season all sides.

4. Using mesquite or hickory pellets set the wood pellet smoker and grill to indirect heating and preheat to 225°F.
5. Insert a wood pellet smoker and grill or remote meat probe into the thickest part of the rib bone plank. If your grill does not have a meat probe or you do not have a remote meat probe, use an instant reading digital thermometer to read the internal temperature while cooking.
6. Place the short rib bone on the grill with the bone side down and smoke at 225°F for 5 hours.
7. If the ribs have not reached an internal temperature of at least 195°F after 5 hours, increase the pit temperature to 250°F until the meat's internal temperature reaches 195° to 205°F (as read by a meat thermometer).
8. Place the smoked short rib bone under the loose foil tent for 15 minutes before serving.

Nutrition: Calories: 357 kCal, Carbs: 0 g, Protein: 37 g, Fat: 22 g

13. Balsamic Vinegar Molasses Steak

Preparation Time: 15 minutes + marinating
Cooking Time: 20-30 minutes
Servings: 4
Ingredients:
- Pepper
- Salt
- 1 tablespoon balsamic vinegar
- 2 tablespoons molasses
- 1 tablespoon red wine vinegar
- 1 cup beef broth
- 2 1/2 pounds steak of choice

Directions:
1. Lay the steaks in a zip-top bag.
2. Add the balsamic vinegar, red wine vinegar, molasses, and beef broth to a bowl. Combine thoroughly by stirring.
3. On the top of the steaks, drizzle this mixture.
4. Place into the refrigerator for eight hours.
5. Add wood pellets to your smoker and follow your cooker's startup procedure. Preheat your smoker, with your lid closed, until it reaches 350°F.
6. Take the flounced steaks out of the refrigerator 30 minutes before you are ready to grill.

7. Place on the grill, cover, and smoke for ten minutes per side, or until meat is tender.
8. Place onto plates and let them rest for ten minutes.

Nutrition: Calories: 164 kCal, Carbs: 6 g, Protein: 22 g, Fat: 5 g

14. Dijon Corned Beef Brisket

Preparation Time: 15 minutes
Cooking Time: 5 hours
Servings: 5 to 8
Ingredients:
- 1 (3 pounds / 1.4 kg) flat cut corned beef brisket, fat cap at least 1/4 inch thick
- 1/4 cup Dijon mustard
- 1 bottle Apricot BBQ Sauce

Directions:
- Remove the brisket from its packaging and discard the spice packet, if any. Soak the brisket in water for at least 8 hours, changing the water every 2 hours.
- When ready to cook, preheat your pellet grill lid closed for 15 minutes at 300ºF.
- Place the brisket, fat-side up, directly on the grill and cook for 2 hours.
- Pour the remaining ingredients together in a medium bowl. Pour half of the sauce mixture into the bottom of a disposable aluminum foil pan.
- Using tongs, transfer the brisket, fat-side up, to the pan. Cover the pan tightly with aluminum foil.
- Return the brisket to the grill and cook for an additional 2 to 3 hours, or until the brisket is tender and reaches an internal temperature of 203ºF (95ºC), as read by a meat thermometer.
- Let the brisket cool for 15 minutes. Slice and serve warm.

Nutrition: Calories: 385 kCal, Carbs: 2 g, Protein: 23 g, Fat: 30 g

15. George's Smoked Tri-Tip

Preparation Time: 25 minutes
Cooking Time: 5 hours
Servings: 4
Ingredients:
- 11/2 pounds tri-tip roast
- Salt
- Freshly ground black pepper
- 2 teaspoons garlic powder
- 2 teaspoons lemon pepper
- 1/2 cup apple juice

Directions:
1. Supply your smoker w/ wood pellets and follow the manufacturer's specific start-up procedure. Allow your grill to preheat with the lid closed, to 180°F.
2. Season the tri-tip roast with salt, pepper, garlic powder, and lemon pepper. Using your two hands, work on the seasoning into the meat.
3. Place the meat to roast directly on the grill grate and smoke for 4 hours.
4. Pull the tri-tip from the grill and place it on enough aluminum foil to wrap it completely.
5. Increase the grill's temperature to 375°F.
6. Fold in three sides of the foil around the roast and add the apple juice. Fold in the last side, completely enclosing the tri-tip and liquid. Return the wrapped tri-tip to the grill and cook for 45 minutes more.
7. Remove the tri-tip roast from the grill and let it rest for 10 to 15 minutes, before unwrapping, slicing, and serving.

Nutrition: Calories: 155 kCal, Carbs: 0 g, Protein: 23 g, Fat: 7 g

16. Almond Crusted Beef Fillet

Preparation Time: 15 minutes
Cooking Time: 55 minutes
Servings: 4
Ingredients:
- 1/4 cup chopped almonds
- 1 tablespoon Dijon mustard
- 1 cup chicken broth
- Salt
- 1/3 cup chopped onion
- 1/4 cup olive oil
- Pepper
- 2 tablespoons curry powder
- 3 pounds beef fillet tenderloin

Directions:
1. Rub the pepper and salt into the tenderloin.
2. Place the almonds, mustard, chicken broth, curry, onion, and olive oil into a bowl. Stir well to combine.
3. Take this mixture and rub the tenderloin generously with it.
4. Add wood pellets to your smoker and follow your cooker's startup procedure. Preheat your smoker, with your lid closed, until it reaches 450°F.
5. Lie on the grill, cover, and smoke for ten minutes on both sides.
6. Continue to cook until it reaches your desired doneness.
7. Take the entire grill and let it rest for at least ten minutes.

Nutrition: Calories: 118 kCal, Carbs: 3 g, Protein: 20 g, Fat: 3 g

17. La Rochelle Steak

Preparation Time: 4 hours and 10 minutes
Cooking Time: 20 minutes
Servings: 4
Ingredients:
- 1 tablespoon red currant jelly
- 1/2 teaspoon salt
- 3 teaspoon curry powder
- 8 ounces pineapple chunks in juice
- 1 1/2 pounds flank steak
- 1/4 cup olive oil

Directions:
1. Put the flank steak into a large bag.
2. Mix the pepper, salt, red currant jelly, curry powder, pineapple chunks with juice, and olive oil together.
3. Pour this mixture over the flank steak.
4. Place into the refrigerator for four hours.
5. Add wood pellets to your smoker and follow your cooker's startup procedure. Preheat your smoker, with your lid closed, until it reaches 350°F.
6. Then you are ready to cook the steak, remove the steak from the refrigerator 30 minutes before ready to cook.

7. Lay the steaks on the grill, cover, and smoke for ten minutes on both sides, or done to your liking.
8. Remove your roasted food from the grill and allow it to cool for about ten minutes.

Nutrition: Calories: 200 kCal, Carbs: 0 g, Fat: 7 g, Protein: 33 g

18. Beer Honey Steaks

Preparation Time: 10 minutes
Cooking Time: 20 minutes
Servings: 4
Ingredients:

- Pepper
- Juice of one lemon
- 1 cup beer of choice
- 1 tablespoon honey
- Salt
- 2 tablespoons olive oil
- 1 teaspoon thyme
- 4 steaks of choice

Directions:
1. Season the steaks with pepper and salt.
2. Combine together with olive oil, lemon juice, honey, thyme, and beer.
3. Rub the steaks with this mixture generously.
4. Add wood pellets to your smoker and follow your cooker's startup procedure. Preheat your smoker, with your lid closed, until it reaches 450°F.
5. Place the steaks onto the grill, cover, and smoke for ten minutes per side.
6. For about 10 minutes, let it cool after removing from the grill.

Nutrition: Calories: 245 kCal, Carbs: 8 g, Fat: 5 g, Protein: 40 g

19. Sweetheart Steak

Preparation Time: 5 minutes
Cooking Time: 15 minutes
Servings: 1
Ingredients:

- 20 ounces boneless strip steak, butterflied
- 2 ounces pure sea salt
- Two teaspoons black pepper
- Two tablespoons raw dark chocolate, finely chopped

- 1/2 tablespoon extra-virgin olive oil

Directions:
1. On a cutting board, trim the meat into a heart shape using a sharp knife. Set aside.
2. In a lighter bowl, combine the rest of the fixings to create a spice rub mix.
3. Rub onto the steak and massage until well-seasoned.
4. When ready to cook, fire the pellet grill to 450°F.
5. Closed the lid and preheat for 15 minutes.
6. Grill each side of the steak for 7 minutes.
7. Allow resting for 5 minutes before slicing.

Nutrition: Calories: 727 kCal, Carbs: 8.8 g, Protein: 133 g, Fat: 18.5 g

20. Beef Jerky

Preparation Time: 6 hours and 15 minutes
Cooking Time: 5 hours
Servings: 10
Ingredients:

- 3 lb. sirloin steaks
- 2 cups soy sauce
- 1 cup pineapple juice
- 1/2 cup brown sugar
- 2 tbsps. sriracha
- 2 tbsps. hoisin
- 2 tbsps. red pepper flake
- 2 tbsps. rice wine vinegar
- 2 tbsps. onion powder

Directions:
1. Mixed the marinade in a zip lock bag and add the beef. Mix until well coated and remove as much air as possible.
2. Placed the bag in a fridge and let marinate overnight or for 6 hours. Remove the bag from the fridge an hour prior to cooking.
3. Startup the Wood Pellet Grill and set it on the smoking settings or at 190°F.
4. Lay the meat on the grill leaving a half-inch space between the pieces. Let cool for 5 hours and turn after 2 hours.
5. Remove from the grill and let cool. Serve or refrigerate.

Nutrition: Calories: 309 kCal, Carbs: 20 g, Fat: 7 g, Protein: 34 g

21. Smoked Roast Beef

Preparation Time: 10 minutes
Cooking Time: 12 to 14 hours
Servings: 5 to 8
Ingredients:
- 1 (4-pound) top round roast
- 1 batch Espresso Brisket Rub
- 1 tablespoon butter

Directions:
1. Supply your smoker with wood pellets and follow the manufacturer's specific start-up procedure. With the lid closed, let the grill heat to 180°F.
2. Season the top round roast with the rub. With the use of your hands, put the rub on the meat.
3. Place the roast directly on the grill grate and smoke until its internal temperature reaches 140°F. Take the roast off the grill.
4. Place a cast-iron skillet on the grill grate and increase the grill's temperature to 450°F. Place the roast in the skillet, add the butter, and cook until its internal temperature reaches 145°F, flipping once after about 3 minutes.
5. Take the roast off the grill and leave it within 10 to 15 minutes, before slicing and serving.

Nutrition: Calories: 241 kCal, Carbs: 1g, Fat: 19g, Protein: 29g

22. Smoked Burgers

Preparation Time: 15 minutes
Cooking Time: 45 minutes
Servings: 4
Ingredients:
- 1 pound ground beef
- 1 egg
- Wood-Fired Burger Shake, for seasoning

Directions:
1. Supply your smoker with wood pellets and follow the manufacturer's specific start-up procedure. With the lid closed, let the grill heat to 180°F.
2. In a medium bowl, thoroughly mix the ground beef and egg. Divide the meat into 4 portions and shape each into a patty. Season the patties with the burger shake.
3. Place the burgers directly on the grill grate and smoke for 30 minutes.

4. Increase the grill's temperature to 400°F and continue to cook the burgers until their internal temperature reaches 145°F. Take the burgers off the grill and serve as you like.

Nutrition: Calories: 215 kCal, Carbs: 1.1g, Fat: 20g, Protein: 18g

23. Smoked Beef Ribs

Preparation Time: 25 minutes
Cooking Time: 4 to 6 hours
Servings: 4 to 8
Ingredients:
- 2 (2- or 3-pound) racks beef ribs
- 2 tablespoons yellow mustard
- 1 batch Sweet and Spicy Cinnamon Rub

Directions:
1. Supply your smoker with wood pellets and follow the manufacturer's specific start-up procedure. With the lid closed, let the grill heat to 225°F.
2. Remove the membrane from the backside of the ribs. This can be done by cutting just through the membrane in an X pattern and working a paper towel between the membrane and the ribs to pull it off.
3. Coat the ribs all over with mustard and season them with the rub. With the use of your hands, put the rub on the meat.
4. Place the ribs directly on the grill grate and smoke until their internal temperature reaches between 190°F and 200°F.
5. Remove the racks from the grill and cut them into individual ribs. Serve immediately.

Nutrition: Calories: 300 kCal, Carbs: 2g, Fat: 30g, Protein: 40g

24. Pellet Grill Meatloaf

Preparation Time: 30 minutes
Cooking Time: 6 hours
Servings: 8
Ingredients:

- 1 cup breadcrumbs
- 2 pounds ground beef
- ¼ pound ground sausage
- 2 large eggs (beaten)
- 2 garlic cloves (grated)
- ½ teaspoon ground black pepper
- ¼ teaspoon red pepper flakes
- ½ teaspoon salt or to taste
- 1 teaspoon dried parsley
- 1 green onion (chopped)
- 1 teaspoon paprika
- ½ teaspoon Italian seasoning
- 1 small onion (chopped)
- 1 cup milk
- 1 cup BBQ sauce
- ½ cup apple juice

Directions:

1. Preheat the grill to 225°F with the lid closed for 15 minutes, using an apple pellet
2. In a large mixing bowl, combine the egg, milk, parsley, onion, green onion, paprika, Italian seasoning, breadcrumbs, ground beef, ground sausage, salt, pepper flakes, black pepper, and garlic. Mix thoroughly until the ingredients are well combined.
3. Form the mixture into a loaf and wrap the loaf loosely in tin foil and use a knife to poke some holes in the foil. The holes will allow the smoke flavor to enter the loaf.
4. Place the wrapped loaf on the grill grate and grill for 1 hour 30 minutes.
5. Meanwhile, combine the BBQ sauce and apple juice in a mixing bowl.
6. Tear off the top half of the tin foil to apply the glaze. Apply the glaze over the meatloaf. Continue grilling until the internal temperature of the meatloaf is 160°F.
7. Remove the meatloaf from the grill and let it sit for a few minutes to cool.
8. Cut and serve.

Nutrition: Calories: 298 kCal, Carbs: 22g, Protein: 28g, Fat: 6g

25. BBQ Brisket

Preparation Time: 30 minutes
Cooking Time: 6 hours
Servings: 8
Ingredients:

- 1 (12-14) packer beef brisket
- 1 teaspoon cayenne pepper
- 1 teaspoon cumin
- 2 tablespoons paprika
- 1 tablespoon smoked paprika
- 1 tablespoon onion powder
- ½ tablespoon maple sugar
- 2 teaspoon ground black pepper
- 2 teaspoon kosher salt

Directions:

1. Combine all the ingredients except the brisket in a mixing bowl.
2. Season all sides of the brisket with the seasoning mixture as needed and wrap the brisket in plastic wrap. Refrigerate for 12 hours or more.
3. Unwrap the brisket and let it sit for about 2 hours or until the brisket is at room temperature.
4. Preheat the pellet grill to 225°F with lid close, using mesquite or oak wood pellet.
5. Place the brisket on the grill grate and grill for about 6 hours. Remove the brisket from the grill and wrap it with foil.
6. Return brisket to the grill and cook for about 4 hours or until the brisket's temperature reaches 204°F.
7. Remove the brisket from the grill and let it sit for about 40 minutes to cool.
8. Unwrap the brisket and cut it into slices.

Nutrition: Calories: 350 kCal, Carbs: 22g, Protein: 28g, Fat: 6g

26. Tri-Tip Roast

Preparation Time: 30 minutes
Cooking Time: 50 minutes
Servings: 8
Ingredients:

- 2 pounds tri-tip roast (silver skin and fat cap removed)
- 1 teaspoon salt
- 1 teaspoon ground black pepper
- ½ teaspoon paprika
- 1 teaspoon fresh rosemary
- 1 teaspoon garlic powder
- 1 tablespoon olive oil

Directions:

1. Combine salt, pepper, garlic, paprika, and rosemary.
2. Brush the tri-tip generously with olive oil. Season the roast with seasoning mixture generously.
3. Preheat the grill smoker 225°F with the lid closed for 15 minutes, using hickory, mesquite, or oak wood pellet.
4. Place the tri-tip roast on the grill grate directly and cook for about 1 hour or until the tri tip's temperature reaches 135°F.
5. Remove the tri-tip from the grill and wrap it with heavy-duty foil. Set aside in a cooler.
6. Adjust the grill temperature to high and preheat with lid closed for 15 minutes.
7. Remove the tri-tip from the foil and place it on the grill cook for 8 minutes, turning the tri-tip after the first 4 minutes.
8. Remove the tri-tip from the grill and let it rest for a few minutes to cool.
9. Cut them into slices against the grain and serve.

Nutrition: Calories: 362 kCal, Carbs: 22g, Protein: 28g, Fat: 6g

27. Fully Loaded Beef Nachos

Preparation Time: 10 minutes
Cooking Time: 25 minutes
Servings: 6
Ingredients:

- Ground beef (1-lbs, 0.45-kgs)
- 1 large bag of tortilla chips
- 1 green bell pepper, seeded and diced
- Scallions, sliced – ½ cup
- Red onion, peeled and diced – ½ cup
- Cheddar cheese, shredded – 3 cups
- Sour cream, guacamole, salsa – to serve

Directions:

1. In a cast-iron pan, arrange a double layer of tortilla chips.
2. Scatter over the ground beef, bell pepper, scallions, red onion, and finally the Cheddar cheese.
3. Place the cast-iron pan on the grill and cook for approximately 10 minutes until the cheese has melted completely.
4. Take off the grill and serve with sour cream, guacamole, and salsa on the side.

Nutrition: Calories: 160 kCal, Carbs: 7g, Protein: 10g, Fat: 10g

28. Whole Smoked Bologna Roll

Preparation Time: 10 minutes
Cooking Time: 4 hours 20 minutes
Servings: 12
Ingredients:

- Whole beef bologna roll (3-lbs, 1.4-kgs)
- Black pepper freshly cracked – 2 tablespoons
- Brown sugar – ¾ cup
- Yellow mustard – ¼ cup

Directions:

1. Combine the black pepper and brown sugar.
2. Score the outside of the bologna with a diamond pattern.
3. Spread mustard over the outside of the bologna and then rub in the black pepper/sugar until thoroughly and evenly coated.
4. Arrange the bologna on the smoker's upper rack and cook for 3-4 hours until the outside caramelizes.
5. Slice the bologna into medium-thick slices and serve.

Nutrition: Calories: 210 kCal, Carbs: 19g, Protein: 10g, Fat: 14g

29. Honey-Apple BBQ Ribs

Preparation Time: 15 minutes
Cooking Time: 2 hours 40 minutes
Servings: 4-6
Ingredients:
- 4 slabs baby back ribs
- Paprika – ½ cup
- Brown sugar - 2/3 cup
- Onion powder – 2 tablespoons
- Garlic powder - 1/3 cup
- Cayenne pepper – 1 tablespoon
- Chili powder – 2 tablespoons
- White pepper – 1 tablespoon
- Black pepper – 1 tablespoon
- Ground cumin – 1½ teaspoons
- Dried oregano – 1½ teaspoons
- White grape juice – ½ cup
- Apple juice – ½ cup
- Honey
- BBQ sauce

Directions:
1. First, prepare the rub. Combine the paprika, brown sugar, onion powder, garlic powder, cayenne pepper, chili powder, white pepper, black pepper, cumin, and oregano.
2. Sprinkle the rub mixture evenly over the ribs on both sides.
3. Place the ribs on the hot grill, close the lid, and cook for 45 minutes.
4. In the meantime, stir together the grape and apple juice and set to one side.
5. Take the ribs off the grill and transfer them to a disposable aluminum tray lined with aluminum kitchen foil.
6. Pour the grape-apple juice over the ribs. Drizzle a generous amount of honey over the rubs. Wrap the ribs with the foil, sealing the edges tightly.
7. Return the ribs to the grill and cook for another hour.
8. Take the ribs out of the foil and place them directly on the grates. Increase Preferred Wood Pellet to 350°F (175°C) and cook for another half an hour.
9. Brush the ribs with lashings of BBQ sauce, grill for a final 5 minutes before transferring to a chopping board to rest for 10 minutes.
10. Slice into single Servings and enjoy.

Nutrition: Calories: 529 kCal, Carbs: 36g, Fat: 25g, Protein: 40g

30. Smoked Rib-Eye Steaks

Preparation Time: 5 minutes
Cooking Time: 50 minutes
Servings: 2
Ingredients:
- 2 thick rib-eye steaks (1.5-lbs, 0.68-kgs)
- Salt and black pepper
- Steak rubs, of choice

Directions:
1. Allow the steaks to sit out at room Smoke Temperature for half an hour.
2. Season the steaks with salt, black pepper, and your choice of rub. Arrange the steaks directly on the grill and cook for just over 20 minutes.
3. Take the steaks off the grill and set the Smoke Temperature to 400°F (205°C).
4. Sear the cooked steaks on the hotter grill for 5 minutes on each side.
5. Wrap the steaks in kitchen foil and set aside for 10 minutes to rest.
6. Slice and serve with your choice of sides.

Nutrition: Calories: 200 kCal, Carbs: 0g, Protein: 24g, Fat: 12g,

31. Texan-Style Smoke Beef Brisket

Preparation Time: 30 minutes
Cooking Time: 15 hours
Servings: 18
Ingredients:
- 1 whole packet brisket, refrigerated (14-lb, 6.3-kgs)
- Sea salt – 2 tablespoons
- Garlic powder – 2 tablespoons
- Coarsely ground black pepper – 2 tablespoons

Directions:
1. Remove the brisket from the fridge and flip it over so that the pointed end is directly on the worktop. Remove and discard any excess fat or silver skin from the muscle. Carefully, trim the fat piece until smooth between the pointed end and the flat end. Trim and discard loose fat or meat from the point. Square both the edges and the end of the flat. Finally, flip the meat over and

trim the top to an approximate thickens ½-ins (1.25-cms) across the surface of the meat.
2. In a bowl, combine the rub ingredients, sea salt, garlic powder, and black pepper. Rub the seasoning all over the brisket.
3. Arrange the meat on the smoker with the pointed end facing towards the main heat source. Close the smoker lid and smoke for approximately 8 hours, or until a meat thermometer registers 165°F (74°C).
4. On a large, clean work surface roll out a large piece of aluminum foil and place your brisket in the middle. Wrap the meat, by folding the foil edge over the edge to create a leaf-proof seal all the way around. Return the foil-wrapped brisket to the smoker, seam side facing downwards.
5. Close the smoker's lid and continue to cook at 225°F (110°C). A meat thermometer inserted in the thickest part of the brisket needs to register 202°F (108°C). This will take between 5-8 hours.
6. When cooked, transfer the meat to a chopping board and set it to one side to rest for 60 minutes before slicing.
7. When you are ready to serve, slice the point and flat against the grain. Serve.
Nutrition: Calories: 282 kCal, Carbs: 1g, Protein: 36g, Fat: 1g

32. Delicious Soy Marinated Steak

Preparation Time: 20 minutes
Cooking Time: 55 minutes
Servings: 4
Ingredients:
- ½ chopped onion
- 0.3 chopped cloves of garlic
- ¼ cup of olive oil
- ¼ cup of balsamic vinegar
- ¼ cup of soy sauce
- 1 tablespoon of Dijon mustard
- 1 tablespoon of rosemary
- 1 teaspoon of salt to taste
- ½ teaspoon of ground black pepper to taste
- 1 ½ pound of flank steak

Directions:
1. Using a large mixing bowl, add in all the ingredients on the list aside from the steak then mix properly to combine.

2. Place the steak in a Ziploc bag, pour in the prepared marinade then shake properly to coat.
3. Place the bag in the refrigerator and let the steak marinate for about thirty minutes to two full days.
4. Preheat the Wood Pellet Smoker and Grill to 350-400 degrees F, remove the steak from its marinade then set the marinade aside for blasting.
5. Place the steak on the preheated grill then grill for about six to eight minutes until the beef is heated through.
6. Flip the steak over and cook for an additional six minutes until an inserted thermometer reads 150 degrees F.
7. Place the steak on a cutting board and let rest for about five minutes. Slice and serve.
Nutrition: Calories: 300 kCal, Carbs: 8g, Fat: 20g, Protein: 22g

33. Grilled Steak and Vegetable Kebabs

Preparation Time: 15 minutes
Cooking Time: 20 minutes
Servings: 5
Ingredients:
Marinade
- ¼ cup of olive oil
- ¼ cup of soy sauce
- 1 ½ tablespoon of fresh lemon juice
- 1 ½ tablespoon of red wine vinegar
- 2 ½ tablespoons of Worcestershire sauce
- 1 tablespoon of honey
- 2 teaspoons of Dijon mustard
- 1 tablespoon of garlic
- 1 teaspoon of freshly ground black pepper to taste

Kebabs:
- 1 3/4 lbs. of sirloin steak
- 1 sliced zucchini.
- 3 sliced bell peppers
- 1 large and sliced red onion
- 1 tablespoon of olive oil
- Salt and freshly ground black pepper to taste
- ½ teaspoon of garlic powder

Directions:
1. Using a large mixing bowl, add in the oil, soy sauce, lemon juice, red wine vinegar,

Worcestershire sauce, Dijon, honey, garlic, and pepper to taste then mix properly to combine.

2. Using a sharp knife, cut the steak into smaller pieces or cubes then add to a resealable bag.
3. Pour the marinade into the bag with steak then shake to coat. Let the steak marinate for about three to six hours in the refrigerator.
4. Preheat the Wood Pellet Smoker and Grill to 425 degrees F, place the veggies into a mixing bowl, add in oil, garlic powder, salt, and pepper to taste then mix to combine.
5. Thread the veggies and steak alternately unto skewers, place the skewers on the preheated grill, and grill for about eight to nine minutes until it is cooked through.
6. Make sure you turn the kebabs occasionally as you cook. Serve.

Nutrition: Calories: 350 kCal, Carbs: 18g, Fat: 14g, Protein: 34g

34. Grilled Barbecue Beef Ribs

Preparation Time: 30 minutes
Cooking Time: 1 hour
Servings: 4
Ingredients:
- ½ cup of Dijon mustard
- 2 tablespoons of cider vinegar
- 3 lbs. of spareribs
- 4 tablespoons of paprika powder
- ½ tablespoon of chili powder
- 1 ½ tablespoon of garlic powder
- 2 teaspoons of ground cumin
- 2 teaspoon of onion powder
- 1 ½ tablespoon of ground black pepper to taste
- 2 tablespoons of salt to taste
- 2 tablespoons of butter (optional)

Directions:
1. Preheat a Wood Pellet Smoker and Grill to 350 degrees F, using a small mixing bowl, add in the mustard and the vinegar then mix properly to combine.
2. Rub the mixture on the spareribs, coating all sides. Using another mixing bowl, add in the paprika powder, chili powder, garlic powder, cumin, onion powder, salt, and pepper to taste then mix properly to combine.

3. Reserve a small quantity of the mixture, seasoned the spareribs with the rest of the spice mixture, coating all sides.
4. Wrap the seasoned ribs in aluminum foil, top with the butter if desired then place the ribs on the preheated grill.
5. Grill the ribs for about one hour until it is cooked through. Make sure you flip after every twenty minutes.
6. Once the ribs are cooked through, remove from the grill, unwrap the aluminum foil then grill the ribs for another two to five minutes until crispy.
7. Let the ribs cool for a few minutes, slice, and serve.

Nutrition: Calories: 280 kCal, Carbs: 6g, Fat: 42g, Protein: 55g

35. Garlic Butter Grilled Steak

Preparation Time: 15 minutes
Cooking Time: 25 minutes
Servings: 4
Ingredients:
- 3 tablespoons of unsalted butter
- 4 cloves of garlic
- 1 tablespoon of chopped parsley
- 1 tablespoon of olive oil
- 4 strip steaks
- Salt and pepper to taste

Directions:
1. Using a large mixing bowl, add in the butter, garlic, and parsley then mix properly to combine, set aside in the refrigerator.
2. Preheat a Wood Pellet Smoker and Grill to 400 degrees F, use paper towels to pat the steak dry, rub oil on all sides then season with some sprinkles of salt and pepper to taste.
3. Place the seasoned steak on the preheated grill and grill for about four to five minutes.
4. Flip the steak over and grill for an additional four to five minutes until it becomes brown and cooked as desired.
5. Rub the steak with the butter mixture, heat on the grill for a few minutes, slice and serve.

Nutrition: Calories: 543 kCal, Carbs: 1g, Fat: 25g, Protein: 64g

36. Grilled Coffee Rub Brisket

Preparation Time: 30 minutes
Cooking Time: 15 hours
Servings: 4
Ingredients:

- 1 (14 pounds) whole brisket

Coffee Rub

- 2 tablespoons of coarse salt to taste
- 2 tablespoons of instant coffee
- 2 tablespoons of garlic powder
- 2 tablespoons of smoked paprika
- 1 tablespoon of pepper to taste
- 1 tablespoon of crushed coriander
- 1 tablespoon of onion powder
- 1 teaspoon of chili powder
- ½ teaspoon of cayenne

Directions:

1. Using a large mixing bowl, add in the instant coffee, garlic powder, paprika, coriander, onion powder, chili powder, cayenne, salt, and pepper to taste then mix properly to combine.
2. Rub the brisket with the prepared rub, coating all sides then set aside.
3. Preheat a Wood Pellet Smoker and Grill to 225 degrees F, add in the seasoned brisket, cover the smoker, and smoke for about eight hours until a thermometer reads 165 degrees for the briskets.
4. Place the brisket in an aluminum foil then wrap up. Place the foil-wrapped brisket on the wood Pellet smoker and cook for another five to eight hours until the meat reaches an internal temperature of 225 degrees F.
5. Once cooked, let the brisket rest on the cutting board for about one hour, slice against the grain then serve.

Nutrition: Calories: 420 kCal, Carbs: 15g, Fat: 11g, Protein: 58g

37. Grilled Herb Steak

Preparation Time: 15 minutes
Cooking Time: 20 minutes
Servings: 4
Ingredients:

- 1 tablespoon of peppercorns
- 1 teaspoon of fennel seeds
- 3 large and minced cloves of garlic
- 2 teaspoons of kosher salt to taste
- 1 tablespoon of chopped rosemary
- 1 tablespoon of chopped thyme
- 2 teaspoons of black pepper to taste
- 2 teaspoons of olive oil
- 1 pound of flank steak

Directions:

1. Using a grinder or a food processor, add in the peppercorns and the fennel seeds then blend until completely crushed then add to a mixing bowl.
2. Add in the garlic, rosemary, thyme, salt, and pepper to taste then mix properly to combine, set aside.
3. Rub the steak with oil, coating all sides then coat with half of the peppercorn mixture. Make sure the steak is coated all around.
4. Place the steak in a Ziploc plastic bag then let marinate in the refrigerator for about 2 to 8 minutes.
5. Preheat a Wood Pellet Smoker and Grill to 450 degrees F, place the coated steak on the grill and cook for about five to six minutes.
6. Flip the steak over and cook for another five to six minutes until cooked through.
7. Once cooked, let the steak cool for a few minutes, slice, and serve.

Nutrition: Calories: 440 kCal, Carbs: 20g, Fat: 25g, Protein: 35g

38. Brisket Baked Beans

Preparation Time: 15 minutes
Cooking Time: 1 to 2 hours
Servings: 5
Ingredients:

- 2 tablespoons extra-virgin olive oil 1 large yellow onion, diced
- 1 medium green bell pepper, diced
- 1 medium red bell pepper, diced
- 2 to 6 jalapeño peppers, diced
- 3 cups chopped Texas-Style Brisket Flat (page 91) 1 (28-ounce) can baked beans, like Bush's Country
- Style Baked Beans 1 (28-ounce) can pork and beans
- 1 (14-ounce) can red kidney beans, rinsed and drained 1 cup barbecue sauce, like Sweet Baby Ray's
- Barbecue Sauce ½ cup packed brown sugar
- 3 garlic cloves, chopped
- 2 teaspoons ground mustard
- ½ teaspoon kosher salt
- ½ teaspoon black pepper

Directions:

1. In a skillet over medium heat, warm the olive oil and then add the diced onion, peppers, and jalapeños. Cook until the onions are translucent, about 8 to 10 minutes, stirring occasionally.
2. In a 4-quart casserole dish, mix the chopped brisket, baked beans, pork and beans, kidney beans, cooked onion and peppers, barbecue sauce, brown sugar, garlic, ground mustard, salt, and black pepper.
3. Configure your Pit Boss smoker-grill for indirect cooking and preheat to 325°F using your Pit Bosss of choice. Cook the brisket baked beans uncovered for 1½ to 2 hours, until the beans are thick and bubbly. Allow to rest for 15 minutes before serving.

Nutrition: Calories: 200 kCal, Carbs: 35g, Fat: 2g, Protein: 9g

39. BBQ Meatloaf

Preparation Time: 25 minutes
Cooking Time: 1 hour and 30 minutes
Servings: 4
Ingredients:

- 1 ½ pound of ground beef
- 1/3 cup of ketchup
- 2 teaspoons of Worcestershire sauce
- 1 large egg
- 1 cup of soft breadcrumbs
- 1 cup of chopped onions
- ½ teaspoon of salt to taste
- ¼ teaspoon of ground black pepper to taste
- Barbecue sauce for a glaze

Directions:

1. Preheat a Wood Pellet Smoker and Grill to 350 degrees F, using a large mixing bowl, add in the beef alongside the rest of the ingredients on the list (aside from the barbecue sauce) then mix properly to combine.
2. Place the beef mixture in an aluminum foil then form it into your desired loaf shape.
3. Unfold the foil, brush the meatloaf with barbecue sauce then warp in.
4. Place the meatloaf on the grill and cook for about 1 hour to 1 hour and 30 minutes until it attains a temperature of 160 degrees F.
5. Slice and serve.

Nutrition: Calories: 370 kCal, Carbs: 20g, Fat: 15g, Protein: 35g

40. Wood Pellet Cocoa Rub Steak

Preparation Time: 20 minutes
Cooking Time: 40 minutes
Servings: 4
Ingredients:

- 4 rib eye steaks
- 2 tablespoons of unsweetened cocoa powder
- 1 tablespoon of dark brown sugar
- 1 tablespoon of smoked paprika
- 1 teaspoon of sea salt to taste
- 1 teaspoon of black pepper
- ½ teaspoon of garlic powder
- ½ teaspoon of onion powder

Directions:

1. Using a large mixing bowl, add in the cocoa powder, brown sugar, paprika, garlic powder, onion powder, and salt to taste then mix properly to combine
2. Rub the steak with about two tablespoons of the spice mixture, coating all sides then let rest for a few minutes.
3. Preheat the Wood Pellet Smoker and Grill to 450 degrees F, place the steak on the grill, and grill for a few minutes on both sides until it is cooked as desired.
4. Once cooked, cover the steak in foil and let rest for a few minutes. Serve and enjoy.

Nutrition: Calories: 480 kCal, Carbs: 4g, Fat: 30g, Protein: 40g

41. Grilled Steak with Mushroom Cream Sauce

Preparation Time: 25 minutes
Cooking Time: 1 hour and 30 minutes
Servings: 6
Ingredients:

- ½ cup of Dijon mustard
- 2 minced cloves of garlic
- 2 tablespoons of bourbon
- 1 tablespoon of Worcestershire sauce
- 4 beefsteak tenderloin
- 1 tablespoon of peppercorns

Others:

- 1 tablespoon of extra-virgin olive oil
- 1 small and diced onion
- 1 minced clove of garlic
- ½ cup of white wine
- ½ cup of chicken stock
- 16 ounces of sliced mushrooms
- ½ cup of heavy cream
- Salt and pepper to taste

Directions:

1. Using a small mixing bowl, add in the mustard, garlic, bourbon, and Worcestershire sauce then mix properly to combine
2. Place the steak in a Ziploc back, pour in the mustard mixture then shake properly to coat. Let the steak sit for about sixty minutes.
3. Using a small mixing bowl, add in the peppercorns, salt, and pepper to taste then mix to combine.
4. Remove the steak from the Ziploc bag, season the steak with the peppercorn mixture then use clean hands to evenly distribute the seasoning.
5. Preheat the Wood Pellet Smoker and grill to 180 degrees F then close the lid for fifteen minutes.
6. Add the seasoned steak to the grill and smoke for about sixty minutes. Take the steak out of the grill, increase the temperature of the grill to 350 degrees, and grill for 20 to 30 minutes until it attains an internal temperature of 130 degrees F.
7. To make the sauce, place a pan on the pellet grill, add in oil and onions then cook for a few minutes.
8. Cook the garlic for one minute. Add in the mushrooms and cook for a few more minutes.
9. Add in the stock, wine, salt, and pepper to taste, stir to combine then bring to a simmer. Simmer the sauce for 5 to 7 minutes then add in the heavy cream.
10. Stir to combine then serve the steak with the sauce, enjoy.

Nutrition: Calories: 470 kCal, Carbs: 10g, Fat: 25g, Protein: 50g

42. Pork Burnt Ends

Preparation Time: 15 minutes
Cooking Time: 4 hours 15 minutes
Serving: 10

Ingredients:

- 4 pounds pork belly
- 4 tbsp. brown sugar
- ¼ tsp. cayenne pepper
- 1 tsp. red pepper flakes
- ½ tsp. onion powder
- ½ tsp. garlic powder
- 1 tbsp. paprika
- 1 tsp. oregano
- 1 tbsp. freshly ground black pepper
- 1 tbsp. salt or to taste
- 1 tsp. dried peppermint
- 1 tbsp. olive oil
- ¼ cup butter
- 1 cup BBQ sauce
- 1 tbsp. maple syrup
- 2 tbsp. chopped fresh parsley

Directions:

1. Trim pork belly of any excess fat and cut off silver skin. Cut the pork into ½ inch cubes.
2. To make rub, combine the sugar, cayenne, pepper flakes, onion powder, garlic, paprika, oregano, black pepper, salt, and peppermint in a mixing bowl.
3. Drizzle oil over the pork and season each pork cubes generously with the rub.
4. Preheat your grill to 205°F with lid closed for 15 minutes.
5. Arrange the pork chunks onto the grill grate and smoke for about 3 hours, or until the pork chunks turn dark red.
6. Meanwhile, combine the BBQ sauce, maple syrup and butter in an aluminum pan.
7. Remove the pork slices from heat and put them in the pan with the sauce. Stir to combine.
8. Cover the pan tightly with aluminum foil and place it on the grill. Cook for 1 hour or until the internal temperature of the pork reaches 200°F.
9. Remove the pork from heat and let it sit for some minutes.
10. Serve and garnish with fresh chopped parsley.

Nutrition: Calories: 477 kCal, Carbs: 19.3g, Fat: 41.8g, Protein: 6.4g

43. Pellet Grilled Pork Chops

Preparation Time: 20 Minutes
Cooking Time: 10 Minutes
Servings: 6

Ingredients:

- Six pork chops, thickly cut
- BBQ rub

Directions:

1. Preheat the wood pellet to 450°F.
2. Season the pork chops generously with the BBQ rub. Place the pork chops on the grill and cook for 6 minutes or until the internal temperature reaches 145°F.
3. Remove from the grill and let sit for 10 minutes before serving.
4. Enjoy.

Nutrition: Calories: 264 kCal, Carbs: 4g, Fat: 13g, Protein: 33g

44. Wood Pellet Blackened Pork Chops

Preparation Time: 5 Minutes
Cooking Time: 20 Minutes
Servings: 6

Ingredients:

- Six pork chops
- 1/4 cup blackening seasoning
- Salt and pepper to taste

Directions:

1. Preheat your grill to 375°F.
2. Meanwhile, generously season the pork chops with the blackening seasoning, salt, and pepper.
3. Place the pork chops on the grill and close the lid.
4. Let grill for 8 minutes, then flip the chops. Cook until the internal temperature reaches 142°F.
5. Remove the chops from the grill and let rest for 10 minutes before slicing.
6. Serve and enjoy.

Nutrition: Calories: 333 kCal, Carbs: 1g, Fat: 18g, Protein: 40g

45. Teriyaki Pineapple Pork Tenderloin Sliders

Preparation Time: 20 Minutes
Cooking Time: 20 Minutes
Servings: 6
Ingredients:

- 1-1/2 lb. pork tenderloin
- One can pineapple ring
- One package king's Hawaiian rolls
- 8 oz teriyaki sauce
- 1-1/2 tbsp salt
- 1 tbsp onion powder
- 1 tbsp paprika
- 1/2 tbsp garlic powder
- 1/2 tbsp cayenne pepper

Directions:

1. Add all the fixings for the rub in a mixing bowl and mix until well mixed. Generously rub the pork loin with the mixture.
2. Heat the pellet to 325°F. Place the meat on a grill and cook while you turn it every 4 minutes.
3. Cook until the internal temperature reaches 145°F.remove from the grill and let it rest for 5 minutes.
4. Meanwhile, open the pineapple can and place the pineapple rings on the grill. Flip the rings when they have a dark brown color.
5. At the same time, half the rolls and place them on the grill and grill them until toasty browned.
6. Assemble the slider by putting the bottom roll first, followed by the pork tenderloin, pineapple ring, a drizzle of sauce, and top with the other roll half. Serve and enjoy.

Nutrition: Calories: 243 kCal, Carbs: 4g, Fat: 5g, Protein: 33g

46. Wood Pellet Grilled Tenderloin with Fresh Herb Sauce

Preparation Time: 10 Minutes
Cooking Time: 15 Minutes
Servings: 4
Ingredients:

- One pork tenderloin, silver skin removed and dried
- BBQ seasoning
- One handful basil, fresh
- 1/4 tbsp garlic powder
- 1/3 cup olive oil
- 1/2 tbsp kosher salt

Directions:

1. Preheat the wood pellet grill to medium heat.
2. Coat the pork with BBQ seasoning, then cook on semi-direct heat of the grill. Turn the pork regularly to ensure even cooking.
3. Cook until the internal temperature is 145°F. Remove from the grill and let it rest for 10 minutes.
4. Meanwhile, make the herb sauce by pulsing all the sauce ingredients in a food processor—pulse for a few times or until well chopped.
5. Slice the pork diagonally and spoon the sauce on top. Serve and enjoy.

Nutrition: Calories: 300 kCal, Carbs: 13g, Fat 22g, Protein: 14g

47. Wood Pellet Grilled Shredded Pork Tacos

Preparation Time: 15 Minutes
Cooking Time: 7 Hours
Servings: 8
Ingredients:

- 5 lb. pork shoulder, bone-in
- 3 tbsp brown sugar
- 1 tbsp salt
- 1 tbsp garlic powder
- 1 tbsp paprika
- 1 tbsp onion powder
- 1/4 tbsp cumin
- 1 tbsp cayenne pepper

Directions:

1. Mix all the dry rub ingredients and rub on the pork shoulder.
2. Preheat the grill to 275°F and cook the pork directly for 6 hours or until the internal temperature has reached 145°F.
3. If you want to fall off the bone tender pork, then cook until the internal temperature is 190°F.
4. Let rest for 10 minutes before serving. Enjoy

Nutrition: Calories: 566 kCal, Carbs: 4g, Fat: 41g, Protein: 44g

48. Baked Pulled Pork Stuffed Potatoes

Preparation Time: 10 minutes
Cooking Time: 50 minutes
Servings 6
Ingredients:

- 4 russet potatoes
- Canola oil, as needed
- Salt, to taste
- 2 tablespoons butter, melted
- 3 cups pulled pork
- 1 cup Cheddar cheese
- 1 cup Mozzarella cheese
- 4 tablespoons Pit Boss Sweet & Heat BBQ Sauce
- Topping:
- Sour cream
- Chopped bacon
- Chopped green onion

Directions:

1. When ready to cook, set Pit Boss temperature to 450 F (232 C) and preheat, lid closed for 15 minutes.
2. Rub the potatoes with canola oil and sprinkle evenly with salt. Place the potatoes directly on the grill grate and cook for 45 minutes, or until fork tender.
3. Cut the potatoes in half and scoop the flesh out, leaving ¼ inch of the potato on the skin. Brush the inside of the skins with the melted butter and place on a baking tray. Place the tray on the grill and cook for 5 minutes, or until golden brown.
4. In a bowl, stir together the pulled pork, cheeses, and Pit Boss Sweet & Heat BBQ Sauce.
5. Fill the potato skins with the mixture and return to the grill. Cook for 30 seconds, lid closed, or until the cheese is melted.
6. Serve topped with the sour cream, bacon, and green onion.

Nutrition: Calories: 320 kCal, Carbs: 49 g, Fat: 6, Protein 18 g

49. Mediterranean Meatballs

Preparation Time: 15 Minutes
Cooking Time: 35 Minutes
Servings: 8
Ingredients:

- Pepper
- Salt
- One t. vinegar
- Two T. olive oil
- Two eggs
- One chopped onion
- One soaked slice of bread
- ½ t. cumin
- One T. chopped basil
- 1 ½ T. chopped parsley
- 2 ½ pounds ground beef

Directions:

1. Use your hands to combine everything until thoroughly combined. If needed, when forming meatballs, dip your hands into some water. Shape into 12 meatballs.
2. Add wood pellets to your smoker.
3. Preheat your smoker, with your lid closed, until it reaches 380.
4. Place the meatballs onto the grill and cook on all sides for eight minutes. Take off the grill and let sit for five minutes.
5. Serve with favorite condiments or a salad.

Nutrition: Calories: 33 kCal, Carbs: 6g, Fat: 0g, Protein: 1g

50. Greek Meatballs

Preparation Time: 10 Minutes
Cooking Time: 40 Minutes
Servings: 6
Ingredients:

- Pepper
- Salt
- Two chopped green onions
- One T. almond flour
- Two eggs
- ½ pound ground pork
- 2 ½ pound ground beef

Directions:

1. Mix all the ingredients using your hands until everything is incorporated evenly. Form mixture into meatballs until all meat is used.
2. Add wood pellets to your smoker and follow your cooker's startup procedure. Preheat your smoker, with your lid closed, until it reaches 380.
3. Brush the meatballs with olive oil and place onto the grill—Cook for ten minutes on all sides.

Nutrition: Calories: 161 kCal, Carbs: 10g, Fat: 6g, Protein: 17g

51. Wood Pellet Togarashi Pork Tenderloin

Preparation Time: 5 Minutes
Cooking Time: 25 Minutes
Servings: 6
Ingredients:
- 1 Pork tenderloin
- 1/2tbsp kosher salt
- 1/4 cup Togarashi seasoning

Directions:
1. Cut any excess silver skin from the pork and sprinkle with salt to taste. Rub generously with the togarashi seasoning
2. Place in a preheated oven at 400°F for 25 minutes or until the internal temperature reaches 145°F.
3. Remove from the grill and let rest for 10 minutes before slicing and serving.
4. Enjoy.

Nutrition: Calories 390 kCal, Carbs: 4g, Fat: 13g, Protein: 33g

52. Wood Pellet Pulled Pork

Preparation Time: 15 Minutes
Cooking Time: 12 Hours
Servings: 12
Ingredients:
- 8 lb. pork shoulder roast, bone-in
- BBQ rub
- 3 cups apple cider, dry hard

Directions:
1. Fire up the wood pellet grill and set it to smoke.
2. Meanwhile, rub the pork with BBQ rub on all sides, then place it on the grill grates. Cook for 5 hours, flipping it every 1 hour.
3. Increase the heat to 225°F and continue cooking for 3 hours directly on the grate.
4. Transfer the pork to a foil pan and place the apple cider at the bottom of the pan.
5. Cook until the internal temperature reaches 200°F then remove it from the grill. Wrap the pork loosely with foil, then let it rest for 1 hour.
6. Remove the fat layer and use forks to shred it.
7. Serve and enjoy.

Nutrition: Calories 912 kCal, Carbs: 7g, Fat: 65g, Protein: 70g

53. Tasty Grilled Pork Chops

Preparation Time: 15 minutes
Cooking Time: 1 hour 30 minutes
Servings: 4
Ingredients:
- Four pork chops.
- 1/4 cup of olive oil.
- 1 1/2 tbsp. of brown sugar
- 2 tsp. of Dijon mustard.
- 1 ½ tbsp. of soy sauce
- 1 tsp. of lemon zest.
- 2 tsp. of chopped parsley.
- 2 tsp. of chopped thyme.
- 1/2 tsp. of salt to taste
- 1/2 tsp. of pepper to taste
- 1 tsp. minced garlic.

Directions:
1. Using a small mixing bowl, add all the ingredients on the list aside from the pork chops, then mix properly to combine. It makes the marinade. Place the chops into a Ziploc bag, pour in the prepared marinade then shake properly to coat. Let the pork chops marinate in the refrigerator for about one to eight hours.
2. Next, preheat a Wood Pellet Smoker and Grill to 300 degrees F, place the marinated pork chops on the grill and cook for about six to eight minutes. Turn over the meat and cook for an additional six to eight minutes until it attains an internal temperature of 165 degrees F.
3. Once cooked, let the pork chops rest for about five minutes, slice, and serve.

Nutrition: Calories: 313 kCal, Carbs: 5g, Protein: 30g, Fat: 14g

54. Delicious Barbeque and Grape Jelly Pork Chops

Preparation Time: 15 minutes
Cooking Time: 20 minutes
Servings: 4
Ingredients:

- Four boneless pork chops.
- 1/2 cup of barbeque sauce.
- 1/4 cup of grape jelly.
- Two minced cloves of garlic.
- 1/2 teaspoon of ground black pepper to taste

Directions:

1. Using a small mixing bowl, add in the barbeque sauce, grape jelly, garlic, and pepper to taste and mix properly. Using a resealable plastic bag, add in the pork chops alongside half of the prepared marinade and shake properly to coat. Let the pork marinate for about four to eight hours in the refrigerator.
2. Preheat a Wood Pellet Smoker and Grill to 350 degrees F, place the marinated pork chops on the grill, and grill for about six to eight minutes. Flip the pork over, blast with the reserved marinade, then grill for an additional six to eight hours until it is cooked through and attains an internal temperature of 145 degrees F.
3. Once cooked, let the pork rest for about five minutes, slice and serve with your favorite sauce.

Nutrition: Calories: 302 kCal, Carbs: 22g, Protein: 29g, Fat 9g

55. Wrapped Jalapeno Poppers

Preparation Time: 15 minutes
Cooking Time: 1 hour 45 minutes
Servings: 8
Ingredients:

- Eight jalapeno peppers.
- 8 oz. of softened cream cheese
- One minced green onion.
- 3/4 teaspoon of garlic powder.
- 1/2 cup of shredded cheddar cheese
- 16 bacon slices.

Directions:

1. Use a knife to cut off the steam of each jalapeno, and then slice lengthwise. Scoop out the seeds, discard then set the jalapenos aside. Using a small mixing bowl, add cream cheese, green onion, garlic powder, and cheese, then mix properly to combine.
2. Stuff each jalapeno with the cheese mixture, and then wrap up with a piece of bacon. Make sure to secure the bacon wraps with toothpicks. Place the stuffed jalapenos into the refrigerator and let rest for about one hour. This step will prevent the cheese from melting when grilling.
3. Preheat Wood Pellet Smoker and Grill to 275 degrees F, add in the jalapenos, and grill for about forty-five minutes. Just check the doneness of the jalapenos halfway through the cooking process. Serve.

Nutrition: Calories 345 kCal, Carbs 3g, Protein 11g, Fat 32g

56. Barbeque Baby Back Ribs

Preparation Time: 15 minutes
Cooking Time: 1 hour 30 minutes
Servings: 6
Ingredients:

- Two racks of baby back ribs
- 3/4 cup of chicken broth.
- 3/4 cup of soy sauce.
- 1 cup of sugar.
- 6 tbsp. cider vinegar.
- 6 tbsp. of olive oil.
- Three minced garlic cloves.
- 2 tsp. of salt to taste
- 1 tbsp. of paprika.
- 1/2 teaspoon of chili powder.
- 1/2 teaspoon of pepper to taste
- 1/4 teaspoon of garlic powder.
- A dash of cayenne pepper.
- Barbecue sauce.

Directions:

1. Using a large mixing bowl, add in half of the sugar, soy sauce, vinegar, oil, and garlic, then mix properly to combine. That makes the marinade. Place the pork ribs in a Ziploc bag; pour in about 2/3 of the prepared marinade, then sake properly to coat. Marinate the ribs overnight in the refrigerator.
2. Using another mixing bowl, add in the rest of the sugar, salt, and seasonings on the list, then mix properly to combine. Rub the ribs with the mixture, coating all sides, and then set aside. Preheat a Wood Pellet Smoker Grill to 250

degrees F, place the ribs on the preheated grill, and grill for about two hours.

3. Blast the ribs with the reserved marinade and cook for an additional one hour. Once cooked, let rest for about five to ten minutes, slice, and serve.

Nutrition: Calories 647 kCal, Fat 41g, Carbs 30g, Protein 37g

57. Delicious Grilled Pulled Pork

Preparation Time: 15 minutes
Cooking Time: 8 hours
Servings: 6
Ingredients:
- 1 (5 to 6 pounds) boneless pork butt.

For the Rub:
- 2 tbsp. of paprika.
- 2 tsp. of salt to taste
- 2 tsp. of dried oregano.
- 2 tsp. of garlic powder.
- 2 tsp. of dried thyme.
- 1/2 teaspoon of ground red pepper to taste
- 1/2 teaspoon of ground black pepper to taste

Directions:
1. Using a small mixing bowl, add in the paprika, oregano, garlic powder, thyme, red pepper, black pepper, and salt to taste and mix properly. Place the pork meat into a large mixing bowl, add the prepared rub, and then toss it to coat. Cover the mixing bowl with a plastic wrap, then let the pork marinate for about one to three hours in the refrigerator.
2. Next, preheat a Wood Pellet Smoker and Grill to 255 degrees F, place pork on the smoker, and cook for about six hours. Wrap the pork in two aluminum foil pieces, increase the grill temperature to 250 degrees F and cook the pork for an additional two hours until it is cooked through and tender.
3. Make sure the pork reads an internal temperature of 204 degrees F. Once cooked, let the pork cool for a few minutes, un-warp the foil then shreds with a fork. Serve.

Nutrition: Calories 859 kCal, Fat 52g, Carbs 2g, Protein 91g

58. Grilled Honey Pork loin

Preparation Time: 15 minutes
Cooking Time: 1 hour
Servings: 12
Ingredients:
- (1 3 lbs.) boneless pork loin.
- 2/3 cup of soy sauce.
- 1 tsp. of ground ginger.
- Three crushed garlic cloves.
- 1/4 cup of packed brown sugar
- 1/3 cup of honey.
- 1 1/2 tablespoons of sesame oil
- Vegetable oil.

Directions:
1. Use a kitchen knife to trim the fat off the pork loin, then add into a Ziploc bag, set aside. Using a small mixing bowl, add in the soy sauce, ginger, and garlic, then mix properly. Pour the mixture into the bag containing the pork loin, then shake properly to coat. To marinate place the pork in the refrigerator for about three hours. Make sure you turn the meat occasionally.
2. Using another mixing bowl, add sugar, honey, and sesame oil to combine. Preheat a Wood Pellet Smoker and Grill to 250 to 275 degrees F, place a pan on the griddle, pour in the sugar mixture, then cook for few minutes until the sugar dissolves, set aside. Place the pork loin on the grill and cook for about one hour.
3. Next, brush the loin with the sugar mixture and cook for an additional forty-five minutes until the internal temperature reads 145 degrees F. Once cooked, let the pork rest for about five minutes, slice, and serve.

Nutrition: Calories 260.5 kCal, Fat 11.2g, Carbs 13.5g, Protein 26g

59. The Best Pork Shoulder Steak

Preparation Time: 15 minutes
Cooking Time: 35 minutes
Servings: 4
Ingredients:

- 4 (12 oz.) pork shoulder steaks.
- 1/3 cup of olive oil.
- 1 tbsp. of apple cider vinegar
- 1 tsp. of salt to taste
- 1/2 teaspoon of black pepper to taste
- One sliced onion.
- 2 tbsp. of chopped parsley.
- 1/2 teaspoon of chopped thyme.
- 1 tsp. of ground cumin.
- 1 tsp. of paprika.
- 1 tsp. of oregano.

Directions:

1. Start by pounding the pork to an even thickness using a meat mallet, then trim off any present fat. Put the pork inside a Ziploc bag and add other ingredients like the oil, vinegar, onion, parsley, thyme, cumin, paprika, oregano, salt, and pepper taste, then mix/shake properly to coat. Place the pork into the refrigerator and let sit for about twenty-four hours.
2. Next, set a Wood Pellet Smoker and Grill to 180 degrees F, then preheat for about fifteen minutes. Make sure the lid is closed. Put the pork on the grill and smoke for about one hour thirty minutes. Wrap the pork with aluminum foil, then cook for another forty-five minutes.
3. Remove the foil, place the pork back on the grill and cook for another fifteen minutes until cooked through tender and attains an internal temperature of 160 degrees F. Once cooked, let the pork cool for a few minutes, slice, and serve.

Nutrition: Calories 384 kCal, Carbs 3g, Fat 27g, Protein 29g

60. Competition Style Barbecue Pork Ribs

Preparation Time: 20 minutes
Cooking Time: 2 hours
Servings: 6
Ingredients:

- 2 racks of St. Louis-style ribs
- cup Pit Boss Pork and Poultry Rub
- 1/8 cup brown sugar
- 4 tablespoons butter
- 4 tablespoons agave
- 1 bottle Pit Boss Sweet and Heat BARBECUE Sauce

Directions:

1. Place the ribs in working surface and remove the thin film of connective tissues covering it. In a smaller bowl, combine the Pit Boss Pork and Poultry Rub, brown sugar, butter, and agave. Mix until well combined.
2. Massage the rub onto the ribs and allow to rest in the fridge for at least 2 hours.
3. When ready to cook, fire the Pit Boss Grill to 2250F. Use desired Pit Bosss when cooking the ribs. Close the lid and preheat for 15 minutes.
4. Place the ribs on the grill grate and close the lid. Smoke for 1 hour and 30 minutes. Make sure to flip the ribs halfway through the cooking time.
5. Ten minutes before the cooking time ends, brush the ribs with Barbecue sauce.
6. Remove from the grill and allow to rest before slicing.

Nutrition: Calories 399 kCal, Carbs: 3.5g, Protein: 47.2g, Fat: 20.5g

61. Smoked Apple Barbecue Ribs

Preparation Time: 25 minutes
Cooking Time: 2 hours
Servings: 6
Ingredients:

- 2 racks St. Louis-style ribs
- ¼ cup Pit Boss Big Game Rub
- cup apple juice
- A bottle of Pit Boss BARBECUE Sauce

Directions:

- Place the ribs on a working surface and remove the film of connective tissues covering it.
- In another bowl, mix the Game Rub and apple juice until well-combined.
- Massage the rub on to the ribs and allow to rest in the fridge for at least 2 hours.
- When ready to cook, fire the Pit Boss Grill to 2250F. Use apple Pit Bosss when cooking the ribs. Close the lid and preheat for 15 minutes.
- Place the ribs on the grill grate and close the lid. Smoke for 1 hour and 30 minutes. Make sure to flip the ribs halfway through the cooking time.

- Ten minutes before the cooking time ends, brush the ribs with BARBECUE sauce.
- Remove from the grill and allow to rest before slicing.

Nutrition: Calories: 337 kCal; Carbs: 4.7 g, Protein: 47.1g; Fat: 12.9g

62. Smoked Pork Shoulder

Preparation Time: 30 minutes
Cooking Time: 1 hour 30 minutes
Servings: 6
Ingredients:
- 3 pounds pork shoulder, roasts

Shoulder Rub Ingredients
- 1/4 cup brown sugar
- ¼ cup white sugar
- 1 tablespoon paprika
- 1 tablespoon garlic powder
- Salt, to taste
- ½ tablespoon chili powder
- 1 teaspoon cayenne pepper
- ¼ teaspoon black pepper
- 2 teaspoons dried oregano
- 2 teaspoons cumin

Liquid Ingredients to Be Injected
- 3/4 cup apple juice
- 1 cup of water
- 1/2 cup sugar
- Salt, to taste
- 6 tablespoons Worcestershire sauce

Directions:
1. Take a large bowl and add all the shoulder spice rub ingredients and mix well.
2. Take a separate bowl and add all the liquid ingredients.
3. Now use an injector to inject the mixed liquid into the meat.
4. Pat dry it from the top with a paper towel.
5. Rub the spice mixture on top and left for a few hours before cooking.
6. Preheat the smoker grill for 50 minutes at 220 degrees F.
7. Put the meat onto the grill grate and cook for 2 hours at 225 degrees.
8. Serve and enjoy.

Nutrition: Calories: 236 kCal, Carbs: 0g, Protein: 17 g, Fat: 18 g

63. Zesty Herbal Smoke Pork Tenderloin

Preparation Time: 30 minutes
Cooking Time: 3 hours
Servings: 4
Ingredients:
- 2-4 pork tenderloins
- 6 tablespoons of BBQ sauce

Pork Rub Ingredients
- The ½ cup of cane sugar
- 1/3 teaspoon of chili powder
- ¼ tablespoon of granulated onion
- ½ tablespoon of granulated garlic
- 1 tablespoon of dried chilies
- 1 tablespoon of dill weed
- 1 tablespoon of lemon powder
- 1 tablespoon mustard powder

Directions:
1. Take a large mixing bowl and combine all the poke rub ingredients in it.
2. Now preheat the smoker grill at 225 degrees Fahrenheit until the smoke started to form
3. Cooking Time for 3 hours, until the internal temperature reaches 150 degrees Fahrenheit.
4. After 3 hours a brush generous amount of the barbecue sauce and then left it to sit for 20 minutes before serving.
5. Serve and enjoy.

Nutrition: Calories: 147 kCal, Carbs: 2g, Protein: 26 g Fat: 4 g

64. Pulled Hickory-Smoked Pork Butts

Preparation Time: 30 to 45 minutes
Cooking Time: 6 hours
Servings: 20
Ingredients:
- Pit Boss: Hickory
- 2 (10-pound) boneless pork butts, vacuum-stuffed or fresh
- 1 cup roasted garlic–seasoned extra-virgin olive oil
- ¾ cup Pork Dry Rub, Jan's Original Dry Rub, or your preferred pork rub

Directions:
1. Trim the fat cap and any effectively available enormous segments of abundance fat from every pork butt as you see fit.
2. Remove the pork butts from the grill and double wrap everyone in heavy-duty aluminum foil.

Take care to ensure that you keep your meat probes in the butts as you double-wrap them.

3. Return the wrapped pork butts to your 350°F Pit Boss smoker-grill.
4. Keep cooking the foil-wrapped pork butts until the internal temperature of the pork butts arrives at 200°F to 205°F.
5. Remove the pork butts and FTC them for 3 to 4 hours before pulling and serving.
6. Force the smoked pork butts into minimal succulent shreds utilizing your preferred pulling technique. I prefer utilizing my hands while wearing heat-safe gloves.
7. On the off chance that you'd like, blend the pulled pork butts with any remaining fluids.
8. Serve the pulled pork with grill sauce on a fresh-prepared move topped with coleslaw, or serve the pulled pork with fixings like lettuce, tomato, red onion, mayo, cheese, and horseradish.

Nutrition: Calories: 267 kCal, Carbs: 0g, Protein: 25 g Fat: 18 g

65. Pork Sirloin Tip Roast Three Ways

Preparation Time: 20 minutes
Cooking Time: 1½ to 3 hours
Servings: 4 to 6
Ingredients:
- Pit Boss: Apple, Hickory
- Apple-injected Roasted Pork Sirloin Tip Roast
- 1 (1½ to 2 pounds) pork sirloin tip roast
- ¾ cup 100% apple juice
- 2 tablespoons roasted garlic–seasoned extra-virgin olive oil
- 5 tablespoons Pork Dry Rub or a business rub, for example, Plowboys BBQ Bovine Bold

Directions:
1. Dry the roast with a piece of paper
2. Utilize a flavor/marinade injector to infuse all zones of tip roast with the apple juice.
3. Rub the whole roast with the olive oil and afterward cover generously with the rub.
4. Utilize 2 silicone nourishment grade cooking groups or butcher's twine to support the roast.
5. Roast the meat until the internal temperature arrives at 145°F, about 1½ hours.
6. Rest the roast under a free foil tent for 15 minutes.

7. Remove the cooking groups or twine and cut the roast contrary to what would be expected.

Nutrition: Calories: 354 kCal, Carbs: 0g, Protein: 22 g, Fat: 30 g

66. Teriyaki-Marinated Pork Sirloin Tip Roast

Preparation Time: 45 minutes
Cooking Time: 2 hours 30 minutes
Servings: 4
Ingredients:
- 1 (1½ to 2 pounds) pork sirloin tip roast
- Teriyaki marinade, for example, Mr. Yoshida's Original Gourmet Marinade

Directions:
1. Dry the roast with a piece of paper
2. Utilizing a 1-gallon cooler stockpiling sack or a sealable compartment, spread the roast with the teriyaki marinade.
3. Refrigerate medium-term, turning at regular intervals whenever the situation allows.
4. Smoke the meat for 1 hour at 180°F.
5. After 60 minutes, increase your pit temperature to 325°F.
6. Cook the roast until the internal temperature, at the thickest part of the roast, arrives at 145°F, around 1 to 1½ hours.
7. Rest the roast under a free foil tent for 15 minutes.
8. Remove the cooking groups or twine and cut the roast contrary to what would be expected.

Nutrition: Calories: 214 kCal, Carbs: 0g, Protein: 17 g, Fat: 19 g

67. Hickory-Smoked Pork Sirloin Tip Roast

Preparation Time: 30 minutes
Cooking Time: 3 hours
Servings: 3
Ingredients:
- 1 (1½ to 2 pounds) pork sirloin tip roast
- 2 tablespoons roasted garlic–seasoned extra-virgin olive oil
- 5 tablespoons Jan's Original Dry Rub, Pork Dry Rub, or your preferred pork rub

Directions:
1. Pat the roast dry with a paper towel.
2. Rub the whole roast with the olive oil. Coat the roast with the rub.

3. Support the roast utilizing 2 to 3 silicone nourishment grade cooking groups or butcher's twine to ensure the roast keeps up its shape during cooking.
4. Wrap the tip roast in plastic wrap and refrigerate medium-term.
5. Place the roast directly on the grill grates and smoke the roast until the internal temperature, at the thickest part of the roast, arrives at 145°F, around 3 hours.
6. Rest the roast under a free foil tent for 15 minutes.
7. Remove the cooking groups or twine and cut the roast contrary to what would be expected.

Nutrition: Calories: 276 kCal, Carbs: 0g, Protein: 28 g, Fat: 12 g

68. Double-Smoked Ham

Preparation Time: 15 minutes
Cooking Time: 2½ to 3 hours
Servings: 8 to 12
Ingredients:
- Pit Boss: Apple, Hickory
- 1 (10-pound) applewood-smoked, boneless, wholly cooked, ready-to-eat ham or bone-in smoked ham

Directions:
1. Remove the ham from its bundling and let sit at room temperature for 30 minutes.
2. Arrange the Pit Boss smoker-grill for a non-direct cooking and preheat to 180°F utilizing apple or hickory Pit Bosss relying upon what sort of wood was utilized for the underlying smoking.
3. Place the ham directly on the grill grates and smoke the ham for 1 hour at 180°F.
4. After 60 minutes, increase pit temperature to 350°F.
5. Cooking Time the ham until the internal temperature arrives at 140°F, about 1½ to 2 additional hours.
6. Remove the ham and wrap in foil for 15 minutes before cutting contrary to what would be expected.

Nutrition: Calories: 215 kCal, Carbs: 0g, Protein: 21 g, Fat: 19 g

69. Hickory-Smoked Prime Rib of Pork

Preparation Time: 30 minutes
Cooking Time: 3 hours
Servings: 6
Ingredients:
- Pit Boss: Hickory
- 1 (5-pound) rack of pork, around 6 ribs
- ¼ cup roasted garlic–enhanced extra-virgin olive oil
- 6 tablespoons Jan's Original Dry Rub, Pork Dry Rub, or your preferred pork roast rub

Directions:
1. Trim of the fat cap and silver skin from the rack of pork. Much the same as a chunk of ribs a rack of pork has a membrane on the bones. Remove the membrane from the bones by working a spoon handle under the bone membrane until you can get the membrane with a paper towel to pull it off.
2. Rub the olive oil generously on all sides of the meat. Season with the rub, covering all sides of the meat.
3. Double wrap the seasoned rack of pork in plastic wrap and refrigerate for 2 to 4 hours or medium-term.
4. Remove the seasoned rack of pork from the refrigerator and let sit at room temperature for 30 minutes before cooking.
5. Arrange the Pit Boss smoker-grill for a non-direct cooking and preheat to 225°F utilizing hickory Pit Bosss.
6. Add your Pit Boss smoker-grill meat probe or a remote meat probe into the thickest part of the rack of pork. On the off chance that your grill doesn't have meat probe capabilities or you don't claim a remote meat probe at that point, utilize a moment read computerized thermometer during the cook for internal temperature readings.
7. Place the rack rib-side down directly on the grill grates.
8. Smoke the rack of pork for 3 to 3½ hours, until the internal temperature arrives at 140°F.
9. Remove from the meat from the smoker, and let it rest under a free foil tent for 15 minutes before cutting.

Nutrition: Calories: 189 kCal, Carbs: 0g, Protein: 17 g, Fat: 12 g

70. Tender Grilled Loin Chops

Preparation Time: 10 minutes
Cooking Time: 12 to 15 minutes
Servings: 6
Ingredients:

- Pit Boss: Any
- 6 boneless focus cut midsection pork cleaves, 1 to 1½ inches thick 2 quarts Pork Brine
- 2 tablespoons roasted garlic–seasoned extra-virgin olive oil
- 2 teaspoons black pepper

Directions:
1. Trim abundance fat and silver skin from the pork slashes.
2. Place the pork slashes and brine in a 1-gallon sealable pack and refrigerate for in any event 12 hours or medium-term.
3. Remove the pork slashes from the brine and pat them dry with paper towels.
4. Brined pork hacks cook quicker than un-brined cleaves, so be mindful so as to screen internal temperatures.
5. Rest the pork slashes under a foil tent for 5 minutes before serving.

Nutrition: Calories: 211 kCal, Carbs: 0g, Protein: 17 g, Fat: 21 g

71. Florentine Ribeye Pork Loin

Preparation Time: 30 minutes
Cooking Time: 60 to 75 minutes
Servings: 6 to 8
Ingredients:

- 1 (3-pound) boneless ribeye pork loin roast
- 4 tablespoons extra-virgin olive oil, divided
- 2 tablespoons Pork Dry Rub or your favorite pork seasoning
- 4 bacon slices
- 6 cups fresh spinach
- 1 small red onion, diced
- 6 cloves garlic, cut into thin slivers
- ¾ cup shredded mozzarella cheese

Directions:
1. Trim away any abundance fat and silver skin.
2. Butterfly the pork loin or approach your butcher to butterfly it for you. There are numerous phenomenal recordings online with nitty gritty directions on the various systems for butterflying a loin roast.

3. Rub 2 tablespoons of the olive oil on each side of the butterflied roast and season the two sides with the rub.
4. Cook the bacon in a large skillet over medium heat. Disintegrate and set aside. Reserve the bacon fat.
5. Grill the pork loin for 60 to 75 minutes, or until the internal temperature at the thickest part arrives at 140°F.
6. Rest the pork loin under a free foil tent for 15 minutes before cutting contrary to what would be expected.

Nutrition: Calories: 365 kCal, Carbs: 0g, Protein: 32.1 g Fat: 22 g

72. Naked St. Louis Ribs

Preparation Time: 30 minutes
Cooking Time: 5 to 6 hours
Servings: 6 to 8
Ingredients:

- Pit Boss: Hickory, Apple
- 3 St. Louis–style pork rib racks
- 1 cup in addition to 1 tablespoon Jan's Original Dry Rub or your preferred pork rub

Directions:
1. Remove the membrane on the underside of the rib racks by embedding a spoon handle between the membrane and rib bones. Get the membrane with a paper towel and gradually dismantle it down the rack to remove.
2. Rub the two sides of the ribs with a liberal measure of the rub.
3. Arrange the Pit Boss smoker-grill for a non-direct cooking and preheat to 225°F utilizing hickory or apple Pit Bosss.
4. In the event of utilizing a rib rack, place the ribs in the rack on the grill grates. Else you can utilize Teflon-covered fiberglass tangles or place the ribs directly on the grill grates.
5. Smoke the ribs at 225°F for 5 to 6 hours with hickory Pit Bosss until the internal temperature, at the thickest part of the ribs, arrives at 185°F to190°F.
6. Rest the ribs under a free foil tent for 10 minutes before cutting and serving.

Nutrition: Calories: 241 kCal, Carbs: 0g, Protein: 23.6 g, Fat: 13 g

73. Buttermilk Pork Sirloin Roast

Preparation Time: 20 minutes
Cooking Time: 3 to 3½ hours
Servings: 4 to 6
Ingredients:
- Pit Boss: Apple, Cherry
- 1 (3 to 3½-pound) pork sirloin roast

Directions:
1. Trim all fat and silver skin from the pork roast.
2. Place the roast and buttermilk brine in a 1-gallon sealable plastic sack or brining holder.
3. Refrigerate medium-term, turning the roast like clockwork whenever the situation allows.
4. Remove the brined pork sirloin roast from the brine and pat dry with a paper towel.
5. Supplement a meat probe into the thickest part of the roast.
6. Design the Pit Boss smoker-grill for a non-direct cooking and preheat to 225°F utilizing apple or cherry Pit Boss.
7. Smoke the roast until the internal temperature arrives at 145°F, 3 to 3½ hours.
8. Rest the roast under a free foil tent for 15 minutes, at that point cut contrary to what would be expected.

Nutrition: Calories: 311 kCal, Carbs: 0g, Protein: 25 g, Fat: 18 g

74. Pierna Criolla

Preparation Time: 12 Hours
Cooking Time: 2.5 Hours
Servings: 18
Ingredients:
- 1 - 8 lbs. pork shoulder
- 8 slices bacon
- 1/2 lb. ham
- 1 bottle Malta
- 1 cup guava shells
- 1 cup Mojo (pg. 125)
- 1 cup prunes
- 4 Tbsp. Adobo Spices
- 2 cups brown sugar
- 2 Tbsp. sea salt

Directions:
1. Debone and flatten meat so that it may be rolled.
2. If the pork shoulder is very fatty, a small amount may be removed.
3. Score fat well and marinate for a minimum of 12 hours in the Mojo, and Adobo.
4. Sear both sides of roast on a very hot grate until dark brown and charred in spots, using apple-Pit Boss for a smoky flavor.
5. Remove roast to cutting board, and line unrolled roast with ham slices, bacon slices, prunes and guava shells. Roll meat carefully to keep the filling inside. Tie firmly with a butcher cord.
6. Cover with brown sugar and 1/2 bottle of Malta.
7. Cook for one hour in the Pit Boss smoker at 325.
8. At this point, turn the meat, cover with the remaining Malta and cook for an extra hour, or until you reach a meat temperature of 180.
9. Allow to cool at least 30 minutes and cut into fine slices. Pour the drippings over the meat after slicing the meat.
10. These ingredients can be found at most Hispanic grocery stores.

Nutrition: Calories: 83 kCal, Carbs: 19g, Fat: 0g, Protein: 3g

75. Sweet & Spicy Pork Kabobs

Preparation Time: 24 Hours
Cooking Time: 10 minutes
Servings: 6
Ingredients:
- 2lbs. boneless pork, 1-inch cubes
- ¾ C olive oil
- 1 Tbsp. Worcestershire sauce
- 1 tsp dried thyme
- 2 tsp black pepper
- ½ tsp cayenne
- ¾ C cider vinegar
- ¼ C sugar
- 4 Tbsp. lemon juice
- 1 Tbsp. oregano
- 2 cloves garlic, minced
- 1 tsp salt

Directions:
1. Mix together first 11 ingredients, place in sealable bag and refrigerate 24 hours: thread onto skewers.
2. Grill on high heat, basting with reserved marinade, for 4-5 minutes; turn and grill another 4-5 minutes.
3. Sprinkle with salt and serve.

Nutrition: Calories: 190 kCal, Carbs: 2.5 g, Fat: 13 g, Protein: 14 g

76. Big Island Pork Kabobs

Preparation Time: 24 Hours
Cooking Time: 15 minutes
Servings: 6
Ingredients:
- 3 lbs. Pork tenderloin
- 3 C margarita mix
- 3 clove garlic – minced
- 2 lg bell peppers
- 4 lbs. whole mushrooms
- ¼ C butter - softened
- 4 tsp lime juice
- 1 teaspoon sugar
- 3 Tbsp. minced parsley

Directions:
1. Cut pork into 1-inch cubes, place in a sealable plastic bag; pour marinade over to cover. Marinate overnight.
2. Blend together the butter, lime juice, Splenda, and parsley; set aside.
3. Thread pork cubes onto skewers, alternating with mushrooms and pepper, cut into eighths.
4. Grill over high heat, basting with butter mixture, for 10-15 minutes, turning frequently.
5. If you're using bamboo skewers, soak them in water 20-30 minutes before using.

Nutrition: Calories: 160 kCal, Carbs: 2g, Fat: 5g, Protein: 28g

77. Asian Pork Sliders

Preparation Time: 24 Hours
Cooking Time: 15 minutes
Servings: 8
Ingredients:
- 2 lbs. ground pork
- 1 C diced green onion
- 2 tsp garlic powder
- 2 Tbsp. soy sauce
- 2 tsp brown sugar
- 1 C shredded lettuce
- 1 tsp cornstarch
- Honey-mustard dressing
- 16 sesame rolls, split

Directions:
1. Mix all ingredients (except soy sauce) and form 16 equal patties. Brush each patty with soy sauce, and grill over high heat, turning once.

2. Serve with honey mustard and cucumber spears.
3. I like to chill the seasoned meat and then spread it on an oiled cutting board, using a rolling pin for an even 1/4-inch thickness.
4. Then, I just grab a biscuit cutter, and voila...perfectly round sliders!

Nutrition: Calories: 280 kCal, Carbs: 31g, Fat: 9g, Protein: 26g

78. Luau Pork

Preparation Time: 12 Hours
Cooking Time: 12 Hours
Servings:50
Ingredients:
- 2 - boneless pork shoulders (6 lbs.)
- 2 C hot water
- 3 Qtrs. gal Hawaiian Mojo
- 2 Tbsp. seasoned salt
- ¼ C Stubbs liquid smoke
- 4 Tbsp. garlic powder
- ½ C Adobo Criollo spices

Directions:
1. Marinate pork in Hawaiian Mojo overnight. Remove from marinade, pat dry, and inject each shoulder with 6-8ozs of remaining marinade.
2. Score pork on all sides, rub with salt, then brush with liquid smoke, and sprinkle with garlic. Wrap entirely in banana leaves, tie with string.
3. Heat one side of your Pit Boss grill to high, covered.
4. Once pre-heated, place the butts on the "cool" side of the grill, roast 3 hours with oak Pit Boss, and then remove banana leaves. Baste with mojo every 45 minutes throughout the rest of the cooking time. The shoulders should not be over any exposed flame.
5. Cover the grill and vent slightly. Slow cook the shoulders for a total of 6 to 8 hours, until the meat is very tender, or you reach 195 F on the meat thermometer.
6. Chop the meat and then mix with a wash of 1/2 cup liquid smoke, 4 cups hot water, 1/4 cup Adobo Criollo spices, and 2 Tbsp. seasoned salt.
7. Let that sit about 15 minutes, drain remaining liquid, and serve with Sweet Hawaiian Pork Sauce

Nutrition: Calories: 116 kCal, Carbs: 4g, Fat: 5g, Protein: 12g

79. Carolina Pork Ribs

Preparation Time: 12 Hours
Cooking Time: 3 Hours
Servings: 6
Ingredients:
- 2 racks of pork spareribs
- ½ C of "Burning' Love" Rub
- 1 C Carolina Basting Sauce
- 1 C Carolina BBQ Sauce

Directions:
1. Prepare ribs by removing the membrane from the underside. Trim off any loose fat, and season ribs with rub, wrap in plastic wrap and refrigerate overnight.
2. Allow ribs to warm 1 hour. Preheat Pit Boss grill to 280F.
3. If you want to sauce the ribs, do so 5 minutes before they're done, turning ever minute, and observe.

Nutrition: Calories: 470 kCal, Carbs: 11 g, Fat: 35 g, Protein: 29 g

80. Pork Collar with Rosemary Marinade

Preparation Time: 15 minutes
Cooking Time: 30 minutes
Servings: 6
Ingredients:
- 1 Pork Collar (3 - 4lb.)
- 3 tbsp. Rosemary, fresh
- 3 minced Shallots
- 2 tbsp. chopped Garlic
- ½ cup of Bourbon
- 2 tsp. Coriander, ground
- 1bottle of Apple Ale
- 1 tsp. ground Black pepper
- 2 tsp. Salt
- 3 tbsp. oil

Directions:
1. In a zip lock bag, combine the black pepper, salt, canola oil, apple ale, bourbon, coriander, garlic, shallots, and rosemary.
2. Cut the meat into slabs (2 inches) and marinate in the refrigerator overnight.
3. Preheat the grill to 450F with the lid closed. Grill the meat for 5 minutes and lower the temperature to 325F. Pour the marinade over the meat. Cook 25 minutes more.

4. Cook until the internal temperature of the meat is 160F.
5. Serve and enjoy!

Nutrition: Calories: 420 kCal, Proteins: 30g, Carbs: 4g, Fat: 26g

81. Simple Pork Tenderloin

Preparation Time: 15min
Cooking Time: 20min
Servings: 4 - 6
Ingredients:
- 2 Pork Tenderloins (12 - 15 oz. each)
- 6 tbsp. hot Sauce, Louisiana style
- 6 tbsp. melted butter
- Cajun seasoning as needed

Directions:
1. Trim the silver skin from the meat.
2. In a large bowl, combine the hot sauce and melted butter. Roll the meat in this mixture -- season with Cajun seasoning.
3. Preheat the grill to 400F with the lid closed.
4. Grill the meat for 8 minutes on each side. The internal temperature should be 145F and if you want well – done, cook until 160F.
5. Let it rest for a few minutes before cutting. Serve with your favorite side dish and enjoy!

Nutrition: Calories: 150 kCal, Proteins: 20g, Carbs: 0, Fat: 3g

82. Pork Collar and Rosemary Marinade

Preparation Time: 15 minutes + marinate time
Cooking Time: 30 minutes
Servings: 4
Ingredients:

- 1 pork collar, 3-4 pounds
- 3 tablespoons rosemary, fresh
- 3 shallots, minced
- 2 tablespoons garlic, chopped
- ½ cup bourbon
- 2 teaspoons coriander, ground
- 1 bottle of apple ale
- 1 teaspoon ground black pepper
- 2 teaspoons salt
- 3 tablespoons oil

Directions:

1. Take a zip bag and add pepper, salt, canola oil, apple ale, bourbon, coriander, garlic, shallots, rosemary, and mix well.
2. Cut meat into slabs and add them to the marinade; let it refrigerate overnight
3. Pre-heat your smoker to 450 degrees F
4. Transfer meat to smoker and smoke for 5 minutes, lower temperature to 325 degrees F
5. Pour marinade all over and cook for 25 minutes more until the internal temperature reaches 160 degrees F
6. Serve and enjoy!

Nutrition: Calories: 420 kCal, Fat: 26g, Carbs: 4g, Protein: 51g

83. Roasted Ham

Preparation Time: 15 minutes
Cooking Time: 2 hours 15 minutes
Servings: 4
Ingredients:

- 8-10 pounds' ham, bone-in
- 2 tablespoons mustard, Dijon
- ¼ cup horseradish
- 1 bottle BBQ Apricot Sauce

Directions:

1. Pre-heat your smoker to 325 degrees F
2. Cover a roasting pan with foil and place the ham, transfer to a smoker, and smoke for 1 hour and 30 minutes
3. Take a small pan and add sauce, mustard and horseradish, place it over medium heat and cook for a few minutes

4. Keep it on the side
5. After 1 hour 30 minutes of smoking, glaze ham and smoke for 30 minutes more until the internal temperature reaches 135 degrees F
6. Let it rest for 20 minutes, slice, and enjoy!

Nutrition: Calories: 460 kCal, Fats: 43g, Carbs: 10g, Protein: 19g

84. Pineapple Pork BBQ

Preparation Time: 10 minutes
Cooking Time: 60 minutes
Servings: 4
Ingredients:

- 1-pound pork sirloin
- 4 cups pineapple juice
- 3 cloves garlic, minced
- 1 cup carne asada marinade
- 2 tablespoons salt
- 1 teaspoon ground black pepper

Directions:

1. Place all ingredients in a bowl and massage the pork sirloin to coat. Place inside the fridge to marinate for at least 2 hours.
2. When ready to cook, fire the Pit Boss Grill to 3000F. Use desired Pit Boss when cooking the ribs. Close the lid and preheat for 15 minutes.
3. Place the pork sirloin on the grill grate and cook for 45 to 60 minutes. Make sure to flip the pork halfway through the cooking time.
4. At the same time, when you put the pork on the grill grate, place the marinade in a pan and place it inside the smoker. Allow the marinade to cook and reduce.
5. Baste the pork sirloin with the reduced marinade before the cooking time ends.
6. Allow resting before slicing.

Nutrition: Calories: 347 kCal; Protein: 33.4 g; Carbs: 45.8 g; Fat: 4.2g

85. BBQ Spareribs with Mandarin Glaze

Preparation Time: 10 minutes
Cooking Time: 60 minutes
Servings: 6
Ingredients:
- 3 large spareribs, membrane removed
- 3 tablespoons yellow mustard
- 1 tablespoon Worcestershire sauce
- 1 cup honey
- 1 ½ cup brown sugar
- 13 ounces Pit Boss Mandarin Glaze
- 1 teaspoon sesame oil
- 1 teaspoon soy sauce
- 1 teaspoon garlic powder

Directions:
1. Place the spareribs on a working surface and carefully remove the connective tissue membrane that covers the ribs.
2. In another bowl, mix the rest of the ingredients until well combined.
3. Massage the spice mixture onto the spareribs. Allow resting in the fridge for at least 3 hours.
4. When ready to cook, fire the Pit Boss Grill to 3000F.
5. Use hickory Pit Boss when cooking the ribs.
6. Close the lid and preheat for 15 minutes.
7. Place the seasoned ribs on the grill grate and cover the lid.
8. Cook for 60 minutes.
9. Once cooked, allow resting before slicing.

Nutrition: Calories: 1263 kCal; Protein: 36.9g; Carbs: 110.3g; Fat: 76.8g

86. Smoked Pork Sausages

Preparation Time: 10 minutes
Cooking Time: 1 hour
Servings: 6
Ingredients:
- 3 pounds ground pork
- ½ tablespoon ground mustard
- 1 tablespoon onion powder
- 1 tablespoon garlic powder
- 1 teaspoon pink curing salt
- 1 teaspoon salt
- 1 teaspoon black pepper
- ¼ cup of ice water
- Hog casings, soaked and rinsed in cold water

Directions:
1. Mix all ingredients except for the hog casings in a bowl. Using your hands, mix until all ingredients are well-combined.
2. Using a sausage stuffer, stuff the hog casings with the pork mixture.
3. Measure 4 inches of the stuffed hog casing and twist to form into a sausage. Repeat the process until you create sausage links.
4. When ready to cook, fire the Pit Boss Grill to 2250F. Use apple Pit Boss when cooking the ribs. Close the lid and preheat for 15 minutes.
5. Place the sausage links on the grill grate and cook for 1 hour or until the internal temperature reads at 1550F.
6. Allow resting before slicing.

Nutrition: Calories: 688 kCal; Protein: 58.9g; Carbs: 2.7g; Fat: 47.3g

87. Braised Pork Chile Verde

Preparation Time: 10 minutes
Cooking Time: 40 minutes
Servings: 6
Ingredients:
- 3 pounds' pork shoulder, bone removed and cut into ½ inch cubes
- 1 tablespoon all-purpose flour
- Salt and pepper to taste
- 1-pound tomatillos, husked and washed
- 2 jalapenos, chopped
- 1 medium yellow onion, peeled and cut into chunks
- 4 cloves of garlic
- 4 tablespoons extra virgin olive oil
- 2 cup chicken stock
- 2 cans green chilies
- 1 tablespoon cumin
- 1 tablespoon oregano
- ½ lime, juiced
- ¼ cup cilantro

Directions:
1. Place the pork shoulder chunks in a bowl and toss with flour -season with salt and pepper to taste.
2. Use desired Pit Boss when cooking. Place a large cast-iron skillet on the bottom rack of the grill. Close the lid and preheat for 15 minutes.

3. Place the tomatillos, jalapeno, onion, and garlic on a sheet tray lined with foil and drizzle with two tablespoons olive oil -season with salt and pepper to taste.
4. Place the remaining olive oil in the heated cast iron skillet and cook the pork shoulder. Spread the meat evenly, then close.
5. Before closing the lid, place the vegetables in the tray on the grill rack. Close the lid of the grill.
6. Cook for 20 minutes without opening the lid or stirring the pork. After 20 minutes, remove the vegetables from the grill and transfer to a blender. Pulse until smooth and pour into the pan with the pork. Stir in the chicken stock, green chilies, cumin, oregano, and lime juice - season with salt and pepper to taste. Close the grill lid and cook for another 20 minutes. Once cooked, stir in the cilantro.

Nutrition: Calories: 389 kCal; Protein: 28.5g; Carbs: 4.5g; Fat: 24.3g

88. BQ Pulled Pork Sandwiches

Preparation Time: 10 minutes
Cooking Time: 1 hour 30 minutes
Servings: 6
Ingredients:
- 8-10lbs of bone-in pork butt roast
- 12 Kaiser Rolls
- 1 cup of yellow mustard
- Coleslaw
- 1 bottle of BBQ sauce
- 5 oz. of sugar

Directions:
1. Push the temperature to 225 degrees F and set your smoker to preheat
2. Now take out the pork roast from the packaging and keep it on a cookie sheet
3. Rub it thoroughly with yellow mustard
4. Now take a bowl and mix the BBQ sauce along with sugar in it
5. Use this mix to rub the roast thoroughly and give time for the rub to seep inside and melt in the meat
6. Now place this roast in the smoker and allow it to cook for 6 hours
7. When done, remove it from the smoker and
8. then wrap it in tin foil

9. Push the temperature to 250 degrees F and cook it for a couple of hours. The internal temperature should reach 200 degrees F
10. Let the pork butt rest in the foil for an hour before pulling it out
11. Now take the Kaiser roll and cut it into half
12. Mix the pulled pork with some BBQ sauce and pile on the top of each halved roll
13. Top it with coleslaw and serve

Nutrition: Calories: 426 kCal; Protein: 65.3g; Carbs: 20.4g; Fat: 8.4g

89. Bourbon Honey Glazed Smoked Pork Ribs

Preparation Time: 15 minutes
Cooking Time: 5 hours
Servings: 10
Ingredients:
- Pork Ribs (4-lbs., 1.8-kg.)
- The Marinade
- Apple juice – 1 ½ cups
- Yellow mustard – ½ cup
- The Rub
- Brown sugar – ¼ cup
- Smoked paprika – 1 tablespoon
- Onion powder – ¾ tablespoon
- Garlic powder – ¾ tablespoon
- Chili powder – 1 teaspoon
- Cayenne pepper – ¾ teaspoon
- Salt – 1 ½ teaspoon
- The Glaze
- Unsalted butter – 2 tablespoons
- Honey – ¼ cup
- Bourbon – 3 tablespoons

Directions:
1. Place apple juice and yellow mustard in a bowl, then stir until combined.
2. Apply the mixture over the pork ribs, then marinates for at least an hour.
3. In the meantime, combine brown sugar with smoked paprika, onion powder, garlic powder, chili powder, black pepper, cayenne pepper, and salt, then mix well.
4. After an hour of the marinade, sprinkle the dry spice mixture over the marinated pork ribs, then let it rest for a few minutes.
5. Plug the Pit Boss grill smoker, then fill the hopper with the wood pellet. Turn the switch on.

6. Set the Pit Boss smoker for indirect heat, then adjust the temperature to 250°F (121°C).
7. When the Pit Boss smoker is ready, place the seasoned pork ribs in the Pit Boss smoker and smoke for 3 hours.
8. Meanwhile, place unsalted butter in a saucepan, then melt over very low heat.
9. Once it is melted, remove it from heat, and then add honey and bourbon to the saucepan. Stir until incorporated and set aside.
10. After 3 hours of smoking, baste the honey bourbon mixture over the pork ribs and wrap it with aluminum foil.
11. Return the wrapped pork ribs to the Pit Boss smoker and continue smoking for another 2 hours.
12. Once the smoked pork ribs reach 145°F (63°C), remove the smoked pork ribs from the Pit Boss grill smoker.
13. Unwrap the smoked pork ribs and serve.

Nutrition: Calories: 313 kCal, Carbs: 5g, Fat: 20g, Protein: 26g

90. Lime Barbecue Smoked Pork Shoulder Chili

Preparation Time: 20 minutes
Cooking Time: 6 hours 10 minutes
Servings: 8
Ingredients:
- Pork Shoulder (3.5-lb., 1.6-kg.)
- The Rub
- Brown sugar – 3 tablespoons
- Garlic powder – 1 tablespoon
- Smoked paprika -1 tablespoon
- Ground cumin – 1 tablespoon
- Salt – 1 teaspoon
- Chili powder – 1 ½ teaspoon
- Black pepper – 1 teaspoon
- The Glaze
- Red chili flakes – 1 tablespoon
- Vegetable oil – 2 tablespoons
- Minced garlic – 1 tablespoon
- Ground coriander – 1 ½ teaspoon
- Tomato ketchup – 1 ½ cups
- White sugar – ¼ cup
- Apple juice – ½ cup
- The Topping
- Fresh limes - 2

Directions:
1. Place brown sugar, garlic powder, smoked paprika, ground cumin, salt, chili powder, and black pepper in a bowl, then stir until combined.
2. Rub the spices mixture over and side by side of the pork shoulder, then let it rest for approximately an hour.
3. In the meantime, pour vegetable oil into a saucepan, then preheat over medium heat.
4. Once the oil is hot, stir in minced garlic and sauté until wilted and aromatic. Remove the saucepan from heat.
5. Stir in red chili flakes, ground coriander, and white sugar into the saucepan, then pour apple juice and tomato ketchup over the sauce. Mix well and set aside.
6. Plug the Pit Boss grill smoker, then fill the hopper with the wood pellet. Turn the switch on.
7. Set the Pit Boss smoker for indirect heat, then adjust the temperature to 250°F (121°C).
8. Place the seasoned pork shoulder in the Pit Boss smoker and smoke for 3 hours. The internal temperature should be 165°F (74°C).
9. Take the pork shoulder out of the Pit Boss grill smoker, then place it on a sheet of aluminum foil.
10. Baste the glaze over the pork shoulder, then arrange sliced limes over the pork shoulder.
11. Wrap the pork shoulder with aluminum foil, then return it to the Pit Boss grill smoker.
12. Smoke the wrapped smoked pork shoulder for another 3 hours or until the internal temperature has reached 205°F (96°C).
13. Once it is done, remove the smoked pork shoulder from the Pit Boss smoker and let it rest for approximately 15 minutes.
14. Unwrap the smoked pork shoulder and place it on a serving dish.

Nutrition: Calories: 220 kCal, Carbs: 1g, Fat: 18g, Protein: 16g

91. Chili Sweet Smoked Pork Tenderloin

Preparation Time: 10 minutes
Cooking Time: 3 hours 30 minutes
Servings: 8
Ingredients:

- Pork Tenderloin (3-lb., 1.4-kg.)
- The Rub
- Apple juice – 1 cup
- Honey – ½ cup
- Brown sugar – ¾ cup
- Dried thyme – 2 tablespoons
- Black pepper – ½ tablespoon
- Chili powder – 1 ½ teaspoon
- Italian seasoning – ½ teaspoon
- Onion powder – 1 teaspoon

Directions:

1. Pour apple juice into a container, then stir in honey, brown sugar, dried thyme, black pepper, chili powder, Italian seasoning, and onion powder. Mix well.
2. Rub the pork tenderloin with the spice mixture, then let it rest for an hour.
3. Plug the Pit Boss grill smoker, then fill the hopper with the wood pellet. Turn the switch on.
4. Set the Pit Boss smoker for indirect heat, then adjust the temperature to 250°F (121°C).
5. When the Pit Boss smoker has reached the desired temperature, place the seasoned pork tenderloin in the Pit Boss smoker and smoke for 3 hours.
6. After 3 hours of smoking, increase the Pit Boss grill smoker's temperature to 350°F (177°C) and continue smoking the pork tenderloin for another 30 minutes.
7. Once the smoked pork tenderloin's internal temperature has reached 165°F (74°C), remove it from the Pit Boss smoker and transfer it to a serving dish.
8. Cut the smoked pork tenderloin into thick slices, then serve.

Nutrition: Calories: 318 kCal, Carbs: 7g, Fat: 10g, Protein: 8g

92. Delicious Parmesan Roast Pork

Preparation Time: 10 minutes
Cooking Time: 3 hours 45 minutes
Servings: 10
Ingredients:

- 4 chopped garlic cloves.
- 2 tablespoons of olive oil.
- 1 tablespoon of minced dried basil.
- 1 tablespoon of dried and crushed oregano.
- 1 pound of boneless pork loin.
- 1 cup of bread crumbs.
- 1/4 cup of grated Parmesan cheese.

Directions:

1. Using a small mixing bowl, add in the garlic, olive oil, basil, and oregano, then mix properly to combine. Rub the mixture on the pork loin, coating all sides, then place in the large bowl. Cover the bowl with a plastic wrap, then place in the refrigerator for about two hours to overnight.
2. In another mixing bowl, add in the bread crumbs and cheese, then mix properly to combine. Dredge the pork in the cheese mixture, then set aside. Preheat a Pit Boss smoker and Grill to 225 degrees F, place the pork on the grill, cover the lid and smoke the pork for about three to four hours until an inserted thermometer reads 155 degrees F.
3. Wrap the pork in aluminum foil and let stand for about ten minutes. Slice and serve.

Nutrition: Calories 250 kCal, Fat 10g, Carbs 3g, Protein 34g

93. Bacon-Wrapped Pork Tenderloin

Preparation Time: 15 minutes
Cooking Time: 40 minutes
Servings: 4
Ingredients:
- 1 pork tenderloin.
- 4 strips of bacon.

<u>Rub</u>:
- 8 tablespoons of brown sugar.
- 3 tablespoons of kosher salt to taste.
- 1 tablespoon of chili powder.
- 1 teaspoon of black pepper to taste.
- 1 teaspoon of onion powder.
- 1 teaspoon of garlic powder.

Directions:
1. Using a small mixing bowl, add sugar, chili powder, onion powder, garlic powder, salt, and pepper to taste, mix properly to combine, and set aside. Use a sharp knife to trim off fats present on the pork, then coat with 1/4 of the prepared rub. Make sure you coat all sides.
2. Roll each pork tenderloin with a piece of bacon, lay the meat on a cutting board, then pound with a meat mallet to give an even thickness, secure the ends of the bacon with toothpicks to hold still. Coat the meat again with just a little more of the rub spice, then set aside.
3. Preheat a Pit Boss smoker and Grill to 350 degrees F, place the pork tenderloin on the grill, and grill for about fifteen minutes. Increase the temperature of the grill to 400 degrees F and cook for another fifteen minutes until it is cooked through and reads an internal temperature of 145 degrees F.
4. Once cooked, let the pork rest for a few minutes, slice, and serve.

Nutrition: Calories 236 kCal, Fat 8g, Carbs 10g, Protein 29g

94. Typical Nachos

Preparation Time: 15 minutes
Cooking Time: 10 minutes
Servings: 4
Ingredients:
- 2 cups leftover smoked pulled pork
- 1 small sweet onion, diced
- 1 medium tomato, diced
- 1 jalapeño pepper, seeded and diced
- 1 garlic clove, minced
- 1 teaspoon salt
- 1 teaspoon freshly ground black pepper
- 1 bag tortilla chips
- 1 cup shredded Cheddar cheese
- ½ cup Bill's Best BBQ Sauce, divided
- ½ cup shredded jalapeño Monterey Jack cheese
- Juice of ½ lime
- 1 avocado, halved, pitted, and sliced
- 2 tablespoons sour cream
- 1 tablespoon chopped fresh cilantro

Directions:
1. Supply your smoker with Pit Boss and follow the manufacturer's specific start-up procedure. Preheat, with the lid, closed, to 375°F.
2. Heat the pulled pork in the microwave.
3. In a medium bowl, combine the onion, tomato, jalapeño, garlic, salt, and pepper, and set aside.
4. Arrange half of the tortilla chips in a large cast-iron skillet. Spread half of the warmed pork on top and cover with the Cheddar cheese. Top with half of the onion-jalapeño mixture, then drizzle with ¼ cup of barbecue sauce
5. Layer on the remaining tortilla chips, then the remaining pork and the Monterey Jack cheese. Top with the remaining onion-jalapeño mixture and drizzle with the remaining ¼ cup of barbecue sauce.
6. Place the skillet on the grill, close the lid, and smoke for about 10 minutes, or until the cheese is melted and bubbly. (Watch to make sure your chips don't burn!)
7. Squeeze the lime juice over the nachos, top with the avocado slices and sour cream, and garnish with the cilantro before serving hot.

Nutrition: Calories: 688 kCal; Protein: 58.9g; Carbs: 2.7g; Fat: 47.3g

95. BBQ Breakfast Grist

Preparation Time: 20 minutes
Cooking Time: 30 to 40 minutes
Servings: 8
Ingredients:

- 1 cup of water
- 1 cup quick-cooking grits
- 3 tablespoons unsalted butter
- 2 tablespoons minced garlic
- 1 medium onion, chopped
- 1 jalapeño pepper, stemmed, seeded, and chopped
- 1 teaspoon cayenne pepper
- 2 teaspoons red pepper flakes
- 1 tablespoon hot sauce
- 1 cup shredded Monterey Jack cheese
- 1 cup sour cream
- Salt
- Freshly ground black pepper
- 2 eggs, beaten
- ⅓ cup half-and-half
- 3 cups leftover pulled pork (preferably smoked)

Directions:

1. Supply your smoker with Pit Boss and follow the manufacturer's specific start-up procedure. Preheat, with the lid, closed, to 350°F.
2. On your kitchen stovetop, in a large saucepan over high heat, bring the chicken stock and water to a boil.
3. Add the grits and reduce the heat to low, then stir in the butter, garlic, onion, jalapeño, cayenne, red pepper flakes, hot sauce, cheese, and sour cream. Season with salt and pepper, then cook for about 5 minutes.
4. Temper the beaten eggs and incorporate them into the grits. Remove the saucepan from the heat and stir in the half-and-half and pulled pork.
5. Pour the grits into a greased grill-safe 9-by-13-inch casserole dish or aluminum pan.
6. Transfer to the grill, close the lid, and bake for 30 to 40 minutes, covering with aluminum foil toward the end of cooking if the grits start to get too brown on top.

Nutrition: Calories: 1263 kCal; Protein: 36.9g; Carbs: 110.3g; Fat: 76.8g

96. Pig Pops (Sweet-hot Bacon on Stick)

Preparation Time: 15 minutes
Cooking Time: 25 to 30 minutes
Servings: 24
Ingredients:

- Nonstick cooking spray, oil, or butter, for greasing
- 2 pounds thick-cut bacon (24 slices)
- 24 metal skewers
- 1 cup packed light brown sugar
- 2 to 3 teaspoons cayenne pepper
- ½ cup maple syrup, divided

Directions:

1. Supply your smoker with Pit Boss and follow the manufacturer's specific start-up procedure. Preheat, with the lid, closed, to 350°F.
2. Coat a disposable aluminum foil baking sheet with cooking spray, oil, or butter.
3. Thread each bacon slice onto a metal skewer and place on the prepared baking sheet.
4. In a medium bowl, stir together the brown sugar and cayenne.
5. Baste the top sides of the bacon with ¼ cup of maple syrup.
6. Sprinkle half of the brown sugar mixture over the bacon
7. Place the baking sheet on the grill, close the lid, and smoke for 15 to 30 minutes.
8. Using tongs, flip the bacon skewers. Baste with the remaining ¼ cup of maple syrup and top with the remaining brown sugar mixture.
9. Continue smoking with the lid closed for 10 to 15 minutes, or until crispy. You can eyeball the bacon and smoke to your desired doneness, but the actual ideal internal temperature for bacon is 155°F (if you want to try to get a thermometer into it—ha!).
10. Using tongs, carefully remove the bacon skewers from the grill. Let cool completely before handling.

Nutrition: Calories: 318 kCal Carbs: 7g Fat: 10g Protein: 8g

97. Party Pulled Pork Shoulder

Preparation Time: 30 minutes
Cooking Time: 8 to 9 minutes
Servings: 10
Ingredients:

- 1 (5-pound) Boston butt (pork shoulder)
- ¼ cup prepared table mustard
- ½ cup Our House Dry Rub or your favorite rub, divided
- 2 cups apple juice
- ½ cup of salt

Directions:

1. Slather the meat with the mustard and coat with ¼ cup of the dry rub
2. In a spray bottle, mix the apple juice and salt and shake until the salt is dissolved
3. Supply your smoker with Pit Boss and follow the manufacturer's specific start-up procedure. Preheat, with the lid, closed, to 225°F.
4. Place the pork fat-side up in an aluminum pan, transfer to the grill, close the lid, and smoke for 8 to 9 hours, spritzing well all over with the salted apple juice every hour, until a meat thermometer inserted in the thickest part of the meat reads 205°F. Cover the pork loosely with aluminum foil toward the end of cooking, if necessary, to keep the top from blackening.
5. Drain the liquid from the pan, cover, and allow the meat to cool for a few minutes before using two forks to shred it.
6. Sprinkle the remaining rub over the meat and serve with barbecue sauce.

Nutrition: Calories: 426 kCal; Protein: 65.3g; Carbs: 20.4g; Fat: 8.4g

98. Pineapple-Pepper Pork Kebabs

Preparation Time: 20 minutes
Cooking Time: 10 to 12 minutes
Servings: 6
Ingredients:

- 1 (20-ounce) bottle hoisin sauce
- ½ cup Sriracha
- ¼ cup honey
- ¼ cup apple cider vinegar
- 2 tablespoons canola oil
- 2 teaspoons minced garlic
- 2 teaspoons onion powder
- 1 teaspoon ground ginger
- 1 teaspoon salt
- 1 teaspoon freshly ground black pepper
- 2 pounds thick-cut pork chops or pork loin, cut into 2-inch cubes
- 10 ounces' fresh pineapple, cut into chunks
- 1 red onion, cut into wedges
- 1 bag mini sweet peppers, tops removed and seeded
- 12 metal or wooden skewers (soaked in water for 30 minutes if wooden)

Directions:

1. In a small bowl, stir together the hoisin, Sriracha, honey, vinegar, oil, minced garlic, onion powder, ginger, salt, and black pepper to create the marinade. Reserve ¼ cup for basting.
2. Toss the pork cubes, pineapple chunks, onion wedges, and mini peppers in the remaining marinade. Cover and refrigerate for at least 1 hour or up to 4 hours.
3. Supply your smoker with Pit Boss and follow the manufacturer's specific start-up procedure. Preheat, with the lid, closed, to 450°F.
4. Remove the pork, pineapple, and veggies from the marinade; do not rinse. Discard the marinade.
5. Use the double-skewer technique to assemble the kebabs (see Tip below). Thread each of 6 skewers with pork, a piece of pineapple, a piece of onion, and sweet mini pepper, making sure that the skewer goes through the left side of the ingredients. Repeat the threading on each skewer two more times. Double-skewer the kebabs by sticking another 6 skewers through the right side of the ingredients.
6. Place the kebabs directly on the grill, close the lid, and smoke for 10 to 12 minutes, turning once. They are done when a meat thermometer inserted in the pork reads 160°F.

Nutrition: Calories: 347 kCal; Protein: 33.4 g; Carbs: 45.8 g; Fat: 4.2g

99. Smoked Bacon

Preparation Time: 20 minutes
Cooking Time: 3 hours
Servings: 12
Ingredients:
- Pork belly, fat trimmed – 2 pounds
- Salt – ½ cup
- Brown sugar – ½ cup
- Ground black pepper – 1 tablespoon

Directions:
1. Before preheating the grill, cure the pork and for this, stir together all of the ingredients for it and then rub it well on the pork belly.
2. Place pork belly into a large plastic bag, seal it, and let it rest for 8 days in the refrigerator.
3. Then remove pork belly from the refrigerator, rinse well and pat dry.
4. When the grill has preheated, place the pork belly on the grilling rack and let smoke for 3 hours or until the control panel shows the internal temperature of 150 degrees F, turning halfway.
5. Check the fire after one hour of smoking and add more wood pallets if required.
6. When done, remove pork from the grill, wrap it in plastic wrap, and rest for 1 hour in the freezer until pork is firm and nearly frozen.
7. When ready to eat, cut pork into slices and then serve.

Nutrition: Calories: 688 kCal; Protein: 58.9g; Carbs: 2.7g; Fat: 47.3g

100. Simple Braised Pork Carnitas

Preparation Time: 20 minutes
Cooking Time: 3 hours and 30 minutes
Servings: 6
Ingredients:
- Pork shoulder, boneless, fat trimmed, marbled – 4 pounds
- Beer – 12 ounces
- Salt – 2 teaspoons
- Ground cumin – ½ teaspoon
- Vegetable shortening – 2 tablespoons

Directions:
1. Meanwhile, cut pork into 2-inch pieces and then place them in a Dutch oven.
2. Add salt and cumin, pour in beer, and then pour in water until pork pieces are covered.

3. Place the pot over medium-high heat and then bring the mixture to a boil.
4. When the grill has preheated, place the pot on the grilling rack and let smoke for 3 hours or until pork pieces have turned tender.
5. Check the fire after one hour of smoking and add more wood pallets if required.
6. When done, remove the pot from the grill, drain the cooking liquid, and break it into bite-size pieces using two forks.
7. Add shortening into the pot, return it onto the grilling rack, switch temperature of the grill to 400 degrees F, and continue cooking for 20 minutes until pork has turned nicely brown, stirring frequently.
8. When done, divide pork evenly among tortillas, add servings as desired, and then serve.

Nutrition: Calories: 170 kCal; Protein: 13 g; Carbs: 6 g; Fat: 11 g

101. Pork Belly Tacos

Preparation Time: 20 minutes
Cooking Time: 2 hours and 30 minutes
Servings: 6
Ingredients:
- Pork belly, scored, deskinned – 4 pounds
- Salt – 4 tablespoons
- Ground black pepper – ½ tablespoon
- Brown sugar – 4 tablespoons

Directions:
1. In the meantime, prepare the pork and for this, stir together salt, black pepper, and sugar and then rub this mixture generously on all sides until coated.
2. When the grill has preheated, place pork on a roasting pan, place on a grilling rack, and let smoke for 30 minutes.
3. Then switch the temperature of the grill to 250 degrees F and continue smoking the pork for 2 hours until tender.
4. Check the fire after one hour of smoking and add more wood pallets if required.
5. When done, remove pork from the grill and let it rest for 30 minutes.
6. Then cut pork into slices, divide evenly among tortillas, add cilantro and then serve.

Nutrition: Calories: 230 kCal; Fat: 8 g; Protein: 13 g; Carbs: 26 g

102. Teriyaki Pork Tenderloin

Preparation Time: 30 minutes
Cooking Time: 1 to 2 hours
Servings: 4 to 6
Ingredients:

- 2 (1-pound) pork tenderloins
- 1 batch Easy Teriyaki Marinade
- Smoked salt

Directions:

1. In a large zip-top bag, combine the tenderloins and marinade. Seal the bag, turn to coat, and refrigerate the pork for at least 30 minutes—I recommend up to overnight.
2. Supply your smoker with Pit Boss and follow the manufacturer's specific start-up procedure. Preheat the grill, with the lid closed, to 180°F
3. Remove the tenderloins from the marinade and season them with smoked salt.
4. Place the tenderloins directly on the grill grate and smoke for 1 hour
5. Increase the grill's temperature to 300°F and continue to cook until the pork's internal temperature reaches 145°F
6. Remove the tenderloins from the grill and let them rest for 5 to 10 minutes before thinly slicing and serving.

Nutrition: Calories: 150 kCal, Carbs: 17g, Protein; 23g, Fat: 4g

103. Pork Belly Burnt Ends

Preparation Time: 30 minutes
Cooking Time: 6 hours
Servings: 8 to 10
Ingredients:

- 1 (3-pound) skinless pork belly (if not already skinned, use a sharp boning knife to remove the skin from the belly), cut into 1½- to 2-inch cube
- 1 batch Sweet Brown Sugar Rub
- ½ cup honey
- 1 cup Bill's Best BBQ Sauce
- 2 tablespoons light brown sugar

Directions:

1. Supply your smoker with Pit Boss and follow the manufacturer's specific start-up procedure. Preheat the grill, with the lid closed, to 250°F.
2. Generously season the pork belly cubes with the rub. Using your hands, work the rub into the meat

3. Place the pork cubes directly on the grill grate and smoke until their internal temperature reaches 195°F.
4. Transfer the cubes from the grill to an aluminum pan. Add the honey, barbecue sauce, and brown sugar. Stir to combine and coat the pork.
5. Place the pan in the grill and smoke the pork for 1 hour, uncovered. Remove the pork from the grill and serve immediately.

Nutrition: Calories 1301 kCal, Carbs: 21g, Fat: 5g, Protein: 18g

104. Cajun Doubled-Smoked Ham

Preparation Time: 20 minutes
Cooking Time: 4 to 5 hours
Servings: 10 to 12
Ingredients:

- 1 (5- or 6-pound) bone-in smoked ham
- 1 batch Cajun Rub
- 3 tablespoons honey

Directions:

1. Supply your smoker with Pit Boss and follow the manufacturer's specific start-up procedure. Preheat the grill, with the lid closed, to 225°F.
2. Generously season the ham with the rub and place it either in a pan or directly on the grill grate. Smoke it for 1 hour.
3. Drizzle the honey over the ham and continue to smoke it until the ham's internal temperature reaches 145°F.
4. Remove the ham from the grill and let it rest for 5 to 10 minutes before thinly slicing and serving.

Nutrition: Calories: 60 kCal, Carbs 2g, Protein: 10g, Fat: 4g

105. Rub-Injected Pork Shoulder

Preparation Time: 15 minutes
Cooking Time: 16 to 20 hours
Servings: 8 to 12
Ingredients:

- 1 (6- to 8-pound) bone-in pork shoulder
- 2 cups Tea Injectable made with Not-Just-for-Pork Rub
- 2 tablespoons yellow mustard
- 1 batch Not-Just-for-Pork Rub

Directions:

1. Supply your smoker with Pit Boss and follow the manufacturer's specific start-up procedure. Preheat the grill, with the lid closed, to 225°F.
2. Inject the pork shoulder throughout with the tea injectable.
3. Coat the pork shoulder all over with mustard and season it with the rub. Using your hands, work the rub into the meat.
4. Place the shoulder directly on the grill grate and smoke until its internal temperature reaches 160°F and a dark bark has formed on the exterior.
5. Pull the shoulder from the grill and wrap it completely in aluminum foil or butcher paper.
6. Increase the grill's temperature to 350°F.
7. Return the pork shoulder to the grill and cook until its internal temperature reaches 195°F.
8. Pull the shoulder from the grill and place it in a cooler. Cover the cooler and let the pork rest for 1 or 2 hours.
9. Remove the pork shoulder from the cooler and unwrap it. Remove the shoulder bone and pull the pork apart using just your fingers. Serve immediately.

Nutrition: Calories: 688 kCal; Protein: 58.9g; Carbs: 2.7g; Fat: 47.3g

106. Smoked Spare Ribs

Preparation Time: 25 minutes
Cooking Time: 4 to 6 hours
Servings: 4 to 8
Ingredients:

- 2 (2- or 3-pound) racks spare ribs
- 2 tablespoons yellow mustard
- 1 batch Sweet Brown Sugar Rub
- ¼ cup Bill's Best BBQ Sauce

Directions:

1. Supply your smoker with Pit Boss and follow the manufacturer's specific start-up procedure. Preheat the grill, with the lid closed, to 225°F.
2. Remove the membrane from the backside of the ribs. This can be done by cutting just through the membrane in an X pattern and working a paper towel between the membrane and the ribs to pull it off.
3. Coat the ribs on both sides with mustard and season with the rub. Using your hands, work the rub into the meat.
4. Place the ribs directly on the grill grate and smoke until their internal temperature reaches between 190°F and 200°F.
5. Baste both sides of the ribs with barbecue sauce.
6. Increase the grill's temperature to 300°F and continue to cook the ribs for 15 minutes more.
7. Remove the racks from the grill, cut them into individual ribs, and serve immediately.

Nutrition: Calories:277 kCal, Carbs: 4.9g, Fat: 12g, Protein: 16g

107. Slow Smoked Pork Belly Sliders

Preparation Time: 20 minutes
Cooking Time: 4 hours
Servings: 8 to 10
Ingredients:

- 4-5 lbs. of pork belly, cut into 1-inch chunks
- 1 – 2 cups cabbage slaw
- 12 brioche slider
- 2 cups of cherry cola
- 1 tsp of coriander
- ½ cup of dark brown sugar
- 1 tsp of onion powder
- 1 cup of ketchup
- 1 tsp of liquid smoke
- 1 tsp of garlic powder
- ½ cup of molasses
- 1 tbsp. of Worcestershire sauce
- 1 tsp of ground ginger
- Sweet heat rub & grill
- Salt and pepper
- 1 tsp of smoked paprika

Directions:
For the BBQ sauce

1. Take a saucepan and add ketchup along with molasses, liquid smoke, dark brown sugar, onion

powder, coriander, ground ginger, cherry cola, garlic powder, Worcestershire sauce, smoked paprika, and salt-pepper

2. Cook it on medium heat till everything seem to have combined well and begins to bubble
3. Reduce the heat to slow and let the sauce thicken till it simmers properly and keep aside.

For the main course
1. Preheat the grill to 225 degrees F
2. Now cut the surface of the pork belly using a sharp knife and make ¼ inch deep marks
3. Apply sweet heat rub generously on all parts of the pork belly, and then let it sit at room temperature for 20 minutes
4. Place it on the grill and smoke it for nearly 4 hours
5. In between, brush it with BBQ sauce every 30 minutes
6. Remove it from the smoker and cut into small bite-sized portions
7. Place it on the brioche buns and top it with BBQ sauce and coleslaw
8. Serve

Nutrition: Calories: 310 kCal, Carbs: 23g, Fats: 26g Protein: 17g

108. **Chinese BBQ Pork**

Preparation Time: 10 minutes
Cooking Time: 20 minutes
Servings: 6
Ingredients:
Pork & Marinade
- 2 Pork Tenderloins, Silver Skin Removed
- 1/4 Cup Hoisin Sauce
- 1/4 Cup Honey
- 1 1/2 Tbsp. Brown Sugar
- 3 Tbsp. Soy Sauce
- 1 Tbsp. Asian Sesame Oil
- 1 Tbsp. Oyster Sauce, Optional
- 1 Tsp Chinese Five Spice
- 1 Garlic Clove, Minced
- 2 Tsp Red Food Coloring, Optional

Five Spice Dipping Sauce
- 1/4 Cup Ketchup
- 3 Tbsp. Brown Sugar
- 1 Tsp Yellow Mustard
- 1/4 Tsp Chinese Five Spice

Directions:
1. In a medium bowl, whisk together marinade thoroughly, making sure brown sugar is dissolved. Add pork and marinade to a glass pan or resalable plastic bag and marinate for at least 8 hours or overnight, occasionally turning to ensure all pork sides are well coated.
2. When ready to cook, set the temperature to 225°F and preheat, lid closed for 15 minutes.
3. Remove pork from marinade and boil marinade in a saucepan over medium-high heat on the stovetop for 3 minutes to use for basting pork. Cool slightly, then whisk in 2 additional Tablespoons of honey.
4. Arrange the tenderloins on the grill grate and smoke pork until the internal temperature reaches 145°F.
5. Baste pork with reserved marinade halfway through cooking. Remove pork from grill and, if desired, increase the temperature to High and return pork to grill for a few minutes per side to slight char and set the sauce. Alternatively, you can broil in the oven, just a couple of minutes per side.
6. For the 5 Spice Sauce: In a small saucepan over low heat, mix ketchup, brown sugar, mustard, and five-spice until sugar is dissolved and sauce is smooth. Let cool, and serve chilled or at room temperature.
7. Serve pork immediately with Jasmine rice, or cool and refrigerate for future use as an appetizer, served with Five Spice dipping sauce and toasted sesame seeds. Enjoy!
8. In a medium bowl, whisk together marinade thoroughly, making sure brown sugar is dissolved. Add pork and marinade to a glass pan or resalable plastic bag and marinate for at least 8 hours or overnight, occasionally turning to ensure all sides of pork are well coated.
9. When ready to cook, set the temperature to 225°F and preheat, lid closed for 15 minutes.
10. Remove pork from marinade and boil marinade in a saucepan over medium-high heat on the stovetop for 3 minutes to use for basting pork. Cool slightly, then whisk in 2 additional Tablespoons of honey.
11. Arrange the tenderloins on the grill grate and smoke pork until the internal temperature reaches 145°F.

12. Baste pork with reserved marinade halfway through cooking. Remove pork from grill and, if desired, increase the temperature to High and return pork to grill for a few minutes per side to slight char and set the sauce. Alternatively, you can broil in the oven, just a couple of minutes per side.
13. For the 5 Spice Sauce: In a small saucepan over low heat, mix ketchup, brown sugar, mustard, and five-spice until sugar is dissolved and sauce is smooth. Let cool, and serve chilled or at room temperature.
14. Serve pork immediately with Jasmine rice, or cool and refrigerate for future use as an appetizer, served with Five Spice dipping sauce and toasted sesame seeds. Enjoy!

Nutrition: Calories: 324 kCal, Fat: 11.6g, Carbs: 15g, Protein: 41g

109. Bacon Grilled Cheese Sandwich

Preparation Time: 15 minutes
Cooking Time: 5 minutes
Servings: 4
Ingredients:
- 1 Lb. Applewood Smoked Bacon Slices, Cooked
- 8 Slices Texas Toast
- 16 Slices Cheddar Cheese
- Mayonnaise
- Butter

Directions:
1. When ready to cook, set the temperature to 350°F and preheat, lid closed for 15 minutes.
2. Spread a little bit of mayonnaise on each piece of bread, place 1 piece of cheddar on a slice then top with a couple of slices of bacon. Add another slice of cheese, then top with the other piece of bread. Spread softened butter on the exterior of the top piece of bread.
3. When the grill is hot, place the grilled cheese directly on a cleaned, oiled grill grate buttered side down. Then spread softened butter on the exterior of the top slice.
4. Cook the grilled cheese on the first side for 5-7 minutes until grill marks develop and the cheese has begun to melt. Flip the sandwich and repeat on the other side.
5. Remove from the grill when the cheese is melted, and the exterior is lightly toasted. Enjoy!

Nutrition: Calories: 500 kCal, Carbs: 30g, Fat: 29g, Protein: 28g

110. Apple Cider Braised Smoked BBQ Pulled Pork

Preparation Time: 20 minutes
Cooking Time: 6 to 7 hours
Servings: 4
Ingredients:
- 7–9 lb. bone-in pork butt/shoulder roast

RUB
- 4 tablespoons brown sugar
- 1 tablespoon garlic powder
- 1 tablespoon onion powder
- 1 tablespoon kosher salt
- 1/2 tablespoon pepper
- 1.5 tablespoons smoked paprika
- 2 teaspoons dry mustard
- 1 tablespoon coriander
- 1 tablespoon chili powder

SPRAY
- 1/2 cup apple cider
- 1/2 cup apple cider vinegar

BRAISING
- 2 cups apple cider
- 3–4 sweet, crisp red apples, peeled and sliced
- 2 onions, sliced

SAUCE
- 1 cup ketchup
- 1/2 cup apple jelly
- 1/4 cup apple cider
- 1 tablespoon apple cider vinegar
- 1 teaspoon liquid smoke
- 1/2 tablespoon Worcestershire sauce
- 1 teaspoon chili powder
- 1/2 teaspoon onion powder
- 1 cup pan juices from the roast (fat separated)

Directions:
1. Pat roast dry. Combine all rub ingredients and a pat on all sides of the roast, rubbing in well. Cover roast and let sit overnight in the fridge.
2. When ready to cook, preheat smoker to 225 degrees and smoke roast directly on the grill for 5 hours. While cooking, combine spray ingredients in a clean spray bottle and spritz roast all over once every hour.

3. While roast is smoking, combine all sauce ingredients and whisk them together in a pan. Set aside until pan juices are ready.

4. After smoking, transfer your roast to either your slow cooker (if it fits, remember you have more stuff going in there!) or a roasting pan or disposable roasting pan (if you'll continue cooking on the smoker.)

5. Place apples, onions, and 2 cups apple cider around the roast in the roasting pan. Cover with a lid or tightly with foil. Cook in the slow cooker on high for 6-7 hours (or low for more like 8-10 if you want/need to drag it out, overnight, for example.) If you are cooking in the oven, set the temperature to 275 degrees. In the smoker, you can increase the temperature to 275 as well. Cook until internal temperature reaches 200-210 degrees, usually about 6-7 hours.

6. Let pork rest, covered for at least 15 minutes (longer is just fine) before discarding bones, separating fat, etc.

7. Pour pan juices into a fat separator. Pour 1 cup of juices into your BBQ sauce and bring to a simmer. Simmer for about 15 minutes until slightly thickened.

8. Pour a little of the remaining juices over shredded pork. Use a slotted spoon to grab the onions and apples and mix them in with the pork. Serve alone or on rolls or over rice. Freezes great! Excellent on nachos, pizzas, and more.

Nutrition: Calories: 426 kCal; Protein: 65.3g; Carbs: 20.4g; Fat: 8.4g

111. Pigs in a Blanket

Preparation Time: 10 minutes
Cooking Time: 45 minutes
Servings: 4
Ingredients:
- Pork sausages - 1 pack
- Biscuit dough - 1 pack

Directions:
1. Preheat your Pit Boss grill to 350 degrees.
2. Cut the sausages and the dough into thirds.
3. Wrap the dough around the sausages. Place them on a baking sheet.
4. Grill with a closed lid for 20-25 minutes or until they look cooked.
5. Take them out when they are golden brown.
6. Serve with a dip of your choice.

Nutrition: Calories: 275 kCal, Cabs: 14g, Protein: 9g, Fat: 22g,

112. Smoked, Candied, and Spicy Bacon

Preparation Time: 10 minutes
Cooking Time: 45 minutes
Servings: 4
Ingredients:
- Center-cut bacon - 1 lb.
- Brown sugar - ½ cup
- Maple syrup - ½ cup
- Hot sauce - 1 tablespoon
- Pepper - ½ tablespoon

Directions:
1. Mix the maple syrup, brown sugar, hot sauce, and pepper in a bowl.
2. Preheat your Pit Boss grill to 300 degrees.
3. Line a baking sheet and place the bacon slices on it.
4. Generously spread the brown sugar mix on both sides of the bacon slices.
5. Place the pan on the Pit Boss grill for 20 minutes. Flip the bacon pieces.
6. Leave them for another 15 minutes until the bacon looks cooked, and the sugar is melted.
7. Remove from the grill and let it stay for 10-15 minutes.
8. Voila! Your bacon candy is ready!

Nutrition: Calories: 218 kCal, Carbs: 14 g Protein: 8 Fat: 14.6 g

113. Stuffed Pork Crown Roast

Preparation Time: 10 minutes
Cooking Time: 3 hours 5 minutes
Servings: 4
Ingredients:

- 12-14 ribs or 1 Snake River Pork Crown Roast
- Apple cider vinegar - 2 tablespoon
- Apple juice - 1 cup
- Dijon mustard - 2 tablespoon
- Salt - 1 teaspoon
- Brown sugar - 1 tablespoon
- Freshly chopped thyme or rosemary - 2 tablespoon
- Cloves of minced garlic - 2
- Olive oil - ½ cup
- Coarsely ground pepper - 1 teaspoon
- Your favorite stuffing - 8 cups

Directions:

1. Set the pork properly in a shallow roasting pan on a flat rack. Cover both ends of the bone with a piece of foil.
2. To make the marinade, boil the apple cider or apple juice on high heat until about half its quantity. Remove the content from the heat and whisk in the mustard, vinegar, thyme, garlic, brown sugar, pepper, and salt. Once all that is properly blended, whisk in the oil slowly.
3. Use a pastry brush to apply the marinade to the roast. Ensure that you coat all the surfaces evenly. Cover it on all sides using plastic wrap. Allow it to sit for about 60 minutes until the meat has reached room temperature.
4. At this time, feel free to brush the marinade on the roast again. Cover it and return it to the refrigerator until it is time to cook it. When you are ready to cook it, allow the meat to reach room temperature, then put it on the pellet grill. Ensure that the grill is preheated for about 15 minutes before you do.
5. Roast the meat for 30 minutes, then reduce the temperature of the grill. Fill the crown loosely with the stuffing and mound it at the top. Cover the stuffing properly with foil. You can also bake the stuffing separately alongside the roast in a pan.
6. Roast the pork thoroughly for 90 more minutes. Get rid of the foil and continue to roast the stuffing for 30-90 minutes until the pork reaches an internal temperature of 150 degrees Fahrenheit. Ensure that you do not touch the bone of the meat with the temperature probe or get a false reading.
7. Remove the roast from the grill. Allow it to rest for around 15 minutes so that the meat soaks in all the juices. Remove the foil covering the bones. Leave the butcher's string on until you are ready to carve it. Now, transfer it to a warm platter, carve between the bones, and enjoy!

Nutrition: Calories: 1010 kCal Carbs: 6 g Protein: 108 g Fat: 59 g

114. St. Louis BBQ Ribs

Preparation Time: 10 minutes
Cooking Time: 4 hours 5 minutes
Servings: 4
Ingredients:

- Pit Boss pork as well as a poultry rub - 6 oz.
- St. Louis bone in the form of pork ribs - 2 racks
- Pit Boss Heat and Sweet BBQ sauce - 1 bottle
- Apple juice - 8 oz.

Directions:

1. Trim the ribs and peel off their membranes from the back.
2. Apply an even coat of the poultry rub on the front and back of the ribs. Let the coat sit for at least 20 minutes. If you wish to refrigerate it, you can do so for up to 4 hours.
3. Once you are ready to cook it, preheat the pellet grill for around 15 minutes. Place the ribs on the grill grate, bone side down. Put the apple juice in an easy spray bottle and then spray it evenly on the ribs.
4. Smoke the meat for 1 hour.
5. Remove the ribs from the pellet grill and wrap them securely in aluminum foil. Ensure that there is an opening in the wrapping at one end. Pour the remaining 6 oz. of apple juice into the foil. Wrap it tightly.
6. Place the ribs on the grill again, meat side down. Smoke the meat for another 3 hours.
7. Once the ribs are done and cooked evenly, get rid of the foil. Gently brush a layer of the sauce on both sides of the ribs. Put them back on the grill to cook for another 10 minutes to ensure that the sauce is set properly.

8. Once the sauce sets, take the ribs off the pellet grill and let them rest for at least 10 minutes so that they can soak in all the juices.
9. Slice the ribs to serve and enjoy!

Nutrition: Calories: 300 kCal Carbs: 30 g Protein: 13 Fat:13 g

115. Lemon Pepper Pork Tenderloin

Preparation Time: 20 minutes
Cooking Time: 20 minutes
Servings: 6
Ingredients:
- 2 pounds' pork tenderloin, Fat: trimmed

For the Marinade:
- ½ teaspoon minced garlic
- 2 lemons, zested
- 1 teaspoon minced parsley
- 1/2 teaspoon salt
- 1/4 teaspoon ground black pepper
- 1 teaspoon lemon juice
- 2 tablespoons olive oil

Directions:
1. Prepare the marinade and for this, take a small bowl, place all of its ingredients in it and whisk until combined.
2. Take a large plastic bag, pour marinade in it, add pork tenderloin, seal the bag, turn it upside down to coat the pork, and let it marinate for a minimum of 2 hours in the refrigerator.
3. When ready to cook, switch on the Pit Boss grill, fill the grill hopper with apple-flavored pellets, power the grill on by using the control panel, select 'smoke' on the temperature dial, or set the temperature to 375 degrees F and let it preheat for a minimum of 15 minutes.
4. When the grill has preheated, open the lid, place pork tenderloin on the grill grate, shut the grill, and smoke for 20 minutes until the internal temperature reaches 145 degrees F, turning pork halfway.
5. When done, transfer pork to a cutting board, let it rest for 10 minutes, then cut it into slices and serve.

Nutrition: Calories: 288.5 kCal Fat: 16.6 g Carbs: 6.2 g Protein: 26.4 g

116. Porchetta

Preparation Time: 30 minutes
Cook time: 3 hours
Servings: 12
Ingredients:
- 6 pounds' skin-on pork belly
- 4 pounds' center-cut pork loin
- 4 tbsp. olive oil
- 1 cup apple juice
- 2 garlic cloves (minced)
- 1 onion (diced)
- 1 ¼ cups grated pecorino Romano cheese
- 1 tsp ground black pepper
- 2 tsp kosher salt - 3 tbsp. fennel seeds
- 1 tbsp. freshly chopped rosemary
- 1 tbsp. freshly chopped sage
- 1 tbsp. freshly chopped thyme
- 1 tbsp. grated lemon zest

Rub:
- 1 tbsp. chili powder - 2 tsp grilling seasoning
- 1 tsp salt or to taste
- ½ tsp cayenne
- 1 tsp oregano - 1 tsp paprika
- 1 tsp mustard powder

Directions:
1. Butterfly the pork loin and place it in the middle of two plastic wraps. On a flat surface, pound the pork evenly until it is ½ inch thick.
2. Combine all the rub ingredients in a small mixing bowl.
3. Place the butterflied pork on a flat surface, cut side up. Season the cut side generously with 1/3 of the rub.
4. Heat 1 tbsp. olive oil in a frying pan over medium to high heat. Add the onion, garlic, and fennel seed. Sauté until the veggies are tender.
5. Stir the black pepper, 1 tsp kosher salt, rosemary, sage, thyme, and lemon zest. Cook for 1 minute and stir in the cheese.
6. Put the sautéed ingredients on the flat pork and spread evenly. Roll up the pork like you are rolling a burrito.
7. Brush the rolled pork loin with 1 tbsp. oil and season with the remaining rub. The loin with butcher's string at the 1-inch interval.
8. Roll the pork belly around the pork, skin side out. Brush the pork belly with the remaining oil and season with 1 tsp salt.

9. Set a rack into a roasting pan and place the Porchetta on the rack. Pour the wine into the bottom of the roasting pan.
10. Start your grill on smoke mode, leaving the lid opened for 5 minutes until the fire starts.
11. Close the lid and preheat the grill to 325°F, using maple or apple hard pellets.
12. Place the roasting pan on the grill and roast Porchetta for about 3 hours or until the Porchetta's internal temperature reaches 155°F.
13. Remove the Porchetta from heat and let it rest for a few minutes to cool.
14. Remove the butcher's string. Slice Porchetta into sizes and serve.

Nutrition: Calories: 611 kCal Fat: 22.7g Carbs: 6.6g Protein: 89.4g

117. Pork Jerky

Preparation Time: 15 minutes
Cook time: 2 hours 30 minutes
Servings: 12
Ingredients:
- 4 pounds' boneless center-cut pork (trimmed of excess fat and sliced into ¼ inch thick slices)

Marinade:
- 1/3 cup soy sauce
- 1 cup pineapple juice
- 1 tbsp. rice wine vinegar
- 2 tsp black pepper
- 1 tsp red pepper flakes
- 5 tbsp. brown sugar
- 1 tsp paprika
- 1 tsp onion powder
- 1 tsp garlic powder
- 2 tsp salt or to taste

Directions:
1. Combine and mix all the marinade ingredients in a mixing bowl.
2. Put the sliced pork in a gallon-sized zip-lock bag and pour the marinade into the bag. Massage the marinade into the pork. Seal the bag and refrigerate for 8 hours.
3. Activate the pellet grill smoker setting and leave the lip open for 5 minutes until the fire starts.
4. Close the lid and preheat your pellet grill to 180°F, using a hickory pellet.
5. Remove the pork slices from the marinade and pat them dry with a paper towel.

6. Arrange the pork slices on the grill in a single layer. Smoke the pork for about 2 ½ hours, often turning after the first 1 hour of smoking. The jerky should be dark and dry when it is done.
7. Remove the jerky from the grill and let it sit for about 1 hour to cool.
8. Serve immediately or store in airtight containers and refrigerate for future use.

Nutrition: Calories: 260 kCal Fat: 11.4g Carbs: 8.6g Protein: 28.1g

118. Grilled Carnitas

Preparation Time: 20 minutes
Cook time: 10 hours
Servings: 12
Ingredients:
- 1 tsp paprika
- 1 tsp oregano
- 1 tsp cayenne pepper
- 2 tsp brown sugar
- 1 tsp mint
- 1 tbsp. onion powder
- 1 tsp cumin
- 1 tsp chili powder
- 2 tbsp. salt
- 1 tsp garlic powder
- 1 tsp Italian seasoning
- 2 tbsp. Olive oil.
- 5 pounds' pork shoulder roast

Directions:
1. Trim the pork of any excess fat.
2. To make a rub, combine the paprika, oregano, cayenne, sugar, mint, onion powder, garlic powder, cumin, chili, salt, and Italian seasoning in a small mixing bowl.
3. Rub all sides of the pork with the rub.
4. Start your grill for smoking, leaving the lid open until the fire starts.
5. Close the lid and preheat the grill to 325°F with the lid closed for 15 minutes.
6. Place the pork in a foil pan and place the pan on the grill—Cook for about 2 hours.
7. After 2 hours, increase the heat to 325°F and smoke pork for an additional 8 hours or until the pork's internal temperature reaches 190°F.
8. Remove pork from it and let it sit until it is cook and easy to handle.
9. Shred the pork with two forks.

10. Place a cast-iron skillet on the grill grate and add the olive oil.
11. Add the pork and sear until the pork is brown and crispy.
12. Remove pork from heat and let it rest for a few minutes. Serve!

Nutrition: Calories: 514 kCal, Fat: 41.1g, Carbs: 1.6g Protein: 32g

119. Stuffed Tenderloin

Preparation Time: 15 minutes
Cook time: 3 hours
Servings: 8
Ingredients:
- 1 pork tenderloin
- 12 slices of bacon
- ¼ cup cheddar cheese
- ¼ cup mozzarella cheese
- 1 small onion (finely chopped)
- 1 carrot (finely chopped)

Rub:
- ½ tsp granulated garlic (not garlic powder)
- ½ tsp cayenne pepper
- 1 tsp paprika
- ½ tsp ground pepper
- 1 tsp chili
- ½ tsp onion powder
- ¼ tsp cumin
- 1 tsp salt

Directions:
1. Butterfly the pork tenderloin and place between 2 plastic wraps. Pound the tenderloin evenly with a mallet until it is ½ inch thick.
2. Place the cheddar, mozzarella, onion, and carrot on one end of the flat pork. Roll up the pork like a burrito.
3. Combine all the ingredients for the rub in a mixing bowl. Rub the seasoning mixture all over the pork.
4. Wrap the pork with bacon slices.
5. Preheat the grill to 275°F for 10-15 minutes. Use apple, hickory, or mesquite hard pellets.
6. Place the pork on the grill and smoke for 3 hours, or until the pork's internal temperature reaches 165°F and the bacon wrap is crispy.
7. Remove the pork from heat and let it rest for about 10 minutes.
8. Cut into sizes and serve.

Nutrition: Calories: 241 kCal, Fat: 14.8g, Carbs: 2.7g, Protein: 22.9g

120. Maplewood Bourbon BBQ Ham

Preparation Time: 15 minutes
Cook time: 2 hours 30 minutes
Servings: 8
Ingredients:
- 1 large ham
- 1/2 cup brown sugar
- 3 tbsp. bourbon
- 2 tbsp. lemon
- 2 tbsp. Dijon mustard
- ¼ cup apple juice
- ¼ cup maple syrup
- 1 tsp salt
- 1 tsp freshly ground garlic
- 1 tsp ground black pepper

Directions:
1. Start your grill on a smoke setting, leaving for 5 minutes, until the fire starts.
2. Close the lid and preheat the grill to 325°F.
3. Place the ham on a smoker rack and place the rack on the grill. Smoke for 2 hours or until the internal temperature of the ham reaches 125°F.
4. Combine the sugar, bourbon, lemon, mustard, apple juice, salt, pepper, and maple in a saucepan over medium to high heat.
5. Bring mixture to a boil, reduce the heat and simmer until the sauce thickens.
6. Glaze the ham with maple mixture.
7. Increase the grill temperature to 375°F and continue cooking until the internal temperature of the ham reaches 140°F.
8. Remove the glazed ham from the grill and let it rest for about 15 minutes.
9. Cut ham into small sizes and serve.

Nutrition: Calories: 163 kCal, Fat: 4.6g, Carbs: 19g Protein: 8.7g

121. Pork Steak

Preparation Time: 10 minutes
Cooking Time: 20 minutes
Servings: 4
Ingredients:
For the Brine:

- 2-inch piece of orange peel
- 2 sprigs of thyme
- 4 tablespoons salt
- 4 black peppercorns
- 1 sprig of rosemary
- 2 tablespoons brown sugar
- 2 bay leaves
- 10 cups water

For Pork Steaks:

- 4 pork steaks, fat trimmed
- Game rub as needed

Directions:

1. Prepare the brine and for this, take a large container, place all of its ingredients in it and stir until sugar has dissolved.
2. Place steaks in it, add some weights to keep steak submerge into the brine, and let soak for 24 hours in the refrigerator.
3. Fill the grill hopper with hickory flavored pellets, power the grill on by using the control panel, select 'smoke' on the temperature dial, or set the temperature to 225ºF and let it preheat for a minimum of 15 minutes.
4. Remove steaks from the brine, rinse well, and pat dry with paper towels and then season well with game rub until coated.
5. When the grill has preheated, open the lid, place steaks on the grill grate, shut the grill, and smoke for 10 minutes per side until the internal temperature reaches 140ºF.
6. Transfer steaks to a cutting board, rest for 10 minutes, and then cut into slices and serve.

Nutrition: Calories: 260 kCal, Fat: 21g, Carbs: 1g, Protein: 17g

122. Carolina Smoked Ribs

Preparation Time: 30 minutes
Cooking Time: 4 hours 30 minutes
Serving: 10
Ingredients:

- 1/2 a cup of brown sugar
- 1/3 cup of fresh lemon juice
- ¼ cup of white vinegar
- 1/4 cup of apple cider vinegar
- 1 tablespoon of Worcestershire sauce
- ¼ cup of molasses
- 2 cups of prepared mustard
- 2 teaspoons of garlic, minced
- 2 teaspoons of salt
- 1 teaspoon of ground black pepper
- 1 teaspoon of crushed red pepper flakes
- ½ a teaspoon of white pepper
- ¼ teaspoon of cayenne pepper
- 2 racks of pork spare ribs
- ½ a cup of barbeque seasoning

Directions:

1. Take a medium-sized bowl and whisk in brown sugar, white vinegar, lemon juice, mustard, Worcestershire sauce, mustard, molasses
2. Mix well and season the mixture with granulated garlic, pepper, salt, red pepper flakes, white pepper flakes, cayenne pepper
3. Take your drip pan and add water; cover with aluminum foil. Pre-heat your smoker to 225 degrees F
4. Use water fill water pan halfway through and place it over drip pan. Add wood chips to the side tray
5. Rub the ribs with your prepared seasoning and transfer to your smoker
6. Cover the meat with aluminum foil and smoke for 4 hours, making sure to add chips after every 60 minutes
7. After the first 3 and a ½ hours, make sure to uncover the meat and baste it generously with the prepared mustard sauce
8. Take the meat out and serve with remaining sauce
9. Enjoy!

Nutrition: Calories: 750 kCal, Fat: 35g, Carbs: 14g, Protein: 29g

123. Hearty Pig Candies

Preparation Time: 20 minutes
Cooking Time: 2 hours
Servings: 10
Ingredients:
- Nonstick cooking spray
- 2 pound of bacon slices
- 1 cup of firmly packed brown sugar
- 2-3 teaspoon of cayenne pepper
- ½ a cup of maple syrup

Directions:
1. Take your drip pan and add water; cover with aluminum foil. Pre-heat your smoker to 225 degrees F
2. Use water fill water pan halfway through and place it over drip pan. Add wood chips to the side tray
3. Remove the grill rack from your smoker and cover with aluminum foil; spray the foils with cooking spay
4. Lay the bacon in a single layer, making sure to leave a bit of space in between
5. Take a small bowl and add brown sugar, cayenne, and mix
6. Baste the bacon with ¼ cup of maple syrup
7. Sprinkle half of the rub on top of the bacon
8. Transfer the rack to the smoker alongside the bacon and smoke for 1 hour
9. Flip the bacon and baste with another ¼ cup of maple syrup, sprinkle more rub, and a smoker for 1 hour more
10. Once the bacon is brown and firm, it's ready to be served!

Nutrition: Calories: 152 kCal, Fat: 10g, Carbs: 13g, Protein: 9g

124. Lamb Rack Wrapped In Apple Wood Walnut

Preparation Time: 25 minutes
Cooking Time: 60 to 90 minutes
Servings: 4
Ingredients:
- 3 tablespoons of Dijon mustard
- 2 pieces of garlic, chopped or 2 cups of crushed garlic
- ½ teaspoon of garlic
- ½ teaspoon kosher salt
- ½ teaspoon black pepper
- ½ teaspoon rosemary
- 1 (1½ pound) ram rack, French
- 1 cup crushed walnut

Directions:
1. Put mustard, garlic, garlic powder, salt, pepper and rosemary in a small bowl.
2. Spread the seasoning mix evenly on all sides of the lamb and sprinkle with crushed walnuts. Lightly press the walnuts by hand to attach the nuts to the meat.
3. Wrap the walnut-coated lamb rack loosely in plastic wrap and refrigerate overnight to allow the seasoning to penetrate the meat.
4. Remove the walnut-covered lamb rack from the refrigerator and let it rest for 30 minutes to reach room temperature.
5. Set the wood pellet r grill for indirect cooking and preheat to 225 ° F using apple pellets.
6. Lay the grill directly on the rack with the lamb bone down.
7. Smoke at 225 ° F until the thickest part of the ram rack reaches the desired internal temperature. This is measured with a digital instantaneous thermometer near the time listed on the chart.
8. Place the mutton under a loose foil tent for 5 minutes before eating

Nutrition: Calories: 165 kCal, Carbs: 0g, Fat: 8g, Protein: 20g

125. Roasted Lamb Leg

Preparation Time: 20 Minutes
Cooking Time: 1.5 Hours to 2 Hours
Servings: 6
Ingredients:

- 1 boneless leg of a lamb
- ½ cup of roasted garlic flavored extra virgin olive oil
- ¼ cup dried parsley
- 3 garlics, chopped
- 2 tablespoons of a fresh lemon juice or 1 tablespoon of lemon zest (from 1 medium lemon)
- 2 tablespoons of dried oregano
- 1 tablespoon dried rosemary
- ½ teaspoon black pepper

Directions:

1. Remove the net from the lamb's leg. Cut off grease, silver skin, and large pieces of fat.
2. In a small bowl, mix olive oil, parsley, garlic, lemon juice or zest, oregano, rosemary, and pepper.
3. Spice the inside and outside surfaces of the lamb's boneless legs.
4. Secure the boneless lamb leg using a silicone food band or butcher twine. Use a band or twine to form and maintain the basic shape of the lamb
5. Wrap the lamb loosely in plastic wrap and refrigerate overnight to allow the seasoning to penetrate the meat.
6. Remove the rum from the refrigerator and leave at room temperature for 1 hour.
7. Set up a wood pellet smoker and grill for indirect cooking and preheat to 400 ° F using selected pellets.
8. Remove the wrap from the ram.
9. Insert a wood pellet smoker and grill meat probe or remote meat probe into the thickest part of the lamb. If your grill does not have a meat probe or you do not have a remote meat probe, use an instant reading digital thermometer to read the internal temperature while cooking. Roast the lamb at 400 ° F until the internal temperature of the thickest part reaches the desired finish.
10. Place the lamb under the loose foil tent for 10 minutes, then cut it against the grain and eat.

Nutrition: Cal: 200 kCal Carbs: 1g Fat: 13g Protein: 20g

126. Greek Leg of Lamb

Preparation Time: 15 minutes
Cooking Time: 25 minutes
Servings: 6
Ingredients:

- 2 tablespoons finely chopped fresh rosemary
- 1 tablespoon ground thyme
- 5 garlic cloves, minced
- 2 tablespoons sea salt
- 1 tablespoon freshly ground black pepper
- Butcher's string
- 1 whole boneless (6- to 8-pound) leg of lamb
- ¼ cup extra-virgin olive oil
- 1 cup red wine vinegar
- ½ cup canola oil

Directions:

1. In a container, combine the rosemary, thyme, garlic, salt, and pepper; set aside.
2. Using butcher's string, tie the leg of lamb into the shape of a roast. Your butcher should also be happy to truss the leg for you.
3. Rub the lamb generously with the olive oil and season with the spice mixture. Put it to a plate, cover with plastic wrap, and refrigerate for 4 hours.
4. Remove the lamb from the refrigerator but do not rinse.
5. Supply your smoker with wood pellets and follow the manufacturer's specific start-up procedure. Preheat, with the lid closed, to 325°F.
6. In a small bowl, combine the red wine vinegar and canola oil for basting.
7. Place the lamb directly on the grill, close the lid, and smoke for 20 to 25 minutes per pound (depending on desired doneness), basting with the oil and vinegar mixture every 30 minutes. Lamb is generally served medium-rare to medium, so it will be done when a meat thermometer where inserted in the thickest part reads 140°F to 145°F.
8. Let the lamb meat rest for about 15 minutes before slicing to serve.

Nutrition: Calories: 130 kCal Carbs: 2g Fat: 5g Protein: 19g

127. Smoked Christmas Crown Roast of Lamb

Preparation Time: 1 hour
Cooking Time: 2 hours
Servings: 4
Ingredients:

- 2 racks of lamb, trimmed, drenched, and tied into a crown
- 1¼ cups extra-virgin olive oil, divided
- 2 tablespoons chopped fresh basil
- 2 tablespoons chopped fresh rosemary
- 2 tablespoons ground sage
- 2 tablespoons ground thyme
- 8 garlic cloves, minced
- 2 teaspoons salt
- 2 teaspoons freshly ground black pepper

Directions:

1. Set the lamb out in the counter to take the chill off, about an hour.
2. In a container, combine 1 cup of olive oil, the basil, rosemary, sage, thyme, garlic, salt, and pepper.
3. Baste the entire crown with the herbed olive oil and wrap the exposed drenched bones in aluminum foil.
4. Supply your smoker with wood pellets and follow the manufacturer's specific start-up procedure. Preheat, with the lid closed, to 275°F.
5. Put the lamb directly on the grill, close the lid, and smoke for 1 hour 30 minutes to 2 hours, or wait until a meat thermometer inserted in the thickest part reads 140°F.
6. Remove the lamb from the heat, tent with foil, and let rest for about 15 minutes before serving. The temperature will rise about 5°F during the rest period, for a finished temperature of 145°F.

Nutrition: Calories: 206 kCal Carbs: 4g Fat: 9g Protein: 32g

128. Succulent Lamb Chops

Preparation Time: 15 minutes
Cooking Time: 20 minutes
Servings: 4
Ingredients:
For The Marinade

- ½ cup rice wine vinegar
- 1 teaspoon liquid smoke
- 2 tablespoons extra-virgin olive oil

- 2 tablespoons dried minced onion
- 1 tablespoon chopped fresh mint

For The Lamb Chops

- 8 (4-ounce) lamb chops
- ½ cup hot pepper jelly
- 1 tablespoon Sriracha
- 1 teaspoon salt
- 1 teaspoon freshly ground black pepper

Directions:

1. In a small container, whisk together the rice wine vinegar, liquid smoke, olive oil, minced onion, and mint.
2. Place the lamb chops in an aluminum roasting pan. Pour the marinade over the meat, turning to coat thoroughly. Cover it with a plastic wrapper and marinate in the refrigerator for 2 hours.
3. Supply your smoker with wood pellets and follow the manufacturer's specific start-up procedure. Preheat, with the lid closed, to 165°F, or the "Smoke" setting.
4. Put your saucepan top of the stove then low heat, combine the hot pepper jelly and Sriracha and keep warm.
5. When you are going to cook the chops, remove them from the marinade and pat dry. Discard the marinade.
6. Season all the chops with a salt and pepper, then place them directly on the grill grate, close the lid, and smoke for 5 minutes to "breathe" some smoke into them.
7. Remove the chops from the grill. Increase the pellet cooker temperature to 450°F, or the "High" setting. Once your griller is up to temperature, place the chops on the grill and sear, cooking for 2 minutes per side to achieve medium-rare chops. A meat thermometer that usually inserted in the thickest part of the meat should read 145°F. Continue grilling, if necessary, to your desired doneness.
8. Serve the chops with the warm Sriracha pepper jelly on the side.

Nutrition: Calories: 277 kCal Carbs: 0g Fat: 26g Protein: 18g

129. Roasted Rosemary Lamb

Preparation Time: 15 minutes
Cooking Time: 4 hours
Servings: 2
Ingredients:
- 1 lamb rack
- 2 rosemary sprigs, chopped
- Salt and pepper to taste
- 12 baby potatoes
- 1/2 cup butter
- 1 bunch asparagus
- 2 tablespoons olive oil

Directions:
1. Set your wood pellet grill to 225 degrees F. Sprinkle the lamb with the rosemary, salt and pepper.
2. In a baking pan, add the potatoes and coat with the butter. Add the lamb to the grill.
3. Place the pan with potatoes beside the lamb. Roast for 3 hours.
4. Coat the asparagus with the olive oil. In your last twenty minutes of cooking, stir the asparagus into the potatoes.
5. Serve the lamb with the asparagus and baby potatoes.

Nutrition: Calories: 197 kCal Carbs: 3g Fat: 14g Protein: 15g

130. Grilled Lamb

Preparation Time: 10 minutes
Cooking Time: 1 hour
Servings: 6
Ingredients:
- 2 racks of lamb, fat trimmed
- 2 tablespoons Dijon mustard
- Steak seasoning
- 1 teaspoon fresh rosemary, chopped
- 1 tablespoon fresh parsley, chopped

Directions:
1. Coat the lamb with the mustard.
2. Sprinkle all sides with the seasoning, rosemary and parsley.
3. Set your wood pellet grill to 400 degrees F.
4. Sear the meat side of the lamb for 6 minutes.
5. Reduce temperature to 300 degrees F.
6. Grill it for about 20 minutes, turning once or twice.

7. Let rest for 10 minutes before slicing and serving.

Nutrition: Calories: 241 kCal Carbs: 0g Fat: 17g Protein: 21g

131. Chipotle Lamb

Preparation Time: 15 minutes
Cooking Time: 2 hours 30 minutes
Servings: 6
Ingredients:
- 1 rack lamb ribs
- 3/4 cup olive oil
- Pepper to taste
- 1 tablespoon chipotle powder
- 3 cloves, garlic
- 1/4 cup Apple wood bacon rub
- 2 tablespoons rosemary, chopped
- 2 tablespoons thyme, chopped
- 2 tablespoons sage, chopped
- 2 tablespoons parsley

Directions:
1. Coat the lamb ribs with olive oil. Season with the pepper and chipotle powder.
2. Marinate for 15 minutes. Set your wood pellet grill to 275 degrees F.
3. Combine the rest of the ingredients. Spread the mixture on all sides of the lamb.
4. Cook the lamb for 2 hours. Allow it to rest about ten minutes before carving and serving.

Nutrition: Calories: 210 kCal Carbs: 0g Fat: 13g Protein: 22g

132. Hickory Rack of Lamb

Preparation Time: 10 minutes
Cooking Time: 2 hours
Servings: 3
Ingredients:
- 1 (3 pounds) rack of lamb (drenched)

Marinade Ingredients:
- 1 lemon (juiced)
- 1 teaspoon ground black pepper
- 1 teaspoon thyme
- ¼ cup balsamic vinegar
- 1 teaspoon dried basil
- 2 tablespoons Dijon mustard
- 2 cloves garlic (crushed)

Rub:
- ½ teaspoon cayenne pepper
- ½ teaspoon ground black pepper
- ¼ teaspoon Italian seasoning
- 1 teaspoon oregano
- 1 teaspoon dried mint
- 1 teaspoon paprika
- 1 teaspoon garlic powder
- 1 teaspoon onion powder
- 1 teaspoon dried parsley
- 1 teaspoon dried basil
- 1 teaspoon dried rosemary
- 4 tablespoons olive oil

Directions:
1. Put all the marinade ingredients in an empty container. Pour the marinade into a gallon zip-lock bag. Add the rack of lamb and massage the marinade into the rack. Seal the bag and place it in a refrigerator. Refrigerate for 8 hour or overnight.
2. When ready to roast, remove the rack of lamb from the marinade and let it sit for about 2 hour or until it is at room temperature.
3. Meanwhile, combine all the rub ingredients except the olive oil in a mixing bowl.
4. Rub the rub mixture over the rack of lamb generously. Drizzle rack with the olive oil.
5. Start your grill on smoke with the lid opened until fire starts.
6. Close the lid and preheat grill to 225°F using hickory wood pellets.
7. Place the rack of your lamb on the grill grate, bone side down. Smoke it for about two hours or until the internal temperature of the meat reaches 140-145°F.
8. Take off the rack of lamb from the grill and let it rest for about 10 minutes to cool.

Nutrition: Calories: 800 kCal, Fat: 41.1g, Carbs: 6.7g, Protein 93.8g

133. Leg of Lamb

Preparation Time: 10 minutes
Cooking Time: 2 hours
Servings: 6
Ingredients:
- 1 (2 pounds) leg of lamb
- 1 teaspoon dried rosemary
- 2 teaspoon freshly ground black pepper
- 4 cloves garlic (minced)
- 2 teaspoon salt or more to taste
- ½ teaspoon paprika
- 1 teaspoon thyme
- 2 tablespoons olive oil
- 1 teaspoon brown sugar
- 2 tablespoons oregano

Directions:
1. Trim the meat of excess fat and remove silver-skin.
2. In a mixing bowl, combine the thyme, salt, sugar, oregano, paprika, black pepper, garlic and olive oil.
3. Generously, rub the mixture over the leg of lamb. Cover seasoned leg of lamb with foil and let it sit for 1 hour to marinate.
4. Start your grill on smoke and leave the lid open for 5 minutes, or until fire starts. Cover the lid and preheat grill to 250°F using hickory, maple or apple wood pellets.
5. Remove the foil and place the leg of lamb on a smoker rack. Place the rack on the grill and smoke the leg of lamb for about 4 hours or until it reaches the internal temperature of your meat 145°F. Take off the leg of lamb from the grill and let it rest for a few minutes to cool. Cut into sizes and serve.

Nutrition: Calories 334 kCal Fat: 16g Carbs: 2.9g Protein 42.9g

134. Smoked Lamb Chops

Preparation Time: 10 minutes
Cooking Time: 50 minutes
Servings: 4
Ingredients:
- 1 rack of lamb, fat trimmed
- 2 tablespoons rosemary, fresh
- 2 tablespoons sage, fresh
- 1 tablespoon garlic cloves, roughly chopped
- 1/2 tablespoon salt
- 1/2 tablespoon pepper, coarsely ground
- 1/4 cup olive oil
- 1 tablespoon honey

Directions:
1. Preheat your wood pellet smoker to 225°F using a fruitwood.
2. Put all your ingredients except the lamb in a food processor. Liberally apply the mixture on the lamb.
3. Place the lamb on the smoker for 45 minutes or until the internal temperature reaches 120°F.
4. Sear the lamb on the grill for 2 minutes per side. Let rest for 5 minutes before serving. Slice and enjoy.

Nutrition: Calories 704 kCal Fat 56g Carbs 24g Protein 27g

135. Wood Pellet Smoked Lamb Shoulder

Preparation Time: 10 minutes
Cooking Time: 1 hour 30 minutes
Servings: 7
Ingredients:
For Smoked Lamb Shoulder
- 5 pounds lamb shoulder, boneless and excess fat trimmed
- 2 tablespoons kosher salt
- 2 tablespoons black pepper
- 1 tablespoon rosemary, dried

The Injection
- 1 cup apple cider vinegar

The Spritz
- 1 cup apple cider vinegar
- 1 cup apple juice

Directions:
1. Preheat the wood pellet smoker with a water pan to 2250 F.
2. Rinse the lamb in cold water then pat it dry with a paper towel. Inject vinegar to the lamb.
3. Pat the lamb dry again and rub with oil, salt black pepper and rosemary. Tie with kitchen twine.
4. Smoke uncovered for 1 hour then spritz after every 15 minutes until the internal temperature reaches 1950 F.
5. Take off the lamb from the grill and place it on a platter. Let cool before shredding it and enjoying it with your favorite side.

Nutrition: Calories 243 kCal Fat 19g Carbs 0g Protein 17g

136. Wood Pellet Smoked Pulled Lamb Sliders

Preparation Time: 10 minutes
Cooking Time: 7 hours
Servings: 7
Ingredients:
For the Lamb's shoulder
- 5 pounds lamb shoulder, boneless
- 1/2 cup olive oil
- 1/4 cup dry rub
- 10 ounces spritz

The Dry Rub
- 1/3 cup kosher salt
- 1/3 cup pepper, ground
- 1-1/3 cup garlic, granulated

The Spritz
- 4 ounces Worcestershire sauce
- 6 ounces apple cider vinegar

Directions:
1. Preheat the wood pellet smoker with a water bath to 2500 F.
2. Trim any fat from the lamb then rub with oil and dry rub.
3. Place the lamb on the smoker for 90 minutes then spritz with a spray bottle every 30 minutes until the internal temperature reaches 1650 F.
4. Transfer the lamb shoulder to a foil pan with the remaining spritz liquid and cover tightly with foil.
5. Place back in the smoker and smoke until the internal temperature reaches 2000 F.
6. Remove from the smoker and let rest for 30 minutes before pulling the lamb and serving with slaw, bun, or aioli. Enjoy

Nutrition: Calories 339 kCal, Fat 22g, Carbs 16g Protein 18g

137. Smoked Lamb Meatballs

Preparation Time: 10 minutes
Cooking Time: 1 hour
Servings: 5
Ingredients:
- 1 pound lamb shoulder, ground
- 3 garlic cloves, finely diced
- 3 tablespoons shallot, diced
- 1 tablespoon salt
- 1 egg
- 1/2 tablespoon pepper
- 1/2 tablespoon cumin
- 1/2 tablespoon smoked paprika
- 1/4 tablespoon red pepper flakes
- 1/4 tablespoon cinnamon, ground
- 1/4 cup panko breadcrumbs

Directions:
1. Set the wood pellet smoker to 2500 F using a fruitwood.
2. In a mixing bowl, combine all meatball ingredients until well mixed.
3. Form small-sized balls and place them on a baking sheet. Place the baking sheet in the smoker and smoke until the internal temperature reaches 1600 F.
4. Remove from the smoker and serve. Enjoy.

Nutrition: Calories 73 kCal Fat 5.2g Carbs 2g Protein 4.9g

138. Crown Rack of Lamb

Preparation Time: 10 minutes
Cooking Time: 30 minutes
Servings: 6
Ingredients:
- 2 racks of lamb, drenched
- 1 tablespoon garlic, crushed
- 1 tablespoon rosemary, finely chopped
- 1/4 cup olive oil
- 2 feet twine

Directions:
1. Rinse the racks with cold water then pat them dry with a paper towel.
2. Lay the racks on a flat board then score between each bone, about ¼ inch down.
3. In a mixing bowl, mix garlic, rosemary, and oil then generously brush on the lamb.
4. Take each lamb rack and bend it into a semicircle forming a crown-like shape.

5. Use the twine to wrap the racks about 4 times starting from the base to the top. Make sure you tie the twine tightly to keep the racks together.
6. Preheat the wood pellet to 400-4500 F then place the lamb racks on a baking dish. Place the baking dish on the pellet grill.
7. Cook for 10 minutes then reduce temperature to 3000 F. cook for 20 more minutes or until the internal temperature reaches 1300 F.
8. Remove the lamb rack from the wood pellet and let rest for 15 minutes.
9. Serve when hot with veggies and potatoes. Enjoy.

Nutrition: Calories 390 kCal Fat 35g Carbs 0g Protein 17g

139. Wood Pellet Smoked Leg of Lamb

Preparation Time: 15 minutes
Cooking Time: 3 hours
Servings: 6
Ingredients:
- 1 leg lamb, boneless
- 4 garlic cloves, minced
- 2 tablespoons salt
- 1 tablespoon black pepper, freshly ground
- 2 tablespoons oregano
- 1 tablespoon thyme
- 2 tablespoons olive oil

Directions:
1. Cut off any excess of fat from the lamb and tie the lamb using twine to form a nice roast.
2. In a mixing bowl, mix garlic, spices, and oil. Rub all over the lamb, wrap with a plastic bag then refrigerate for an hour to marinate.
3. Place the lamb on a smoker set at 2500 F. smoke the lamb for 4 hours or until the internal temperature reaches 1450 F.
4. Remove from the smoker and let rest to cool. Serve and enjoy.

Nutrition: Calories: 356 kCal Fat 16g Carbs 3g Protein 49g

140. Wood Pellet Grilled Aussie Leg of Lamb Roast

Preparation Time: 30 minutes
Cooking Time: 2 hours
Serving: 8
Ingredients:

- 5 pounds Aussie leg of lamb, boneless
- Smoked Paprika Rub
- 1 tablespoon raw sugar
- 1 tablespoon kosher salt
- 1 tablespoon black pepper
- 1 tablespoon smoked paprika
- 1 tablespoon garlic powder
- 1 tablespoon rosemary, dried
- 1 tablespoon onion powder
- 1 tablespoon cumin
- 1/2 tablespoon cayenne pepper
- Roasted Carrots
- 1 bunch rainbow carrots
- Olive oil
- Salt
- Pepper

Directions:

1. Heat the wood pellet grill to 3750 F.
2. Trim any excess fat from the lamb.
3. Put all your rub ingredients and rub all over the lamb. Place the lamb on the grill and smoke for 2 hours.
4. Toss the carrots in oil, salt, and pepper then add to the grill after the lamb has cooked for 1 ½ hour.
5. Cook until the roast internal temperature reaches 1350 F. remove the lamb from the grill and cover with foil. Let rest for 30 minutes.
6. Remove the carrots from the grill once soft and serve with the lamb. Enjoy.

Nutrition: Calories 257 kCal Fat 8g Carbs 6g Protein 37g

141. Simple Grilled Lamb Chops

Preparation Time: 10 minutes
Cooking Time: 6 minutes
Servings: 6
Ingredients:

- 1/4 cup distilled white vinegar
- 2 tablespoons salt
- 1/2 tablespoon black pepper
- 1 tablespoon garlic, minced

- 1 onion, thinly sliced
- 2 tablespoons olive oil
- 2 pounds lamb chops

Directions:

1. In a reseal able bag, mix vinegar, salt, black pepper, garlic, sliced onion, and oil until all salt has dissolved.
2. Add the lamb chops and toss until well coated. Place in the fridge to marinate for 2 hours.
3. Preheat the wood pellet grill to high heat.
4. Remove the lamb from the fridge and discard the marinade. Wrap any exposed bones with foil.
5. Grill your lamb meat for three minutes per side. You can also broil in a broiler for more crispness. Serve and enjoy

Nutrition: Calories: 519 kCal, Fat: 45 g, Carbs: 2.3 g, Protein: 25g

142. Wood Pellet Grilled Lamb with Brown Sugar Glaze

Preparation Time: 15 minutes
Cooking Time: 10 minutes
Servings: 4
Ingredients:

- 1/4 cup brown sugar
- 2 tablespoons ginger, ground
- 2 tablespoons tarragon, dried
- 1 teaspoon cinnamon, ground
- 1 tablespoons black pepper, ground
- 1 tablespoons garlic powder
- 1/2 tablespoons salt
- 4 lamb chops

Directions:

1. In a mixing bowl, mix sugar, ginger, dried tarragon, cinnamon, black pepper, garlic, and salt.
2. Rub the lamb chops with the seasoning and place it on a plate. Refrigerate for an hour to marinate.
3. Preheat the grill to high heat then brush the grill grate with oil.
4. Arrange the lamb chops on the grill grate in a single layer and cook for 5 minutes on each side. Serve and enjoy.

Nutrition: Calories 241 kCal Fat 13.1g Carbs 15.8g Protein 14.6g

143. Grilled Leg of Lambs Steaks

Preparation Time: 10 minutes
Cooking Time: 10 minutes
Servings: 4

Ingredients:

- 4 lamb steaks, bone-in
- 1/4 cup olive oil
- 4 garlic cloves, minced
- 1 tablespoon rosemary, freshly chopped
- Salt and black pepper

Directions:

1. Put the lamb in a shallow container in a single layer. Top with oil, garlic cloves, rosemary, salt, and black pepper then flip the steaks to cover on both sides.
2. Let sit for 30 minutes to marinate.
3. Preheat the wood pellet grill to high and brush the grill grate with oil.
4. Place the lamb steaks on the grill grate and cook until browned and the internal are slightly pink. The internal temperature should be 1400 F.
5. Let rest for 5 minutes before serving. Enjoy.

Nutrition: Calories   327 kCal   Fat   21.9g Carbs 1.7g Protein 29.6g

Chapter 3:   Poultry Recipes

144.   Cajun Patch Cock Chicken

Preparation Time: 30 minutes (additional 3 hours marinade)
Cooking Time: 2.5 hours
Servings: 4
Ingredients:

- 4-5 pounds of fresh or thawed frozen chicken
- 4-6 glasses of extra virgin olive oil
- Cajun Spice Lab 4 tablespoons or Lucile Bloody Mary Mix Cajun Hot Dry Herb Mix Seasoning

Directions:

1. Use hickory, pecan pellets, or blend to configure a wood pellet smoker grill for indirect cooking and preheat to 225 ° F.
2. If the unit has a temperature meat probe input, such as a MAK Grills 2 Star, insert the probe into the thickest part of the breast.
3. Make chicken for 1.5 hours.
4. After one and a half hours at 225 ° F, raise the pit temperature to 375 ° F and roast until the inside temperature of the thickest part of the chest reaches 170 ° F and the thighs are at least 180 ° F.
5. Place the chicken under a loose foil tent for 15 minutes before carving.

Nutrition: Calories 956 kCal, Total fat 47g, Carbs 1g, Protein 124g

145.   Chicken Breast with Lemon

Preparation Time: 15min
Cooking Time: 15min
Servings: 6
Ingredients:

- 6 Chicken breasts, skinless and boneless
- ½ cup Oil
- 1 - 2 Fresh thyme sprigs
- 1 tsp. ground black pepper
- 2 tsp. Salt
- 2 tsp. of Honey
- 1 Garlic clove, chopped
- 1 Lemon the juice and zest
- For service: Lemon wedges

Directions:

1. In a bowl combine the thyme, black pepper, salt, honey, garlic, and lemon zest and juice. Stir until dissolved and combined. Add the oil and whisk to combine.
2. Clean the breasts and pat dry. Place them in a plastic bag. Pour the pre-made marinade and massage to distribute evenly. Place in the fridge, 4 hours.
3. Preheat the grill to 400F with the lid closed.
4. Drain the chicken and grill until the internal temperature reaches 165F, about 15 minutes.
5. Serve with lemon wedges and a side dish of your choice.

Nutrition: Calories: 230 kCal Proteins: 38g Carbs: 1g Fat: 7g

146.   Pit Boss Smoked Chicken Burgers

Preparation Time: 20 minutes
Cooking Time: 1 hour and 10 minutes
Servings: 6
Ingredients:

- 2 lb. ground chicken breast
- 2/3 cup of finely chopped onions
- 1 Tbsps. of cilantro, finely chopped
- 2 Tbsp. fresh parsley, finely chopped
- 2 Tbsp. of olive oil
- 1/2 tsp of ground cumin
- 2 Tbsps. of lemon juice freshly squeezed
- 3/4 tsp of salt and red pepper to taste

Directions:

1. In a bowl add all ingredients; mix until combined well.
2. Form the mixture into 6 patties.
3. Start your Pit Boss grill on SMOKE (oak or apple Pit Boss) with the lid open until the fire is established. Set the heat to 350F and preheat, lid closed, for 10 to 15 minutes.
4. Smoke the chicken burgers for 45 - 50 minutes or until cooked through, turning every 15 minutes.
5. Your burgers are ready when internal temperature reaches 165 F
6. Serve hot.

Nutrition: Calories: 221 kCal Carbs: 2.12g Fat: 8.5g Protein: 32.5g

147. Perfect Smoked Chicken Patties

Preparation Time: 20 minutes
Cooking Time: 50 minutes
Servings: 6
Ingredients:
- 2 lb. ground chicken breast
- 2/3 cup minced onion
- 1 Tbsps. cilantro (chopped)
- 2 Tbsp. fresh parsley, finely chopped
- 2 Tbsp. olive oil
- 1/8 tsp crushed red pepper flakes
- 1/2 tsp ground cumin
- 2 Tbsps. fresh lemon juice
- 3/4 tsp kosher salt
- 2 tsp paprika
- Hamburger buns for serving

Directions:
1. In a bowl combine all ingredients from the list.
2. Using your hands, mix well. Form mixture into 6 patties. Refrigerate until ready to grill (about 30 minutes).
3. Start your Pit Boss grill on SMOKE with the lid open until the fire is established). Set the temperature to 350F and preheat for 10 to 15 minutes.
4. Arrange chicken patties on the grill rack and cook for 35 to 40 minutes turning once.
5. Serve hot with hamburger buns and your favorite condiments.

Nutrition: Calories: 258 kCal Carbs: 2.5g Fat: 9.4g Protein: 39g

148. Smoked Chicken Breasts with Dried Herbs

Preparation Time: 15 minutes
Cooking Time: 40 minutes
Servings: 4
Ingredients:
- 4 chicken breasts boneless
- 1/4 cup garlic-infused olive oil
- 2 clove garlic minced
- 1/4 tsp of dried sage
- 1/4 tsp of dried lavender
- 1/4 tsp of dried thyme
- 1/4 tsp of dried mint

- 1/2 Tbsps. dried crushed red pepper
- Kosher salt to taste

Directions:
1. Place the chicken breasts in a shallow plastic container.
2. In a bowl, combine all remaining ingredients, and pour the mixture over the chicken breast and refrigerate for one hour.
3. Remove the chicken breast from the sauce (reserve sauce) and pat dry on kitchen paper.
4. Start your Pit Boss grill on SMOKE (hickory Pit Boss) with the lid open until the fire is established). Set the temperature to 250F and preheat for 10 to 15 minutes.
5. Place chicken breasts on the smoker. Close Pit Boss grill lid and cook for about 30 to 40 minutes or until chicken breasts reach 165F.
6. Serve hot with reserved marinade.

Nutrition: Calories: 391 kCal Carbs: 1g Fat: 3g Protein: 20g

149. Grilled Chicken with Pineapple

Preparation Time: 1 hour
Cooking Time: 1 hr. 15 mins
Servings: 6
Ingredients:
- 2 lbs. Chicken tenders
- 1 c. sweet chili sauce
- ¼ c. fresh pineapple juice
- ¼ c. honey

Directions:
1. Combine the honey, pineapple juice, and sweet chili sauce in a medium bowl. Whisk together thoroughly.
2. Put ¼ cup of the mixture to one side.
3. Coat the chicken in the sauce.
4. Place a lid over the bowl and leave it in the fridge for 30 minutes to marinate.
5. Heat the grill to high heat.
6. Separate the chicken from the marinade and grill for 5 minutes on each side.
7. Use the reserved sauce to brush over the chicken.
8. Continue to grill for a further 1 minute on each side.
9. Take the chicken off the grill and let it rest for 5 minutes before servings.

Nutrition: Calories: 270 kCal Fat: 2 g, Carbs: 25 g, Protein: 33 g

150. Whole Orange Chicken

Preparation Time: 15 minutes + marinate time
Cooking Time: 45 minutes
Servings: 4
Ingredients:

- 1 whole chicken, 3-4 pounds' backbone removed
- 2 oranges
- ¼ cup oil
- 2 teaspoons Dijon mustard
- 1 orange, zest
- 2 tablespoons rosemary leaves, chopped
- 2 teaspoons salt

Directions:

1. Clean and pat your chicken dry
2. Take a bowl and mix in orange juice, oil, orange zest, salt, rosemary leaves, Dijon mustard and mix well
3. Marinade chicken for 2 hours or overnight
4. Pre-heat your grill to 350 degrees F
5. Transfer your chicken to the smoker and smoke for 30 minutes' skin down. Flip and smoke until the internal temperature reaches 175 degrees F in the thigh and 165 degrees F in the breast
6. Rest for 10 minutes and carve
7. Enjoy!

Nutrition: Calories: 290 kCal Fats: 15g Carbs: 20g Protein: 7g

151. Smoked Turkey Patties

Preparation Time: 20 minutes
Cooking Time: 40 minutes
Servings: 6
Ingredients:

- 2 lbs. turkey minced meat
- 1/2 cup of parsley finely chopped
- 2/3 cup of onion finely chopped
- 1 red bell pepper finely chopped
- 1 large egg at room temperature
- Salt and pepper to taste
- 1/2 tsp dry oregano
- 1/2 tsp dry thyme

Directions:

1. In a bowl, combine well all ingredients.
2. Make from the mixture patties.
3. Start Pit Boss grill on (recommended apple or oak Pit Boss) lid open, until the fire is established

(4-5 minutes). Increase the temperature to 350F and allow to pre-heat, lid closed, for 10 - 15 minutes.

4. Place patties on the grill racks and cook with lid covered for 30 to 40 minutes.
5. Your turkey patties are ready when you reach a temperature of 130F
6. Serve hot.

Nutrition: Calories: 251 kCal Carbs: 3.4g Fat: 12.5g Protein: 31.2g

152. Apple Smoked Turkey

Preparation Time: 30 Minutes
Cooking Time: 3 Hours
Servings: 5
Ingredients:

- 4 Cups Applewood chips
- 1 Fresh or frozen turkey of about 12 pounds
- 3 Tablespoons of extra-virgin olive oil
- 1 tablespoon of chopped fresh sage
- 2 and ½ teaspoons of kosher salt
- 2 Teaspoons of freshly ground black pepper
- 1 and ½ teaspoons of paprika
- 1 Teaspoon of chopped fresh thyme
- 1 Teaspoon of chopped fresh oregano
- 1 Teaspoon of garlic powder
- 1 Cup of water
- ½ Cup of chopped onion
- ½ Cup of chopped carrot
- ½ Cup of chopped celery

Directions:

1. Soak the wood chips into the water for about 1 hour; then drain very well.
2. Remove the neck and the giblets from the turkey; then reserve and discard the liver. Pat the turkey dry; then trim any excess of fat and start at the neck's cavity
3. Loosen the skin from the breast and the drumstick by inserting your fingers and gently push it between the meat and skin and lift the wingtips, then over back and tuck under the turkey
4. Combine the oil and the next 7 ingredients in a medium bowl and rub the oil under the skin; then rub it over the breasts and the drumsticks
5. Tie the legs with the kitchen string.

6. Pour 1 cup of water, the onion, the carrot, and the celery into the bottom of an aluminum foil roasting pan
7. Place the roasting rack into a pan; then arrange the turkey with the breast side up over a roasting rack; then let stand at the room temperature for about 1 hour
8. Remove the grill rack; then preheat the charcoal smoker grill to medium-high heat.
9. After preheating the smoker to a temperature of about 225°F
10. Place 2 cups of wood chips on the heating element on the right side.
11. Replace the grill rack; then place the roasting pan with the turkey over the grill rack over the left burner.
12. Cover and smoke for about 3 hours and turn the chicken halfway through the cooking time; then add the remaining 2 cups of wood chips halfway through the cooking time.
13. Place the turkey over a cutting board; then let stand for about 30 minutes
14. Discard the turkey skin; then serve and enjoy your dish!

Nutrition: Calories: 530 kCal, Fat: 22g, Carbs: 14g, Protein: 41g

153. Special Occasion's Dinner Cornish Hen

Preparation Time: 15 minutes
Cooking Time: 1 hour
Servings: 4
Ingredients:
- 4 Cornish game hens
- 4 fresh rosemary sprigs
- 4 tbsp. butter, melted
- 4 tsp. chicken rub

Directions:
1. Set the temperature of Grill to 375 degrees F and preheat with closed lid for 15 mins.
2. With paper towels, pat dry the hens.
3. Tuck the wings behind the backs and with kitchen strings, tie the legs together.
4. Coat the outside of each hen with melted butter and sprinkle with rub evenly.
5. Stuff each hen with a rosemary sprig.
6. Place the hens onto the grill and cook for about 50-60 mins.

7. Remove the hens from grill and place onto a platter for about 10 mins.
8. Cut each hen into desired-sized pieces and serve.

Nutrition: Calories: 430 kCal Carbs: 2.1g Protein: 25.4g Fat: 33g

154. Crispy & Juicy Chicken

Preparation Time: 15 minutes
Cooking Time: 5 hours
Servings: 6
Ingredients:
- ¾ C. dark brown sugar
- ½ C. ground espresso beans
- 1 tbsp. ground cumin
- 1 tbsp. ground cinnamon
- 1 tbsp. garlic powder
- 1 tbsp. cayenne pepper
- Salt and ground black pepper, to taste
- 1 (4-lb.) whole chicken, neck and giblets removed

Directions:
1. Set the temperature of Grill to 200-225 degrees F and preheat with closed lid for 15 mins.
2. In a bowl, mix together brown sugar, ground espresso, spices, salt and black pepper.
3. Rub the chicken with spice mixture generously.
4. Put the chicken onto the grill and cook for about 3-5 hours.
5. Remove chicken from grill and place onto a cutting board for about 10 mins before carving.
6. Cut the chicken into desired-sized pieces and serve.

Nutrition: Calories: 540 kCal Carbs: 20.7g Protein: 88.3g Fat: 9.6g

155. Ultimate Tasty Chicken

Preparation Time: 15 minutes
Cooking Time: 3 hours
Servings: 5
Ingredients:
For Brine:
- 1 C. brown sugar
- ½ C. kosher salt
- 16 C. water

For Chicken:
- 1 (3-lb.) whole chicken
- 1 tbsp. garlic, crushed
- 1 tsp. onion powder
- Salt
- Ground black pepper, to taste
- 1 medium yellow onion, quartered
- 3 whole garlic cloves, peeled
- 1 lemon, quartered
- 4-5 fresh thyme sprigs

Directions:
1. For brine: in a bucket, dissolve brown sugar and kosher salt in water.
2. Place the chicken in brine and refrigerate overnight.
3. Set the temperature of Grill to 225 degrees F and preheat with closed lid for 15 mins.
4. Remove the chicken from brine and with paper towels, pat it dry.
5. In a small bowl, mix together crushed garlic, onion powder, salt and black pepper.
6. Rub the chicken with garlic mixture evenly.
7. Stuff the inside of the chicken with onion, garlic cloves, lemon and thyme.
8. With kitchen strings, tie the legs together.
9. Place the chicken onto grill and cook, covered for about 2½-3 hours.
10. Remove chicken from pallet grill and transfer onto a cutting board for about 10 mins before carving.
11. Cut the chicken in desired sized pieces and serve.

Nutrition: Calories: 641 kCal Carbs: 31.7g Protein: 79.2g Fat: 20.2g

156. South-East-Asian Chicken Drumsticks

Preparation Time: 15 minutes
Cooking Time: 2 hours
Servings: 6
Ingredients:
- 1 C. fresh orange juice
- ¼ C. honey
- 2 tbsp. sweet chili sauce
- 2 tbsp. hoisin sauce
- 2 tbsp. fresh ginger, grated finely
- 2 tbsp. garlic, minced
- 1 tsp. Sriracha
- ½ tsp. sesame oil
- 6 chicken drumsticks

Directions:
1. Set the temperature of Grill to 225 degrees F and preheat with closed lid for 15 mins, using charcoal.
2. Mix all the ingredients except for chicken drumsticks and mix until well combined.
3. Set aside half of honey mixture in a small bowl.
4. In the bowl of remaining sauce, add drumsticks and mix well.
5. Arrange the chicken drumsticks onto the grill and cook for about 2 hours, basting with remaining sauce occasionally.
6. Serve hot.

Nutrition: Calories: 385 kCal Carbs: 22.7g Protein: 47.6g Fat: 10.5g

157. Game Day Chicken Drumsticks

Preparation Time: 15 minutes
Cooking Time: 1 hour
Servings: 8
Ingredients:
For Brine:
- ½ C. brown sugar
- ½ C. kosher salt
- 5 C. water
- 2 (12-oz.) bottles beer
- 8 chicken drumsticks

For Coating:
- ¼ C. olive oil
- ½ C. BBQ rub
- 1 tbsp. fresh parsley, minced
- 1 tbsp. fresh chives, minced
- ¾ C. BBQ sauce
- ¼ C. beer

Directions:
1. For brine: in a bucket, dissolve brown sugar and kosher salt in water and beer.
2. Place the chicken drumsticks in brine and refrigerate, covered for about 3 hours.
3. Set the temperature of Grill to 275 degrees F and preheat with closed lid for 15 mins.
4. Remove chicken drumsticks from brine and rinse under cold running water.
5. With paper towels, pat dry chicken drumsticks.
6. Coat drumsticks with olive oil and rub with BBQ rub evenly.
7. Sprinkle the drumsticks with parsley and chives.
8. Arrange the chicken drumsticks onto the grill and cook for about 45 mins.
9. Meanwhile, in a bowl, mix together BBQ sauce and beer.
10. Remove from grill and coat the drumsticks with BBQ sauce evenly.
11. Cook for about 15 mins more.
12. Serve immediately.

Nutrition: Calories: 448 kCal Carbs: 20.5g Protein: 47.2g Fat: 16.1g

158. Glazed Chicken Thighs

Preparation Time: 15 minutes
Cooking Time: 2 hours and 5 minutes
Servings: 4
Ingredients:
- 2 garlic cloves, minced
- ¼ C. honey
- 2 tbsp. soy sauce
- ¼ tsp. red pepper flakes, crushed
- 4 (5-oz.) skinless, boneless chicken thighs
- 2 tbsp. olive oil
- 2 tsp. sweet rub
- ¼ tsp. red chili powder
- Freshly ground black pepper, to taste

Directions:
1. Set the temperature of Grill to 400 degrees F and preheat with closed lid for 15 mins.
2. In a bowl, add garlic, honey, soy sauce and red pepper flakes and with a wire whisk, beat until well combined.
3. Coat chicken thighs with oil and season with sweet rub, chili powder and black pepper generously.
4. Arrange the chicken drumsticks onto the grill and cook for about 15 mins per side.
5. In the last 4-5 mins of cooking, coat the thighs with garlic mixture.
6. Serve immediately.

Nutrition: Calories: 309 kCal Carbs: 18.7g Protein: 32.3g; Fat: 12.1g

159. Cajun Chicken Breasts

Preparation Time: 10 minutes
Cooking Time: 6 hours
Servings: 6
Ingredients:
- 2 lb. skinless, boneless chicken breasts
- 2 tbsp. Cajun seasoning
- 1 C. BBQ sauce

Directions:
1. Set the temperature of Grill to 225 degrees F and preheat with closed lid for 15 mins.
2. Rub the chicken breasts with Cajun seasoning generously.
3. Put the chicken breasts onto the grill and cook for about 4-6 hours.
4. During last hour of cooking, coat the breasts with BBQ sauce twice.

5. Serve hot.

Nutrition: Calories: 252 kCal Carbs: 15.1g Protein: 33.8g; Fat: 5.5g

160. BBQ Sauce Smothered Chicken Breasts

Preparation Time: 15 minutes
Cooking Time: 30 minutes
Servings: 4
Ingredients:
- 1 tsp. garlic, crushed
- ¼ C. olive oil
- 1 tbsp. Worcestershire sauce
- 1 tbsp. sweet mesquite seasoning
- 4 chicken breasts
- 2 tbsp. regular BBQ sauce
- 2 tbsp. spicy BBQ sauce
- 2 tbsp. honey bourbon BBQ sauce

Directions:
1. Set the temperature of Grill to 450 degrees F and preheat with closed lid for 15 mins.
2. In a large bowl, mix together garlic, oil, Worcestershire sauce and mesquite seasoning.
3. Coat chicken breasts with seasoning mixture evenly.
4. Put the chicken breasts onto the grill and cook for about 20-30 mins.
5. Meanwhile, in a bowl, mix together all 3 BBQ sauces.
6. In the last 4-5 mins of cooking, coat breast with BBQ sauce mixture.
7. Serve hot.

Nutrition: Calories: 421 kCal Carbs: 10.1g Protein: 41,2g Fat: 23.3g

161. Budget Friendly Chicken Legs

Preparation Time: 15 minutes
Cooking Time: 1 hour and 30 minutes
Servings: 6
Ingredients:
For Brine:
- 1 C. kosher salt
- ¾ C. light brown sugar
- 16 C. water
- 6 chicken leg quarters

For Glaze:
- ½ C. mayonnaise
- 2 tbsp. BBQ rub

- 2 tbsp. fresh chives, minced
- 1 tbsp. garlic, minced

Directions:
1. For brine: in a bucket, dissolve salt and brown sugar in water.
2. Place the chicken quarters in brine and refrigerate, covered for about 4 hours.
3. Set the temperature of Grill to 275 degrees F and preheat with closed lid for 15 mins.
4. Remove chicken quarters from brine and rinse under cold running water.
5. With paper towels, pat dry chicken quarters.
6. For glaze: in a bowl, add all ingredients and mix till ell combined.
7. Coat chicken quarters with glaze evenly.
8. Place the chicken leg quarters onto grill and cook for about 1-1½ hours.
9. Serve immediately.

Nutrition: Calories: 399 kCal Carbs: 17.2g Protein: 29.1g Fat: 24.7g

162. Roasted Tuscan Thighs

Preparation Time: 20 minutes (plus 1-2 hours marinade)
Cooking Time: 40-60 minutes
Servings: 4
Ingredients:
- 8 chicken thighs, with bone, with skin
- 3 extra virgin olive oils with roasted garlic flavor
- 3 cups of Tuscan or Tuscan seasoning per thigh

Directions:
1. Set the wood pellet smoker grill for indirect cooking and use the pellets to preheat to 375 degrees Fahrenheit.
2. Depending on the grill of the wood pellet smoker, roast for 40-60 minutes until the internal temperature of the thick part of the chicken thigh reaches 180 ° F. Place the roasted Tuscan thighs under a loose foil tent for 15 minutes before serving.

Nutrition: Calories 111 kCal, Fat 5g, Carbs 1g, Protein 13.4g

163. Smoked Bone In-Turkey Breast

Preparation Time: 20 minutes
Cooking Time: 3-4 hours
Servings: 6-8
Ingredients:

- 1 (8-10 pounds) boned turkey breast
- 6 tablespoons extra virgin olive oil
- 5 Yang original dry lab or poultry seasonings

Directions:

1. Configure a wood pellet smoker grill for indirect cooking and preheat to 225 ° F using hickory or pecan pellets.
2. Smoke the boned turkey breast directly in a V rack or grill at 225 ° F for 2 hours.
3. After 2 hours of hickory smoke, raise the pit temperature to 325 ° F. Roast until the thickest part of the turkey breast reaches an internal temperature of 170 ° F and the juice is clear.
4. Place the hickory smoked turkey breast under a loose foil tent for 20 minutes, then scrape the grain.

Nutrition: Calories 150 kCal, Fat 7g, Carbs 1g, Protein 20g

164. Teriyaki Smoked Drumstick

Preparation Time: 15 minutes (more marinade overnight)
Cooking Time: 1.5 hours to 2 hours
Servings: 4
Ingredients:

- 3 cup teriyaki marinade and cooking sauce like Yoshida's original gourmet
- Poultry seasoning 3 tsp
- 1 tsp garlic powder
- 10 chicken drumsticks

Directions:

1. Configure a wood pellet smoking grill for indirect cooking.
2. Place the skin on the drumstick and, while the grill is preheating, hang the drumstick on a poultry leg and wing rack to drain the cooking sheet on the counter. If you do not have a poultry leg and feather rack, you can dry the drumstick by tapping it with a paper towel.
3. Preheat wood pellet smoker grill to 180 ° F using hickory or maple pellets.
4. Make marinated chicken leg for 1 hour.

5. After 1 hour, raise the hole temperature to 350 ° F and cook the drumstick for another 30-45 minutes until the thickest part of the stick reaches an internal temperature of 180 ° F.
6. Place the chicken drumstick under the loose foil tent for 15 minutes before serving.

Nutrition: Calories 98 kCal, Fat 3g, Carbs 5g, Protein 13g

165. Hickory Smoke Spatchcock Turkey

Preparation Time: 20 minutes
Cooking Time: 3-4 hours
Servings: 8-10
Ingredients:

- 1 (14 lb.) fresh or thawed frozen young turkey
- ¼ Extra virgin olive oil with cup roasted garlic flavor
- 6 poultry seasonings or original dry lab in January

Directions:

1. Configure a wood pellet smoking grill for indirect cooking and preheat to 225 ° F using hickory pellets.
2. Place the turkey skin down on a non-stick grill mat made of Teflon-coated fiberglass.
3. Suck the turkey at 225 ° F for 2 hours.
4. After 2 hours, raise the pit temperature to 350 ° F.
5. Roast turkey until the thickest part of the chest reaches an internal temperature of 170 ° F and the juice is clear.
6. Place the Hickory smoked roast turkey under a loose foil tent for 20 minutes before engraving.

Nutrition: Calories 1055 kCal, Fat 56g, Carbs 11g, Protein 128g

166. Lemon Cornish Chicken Stuffed with Crab

Preparation Time: 30 minutes (additional 2-3 hours marinade)
Cooking Time: 1 hour 30 minutes
Servings: 2-4

Ingredients:
- 2 Cornish chickens (about 1¾ pound each)
- Half lemon, half
- 4 tbsp western rub or poultry rub
- 2 cups stuffed with crab meat

Directions:
1. Set wood pellet smoker grill for indirect cooking and preheat to 375 ° F with pellets.
2. Place the stuffed animal on the rack in the baking dish. If you do not have a rack that is small enough to fit, you can also place the chicken directly on the baking dish.
3. Roast the chicken at 375 ° F until the inside temperature of the thickest part of the chicken breast reaches 170 ° F, the thigh reaches 180 ° F, and the juice is clear.
4. Test the crab meat stuffing to see if the temperature has reached 165 ° F.
5. Place the roasted chicken under a loose foil tent for 15 minutes before serving.

Nutrition: Calories 510 kCal, Fat 25g, Carbs 26g, Protein 35g

167. Bacon Cordon Bleu

Preparation Time: 30 minutes
Cooking Time: 2 to 2.5 hours
Servings: 6

Ingredients:
- 24 bacon slices
- 3 large boneless, skinless chicken breasts, butterfly
- 3 extra virgin olive oils with roasted garlic flavor
- 3 Yang original dry lab or poultry seasonings
- 12 slice black forest ham
- 12-slice provolone cheese

Directions:
1. Using apple or cherry pellets, configure a wood pellet smoker grill for indirect cooking and preheat (180 ° F to 200 ° F) for smoking.
2. Inhale bacon cordon blue for 1 hour.
3. After smoking for 1 hour, raise the pit temperature to 350 ° F.
4. Bacon cordon blue occurs when the internal temperature reaches 165 ° F and the bacon becomes crispy.
5. Rest for 15 minutes under a loose foil tent before serving.

Nutrition: Calories 388 kCal, Fat 25g, Carbs 2g, Protein 35g

168. Roast Duck à l'Orange

Preparation Time: 30 minutes
Cooking Time: 2 to 2.5 hours
Servings: 3-4

Ingredients:
- 1 (5-6 lb.) Frozen Long Island, Beijing or Canadian ducks
- 3 tbsp west or 3 tbsp
- 1 large orange, cut into wedges
- Three celery stems chopped into large chunks
- Half a small red onion, a quarter

Orange sauce:
- 2 orange cups
- 2 tablespoons soy sauce
- 2 tablespoons orange marmalade
- 2 tablespoons honey
- 3g tsp grated raw

Directions:
1. Set the wood pellet smoker grill for indirect cooking and use the pellets to preheat to 350 ° F.
2. Roast the ducks at 350 ° F for 2 hours.
3. After 2 hours, brush the duck freely with orange sauce.
4. Roast the orange glass duck for another 30 minutes, making sure that the inside temperature of the thickest part of the leg reaches 165 ° F.
5. Place duck under loose foil tent for 20 minutes before serving.
6. Discard the orange wedge, celery and onion. Serve with a quarter of duck with poultry scissors.

Nutrition: Calories 455 kCal, Fat 23g, Carbs 21g, Protein 41g

169. Herb Roasted Turkey

Preparation Time: 30 minutes (additional 2-3 hours marinade)
Cooking Time: 1 hour 30 minutes
Servings: 2-4
Ingredients:
1. 8 Tbsp. Butter, Room Temperature
2. 2 Tbsp. Mixed Herbs Such as Parsley, Sage, Rosemary, And Marjoram, Chopped
3. 1/4 Tsp. Black Pepper, Freshly Ground
4. 1 (12-14 Lbs.) Turkey, Thawed If pre-frozen
5. **3 Tbsp. Butter**

Directions:
1. In a small mixing bowl, combine the 8 tablespoons of softened butter, mixed herbs, and black pepper and beat until fluffy with a wooden spoon.
2. Remove any giblets from the turkey cavity and save them for gravy making, if desired. Wash the turkey, inside and out, under cold running water. Dry with paper towels.
3. Using your fingers or the handle of a wooden spoon, gently push some of the herbed butter underneath the turkey skin onto the breast halves, being careful not to tear the skin.
4. Rub the outside of the turkey with the melted butter and sprinkle with the Pit Boss Pork and Poultry Rub. Pour the chicken broth in the bottom of the roasting pan.
5. When ready to cook, set temperature to 325 F and preheat, lid closed for 15 minutes.

Nutrition: Calories 60 kCal, Fat 1g, Carbs 1g, Protein 13g

170. Smoked Bourbon & Orange Brined Turkey

Preparation Time: 30 minutes
Cooking Time: 1 hour 30 minutes
Servings: 2-4
Ingredients:
- Pit Boss Orange Brine (From Kit)
- Pit Boss Turkey Rub (From Kit)
- 1.25-2.5 Gallons Cold Water
- 1 Cup Bourbon
- 1 Tbsp. Butter, Melted

Directions:
1. Mix Pit Boss Orange Brine seasoning (from Orange Brine & Turkey Rub Kit) with one quart of water. Boil for 5 minutes. Remove from heat, add 1 gallon of cold water and bourbon.
2. Place turkey breast side down in a large container. Pour cooled brine mix over bird. Add cold water until bird is submerged. Refrigerate for 24 hours.
3. Remove turkey and disregard brine. Blot turkey dry with paper towels. Combine butter and Grand Marnier and coat outside of turkey.
4. Season outside of turkey with Pit Boss Turkey Rub (from Orange Brine & Turkey Rub Kit).
5. When ready to cook, set temperature to 225 F and preheat, lid closed for 15 minutes.

Nutrition: Calories 433 kCal, Fat 8g, Carbs 12g, Protein 15g

171. Pit Boss Leftover Turkey Soup

Preparation Time: 30 minutes
Cooking Time: 1 hour 30 minutes
Servings: 2-4
Ingredients:
- 1 Turkey Carcass
- 16 Cups Cold Water
- 2 Large Celery Ribs, Sliced
- 2 Large Carrots, Scraped and Sliced
- 2 Red Onions, Quartered

Directions:
1. Strip a turkey carcass of all meat; set aside in a container.
2. Break up the bones of the turkey carcass and place them in a large pot. Add any turkey skin or other assorted "bits" that are not edible meat.
3. Once the stock has come to a boil, add all remaining Ingredients and turn heat down until the bubbles barely break the surface. Let simmer for 3 to 4 hours, stirring occasionally.
4. When the stock is ready, strain it through a fine-meshed sieve into a large bowl; if your sieve is not fine, line it first with cheesecloth.
5. Refrigerate stock, covered, for several hours or preferably overnight. You can either make soup the then day, or freeze the stock.

Nutrition: Calories 210 kCal, Fat 11g, Carbs 11g Protein 18g

172. Smoked Turkey by Rob cooks

Preparation Time: 30 minutes
Cooking Time: 1 hour 30 minutes
Servings: 2-4
Ingredients:
- Smoked Turkey by Rob cooks
- 1 (12-14 Lb.) Turkey, Fresh or Thawed
- 3/4 Lb. (3 Sticks) Unsalted Butter
- 1 (5 Gal) Bucket or Stock Pot
- Foil Pan, Large Enough for Turkey

Directions:
1. This method requires an overnight brining so collect everything the day before your meal.
2. The afternoon before, prepare your brine by adding the kosher salt and sugar to a medium saucepan. Cover with water and bring to a boil. Stir to dissolve the salt and sugar.
3. Prepare your turkey by removing the neck, gizzards and truss, if pre-trussed. Trim off excess skin and fat near the cavity and neck. Place the turkey in bucket with the brine.
4. When ready to cook, set temperature to 180 F and preheat, lid closed for 15 minutes.
5. Remove your turkey from the brine. Remember there's a cavity full of water so make sure to do this over the sink, otherwise you'll have brine all over the place.

Nutrition: Calories 956 kCal, Total fat 47g, Saturated fat 13g, Total carbs 1g, Net carbs 1g Protein 124g, Sugars 0g, Fiber 0g, Sodium 1750mg

173. Smoked Turkey Legs

Preparation Time: 30 minutes
Cooking Time: 1 hour 30 minutes
Servings: 2-4
Ingredients:
- 1 Gal Warm Water
- 1/2-Gal Cold Water
- 4 Cups Ice
- 1 Cup Pit Boss BBQ Rub
- 1/2 Cup Curing Salt

Directions:
1. In a large stockpot, combine one gallon of warm water, the rub, curing salt, brown sugar, allspice (if using), peppercorns, bay leaves and liquid smoke.
2. Bring to a boil over high heat to dissolve the salt granules. Cool to room temperature.
3. Add cold water and ice; chill in the refrigerator. Add the turkey legs, making sure they're completely submerged in the brine.
4. After 24 hours, drain the turkey legs and discard the brine. Rinse the brine off the legs with cold water, then dry thoroughly with paper towels. Brush off any clinging solid spices.
5. When ready to cook, set temperature to 250 F and preheat, lid closed for 15 minutes.

Nutrition: Calories 589 kCal, Fat 28g, Carbs 0g, Protein 79g

174. Traditional Thanksgiving Turkey

Preparation Time: 30 minutes
Cooking Time: 1 hour 30 minutes
Servings: 2-4
Ingredients:
- 1 (18-20lb) Turkey
- 1/2 Lb. Butter, Softened
- 8 Sprigs Thyme
- 6 Cloves Garlic, Minced
- 1 Sprig Rosemary, Rough Chop

Directions:
1. In a small bowl, combine butter with the minced garlic, thyme leaves, chopped rosemary, black pepper and kosher salt.
2. Prepare the turkey by separating the skin from the breast creating a pocket to stuff the butter-herb mixture in.
3. Cover the entire breast with 1/4" thickness of butter mixture.
4. Season the whole turkey with kosher salt and black pepper. As an option, you can also stuff the turkey cavity with Traditional Stuffing.
5. When ready to cook, set the temperature to 300 F and preheat, lid closed for 15 minutes.

Nutrition: Calories 214 kCal, Fat 8g, Carbs 0g, Protein 32g

175. Turkey Jalapeno Meatballs

Preparation Time: 30 minutes
Cooking Time: 1 hour 30 minutes
Servings: 2-4
Ingredients:
Turkey Jalapeño Meatballs
- 1 1/4 Lbs. Ground Turkey
- 1 Jalapeño Pepper, Deseeded and Finely Diced
- 1/2 Tsp Garlic Salt
- 1 Tsp Onion Powder

Directions:
1. In a separate small bowl, combine the milk and bread crumbs.
2. In a large bowl, mix together turkey, garlic salt, onion powder, salt, pepper, Worcestershire sauce, cayenne pepper, egg and jalapeños.
3. Add the bread crumb milk mixture to the bowl and combine. Cover with plastic and refrigerate for up to 1 hour.
4. When ready to cook, set the temperature to 350°F and preheat, lid closed for 15 minutes
5. Roll the turkey mixture into balls, about one tablespoon each and place the meatballs in a single layer on a parchment lined baking sheet.

Nutrition: Calories 351 kCal, Fat 11g, Carbs 36g, Protein 27g

176. Wild Turkey Southwest Egg Rolls

Preparation Time: 30 minutes
Cooking Time: 1 hour 30 minutes
Servings: 2-4
Ingredients:
- 2 Cups Leftover Wild Turkey Meat
- 1/2 Cup Corn
- 1/2 Cup Black Beans
- 3 Tbsp Taco Seasoning
- 1/2 Cup White Onion, Chopped

Directions:
1. Add olive oil to a large skillet and heat on the stove over medium heat. Add onions and peppers and sauté 2-3 minutes until soft. Add garlic, cook 30 seconds, then Rote and black beans.
2. Pour taco seasoning over meat and add 1/3 cup of water and mix to coat well. Add to veggie mixture and stir to mix well. If it seems dry, add 2 tbsp water. Cook until heated all the way through.
3. Remove from the heat and transfer the mixture to the fridge. The mixture should be completely cooled prior to stuffing the egg rolls or the wrappers will break.
4. Place spoonful of the mixture in each wrapper and wrap tightly. Repeat with remaining wrappers. When ready to cook, set temperature to High and preheat, lid closed for 15 minutes.
5. Brush each egg roll with oil or butter and place directly on the Pit Boss grill grate. Cook until the exterior is crispy, about 20 min per side.

Nutrition: Calories 419 kCal, Total fat 31.2g, Carbs 1g, Net carbs 21.8g Protein 13.6g

177. Smoked Wild Turkey Breast

Preparation Time: 30 minutes
Cooking Time: 1 hour 30 minutes
Servings: 2-4
Ingredients:
Brine
- 2 Lbs. Turkey Breast and Deboned Thigh, Tied with Skin On
- 1 Cup Brown Sugar
- 1/4 Cup Salt
- 2 Tbsp Cracked Pepper
- 4 Cups Cold Water

BBQ Rub
- 2 Tbsp Garlic Powder
- 2 Tbsp Onions, Dried
- 2 Tbsp Black Pepper
- 2 Tbsp Brown Sugar
- 1 Tbsp Cayenne Pepper
- 2 Tbsp Chili Powder
- 1/4 Cup Paprika
- 1 Tbsp Salt
- 2 Tbsp Sugar
- 2 Tbsp Cumin, Ground

Directions:
1. For the Brine: In a large glass bowl combine brown sugar, salt, pepper and water. Add turkey and weigh down to completely submerge if necessary. Transfer to the refrigerator and brine.
2. Remove turkey from the brine and discard the brine.
3. When ready to cook, set the temperature 180 F and preheat lid closed for 15 minutes.

4. Combine Ingredients for the BBQ Rub. Season turkey with rub and place directly on the grill grate skin side up.

5. Smoke for 5-8 hours or until the internal temperature reaches 160 F degrees when an instant read thermometer is inserted into the center.

6. Remove from the smoker and let rest for 10 minutes. Turkey will continue to cook once taken off grill to reach a final temperature of 165 F in the breast.

7. Slice and serve with your favorite sides. Enjoy!

Nutrition: Calories 30 kCal, Fat 1g, Carbs 1g, Protein 5g

178. Grilled Wild Turkey Orange Cashew Salad

Preparation Time: 30 minutes
Cooking Time: 1 hour 30 minutes
Servings: 2-4

Ingredients:

- Turkey Breast
- 2 Wild Turkey Breast Halves, Without Skin
- 1/4 Cup Teriyaki Sauce
- 1 Tsp Fresh Ginger
- 1 (12 Oz) Can Blood Orange Kill Cliff or Similar Citrus Soda
- 2 Tbsp Pit Boss Chicken Rub
- Cashew Salad
- 4 Cups Romaine Lettuce, Chopped
- 1/2 Head Red or White Cabbage, Chopped
- 1/2 Cup Shredded Carrots
- 1/2 Cup Edamame, Shelled
- 1 Smoked Yellow Bell Pepper, Sliced into Circles
- 1 Smoked Red Bell Pepper, Sliced into Circles
- 3 Chive Tips, Chopped
- 1/2 Cup Smoked Cashews
- Blood Orange Vinaigrette
- 1 Tsp Orange Zest
- Juice From 1/2 Large Orange
- 1 Tsp Finely Grated Fresh Ginger
- 2 Tbsp Seasoned Rice Vinegar
- 1 Tsp Honey
- Sea Salt, To Taste
- 1/4 Cup Light Vegetable Oil

Directions:

1. For the Marinade: Combine teriyaki sauce, Kill Cliff soda and fresh ginger. Pour marinade over turkey breasts in a Ziplock bag or dish and seal.

2. When ready to cook, set temperature to 375 F and preheat, lid closed for 15 minutes.

3. Remove turkey from the refrigerator, drain the marinade and pat turkey dry with paper towels.

4. Place turkey into a shallow oven proof dish and season with Pit Boss Chicken Rub.

5. Place dish in the Pit Boss and cook for 30-45 minutes or until the breast reaches an internal temperature of 160 F.

6. Remove the breast from the grill and wrap in Pit Boss Butcher Paper. Let turkey rest for 10 minutes. While turkey is resting, prepare salad.

7. Assemble salad Ingredients in a bowl and toss to mix. Combine all Ingredients in list for vinaigrette.

8. After resting for 10 minutes, slice turkey and serve with cashew salad and blood orange vinaigrette. Enjoy!

Nutrition: Calories 475 kCal, Fat 10g, Carbs 57g, Protein 37g

179. Baked Cornbread Turkey Tamale Pie

Preparation Time: 30 minutes
Cooking Time: 1 hour 30 minutes
Servings: 2-4
Ingredients:
- Filling
- 2 Cups Shredded Turkey
- 2 Cobs of Corn
- 1 (15 Oz) Can Black Beans, Rinsed and Drained
- 1 Yellow Bell Pepper
- 1 Orange Bell Pepper
- 2 Jalapeños
- 2 Tbsp Cilantro
- 1 Bunch Green Onions
- 1/2 Tsp Cumin
- 1/2 Tsp Paprika
- 1 (7 Oz) Can Chipotle Sauce
- 1 (15 Oz) Can Enchilada Sauce
- 1/2 Cup Shredded Cheddar Cheese
- Cornbread Topping
- 1 Cup All-Purpose Flour
- 1 Cup Yellow or White Cornmeal
- 1 Tbsp Sugar
- 2 Tsp Baking Powder
- 1/2 Tsp Salt
- 3 Tbsp Butter
- 1 Cup Buttermilk
- 1 Large Egg, Lightly Beaten

Directions:
1. For the filling: Mix to combine filling Ingredients Place in the bottom of a butter greased 10-inch pan.
2. For the cornbread topping: In a mixing bowl, combine the flour, cornmeal, sugar, baking powder, and salt. Melt the butter in a small saucepan.
3. Add the milk-egg mixture to the dry Ingredients and stir to combine. Do not over mix.
4. To assemble Tamale Pie: Fill the bottom of a butter greased 10-inch pan with the shredded turkey filling. Top with the cornbread topping and smooth to the edges of pan.
5. When ready to cook, set the temperature to 375 F and preheat, lid closed for 15 minutes.
6. Place directly on the grill grate and cook for 45-50 minutes or until the cornbread is lightly browned and cooked through. Enjoy!

Nutrition: Cal 344 kCal, Fat 17g, Carbs 31g, Protein 20g

180. Pit Boss BBQ simple Turkey Sandwiches

Preparation Time: 30 minutes
Cooking Time: 45 minutes
Servings: 10
Ingredients:
- 6 Turkey Thighs, Skin-On
- 1 1/2 Cups Chicken or Turkey Broth
- Pork & Poultry Rub
- 1 Cup barbeque Sauce, Or More as Needed
- 6 Buns or Kaiser Rolls, Split and Buttered

Directions:
1. Season turkey thighs on both sides with the Pork & Poultry rub.
2. When ready to cook, turn temperature to 180 degrees F and preheat, lid closed for 15 minutes.
3. Arrange the turkey thighs exactly on the grill grate and smoke for 30 minutes.
4. Transfer the thighs to sturdy disposable aluminum foil or baking tray. Pour the broth around the thighs and then cover the pan with foil or a lid.
5. Increase temperature to 325 degrees F and preheat, lid closed. Roast the thighs until it reaches an internal temperature of 180 degrees F.
6. Remove pan from the grill, but leave the grill on. Let the turkey thighs cool slightly up to they can be handled comfortably.
7. Let the drops drip off and keep. Remove skin and discard.
8. Pull out the shredded turkey meat with your fingers and return it to the roasting pan.
9. Add a cup or more of your favorite BBQ Sauce along with some of the drippings.
10. Recover the pan with foil and reheat the BBQ turkey on the grill for 20 to 30 minutes.
11. Serve with toasted buns if desired. Enjoy!

Nutrition: Calories: 25 kcal Protein: 0.7 g Fat: 1.53 g Carbs: 2.59 g

181. Roasted Spatchcock Turkey

Preparation Time: 30 minutes
Cooking Time: 3-4 hours
Servings: 4
Ingredients:
- 1 (18-20 Lb.) Whole Turkey
- 4 tbsps. Turkey Rub
- 1 tbsp. Jacobsen Sea Salt
- 4 Cloves Garlic, Minced
- 3 tbsps. Parsley, Chopped
- 1 tbsp. Rosemary, Chopped
- 2 tbsps. Thyme Leaves, Chopped
- 2 Scallions, Chopped
- 3 tbsps. Olive Oil

Directions:
1. When ready to cook, turn temperature to High and preheat, lid closed for 15 minutes.
2. On a cutting board, mix the garlic, parsley, thyme, rosemary and green onions. Chop the mixture until it turns into a paste. Set aside.
3. Spatchcock the turkey: With a large knife or shears, cut the bird open along the backbone on both sides, through the ribs, and remove the backbone.
4. Once the bird is open, split the breastbone to spread the bird flat, allowing it to roast evenly.
5. With the bird's breast facing up, season the outside with half of the Turkey Rub, then follow 2/3 of the herb mixture by rubbing it into the bird. Drizzle with olive oil.
6. Roll over the bird and then season generously with the remaining Turkey Rub.
7. Place the turkey exactly on the grill grate and cook for 30 minutes.
8. Turn to low temperature on the grill to 300 degrees F and continue to cook for 3-4 hours or until the internal temperature reaches 160 degrees F in the breast.
9. The finished inside temperature should reach 165 degrees F, but it will continue to rise after the bird is totally removed it from the grill.
10. Prepare the bird and let it rest 20-25 minutes before carving. Enjoy!

Nutrition: Calories: 532 kcal Protein: 70 g Fat: 25 g Carbs: 2 g

182. Spatchcocked Maple Brined Turkey

Preparation Time: 40 minutes
Cooking Time: 2-3 hours
Servings: 6
Ingredients:
- 1 (12-14 Lbs.) Turkey, Thawed If Frozen
- 5 Qtrs. Hot Water
- 1 1/2 Cups Kosher Salt
- 3/4 cup of Bourbon
- 1 cup of Pure Maple Syrup
- 1/2 Cup of Brown Sugar
- 1 Onion
- 3-4 Strips Orange Peel
- 3 Bay Leaves, Broken into Pieces
- 2 tbsps. Black Peppercorns
- 1 tbsp. Whole Cloves
- 3 Qtrs. Ice
- 1 cup Butter, Melted
- Pork & Poultry Rub, As Needed
- Sprigs of Fresh Sage and Thyme, To Garnish
- Orange Wedges, Lady Apples, Or Kumquats, To Serve

Directions:
Note: Do not use kosher turkey or basting turkey for this recipe as they have already been fortified with saline.
For the Brine:
1. In a large stockpot or container, combine the hot water, kosher salt, bourbon, 3/4 cup of the maple syrup, brown sugar, onion, bay leaves, orange peel, peppercorns, and cloves and stir until well mixed. Add the ice.
2. Rinse or drain the turkey, inside and out, under cold running water. Remove giblets and discard or save for another use. Some turkeys come with a gravy packet as well; remove it before roasting the bird.
3. Add the turkey to the brine and refrigerate 8 to 12 hours, or overnight—weight with an ice pack to keep the bird immerse
4. Rinse and pat dry it with paper towels; discard the brine.
5. Spatchcock the turkey: Using a knife or shears, cut the bird open along the spine on both sides, then through the ribs and removes the backbone.
6. Once the bird is open, split the breastbone to spread the bird flat, allowing it to roast evenly.

7. Mix together the melted butter and the remaining 1/4 cup of maple syrup and divide in half. Brush half of the blend on the bird and then sprinkle with Pork and Poultry Rub or the salt and black pepper.
8. Set aside the other half of the blend mixture until ready to use.
9. Prepare and ready to cook, set the temperature to 350 degrees F and preheat, lid closed for 15 minutes.
10. Roast or cook the turkey until the internal temperature in the thickest part of the breast reaches 165 degrees F, about 2-3 hours.
11. Brush with the remaining butter-maple syrup glaze while having the last 30 minutes of cooking the meat.
12. Let the turkey remain rest for 15 to 20 minutes and then garnish, if desired, with fresh herbs and or kumquats. Enjoy!

Nutrition: Calories: 748 kcal Protein: 18.11 g Fat: 50.92 g Carbs: 55.01 g

183. Home Turkey Gravy

Preparation Time: 30 minutes
Cooking Time: 3-4 hours
Servings: 8
Ingredients:
- 4 cups Homemade Chicken Stock
- 2 Large Onions Cut Into 8th
- 4 Carrots, Rough Chop
- 4 Celery Stalks
- 8 Sprigs Thyme
- 8 Cloves Garlic, Peeled and Smashed
- 1 Turkey Neck
- 1 cup Flour
- 1 Stick Butter, Cut into About 8 Pieces
- 1 tsp. Kosher Salt
- 1 tsp. Cracked Black Pepper

Directions:
1. When all are prepared ready to cook, set the temperature to 350 degrees and preheat with the lid closed for 15 minutes.
2. In a large pan, place turkey neck, plus onion, celery, also carrot, garlic, and thyme. Please add 4 cups of chicken stock and then sprinkle with salt and pepper.

3. Put the prepped turkey on the rack into the roasting pan and place it in the wood pellet grill.
4. Cook for 3-4 hours or until the breast reaches 160 degrees F. When you remove from the grill, the turkey will continue to cook and reach a finished internal temperature of 165degrees F.
5. Rinse the drippings into a saucepan and simmer on low.
6. In a larger saucepan, combine butter and flour with a whisk stirring until golden tan. It takes about 8 minutes, stirring constantly.
7. Next, whisk the drippings into the roux and cook until it comes to a boil. Season with salt and pepper and serve hot. Enjoy!

Nutrition: Calories: 621 kcal Protein: 99.57 g Fat: 13.18 g Carbs: 19.82 g

184. Roasted Honey Bourbon Glazed Turkey

Preparation Time: 40 minutes
Cooking Time: 3-4 hours
Servings: 8
Ingredients:
Turkey
- 1 (16-18 Lbs.) Turkey
- 1/4 Cup of Fin and Feather Rub

Whiskey Glaze
- 1/2 cup Bourbon
- 1/2 Cup Honey
- 1/4 Cup Brown Sugar
- 3 tbsps. Apple Cider Vinegar
- 1 tbsp. Dijon Mustard
- Salt and Pepper, To Taste

Directions:
1. Prepare and ready to cook, set the temperature to 375 degrees F and preheat, lid closed for 15 minutes.
2. Truss the turkey legs together and then season the exterior of the bird and the cavity with Fin and Feather Rub.
3. Place the turkey exactly on the grill grate and cook for 20-30 minutes at 375 degrees F or until the skin begins to brown.
4. After 30 minutes, turn down the temperature to 325 degrees F and continue to cook until the inside temperature registers 165 degrees F when an instant-read thermometer is inserted into the thickest part of the breast, about 3-4 hours.

For the Whiskey Glaze:

1. Blend or mix all ingredients in a small saucepan and bring to a boil. Turn down the heat and simmer for 15-20 minutes or until thick enough to cover the back of a spoon. Remove from heat and set aside.
2. Meanwhile the last ten minutes of cooking, brush the turkey's glaze while on the grill and cook until it is set, 10 minutes.
3. Remove from grill and let it rest 10-15 minutes before carving. Enjoy!

Nutrition: Calories: 333 kcal Protein: 9.77 g Fat: 22 g Carbs: 25.13 g

185. Roasted Autumn Brined Turkey Breast

Preparation Time: 40 minutes
Cooking Time: 3-4 hours
Servings: 6
Ingredients:

- 6 Cups Apple Cider
- 2 Cloves Garlic, Smashed
- 1/3 Cup Brown Sugar
- 1 tbsp. Allspice
- 1/3 cup Kosher Salt
- 3 Bay Leaves
- 4 Cups Ice Water
- 1 Turkey Breast
- 1/2 Cup Plus Two Tbsps. Unsalted Butter, Softened
- Pork and Poultry Rub

Directions:
For the Brine:

1. In a large pot or saucepan, Mix 4 cups of apple cider, the garlic cloves, brown sugar, allspice, salt and bay leaves. Simmer on the stovetop for 5 minutes, stirring often.
2. Take off the stovetop and add in the ice water.
3. Put turkey in the brine and add water as needed until the turkey is fully submerged. Cover and refrigerate overnight.

For the Cider Glaze:

1. Let the remaining 2 cups of apple cider in a saucepan until reduced to 1/4 cup, about 30-45 minutes. Whisk in butter and cool completely.
2. After the turkey has brined overnight, drain the turkey and rinse.
3. Using your fingers, take two tablespoons of the softened butter and smear it under the breast's

skin. Season the breast of the turkey with Pork & Poultry Rub.

4. When ready to cook, turn the temperature to 325 degrees F and preheat, lid closed for 15 minutes.
5. Cook turkey until it reaches an inside temperature of 160 degrees F, about 3-4 hrs. After the first 20 minutes of cooking, rub turkey with the cider glaze.
6. When the breast starts to get too dark you should cover it with foil. Let stand 30 minutes before carving. Enjoy!

Nutrition: Calories: 680 kcal Protein: 62.27 g Fat: 32.92 g Carbs: 30.71 g

186. Ultimate Smoked Turkey

Preparation Time: 30 minutes
Cooking Time: 3-4 hours
Servings: 6
Ingredients:

- 1 (1.8-2.0 Lb.) Turkey
- 1 Turkey Brine Kit
- 1/2 Cup Pork & Poultry Rub
- 1/2 Lb. Softened Butter

Directions:

1. The day before, brine the turkey according to the Turkey Brine Kit package directions.
2. Remove from brine, rinse and pat dry. Season the inside cavity with Pork & Poultry Rub.
3. Prepare the turkey by separating the breast's skin, creating a pocket to stuff the softened butter in. Cover the entire breast with the 1/4-inch thickness of butter.
4. Move to the fridge and let chill for at least 1 hour.
5. Remove from the refrigerator and tie the legs and tuck the wing tips back around the bird.
6. Prepare and ready to cook, turn the temperature to 225 degrees F and preheat, lid closed for 15 minutes.
7. Place directly the turkey in a roasting pan on the grill grate. Cook until the internal temperature reaches 100-110 degrees F.
8. Turn the temperature on the grill up to 350 degrees F and continue to cook until an instant-read thermometer registers 160 degrees F when inserted in the thickest part of the breast, about 3 to 4 hours total cook time. Turkey will also

cook once taken off the grill to reach a final temperature of 165 degrees F in the breast.

9. Put away the bird from the grill and let it rest for at least 15 minutes before carving. Enjoy!

Nutrition: Calories: 630 kcal Protein: 24.87 g Fat: 58.08 g Carbs: 0 g

187. Smoked Wild Turkey Jerky

Preparation Time: 30 minutes
Cooking Time: 20 minutes
Servings: 12
Ingredients:
- 3 Lb. Turkey Breast, Thinly Sliced
- 2 Cups Soy Sauce
- 1 cup Brown Sugar
- 5 Garlic Cloves, Chopped
- 2 tbsps. Fresh Ginger, Chopped
- 1 tbsp. Ground Black Pepper
- 3 tbsps. Honey

Directions:
1. Make all ingredients and combine in a large zip-top bag then mix. Place the zip-top bag in a container and place in the refrigerator for 12 to 24 hours.
2. Prepare and ready to cook, turn temperature up to 180 degrees F and preheat, lid closed for 15 minutes.
3. Rinse the marinade and place the turkey strips on the grill.
4. Leave to smoke for 4 hours or until the jerky is dry. Enjoy!

Nutrition: Calories: 1085 kcal Protein: 127.1 g Fat: 47.44 g Carbs: 29.32 g

188. BBQ Chicken Breasts

Preparation Time: 40 minutes
Cooking Time: 15 minutes
Servings: 6
Ingredients:
- 4-6 Boneless and skinless Chicken Breast
- 1 half Cup of Sweet & Heat BBQ Sauce
- Salt and Pepper
- 1 tbsp. Chopped Parsley, To Garnish

Directions:
1. Put the chicken breasts and a cup of Sweet & Heat BBQ sauce in a Ziploc bag and marinate overnight.

2. Turn temperature to High and preheat, lid closed for 15 minutes.
3. Remove chicken from marinade and season with salt and pepper.
4. Place directly on the grill grate and cook for 10 minutes on each side, flipping once or until the internal temperature reaches 150 degrees F.
5. Brush remaining sauce on chicken while on the grill and continue to cook 5-10 minutes longer or until a finished internal temperature of 165 degrees F.
6. Move away from grill and let rest 5 minutes before serving. Sprinkle with chopped parsley. Enjoy!

Nutrition: Calories: 183 kcal Protein: 29.82 g Fat: 3.48 g Carbs: 7.73 g

189. Buffalo Chicken Wings

Preparation Time: 15 Minutes
Cooking Time: 25 Minutes
Servings: 6
Ingredients:
- 2 lb. chicken wings
- 1/2 cup sweet, spicy dry rub
- 2/3 cup buffalo sauce
- Celery, chopped

Directions:
1. Start your wood pellet grill.
2. Set it to 450 degrees F.
3. Sprinkle the chicken wings with the dry rub.
4. Place on the grill rack.
5. Cook for 10 minutes per side.
6. Brush with the buffalo sauce.
7. Grill for another 5 minutes.
8. Dip each wing in the buffalo sauce.
9. Sprinkle the celery on top.

Nutrition: Calories 88 kCal Fat 7g Protein 5g Carbs 3g

190. Sweet and Sour Chicken

Preparation Time: 30 Minutes
Cooking Time: 5 Hours
Servings: 4
Ingredients:
- Eight chicken drumsticks
- 1/4 cup soy sauce
- 1 cup ketchup
- Two tablespoons rice wine vinegar
- Two tablespoons lemon juice
- Two tablespoons honey
- Two tablespoons garlic, minced
- Two tablespoons ginger, minced
- One tablespoon sweet-spicy dry rub
- Three tablespoons brown sugar

Directions:
1. Combine all the sauce fixings in a bowl.
2. Mix well.
3. Take half of the mixture, transfer to another bowl and refrigerate.
4. Add the chicken to the bowl with the remaining sauce.
5. Toss to coat evenly.
6. Cover and refrigerate for 4 hours.
7. When ready to cook, take the chicken out of the refrigerator.
8. Discard the marinade.
9. Turn on your wood pellet grill.
10. Set it to smoke.
11. Set the temperature to 225 degrees F.
12. Smoke the chicken for 3 hours.
13. Serve the chicken with the reserved sauce.

Nutrition: Calories 140 kCal Fat 3g Protein 11g Carbs 18g

191. Honey Glazed Whole Chicken

Preparation Time: 30 Minutes
Cooking Time: 4 Hours
Servings: 4
Ingredients:
- One tablespoon honey
- Four tablespoons butter
- Three tablespoons lemon juice
- One whole chicken, giblets trimmed
- Four tablespoons chicken seasoning

Directions:
1. Set your wood pellet grill to smoke.
2. Set it to 225 degrees F.

3. In a pan over low heat, increase the honey and butter. Pour in the lemon juice.
4. Add the seasoning.
5. Cook for 1 minute, stirring.
6. Add the chicken to the grill.
7. Smoke for 8 minutes.
8. Flip the chicken and brush with the honey mixture.
9. Smoke for 3 hours, brushing the sauce every 40 minutes.
10. Let rest for 5 minutes before serving.

Nutrition: Calories 550 kCal Fat 25g Protein 44g Carbs 36g

192. Chicken Lollipops

Preparation Time: 30 Minutes
Cooking Time: 2 Hours
Servings: 6
Ingredients:
- 12 chicken lollipops
- Chicken seasoning
- Ten tablespoons butter, sliced into 12 cubes
- 1 cup barbecue sauce
- 1 cup hot sauce

Directions:
1. Turn on your wood pellet grill.
2. Set it to 300 degrees F.
3. Then season, the chicken with the chicken seasoning.
4. Arrange the chicken in a baking pan.
5. Put the butter cubes on top of each chicken.
6. Cook the chicken lollipops for 2 hours, basting with the melted butter in the baking pan every 20 minutes.
7. Pour in the barbecue sauce and hot sauce over the chicken.
8. Grill for 15 minutes.

Nutrition: Calories 88 kCal Fat 7g Protein 5g Carbs 3g

193. Lemon Chicken in Foil Packet

Preparation Time: 5 Minutes
Cooking Time: 25 Minutes
Servings: 4
Ingredients:
- Four chicken fillets
- Three tablespoons melted butter
- One garlic, minced
- 1-1/2 teaspoon dried Italian seasoning
- Salt and pepper to taste
- One lemon, sliced

Directions:
1. Turn on your wood pellet grill.
2. Keep the lid open while burning for 5 minutes.
3. Preheat it to 450 degrees F.
4. Add the chicken fillet on top of foil sheets.
5. In a bowl, mix the butter, garlic, seasoning, salt, and pepper.
6. Brush the chicken with this mixture.
7. Put the lemon slices on top.
8. Wrap the chicken with the foil.
9. Grill each side for 7 to 10 minutes per side.

Nutrition: Calories 297 kCal Fat 12g Protein 40g Carbs 8g

194. Sweet and Spicy Chicken

Preparation Time: 30 Minutes
Cooking Time: 1 Hour and 30 Minutes
Servings: 4
Ingredients:
- 16 chicken wings
- Three tablespoons lime juice
- A sweet, spicy rub

Directions:
1. Arrange the chicken wings in a baking pan.
2. Pour the lime juice over the wings.
3. Sprinkle the wings with the seasoning.
4. Set your wood pellet grill to 350 degrees F.
5. Add the chicken wings to the grill.
6. Grill for 20 minutes per side.

Nutrition: Calories 300 kCal Fat 15g Protein 8g Carbs 32g

195. Teriyaki Turkey

Preparation Time: 30 Minutes
Cooking Time: 4 Hours
Servings: 10
Ingredients:
- Glaze
- 1/4 cup melted butter
- 1/2 cup apple cider
- Two cloves garlic, minced
- 1/2 teaspoon ground ginger
- Two tablespoons soy sauce
- Two tablespoons honey
- Turkey
- Two tablespoons chicken seasoning
- One whole turkey
- Thickener
- One tablespoon cold water
- One teaspoon cornstarch

Directions:
1. Add the glaze ingredients to a pan over medium heat.
2. Bring to a boil and then simmer for 5 minutes.
3. Reserve 5 tablespoons of the mixture.
4. Add the remaining to a marinade injection.
5. Place the turkey in a baking pan.
6. Season with the chicken seasoning.
7. Turn on the wood pellet grill.
8. Set it to 300 degrees F.
9. Add the turkey to the grill.
10. Cook for 3 hours.
11. Add the thickener to the reserved mixture.
12. Brush the turkey with this sauce.
13. Cook for another 1 hour.

Nutrition: Calories 80 kCal Fat 1g Protein 10g Carbs 8g

196. Cheesy Turkey Burger

Preparation Time: 20 Minutes
Cooking Time: 3 Hours
Servings: 8
Ingredients:
- 3 lb. ground turkey
- Burger seasoning
- 7 oz. brie cheese, sliced into cubes
- Eight burger buns, sliced
- Blueberry jam
- Two roasted bell peppers, sliced

Directions:
1. Season the turkey with the burger seasoning.
2. Mix well.
3. Form 8 patties from the mixture.
4. Press cheese into the patties.
5. Cover the top with more turkey.
6. Preheat your wood pellet grill to 350 degrees F.

7. Cook the turkey burgers for 30 to 40 minutes per side.
8. Spread the burger buns with blueberry jam.
9. Add the turkey burger on top.
10. Top with the bell peppers.

Nutrition: Calories 554 kCal Fat 35g Protein 34g Carbs 26g

197. Turkey Sandwich

Preparation Time: 5 Minutes
Cooking Time: 25 Minutes
Servings: 4
Ingredients:
- Eight bread slices
- 1 cup gravy
- 2 cups turkey, cooked and shredded

Directions:
1. Set your wood pellet grill to smoke.
2. Preheat it to 400 degrees F.
3. Place a grill mat on top of the grates.
4. Add the turkey on top of the mat.
5. Cook for 10 minutes.
6. Toast the bread in the flame broiler.
7. Top the bread with the gravy and shredded turkey.

Nutrition: Calories 935 kCal Total fat 53g Saturated fat 15g Protein 107g Sodium 320mg

198. Smoked Turkey

Preparation Time: 30 Minutes
Cooking Time: 6 Hours and 30 Minutes
Servings: 8
Ingredients:
- 1 cup butter
- 1/2 cup maple syrup
- Two tablespoons chicken seasoning
- One whole turkey

Directions:
1. Add the butter to a pan over low heat.
2. Stir in the maple syrup.
3. Simmer for 5 minutes, stirring.
4. Turn off the stove and let cool.
5. Add to a marinade injection.
6. Inject into the turkey.
7. Add the turkey to the wood pellet grill.
8. Set it smoke.
9. Smoke at 275 degrees F for 6 hours.

Nutrition: Calories 324 kCal Fat 13g Protein 21g Carbs 29g

199. Texas Turkey

Preparation Time: 30 Minutes
Cooking Time: 4 Hours and 30 Minutes
Servings: 8
Ingredients:
- One pre-brined turkey
- Salt and pepper to taste
- 1 lb. butter

Directions:
1. Preheat your wood pellet grill to 300 degrees F.
2. Season the turkey with salt and pepper.
3. Grill for 3 hours.
4. Add the turkey to a roasting pan.
5. Cover the turkey with the butter.
6. Cover with foil.
7. Add to the grill and cook for another 1 hour.
8. Let rest for 20 minutes before carving and serving.

Nutrition: Calories 179 kCal Fat 9g Protein 20g Carbs 3g

200. Pit Boss Grilled Chicken

Preparation Time: 10 Minutes
Cooking Time: 1 Hour and 10 Minutes
Servings: 6
Ingredients:
- 5 lb. whole chicken
- 1/2 cup oil
- Pit Boss chicken rub

Directions:
1. Preheat the Pit Boss on the smoke setting with the lid open for 5 minutes. Close the lid, and let it warm for 15 minutes or until it reaches 450.
2. Use bakers' twine to tie the chicken legs together, then rub it with oil. Coat the chicken with the rub and place it on the grill.
3. Grill for 70 minutes with the lid closed or until it reaches an internal temperature of 1650F.
4. Remove the chicken from the Pit Boss and let rest for 15 minutes. Cut and serve.

Nutrition: Calories 246 kCal Fat 5.3g Protein 46g Carbs 0g

201. Pit Boss Chicken Breast

Preparation Time: 10 Minutes
Cooking Time: 15 Minutes
Servings: 6
Ingredients:
- Three chicken breasts
- 1 tbsp avocado oil
- 1/4 tbsp garlic powder
- 1/4 tbsp onion powder
- 3/4 tbsp salt
- 1/4 tbsp pepper

Directions:
1. Preheat your Pit Boss to 3750F
2. Cut the chicken breast into halves lengthwise, then coat with avocado oil.
3. Season with garlic powder, onion powder, salt, and pepper.
4. Place the chicken on the grill and cook for 7 minutes on each side or until the internal temperature reaches 1650F

Nutrition: Calories 120 kCal Fat 4g Protein 19g Carbs 0g

202. Chicken Wings

Preparation Time: 10 minutes
Cooking Time: 15 minutes
Servings: 4
Ingredients:
- Fresh chicken wings
- Salt to taste
- Pepper to taste
- Garlic powder
- Onion powder
- Cayenne
- Paprika
- Seasoning salt
- Barbeque sauce to taste

Directions:
1. Preheat the wood pellet grill to low.
2. Mix seasoning and coat on chicken
3. Put the wings on the grill and cook
4. Place the wings on the grill and cook for 20 minutes or until the wings are fully cooked.
5. Let rest to cool for 5 minutes then toss with barbeque sauce.
6. Serve with orzo and salad. Enjoy.

Nutrition: Calories: 311 kCal Fat: 22 g Carbs: 22g Protein: 22 g

203. Wood Pellet Grilled Chicken Kabobs

Preparation Time: 45 minutes
Cooking Time: 12 minutes
Servings: 6
Ingredients:
- 1/2 cup olive oil
- 2 tbsp white vinegar
- 1 tbsp lemon juice
- 1-1/2 tbsp salt
- 1/2 tbsp pepper, coarsely ground
- 2 tbsp chives, freshly chopped
- 1-1/2 tbsp thyme, freshly chopped
- 2 tbsp Italian parsley freshly chopped
- 1tbsp garlic, minced
- Kabobs
- 1 each orange, red, and yellow pepper
- 1-1/2 pounds chicken breast, boneless and skinless
- 12 mini mushrooms

Directions:
1. In a mixing bowl, add all the marinade ingredients and mix well. Toss the chicken and mushrooms in the marinade then refrigerate for 30 minutes.
2. Meanwhile, soak the skewers in hot water. Remove the chicken from the fridge and start assembling the kabobs.
3. Preheat your wood pellet to 450°F.
4. Grill the kabobs in the wood pellet for 6 minutes, flip them and grill for 6 more minutes.
5. Remove from the grill and let rest. Heat up the naan bread on the grill for 2 minutes.
6. Serve and enjoy.

Nutrition: Calories: 165 kCal Fat: 13g Carbs: 1g Protein: 33 g

204. Wood Pellet Grilled Chicken

Preparation Time: 10 minutes
Cooking Time: 1 hour and 10 minutes
Servings: 6
Ingredients:
- 5 pounds whole chicken
- 1/2 cup oil
- Chicken rub

Directions:
1. Preheat your wood pellet on smoke with the lid open for 5 minutes. Close the lid, increase the

temperature to 450°F and preheat for 15 more minutes.

2. Tie the chicken legs together with the baker's twine then rub the chicken with oil and coat with chicken rub.
3. Place the chicken on the grill with the breast side up.
4. Grill the chicken for 70 minutes without opening it or until the internal temperature reaches 165°F.
5. Once the chicken is out of the grill let it cool down for 15 minutes
6. Enjoy.

Nutrition: Calories: 246 kCal Fat: 5.3 g Carbs: 0 g Protein: 46 g

205. Wood Pellet Chicken Breasts

Preparation Time: 10 minutes
Cooking Time: 15 minutes
Servings: 6
Ingredients:
- 3 chicken breasts
- 1 tbsp avocado oil
- 1/4 tbsp garlic powder
- 1/4 tbsp onion powder
- 3/4 tbsp salt
- 1/4 tbsp pepper

Directions:
1. Preheat your pellet to 375°F.
2. Half the chicken breasts lengthwise then coat with avocado oil.
3. With the spices, drizzle it on all sides to season
4. Drizzle spices to season the chicken
5. Put the chicken on top of the grill and begin to cook until its internal temperature approaches 165 degrees Fahrenheit
6. Put the chicken on top of the grill and begin to cook until it rises to a temperature of 165 degrees Fahrenheit
7. Serve and enjoy.

Nutrition: Calories: 120 kCal Fat: 4 g Carbs: 0 g Protein: 19 g

206. Wood Pellet Smoked Spatchcock Turkey

Preparation Time: 30 minutes
Cooking Time: 1 hour and 45 minutes
Servings: 6
Ingredients:
- 1 whole turkey
- 1/2 cup oil
- 1/4 cup chicken rub
- 1 tbsp onion powder
- 1 tbsp garlic powder
- 1 tbsp rubbed sage

Directions:
1. Preheat your wood pellet grill to high.
2. Meanwhile, place the turkey on a platter with the breast side down then cut on either side of the backbone to remove the spine.
3. Flip the turkey and season on both sides then place it on the preheated grill or on a pan if you want to catch the drippings.
4. Grill on high for 30 minutes, reduce the temperature to 325°F, and grill for 45 more minutes or until the internal temperature reaches 165°F
5. Remove from the grill and let rest for 20 minutes before slicing and serving. Enjoy.

Nutrition: Calories: 156 kCal Fat: 16g Carbs: 1 g Protein: 2g

207. Wood Pellet Smoked Cornish Hens

Preparation Time: 10 minutes
Cooking Time: 1 hour
Servings: 6
Ingredients:
- 6 Cornish hens
- 3 tbsp avocado oil
- 6 tbsp rub of choice

Directions:
1. Fire up the wood pellet and preheat it to 275°F.
2. Rub the hens with oil then coat generously with rub. Place the hens on the grill with the chest breast side down.
3. Smoke for 30 minutes. Flip the hens and increase the grill temperature to 400°F. Cook until the internal temperature reaches 165°F.
4. Remove from the grill and let rest for 10 minutes before serving. Enjoy.

Nutrition: Calories: 696 kCal Fat: 50g Carbs: 1 g Protein: 57 g

208. Smoked and Fried Chicken Wings

Preparation Time: 10 minutes
Cooking Time: 2 hours
Servings: 6
Ingredients:
- 3 pounds chicken wings
- 1 tbsp Goya adobo all-purpose seasoning
- Sauce of your choice

Directions:
1. Fire up your wood pellet grill and set it to smoke.
2. Meanwhile, coat the chicken wings with adobo all-purpose seasoning. Place the chicken on the grill and smoke for 2 hours.
3. Remove the wings from the grill.
4. Preheat oil to 375°F in a frying pan. Drop the wings in batches and let fry for 5 minutes or until the skin is crispy.
5. Drain the oil and proceed with drizzling preferred sauce
6. Drain oil and drizzle preferred sauce
7. Enjoy.

Nutrition: Calories: 755 kCal Fat: 55g Carbs: 24g Protein: 39 g

209. Wood Pellet Grilled Buffalo Chicken Leg

Preparation Time: 5 minutes
Cooking Time: 25 minutes
Servings: 6
Ingredients:
- 12 chicken legs
- 1/2 tbsp salt
- 1 tbsp buffalo seasoning
- 1 cup buffalo sauce

Directions:
1. Preheat your wood pellet grill to 325°F.
2. Toss the legs in salt and buffalo seasoning then place them on the preheated grill.
3. Grill for 40 minutes ensuring you turn them twice through the cooking.
4. Brush the legs with buffalo sauce and cook for an additional 10 minutes or until the internal temperature reaches 165°F.
5. Remove the legs from the grill, brush with more sauce, and serve when hot.

Nutrition: Calories: 87 kCal Fat: 4.7g Carbs: 0g Protein: 10 g

210. Wood Pellet Chile Lime Chicken

Preparation Time: 2 minutes
Cooking Time: 15 minutes
Servings: 1
Ingredients:
- 1 chicken breast
- 1 tbsp oil
- 1 tbsp chile-lime seasoning

Directions:
1. Preheat your wood pellet to 400°F.
2. Brush the chicken breast with oil on all sides.
3. Sprinkle with seasoning and salt to taste.
4. Grill for 7 minutes per side or until the internal temperature reaches 165°F.
5. Serve when hot or cold and enjoy.

Nutrition: Calories: 131 kCal Fat: 5 g Carbs: 4g Protein: 19 g

211. Wood Pellet Sheet Pan Chicken Fajitas

Preparation Time: 10 minutes
Cooking Time: 10 minutes
Servings: 10
Ingredients:
- 2 tbsp oil
- 2 tbsp chile margarita seasoning
- 1 tbsp salt
- 1/2 tbsp onion powder
- 1/2 tbsp garlic, granulated
- 2-pound chicken breast, thinly sliced
- 1 red bell pepper, seeded and sliced
- 1 orange bell pepper
- 1 onion, sliced

Directions:
1. Preheat the wood pellet to 450°F.
2. Meanwhile, mix oil and seasoning then toss the chicken and the peppers.
3. Line a sheet pan with foil then place it in the preheated grill. Let it heat for 10 minutes with the grill's lid closed.
4. Open the grill and place the chicken with the veggies on the pan in a single layer.
5. Cook for 10 minutes or until the chicken is cooked and no longer pink.
6. Remove from grill and serve with tortilla or your favorite fixings.

Nutrition: Calories: 211 kCal Fat: 6 g Carbs: 5 g Protein: 29 g

212. Buffalo Chicken Flatbread

Preparation Time: 5 minutes
Cooking Time: 30 minutes
Servings: 6

Ingredients:
- 6 mini pita bread
- 1-1/2 cups buffalo sauce
- 4 cups chicken breasts, cooked and cubed
- 3 cups mozzarella cheese
- Blue cheese for drizzling

Directions:
1. Preheat the wood pellet grill to 375-400°F.
2. Place the breads on a flat surface and evenly spread sauce over all of them.
3. Toss the chicken with the remaining buffalo sauce and place it on the pita breads.
4. Top with cheese then place the breads on the grill but indirectly from the heat. Close the grill lid.
5. Cook for 7 minutes or until the cheese has melted and the edges are toasty.
6. Remove from grill and drizzle with blue cheese. Serve and enjoy.

Nutrition: Calories: 254 kCal Fat: 13g Carbs: 4g Protein: 33 g

213. Wood Pellet Grilled Buffalo Chicken

Preparation Time: 5 minutes
Cooking Time: 20 minutes
Servings: 6

Ingredients:
- 5 chicken breasts, boneless and skinless
- 2 tbsp homemade barbeque rub
- 1 cup homemade Cholula buffalo sauce

Directions:
1. Preheat the wood pellet grill to 400°F.
2. Slice the chicken into long strips and season with barbeque rub.
3. Place the chicken on the grill and paint both sides with buffalo sauce.
4. Cook for 4 minutes with the grill closed. Cook while flipping and painting with buffalo sauce every 5 minutes until the internal temperature reaches 165°F.
5. Remove from the grill and serve when warm. Enjoy.

Nutrition: Calories: 176 kCal Fat: 4 g Carbs: 1g Protein: 32 g

214. Beer Can Chicken

Preparation Time: 10 minutes
Cooking Time: 1 hour and 15 minutes
Servings: 6

Ingredients:
- 5-pound chicken
- 1/2 cup dry chicken rub
- 1 can beer

Directions:
1. Preheat your wood pellet grill on smoke for 5 minutes with the lid open.
2. The lid must then be closed and then preheated up to 450 degrees Fahrenheit
3. Pour out half of the beer then shove the can in the chicken and use the legs like a tripod.
4. Place the chicken on the grill until the internal temperature reaches 165°F.
5. Remove from the grill and let rest for 20 minutes before serving. Enjoy.

Nutrition: Calories: 882kCal Fat: 51g Carbs: 2g Protein: 94g

215. Wood Pellet Chicken Wings with Spicy Miso

Preparation Time: 15 minutes
Cooking Time: 25 minutes
Servings:6

Ingredients:
- 2-pound chicken wings
- 3/4 cup soy
- 1/2 cup pineapple juice
- 1 tbsp sriracha
- 1/8 cup miso
- 1/8 cup gochujang
- 1/2 cup water
- 1/2 cup oil
- Togarashi

Directions:
1. Mix all ingredients then toss the chicken wings until well coated. Refrigerate for 12 minutes.
2. Preheat your wood pellet grill to 375°F.
3. Place the chicken wings on the grill grates and close the lid. Cook until the internal temperature reaches 165°F.
4. Remove the wings from the grill and sprinkle with togarashi.
5. Serve when hot and enjoy.

Nutrition: Cal: 704kCal Fat: 56g Carbs:24g Protein: 27 g

216. Bacon-wrapped Chicken Tenders

Preparation Time: 25 minutes
Cooking Time: 30 minutes
Servings: 6
Ingredients:
- 1-pound chicken tenders
- 10 strips bacon
- 1/2 tbsp Italian seasoning
- 1/2 tbsp black pepper
- 1/2 tbsp salt
- 1 tbsp paprika
- 1 tbsp onion powder
- 1 tbsp garlic powder
- 1/3 cup light brown sugar
- 1 tbsp chili powder

Directions:
1. Preheat your wood pellet smoker to 350°F.
2. Mix seasonings
3. Sprinkle the mixture on all sides of chicken tenders
4. Wrap each chicken tender with a strip of bacon
5. Place them on the smoker and smoker for 30 minutes with the lid closed or until the chicken is cooked.
6. Serve and enjoy.

Nutrition: Calories: 206 kCal Fat: 7.9g Carbs: 1.5g Protein: 30.3 g

217. Apple Wood-Smoked Whole Turkey

Preparation Time: 10 minutes
Cooking Time: 5 hours
Servings: 6
Ingredients:
- 1 (10- to 12-pound) turkey, giblets removed
- Extra-virgin olive oil, for rubbing
- ¼ cup poultry seasoning
- 8 tablespoons (1 stick) unsalted butter, melted
- ½ cup apple juice
- 2 teaspoons dried sage
- 2 teaspoons dried thyme

Directions:
1. Supply your smoker with wood pellets and follow the manufacturer's specific start-up procedure. Preheat, with the lid closed, to 250°F.

2. Rub the turkey with oil and season with the poultry seasoning inside and out, getting under the skin.
3. In a bowl, combine the melted butter, apple juice, sage, and thyme to use for basting.
4. Put the turkey in a roasting pan, place on the grill, close the lid, and grill for 5 to 6 hours, basting every hour, until the skin is brown and crispy, or until a meat thermometer inserted in the thickest part of the thigh reads 165°F.
5. Let the turkey meat rest for about 15 to 20 minutes before carving.

Nutrition: Calories: 180 kCal Carbs: 3g Fat: 2g Protein: 39g

218. Savory-Sweet Turkey Legs

Preparation Time: 10 minutes
Cooking Time: 5 hours
Servings: 4
Ingredients:
- 1 gallon hot water
- 1 cup curing salt (such as Morton Tender Quick)
- ¼ cup packed light brown sugar
- 1 teaspoon freshly ground black pepper
- 1 teaspoon ground cloves
- 1 bay leaf
- 2 teaspoons liquid smoke
- 4 turkey legs
- Mandarin Glaze, for serving

Directions:
1. In a huge container with a lid, stir together the water, curing salt, brown sugar, pepper, cloves, bay leaf, and liquid smoke until the salt and sugar are dissolved; let come to room temperature.
2. Submerge the turkey legs in the seasoned brine, cover, and refrigerate overnight.
3. When ready to smoke, remove the turkey legs from the brine and rinse them; discard the brine.
4. Supply your smoker with wood pellets and follow the manufacturer's specific start-up procedure. Preheat, with the lid closed, to 225°F.
5. Arrange the turkey legs on the grill, close the lid, and smoke for 4 to 5 hours, or until dark brown and a meat thermometer inserted in the thickest part of the meat reads 165°F.

6. Serve with Mandarin Glaze on the side or drizzled over the turkey legs.

Nutrition: Calories: 190 kCal Carbs: 1g Fat: 9g Protein: 24g

219. Hoisin Turkey Wings

Preparation Time: 15 minutes
Cooking Time: 1 hour
Servings: 8
Ingredients:
- 2 pounds turkey wings
- ½ cup hoisin sauce
- 1 tablespoon honey
- 2 teaspoons soy sauce
- 2 garlic cloves (minced)
- 1 teaspoon freshly grated ginger
- 2 teaspoons sesame oil
- 1 teaspoons pepper or to taste
- 1 teaspoons salt or to taste
- ¼ cup pineapple juice
- 1 tablespoon chopped green onions
- 1 tablespoon sesame seeds
- 1 lemon (cut into wedges)

Directions:
1. In a huge container, combine the honey, garlic, ginger, soy, hoisin sauce, sesame oil, pepper and salt. Put all the mixture into a zip lock bag and add the wings. Refrigerate for 2 hours.
2. Remove turkey from the marinade and reserve the marinade. Let the turkey rest for a few minutes, until it is at room temperature.
3. Preheat your grill to 300°F with the lid closed for 15 minutes.
4. Arrange the wings into a grilling basket and place the basket on the grill.
5. Grill for 1 hour or until the internal temperature of the wings reaches 165°F.
6. Meanwhile, pour the reserved marinade into a saucepan over medium-high heat. Stir in the pineapple juice.
7. Wait to boil then reduce heat and simmer for until the sauce thickens.
8. Brush the wings with sauce and cook for 6 minutes more. Remove the wings from heat.
9. Serve and garnish it with green onions, sesame seeds and lemon wedges.

Nutrition: Calories: 115 kCal Fat: 4.8g Carbs: 11.9g Protein 6.8g

220. Turkey Jerky

Preparation Time: 15 minutes
Cooking Time: 4 hours
Servings: 6
Ingredients:
Marinade:
- 1 cup pineapple juice
- ½ cup brown sugar
- 2 tablespoons sriracha
- 2 teaspoons onion powder
- 2 tablespoons minced garlic
- 2 tablespoons rice wine vinegar
- 2 tablespoons hoisin
- 1 tablespoon red pepper flakes
- 1 tablespoon coarsely ground black pepper flakes
- 2 cups coconut amino
- 2 jalapenos (thinly sliced)

Meat:
- 3 pounds turkey boneless skinless breasts (sliced to ¼ inch thick)

Directions:
1. Pour the marinade mixture ingredients in a container and mix until the ingredients are well combined.
2. Put the turkey slices in a gallon sized zip lock bag and pour the marinade into the bag. Massage the marinade into the turkey. Seal the bag and refrigerate for 8 hours.
3. Remove the turkey slices from the marinade.
4. Activate the pellet grill for smoking and leave lip opened for 5 minutes until fire starts.
5. Close the lid and preheat your pellet grill to 180°F, using hickory pellet.
6. Remove the turkey slices from the marinade and pat them dry with a paper towel.
7. Arrange the turkey slices on the grill in a single layer. Smoke the turkey for about 3 to 4 hours, turning often after the first 2 hours of smoking. The jerky should be dark and dry when it is done.
8. Remove the jerky from the grill and let it sit for about 1 hour to cool. Serve immediately or store in refrigerator.

Nutrition: Calories: 109 kCal Carbs: 12g Fat: 1g Protein: 14g

221. Smoked Turkey Breast

Preparation Time: 10 Minutes
Cooking Time: 1 Hour 30 minutes
Servings: 6
Ingredients:
For the Brine
- 1 Cup of kosher salt
- 1 Cup of maple syrup
- ¼ Cup of brown sugar
- ¼ Cup of whole black peppercorns
- 4 Cups of cold bourbon
- 1 and ½ gallons of cold water
- 1 Turkey breast of about 7 pounds

For the Turkey
- 3 Tablespoons of brown sugar
- 1 and ½ tablespoons of smoked paprika
- 1 ½ teaspoons of chipotle chili powder
- 1 ½ teaspoons of garlic powder
- 1 ½ teaspoons of salt
- 1 and ½ teaspoons of black pepper
- 1 Teaspoon of onion powder
- ½ teaspoon of ground cumin
- 6 Tablespoons of melted unsalted butter

Directions:
1. Before beginning, make sure that the bourbon; the water and the chicken stock are all cold
2. Now to make the brine, combine altogether the salt, the syrup, the sugar, the peppercorns, the bourbon, and the water in a large bucket.
3. Remove any pieces that are left on the turkey, like the neck or the giblets
4. Refrigerate the turkey meat in the brine for about 8 to 12 hours in a reseal able bag
5. Remove the turkey breast from the brine and pat dry with clean paper towels; then place it over a baking sheet and refrigerate for about 1 hour
6. Preheat your pellet smoker to about 300°F; making sure to add the wood chips to the burner
7. In a bowl, mix the paprika with the sugar, the chili powder, the garlic powder, the salt, the pepper, the onion powder and the cumin, mixing very well to combine.
8. Carefully lift the skin of the turkey; then rub the melted butter over the meat
9. Rub the spice over the meat very well and over the skin
10. Smoke the turkey breast for about 1 ½ hours at a temperature of about 375°

Nutrition: Calories: 94 kCal Fat: 2g Carbs: 1g Protein: 18g

222. Whole Turkey

Preparation Time: 10 Minutes
Cooking Time: 7 Hours And 30 Minutes
Servings: 10
Ingredients:
- 1 frozen whole turkey, giblets removed, thawed
- 2 tablespoons orange zest
- 2 tablespoons chopped fresh parsley
- 1 teaspoon salt
- 2 tablespoons chopped fresh rosemary
- 1 teaspoon ground black pepper
- 2 tablespoons chopped fresh sage
- 1 cup butter, unsalted, softened, divided
- 2 tablespoons chopped fresh thyme
- ½ cup water
- 14.5-ounce chicken broth

Directions:
1. Open hopper of the smoker, add dry pallets, make sure ash-can is in place, then open the ash damper, power on the smoker and close the ash damper.
2. Set the temperature of the smoker to 180 degrees F, let preheat for 30 minutes or until the green light on the dial blinks that indicate smoker has reached to set temperature.
3. Meanwhile, prepare the turkey and for this, tuck its wings under it by using kitchen twine.
4. Place ½ cup butter in a bowl, add thyme, parsley, and sage, orange zest, and rosemary, stir well until combined and then brush this mixture generously on the inside and outside of the turkey and season the external of turkey with salt and black pepper.
5. Place turkey on a roasting pan, breast side up, pour in broth and water, add the remaining butter in the pan, then place the pan on the smoker grill and shut with lid.
6. Smoke the turkey for 3 hours, then increase the temperature to 350 degrees F and continue smoking the turkey for 4 hours or until thoroughly cooked and the internal temperature of the turkey reaches to 165

degrees F, basting turkey with the dripping every 30 minutes, but not in the last hour.

7. When you are done, take off the roasting pan from the smoker and let the turkey rest for 20 minutes.
8. Carve turkey into pieces and serve.

Nutrition: Calories: 146 kCal Fat: 8 g Protein: 18 g Carbs: 1 g

223. Herbed Turkey Breast

Preparation Time: 8 hours 10 minutes
Cooking Time: 3 hours
Servings: 12
Ingredients:

- 7 pounds turkey breast, bone-in, skin-on, fat trimmed
- 3/4 cup salt
- 1/3 cup brown sugar
- 4 quarts water, cold

For Herbed Butter:

- 1 tablespoon chopped parsley
- ½ teaspoon ground black pepper
- 8 tablespoons butter, unsalted, softened
- 1 tablespoon chopped sage
- ½ tablespoon minced garlic
- 1 tablespoon chopped rosemary
- 1 teaspoon lemon zest
- 1 tablespoon chopped oregano
- 1 tablespoon lemon juice

Directions:

1. Prepare the brine and for this, pour water in a large container, add salt and sugar and stir well until salt and sugar has completely dissolved.
2. Add turkey breast in the brine, cover with the lid and let soak in the refrigerator for a minimum of 8 hours.
3. Then remove turkey breast from the brine, rinse well and pat dry with paper towels.
4. Open hopper of the smoker, add dry pallets, make sure ash-can is in place, then open the ash damper, power on the smoker and close the ash damper.
5. Set the temperature of the smoker to 350 degrees F, let preheat for 30 minutes or until the green light on the dial blinks that indicate smoker has reached to set temperature.

6. Meanwhile, take a roasting pan, pour in 1 cup water, then place a wire rack in it and place turkey breast on it.
7. Prepare the herb butter and for this, place butter in a heatproof bowl, add remaining ingredients for the butter and stir until just mix.
8. Loosen the skin of the turkey from its breast by using your fingers, then insert 2 tablespoons of prepared herb butter on each side of the skin of the breastbone and spread it evenly, pushing out all the air pockets.
9. Place the remaining herb butter in the bowl into the microwave wave and heat for 1 minute or more at high heat setting or until melted.
10. Then brush melted herb butter on the outside of the turkey breast and place roasting pan containing turkey on the smoker grill.
11. Shut the smoker with lid and smoke for 2 hours and 30 minutes or until the turkey breast is nicely golden brown and the internal temperature of turkey reach to 165 degrees F, flipping the turkey and basting with melted herb butter after 1 hour and 30 minutes smoking.
12. When done, transfer the turkey breast to a cutting board, let it rest for 15 minutes, then carve it into pieces and serve.

Nutrition: Calories: 97 kCal Fat: 4 g Protein: 13 g Carbs: 1 g

224.   Smoked Turkey Mayo with Green Apple

Preparation Time: 20 minutes
Cooking Time: 4 hours 10 minutes
Servings: 10
Ingredients:

- Whole turkey (4-lbs., 1.8-kg.)
- The Rub
- Mayonnaise – ½ cup
- Salt – ¾ teaspoon
- Brown sugar – ¼ cup
- Ground mustard – 2 tablespoons
- Black pepper – 1 teaspoon
- Onion powder – 1 ½ tablespoons
- Ground cumin – 1 ½ tablespoons
- Chili powder – 2 tablespoons
- Cayenne pepper – ½ tablespoon
- Old Bay Seasoning – ½ teaspoon
- The Filling
- Sliced green apples – 3 cups

Directions:

1. Place salt, brown sugar, brown mustard, black pepper, onion powder, ground cumin, chili powder, cayenne pepper, and old bay seasoning in a bowl then mix well. Set aside.
2. Next, fill the turkey cavity with sliced green apples then baste mayonnaise over the turkey skin.
3. Sprinkle the dry spice mixture over the turkey then wrap with aluminum foil.
4. Marinate the turkey for at least 4 hours or overnight and store in the fridge to keep it fresh.
5. On the next day, remove the turkey from the fridge and thaw at room temperature.
6. Meanwhile, plug the wood pellet smoker then fill the hopper with the wood pellet. Turn the switch on.
7. Set the wood pellet smoker for indirect heat then adjust the temperature to 275°F (135°C).
8. Unwrap the turkey and place in the wood pellet smoker.
9. Smoke the turkey for 4 hours or until the internal temperature has reached 170°F (77°C).
10. Remove the smoked turkey from the wood pellet smoker and serve.

Nutrition: Calories: 340 kCal Carbs: 40g Fat: 10g Protein: 21g

225.   Buttery Smoked Turkey Beer

Preparation Time: 15 minutes
Cooking Time: 4 hours
Servings: 6
Ingredients:

- Whole turkey (4-lbs., 1.8-kg.)
- The Brine
- Beer – 2 cans
- Salt – 1 tablespoon
- White sugar – 2 tablespoons
- Soy sauce – ¼ cup
- Cold water – 1 quart
- The Rub
- Unsalted butter – 3 tablespoons
- Smoked paprika – 1 teaspoon
- Garlic powder – 1 ½ teaspoons
- Pepper – 1 teaspoon
- Cayenne pepper – ¼ teaspoon

Directions:

1. Pour beer into a container then add salt, white sugar, and soy sauce then stir well.
2. Put the turkey into the brine mixture cold water over the turkey. Make sure that the turkey is completely soaked.
3. Soak the turkey in the brine for at least 6 hours or overnight and store in the fridge to keep it fresh.
4. On the next day, remove the turkey from the fridge and take it out of the brine mixture.
5. Wash and rinse the turkey then pat it dry.
6. Next, plug the wood pellet smoker then fill the hopper with the wood pellet. Turn the switch on.
7. Set the wood pellet smoker for indirect heat then adjust the temperature to 275°F (135°C).
8. Open the beer can then push it in the turkey cavity.
9. Place the seasoned turkey in the wood pellet smoker and make a tripod using the beer can and the two turkey-legs.
10. Smoke the turkey for 4 hours or until the internal temperature has reached 170°F (77°C).
11. Once it is done, remove the smoked turkey from the wood pellet smoker and transfer it to a serving dish.

Nutrition: Calories: 229 kCal Carbs: 34g Fat: 8g Protein: 3g

226. Barbecue Chili Smoked Turkey Breast

Preparation Time: 15 minutes
Cooking Time: 4 hours 20 minutes
Servings: 8
Ingredients:

- Turkey breast (3-lb., 1.4-kg.)

The Rub

- Salt – ¾ teaspoon
- Pepper – ½ teaspoon

The Glaze

- Olive oil – 1 tablespoon
- Ketchup – ¾ cup
- White vinegar – 3 tablespoons
- Brown sugar – 3 tablespoons
- Smoked paprika – 1 tablespoons
- Chili powder – ¾ teaspoon
- Cayenne powder – ¼ teaspoon

Directions:

1. Score the turkey breast at several places then sprinkle salt and pepper over it.
2. Let the seasoned turkey breast rest for approximately 10 minutes.
3. In the meantime, plug the wood pellet smoker then fill the hopper with the wood pellet. Turn the switch on.
4. Set the wood pellet smoker for indirect heat then adjust the temperature to 275°F (135°C).
5. Place the seasoned turkey breast in the wood pellet smoker and smoke for 2 hours.
6. In the meantime, combine olive oil, ketchup, white vinegar, brown sugar, smoked paprika; chili powder, garlic powder, and cayenne pepper in a saucepan then stir until incorporated. Wait to simmer then remove from heat.
7. After 2 hours of smoking, baste the sauce over the turkey breast and continue smoking for another 2 hours.
8. Once the internal temperature of the smoked turkey breast has reached 170°F (77°C) remove from the wood pellet smoker and wrap with aluminum foil.
9. Let the smoked turkey breast rest for approximately 15 minutes to 30 minutes then unwrap it.
10. Cut the smoked turkey breast into thick slices then serve.

Nutrition: Calories: 290 kCal Carbs: 2g Fat: 3g Protein: 63g

227. Hot Sauce Smoked Turkey Tabasco

Preparation Time: 20 minutes
Cooking Time: 4 hours 15 minutes
Servings: 8
Ingredients:

- Whole turkey (4-lbs., 1.8-kg.)

The Rub

- Brown sugar – ¼ cup
- Smoked paprika – 2 teaspoons
- Salt – 1 teaspoon
- Onion powder – 1 ½ teaspoons
- Oregano – 2 teaspoons
- Garlic powder – 2 teaspoons
- Dried thyme – ½ teaspoon
- White pepper – ½ teaspoon
- Cayenne pepper – ½ teaspoon

The Glaze

- Ketchup – ½ cup
- Hot sauce – ½ cup
- Cider vinegar – 1 tablespoon
- Tabasco – 2 teaspoons
- Cajun spices – ½ teaspoon
- Unsalted butter – 3 tablespoons

Directions:

1. Rub the turkey with 2 tablespoons of brown sugar, smoked paprika, salt, onion powder, garlic powder, dried thyme, white pepper, and cayenne pepper. Let the turkey rest for an hour.
2. Plug the wood pellet smoker then fill the hopper with the wood pellet. Turn the switch on.
3. Set the wood pellet smoker for indirect heat then adjust the temperature to 275°F (135°C).
4. Place the seasoned turkey in the wood pellet smoker and smoke for 4 hours.
5. In the meantime, place ketchup, hot sauce, cider vinegar, Tabasco, and Cajun spices in a saucepan then bring to a simmer.
6. Remove the sauce from heat and quickly add unsalted butter to the saucepan. Stir until melted.
7. After 4 hours of smoking, baste the Tabasco sauce over the turkey then continue smoking for 15 minutes.
8. Once the internal temperature of the smoked turkey has reached 170°F (77°C), remove from the wood pellet smoker and place it on a serving dish.

Nutrition: Calories: 160 kCal Carbs: 2g Fat: 14g Protein: 7g

228. Cured Turkey Drumstick

Preparation Time: 20 minutes
Cooking Time: 2.5 hours to 3 hours
Servings: 3
Ingredients:
- 3 fresh or thawed frozen turkey drumsticks
- 3 tablespoons extra virgin olive oil

Brine component
- 4 cups of filtered water
- ¼Cup kosher salt
- ¼ cup brown sugar
- 1 teaspoon garlic powder
- Poultry seasoning 1 teaspoon
- 1/2 teaspoon red pepper flakes
- 1 teaspoon pink hardened salt

Directions:
1. Put the salt water ingredients in a 1 gallon sealable bag. Add the turkey drumstick to the salt water and refrigerate for 12 hours.
2. After 12 hours, remove the drumstick from the saline, rinse with cold water, and pat dry with a paper towel.
3. Air dry the drumstick in the refrigerator without a cover for 2 hours.
4. Remove the drumsticks from the refrigerator and rub a tablespoon of extra virgin olive oil under and over each drumstick.
5. Set the wood pellet or grill for indirect cooking and preheat to 250 degrees Fahrenheit using hickory or maple pellets.
6. Place the drumstick on the grill and smoke at 250 ° F for 2 hours.
7. After 2 hours, increase grill temperature to 325 ° F.
8. Cook the turkey drumstick at 325 ° F until the internal temperature of the thickest part of each drumstick is 180 ° F with an instant reading digital thermometer.
9. Place a smoked turkey drumstick under a loose foil tent for 15 minutes before eating.

Nutrition: Calories: 278 kCal Carbs: 0g Fat: 13g Protein: 37g

229. Tailgate Smoked Young Turkey

Preparation Time: 20 Minutes
Cooking Time: 4 To 4 Hours 30 Minutes
Servings: 6
Ingredients:
- 1 fresh or thawed frozen young turkey
- 6 glasses of extra virgin olive oil with roasted garlic flavor
- 6 original Yang dry lab or poultry seasonings

Directions:
1. Remove excess fat and skin from turkey breasts and cavities.
2. Slowly separate the skin of the turkey to its breast and a quarter of the leg, leaving the skin intact.
3. Apply olive oil to the chest, under the skin and on the skin.
4. Gently rub or season to the chest cavity, under the skin and on the skin.
5. Set up tailgate wood pellet smoker grill for indirect cooking and smoking. Preheat to 225 ° F using apple or cherry pellets.
6. Put the turkey meat on the grill with the chest up.
7. Suck the turkey for 4-4 hours at 225 ° F until the thickest part of the turkey's chest reaches an internal temperature of 170 ° F and the juice is clear.
8. Before engraving, place the turkey under a loose foil tent for 20 minutes

Nutrition: Calories: 240 kCal Carbs: 27g Fat: 9g Protein: 15g

230. Roast Turkey Orange

Preparation Time: 30 Minutes
Cooking Time: 2 hours 30 minutes
Servings:
Ingredients:
- 1 Frozen Long Island turkey
- 3 tablespoons west
- 1 large orange, cut into wedges
- Three celery stems chopped into large chunks
- Half a small red onion, a quarter

Orange sauce:
- 2 orange cups
- 2 tablespoons soy sauce
- 2 tablespoons orange marmalade
- 2 tablespoons honey
- 3 teaspoons grated raw

Directions:
1. Remove the nibble from the turkey's cavity and neck and retain or discard for another use. Wash the duck and pat some dry paper towel.
2. Remove excess fat from tail, neck and cavity. Use a sharp scalpel knife tip to pierce the turkey's skin entirely, so that it does not penetrate the duck's meat, to help dissolve the fat layer beneath the skin.
3. Add the seasoning inside the cavity with one cup of rub or seasoning.
4. Season the outside of the turkey with the remaining friction or seasoning.
5. Fill the cavity with orange wedges, celery and onion. Duck legs are tied with butcher twine to make filling easier. Place the turkey's breast up on a small rack of shallow roast bread.
6. To make the sauce, mix the ingredients in the saucepan over low heat and cook until the sauce is thick and syrupy. Set aside and let cool.
7. Set the wood pellet smoker grill for indirect cooking and use the pellets to preheat to 350 ° F.
8. Roast the turkey at 350 ° F for 2 hours.
9. After 2 hours, brush the turkey freely with orange sauce.
10. Roast the orange glass turkey for another 30 minutes, making sure that the inside temperature of the thickest part of the leg reaches 165 ° F.
11. Place turkey under loose foil tent for 20 minutes before serving.
12. Discard the orange wedge, celery and onion. Serve with a quarter of turkey with poultry scissors.

Nutrition: Calories: 216 kCal Carbs: 2g Fat: 11g Protein: 34g

231. Thanksgiving Dinner Turkey

Preparation Time: 15 minutes
Cooking Time: 4 hours
Servings: 16
Ingredients:
- ½ lb. butter, softened
- 2 tbsp. fresh thyme, chopped
- 2 tbsp. fresh rosemary, chopped
- 6 garlic cloves, crushed
- 1 (20-lb.) whole turkey, neck and giblets removed
- Salt and ground black pepper

Directions:
1. Set the temperature of Grill to 300 degrees F and preheat with closed lid for 15 minutes, using charcoal.
2. In a bowl, place butter, fresh herbs, garlic, salt and black pepper and mix well.
3. Separate the turkey skin from breast to create a pocket.
4. Stuff the breast pocket with ¼-inch thick layer of butter mixture.
5. Season turkey with salt and black pepper.
6. Arrange the turkey onto the grill and cook for 3-4 hours.
7. Remove the turkey from grill and place onto a cutting board for about 15-20 minutes before carving.
8. Cut the turkey into desired-sized pieces and serve.

Nutrition: Calories: 1753 kCal Carbs: 199g Protein: 72g Fat: 76g

232. Mixed Herbs Turkey

Preparation Time: 15 minutes
Cooking Time: 3 hours 30 minutes
Servings: 12
Ingredients:

- 14 pounds turkey, cleaned
- 2 tablespoons chopped mixed herbs
- Pork and poultry rub as needed
- ¼ teaspoon ground black pepper
- 3 tablespoons butter, unsalted, melted
- 8 tablespoons butter, unsalted, softened
- 2 cups chicken broth

Directions:

1. Clean the turkey by removing the giblets, wash it inside out, pat dry with paper towels, then place it on a roasting pan and tuck the turkey wings by tiring with butcher's string.
2. Switch on the grill, fill the grill hopper with hickory flavored wood pellets, power the grill on by using the control panel, select 'smoke' on the temperature dial, or set the temperature to 325 degrees F and let it preheat for a minimum of 15 minutes.
3. Meanwhile, prepared herb butter and for this, take a small bowl, place the softened butter in it, add black pepper and mixed herbs and beat until fluffy.
4. Place some of the prepared herb butter underneath the skin of turkey by using a handle of a wooden spoon and massage the skin to distribute butter evenly.
5. Then rub the exterior of the turkey with melted butter, season with pork and poultry rub, and pour the broth in the roasting pan.
6. When the grill has preheated, open the lid, place roasting pan containing turkey on the grill grate, shut the grill and smoke for 3 hours and 30 minutes until the internal temperature reaches 165 degrees F and the top has turned golden brown.
7. When done, transfer turkey to a cutting board, let it rest for 30 minutes, then carve it into slices and serve.

Nutrition: Calories: 154.6 kCal Fat: 3.1 g Carbs: 8.4 g Protein: 28.8 g

233. Turkey Legs

Preparation Time: 10 minutes
Cooking Time: 5 hours
Servings: 4
Ingredients:

- 4 turkey legs

For the Brine:

- ½ cup curing salt
- 1 tablespoon whole black peppercorns
- 1 cup BBQ rub
- ½ cup brown sugar
- 2 bay leaves
- 2 teaspoons liquid smoke
- 16 cups of warm water
- 4 cups ice
- 8 cups of cold water

Directions:

1. Prepare the brine and for this, take a large stockpot, place it over high heat, pour warm water in it, add peppercorn, bay leaves, and liquid smoke, stir in salt, sugar, and BBQ rub and bring it to a boil.
2. Remove pot from heat, bring it to room temperature, then pour in cold water, add ice cubes and let the brine chill in the refrigerator.
3. Then add turkey legs in it, submerge them completely, and let soak for 24 hours in the refrigerator.
4. After 24 hours, remove turkey legs from the brine, rinse well and pat dry with paper towels.
5. When ready to cook, switch on the grill, fill the grill hopper with hickory flavored wood pellets, power the grill on by using the control panel, select 'smoke' on the temperature dial, or set the temperature to 250 degrees F and let it preheat for a minimum of 15 minutes.
6. When the grill has preheated, open the lid, place turkey legs on the grill grate, shut the grill, and smoke for 5 hours until nicely browned and the internal temperature reaches 165 degrees F. Serve immediately.

Nutrition: Calories: 416 kCal Fat: 13.3 g Carbs: 0 g Protein: 69.8 g

234. Turkey Breast

Preparation Time: 12 hours
Cooking Time: 8 hours
Servings: 6
Ingredients:
For the Brine:

- 2 pounds turkey breast, deboned
- 2 tablespoons ground black pepper
- ¼ cup salt
- 1 cup brown sugar
- 4 cups cold water

For the BBQ Rub:

- 2 tablespoons dried onions
- 2 tablespoons garlic powder
- ¼ cup paprika
- 2 tablespoons ground black pepper
- 1 tablespoon salt
- 2 tablespoons brown sugar
- 2 tablespoons red chili powder
- 1 tablespoon cayenne pepper
- 2 tablespoons sugar
- 2 tablespoons ground cumin

Directions:

1. Prepare the brine and for this, take a large bowl, add salt, black pepper, and sugar in it, pour in water, and stir until sugar has dissolved.
2. Place turkey breast in it, submerge it completely and let it soak for a minimum of 12 hours in the refrigerator.
3. Meanwhile, prepare the BBQ rub and for this, take a small bowl, place all of its ingredients in it and then stir until combined, set aside until required.
4. Then remove turkey breast from the brine and season well with the prepared BBQ rub.
5. When ready to cook, switch on the grill, fill the grill hopper with apple-flavored wood pellets, power the grill on by using the control panel, select 'smoke' on the temperature dial, or set the temperature to 180 degrees F and let it preheat for a minimum of 15 minutes.
6. When the grill has preheated, open the lid, place turkey breast on the grill grate, shut the grill, change the smoking temperature to 225 degrees F, and smoke for 8 hours until the internal temperature reaches 160 degrees F.
7. When done, transfer turkey to a cutting board, let it rest for 10 minutes, then cut it into slices and serve.

Nutrition: Calories: 250 kCal Fat: 5 g Carbs: 31 g Protein: 18 g

235. Wild Turkey Egg Rolls

Preparation Time: 10 minutes
Cooking Time: 55 minutes
Servings: 1
Ingredients:

- Corn - ½ cup
- Leftover wild turkey meat - 2 cups
- Black beans - ½ cup
- Taco seasoning - 3 tablespoon
- Water ½ cup
- Rotel chilies and tomatoes - 1 can
- Egg roll wrappers- 12
- Cloves of minced garlic- 4
- 1 chopped Poblano pepper or 2 jalapeno peppers
- Chopped white onion - ½ cup

Directions:

1. Add some olive oil to a fairly large skillet. Heat it over medium heat on a stove.
2. Add peppers and onions. Sauté the mixture for 2-3 minutes until it turns soft.
3. Add some garlic and sauté for another 30 seconds. Add the Rotel chilies and beans to the mixture. Keeping mixing the content gently. Reduce the heat and then simmer.
4. After about 4-5 minutes, pour in the taco seasoning and 1/3 cup of water over the meat. Mix everything and coat the meat well. If you feel that it is a bit dry, you can add 2 tablespoons of water. Keep cooking until everything is heated all the way through.
5. Remove the content from the heat and box it to store in a refrigerator. Before you stuff the mixture into the egg wrappers, it should be completely cool to avoid breaking the rolls.
6. Place a spoonful of the cooked mixture in each wrapper and then wrap it securely and tightly. Do the same with all the wrappers.
7. Preheat the Pit Boss grill and brush it with some oil. Cook the egg rolls for 15 minutes on both sides, until the exterior is nice and crispy.

8. Remove them from the grill and enjoy with your favorite salsa!

Nutrition: Calories: 211 kCal Carbs: 26.1 g Protein: 9.2 g Fat: 4.2 g

236. Traeger Smoked Spatchcock Turkey

Preparation time: 30 minutes
Cooking time: 1 hour 15 minutes
Servings: 8
Ingredients:
- turkey
- 1/2 cup melted butter
- 1/4 cup Pit Boss chicken rub
- 1 Tablespoon onion powder
- 1 Tablespoon garlic powder
- 1 Tablespoon rubbed sage

Direction:
1. Preheat your Pit Boss to high temperature.
2. Place the turkey on a chopping board with the breast side down and the legs pointing towards you.
3. Cut either side of the turkey backbone, to remove the spine. Flip the turkey and place it on a pan
4. Season both sides with the seasonings and place it on the grill skin side up on the grill.
5. Cook for 30 minutes, reduce temperature, and cook for 45 more minutes or until the internal temperature reaches 1650F.
6. Remove from the Pit Boss and let rest for 15 minutes before slicing and serving.

Nutrition: Calories 156 kCal, Fat 16g, Protein 2g, Carbs 1g

237. Buttery Apple Smoked Turkey

Preparation time: 30 minutes
Cooking Time: 6 Hours
Servings: 1
Ingredients:
- Whole Turkey - 1 (10-lbs., 4.5-kgs)

The Rub
- Minced garlic – 2 tablespoons
- Salt – 2 ½ tablespoons

The Filling
- Garlic powder – 1 ½ tablespoons
- Black pepper – 1 ½ tablespoons
- Butter – 1 cup

- Unsweetened apple juice – 1 cup
- Fresh apples – 2
- Chopped onion – 1 cup

The Fire
- Preheat the smoker an hour prior to smoking.
- Use charcoal and hickory wood chips for smoking.

Directions:
1. Preheat a smoker to 225°F (107°C) with charcoal and hickory wood chips.
2. Rub the turkey with salt and minced garlic then set aside.
3. After that, cut the apples into cubes then combine with garlic powder, black pepper, butter, and chopped onion.
4. Pour the unsweetened apple juice over the filling mixture then mix well.
5. Fill the turkey's cavity with the filling mixture then cover the turkey with aluminum foil.
6. Place in the smoker once the smoker is ready and smoke it for 10 hours or until the internal temperature has reached 180°F (82°C). Don't forget to check the smoke and add more wood chips if it is necessary.
7. When the turkey is done, remove from the smoker then let it sit for a few minutes.
8. Unwrap the turkey then place on a flat surface.
9. Cut the turkey into pieces or slices then serve.
10. Enjoy.

Nutrition: Calories: 245 kCal Carbs: 2 g Protein: 34 g Fat: 6g

238. Smoked Turkey Legs grill

Preparation Time: 30 minutes
Cooking Time: 6 Hours
Servings: 1
Ingredients:
- 4 turkey legs
- 2 bay leaves
- 1 cup of BBQ rubs
- 1 tablespoon of crushed allspice berries
- 2 teaspoons of liquid smoke
- ½ gal of cold water
- 4 cups of ice
- 1 gal of warm water
- ½ cup of brown sugar
- ½ cup of curing salt
- 1 tablespoon of peppercorns; whole black

Directions:
1. Take a large stockpot and mix a gallon of warm water to curing salt, rub, peppercorns, brown sugar, liquid smoke, allspice and bay leaves
2. Bring this mix to boil by keeping the flame on high heat and let all salt granules dissolve thoroughly
3. Now let it cool to room temperature
4. Now add ice and cold water and let the whole thing chill in the refrigerator
5. Add turkey legs and make sure they are submerged in the brine
6. Let it stay for a day
7. Now drain the turkey legs and get rid of the brine
8. Wash off the brine from the legs with the help of cold water and then pat it dry
9. Set the grill to preheat by keeping the temperature to 250 degrees F
10. Lay the legs directly on the grate of the grill
11. Smoke it for 4 to 5 hours till the internal temperature reaches 165 degrees F
12. Serve and enjoy

Nutrition: Calories: 589 kCal Carbs: 0 g Protein: 79 g Fat: 28g

239. Smoked Turkey in Beer Brine

Preparation time: 30 minutes
Cooking Time: 6 Hours
Servings: 1
Ingredients:
- Whole Turkey - 1 (10-lbs., 4.5-kgs)

The Brine
- Water – 1 liter
- Salt – 2 cups
- Brown sugar – 1 sugar
- Bay leaves – 3 leaves
- Thyme – 1 cup
- Chopped onion – 1 cup
- Cold beer – 1 gallon

The Fire
- Preheat the smoker an hour prior to smoking.
- Use charcoal and hickory wood chips for smoking.

Directions:
1. Pour water into a pot then add salt, brown sugar, bay leaves, thyme, and chopped onion. Bring to boil.
2. Once it is boiled, remove from heat and let it cool. Usually, it will take approximately 30 minutes.
3. When the brine is cool, transfer to a container then pour cold beer into it. Mix until incorporated.
4. Add turkey to the container then refrigerate for 24 hours until the turkey is completely seasoned.
5. After 24 hours, remove from the refrigerator and dry using a paper towel. Set aside.
6. Preheat a smoker to 225°F (107°C) with charcoal and hickory wood chips.
7. Place the turkey in the sm0ker then smoke for 6 hours or until the internal temperature has reached 160°F (71°C).
8. Remove the smoked turkey from the smoker then let it warm.
9. Cut the smoked turkey into pieces or slices then arrange on a serving dish.
10. Serve and enjoy.

Nutrition: Calories: 123 kCal Carbs: 37 g Protein: 9 g Fat: 5g

240. Hot Smoked Turkey with Jelly Glaze

Preparation time: 30 minutes
Cooking Time: 6 Hours
Servings: 1
Ingredients:
- Whole Turkey - 1 (10-lbs., 4.5-kgs)

The Rub
- Olive oil – ½ cup
- Salt – 3 tablespoons
- Pepper – 2 tablespoons

The Glaze
- Hot pepper jelly – ¾ cup
- Rice vinegar – 3 tablespoons
- Red pepper flakes – ¼ cup

The Fire
- Preheat the smoker an hour prior to smoking.
- Use charcoal and hickory wood chips for smoking.

Directions:
1. Preheat a smoker to 225°F (107°C) with charcoal and hickory wood chips. Wait until the smoker is ready.
2. Cut the excess fat of the turkey then brush all sides of the turkey with olive oil,
3. Sprinkle salt and pepper over the turkey then place it in the smoker.
4. Smoke the turkey for 6 hours or until the internal temperature has reached 160°F (71°C).
5. Meanwhile, combine hot pepper jelly with rice vinegar and red pepper flakes then mix well.
6. After 6 hours, brush the smoked turkey with the hot pepper jelly mixture then return to the smoker.
7. Smoke for about 20 minutes then remove from the smoker.
8. Let the smoked turkey warm for a few minutes then cut into slices.
9. Arrange on a serving dish then serve.
10. Enjoy!

Nutrition: Calories: 80 kCal Carbs: 3 g Protein: 13 g Fat 1g

241. Lightly Spiced Smoked Turkey

Preparation time: 30 minutes
Cooking Time: 6 Hours
Servings: 10
Ingredients:
- Whole Turkey - 1 (10-lbs., 4.5-kgs)

- Vegetable oil – ¼ cup

The Injection
- Beer – ¾ cup, at room temperature
- Butter – ½ cup, melted
- Garlic – 6 cloves
- Worcestershire sauce – 2 ½ tablespoons
- Creole seasoning – 1 ½ tablespoons
- Hot sauce – 1 ½ tablespoons
- Salt – 1 ½ tablespoons
- Cayenne pepper – ½ teaspoon

The Rub
- Paprika – 1 ½ teaspoons
- Garlic powder – 1 teaspoon
- Onion powder – 1 teaspoon
- Thyme – ¾ teaspoon
- Oregano – ¼ teaspoon
- Cumin – ¼ teaspoon
- Salt – ½ teaspoon
- Black pepper – 1 teaspoon

The Fire
- Preheat the smoker an hour prior to smoking.
- Use charcoal and hickory wood chips for smoking.

Directions:
1. Preheat a smoker to 225°F (107°C) with charcoal and hickory wood chips. Wait until the smoker is ready.
2. Place garlic, Worcestershire sauce, Creole seasoning, hot sauce, salt, and cayenne pepper in a blender.
3. Pour beer and melted butter into the blender then blend until smooth.
4. Inject all sides of the turkey—give space about 1-inch. Set aside.
5. After that, make the rub by combining paprika with garlic powder, onion powder, thyme, oregano, cumin, salt, and black pepper. Mix well.
6. Rub the turkey with the spice mixture then lightly brush with vegetable oil.
7. When the smoker is ready, place the seasoned turkey in the smoker.
8. Smoke the turkey for 6 hours or until the internal temperature has reached 160°F (71°C).
9. Remove the turkey from the smoker then let it sit for a few minutes.
10. Carve the smoked turkey then serve.
11. Enjoy!

Nutrition: Cal: 126 kCal Carbs: 1g Protein: 26g Fat 2g

242. BBQ Pulled Turkey Sandwiches

Preparation Time: 30 minutes
Cooking Time: 4 Hours
Servings: 1
Ingredients:

- 6 skin-on turkey thighs
- 6 split and buttered buns
- 1 ½ cups of chicken broth
- 1 cup of BBQ sauce
- Poultry rub

Directions:

1. Season the turkey thighs on both the sides with poultry rub
2. Set the grill to preheat by pushing the temperature to 180 degrees F
3. Arrange the turkey thighs on the grate of the grill and smoke it for 30 minutes
4. Now transfer the thighs to an aluminum foil which is disposable and then pour the brine right around the thighs
5. Cover it with a lid
6. Now increase the grill, temperature to 325 degrees F and roast the thigh till the internal temperature reaches 180 degrees F
7. Remove the foil from the grill but do not turn off the grill
8. Let the turkey thighs cool down a little
9. Now pour the dripping and serve
10. Remove the skin and discard it
11. Pull the meat into shreds and return it to the foil
12. Add 1 more cup of BBQ sauce and some more dripping
13. Now cover the foil with lid and re-heat the turkey on the smoker for half an hour
14. Serve and enjoy

Nutrition: Calories: 290 kCal Carbs: 23 g Protein: 26 g Fat 10g

243. Tempting Tarragon Turkey Breasts

Preparation Time: 20 Minutes (Marinating Time: Overnight)
Cooking Time: 3½ to 4 hours
Servings: 4 to 5
Ingredients:
For the marinade

- ¾ cup heavy (whipping) cream
- ¼ cup Dijon mustard
- ¼ cup dry white wine
- 2 tablespoons olive oil
- ½ cup chopped scallions, both white and green parts, divided
- 3 tablespoons fresh tarragon, finely chopped
- 6 garlic cloves, coarsely chopped
- 1 teaspoon salt
- 1 teaspoon freshly ground black pepper

For the turkey

- (6- to 7-pound) bone-in turkey breast
- ¼ cup (½ stick) unsalted butter, melted

Directions:
To make the marinade

1. In a large bowl, whisk together the cream, mustard, wine, and olive oil until blended.
2. Stir in ¼ cup of scallions and the tarragon, garlic, salt, and pepper.
3. Rub the marinade all over the turkey breast and under the skin. Cover and refrigerate overnight.

To make the turkey

1. Following the manufacturer's specific start-up procedure, preheat the smoker to 250°F, and add apple or mesquite wood.
2. Remove the turkey from the refrigerator and place it directly on the smoker rack. Do not rinse it.
3. Smoke the turkey for 3½ to 4 hours (about 30 minutes per pound), basting it with the butter twice during smoking, until the skin is browned and the internal temperature registers 165°F.
4. Remove the turkey from the heat and let it rest for 10 minutes.
5. Sprinkle with the remaining scallions before serving.

Nutrition: Calories: 165 kCal Fat: 14g Carbs: 0.5g Protein: 15.2g

244. Juicy Beer Can Turkey

Preparation Time: 20 Minutes
Cooking Time: 6 hours
Servings: 6-8
Ingredients:
For the rub
- 4 garlic cloves, minced
- 2 teaspoons dry ground mustard
- 2 teaspoons smoked paprika
- 2 teaspoons salt
- 2 teaspoons freshly ground black pepper
- 1 teaspoon ground cumin
- 1 teaspoon ground turmeric
- 1 teaspoon onion powder
- ½ teaspoon sugar

For the turkey
- (10-pound) fresh whole turkey, neck, giblets, and gizzard removed and discarded
- tablespoons olive oil
- 1 large, wide (24-ounce) can of beer, such as Foster's
- 4 dried bay leaves
- 2 teaspoons ground sage
- 2 teaspoons dried thyme
- ¼ cup (½ stick) unsalted butter, melted

Directions:
To make the rub
1. Following the manufacturer's specific start-up procedure, preheat the smoker to 250°F, and add cherry, peach, or apricot wood.
2. In a small bowl, stir together the garlic, mustard, paprika, salt, pepper, cumin, turmeric, onion powder, and sugar.

To make the turkey
1. Rub the turkey inside and out with the olive oil.
2. Apply the spice rub all over the turkey.
3. Pour out or drink 12 ounces of the beer.
4. Using a can opener, remove the entire top of the beer can.
5. Add the bay leaves, sage, and thyme to the beer.
6. Place the can of beer upright on the smoker grate. Carefully fit the turkey over it until the entire can is inside the cavity and the bird stands by itself. Prop the legs forward to aid in stability.
7. Smoke the turkey for 6 hours, basting with the butter every other hour.
8. Remove the turkey from the heat when the skin is browned and the internal temperature registers 165°F. Remove the beer can very carefully—it will be slippery, and the liquid inside extremely hot. Discard the liquid, and recycle the can.
9. Let the turkey rest for 20 minutes before carving.

Nutrition: Calories: 300 kcal Fat: 12g Carbs: 1g Protein: 42g

245. Buttered Thanksgiving Turkey

Preparation Time: 25 minutes
Cooking Time: 5 or 6 hours
Servings: 12 to 14
Ingredients:
- 1 whole turkey (make sure the turkey is not pre-brined)
- 2 batches Garlic Butter Injectable
- 3 tablespoons olive oil
- 1 batch Chicken Rub
- 2 tablespoons butter

Directions:
1. Supply your smoker with Pit Bosss and follow the manufacturer's specific start-up procedure. Preheat the grill, with the lid closed, to 180°F.
2. Inject the turkey throughout with the garlic butter injectable. Coat the turkey with olive oil and season it with the rub. Using your hands, work the rub into the meat and skin.
3. Place the turkey directly on the grill grate and smoke for 3 or 4 hours (for an 8- to 12-pound turkey, cook for 3 hours; for a turkey over 12 pounds, cook for 4 hours), basting it with butter every hour.
4. Increase the grill's temperature to 375°F and continue to cook until the turkey's internal temperature reaches 170°F.
5. Remove the turkey from the grill and let it rest for 10 minutes, before carving and serving.

Nutrition: Calories: 97 kcal Fat: 4g Protein: 13g Carbs: 1g

246. Jalapeno Injection Turkey

Preparation Time: 15 minutes
Cooking Time: 4 hours and 10 minutes
Servings: 6
Ingredients:

- 15 pounds whole turkey, giblet removed
- ½ of medium red onion, peeled and minced
- 8 jalapeño peppers
- 2 tablespoons minced garlic
- 4 tablespoons garlic powder
- 6 tablespoons Italian seasoning
- 1 cup butter, softened, unsalted
- ¼ cup olive oil
- 1 cup chicken broth

Directions:

1. Open hopper of the smoker, add dry pallets, make sure ash-can is in place, then open the ash damper, power on the smoker and close the ash damper.
2. Set the temperature of the smoker to 200 degrees F, let preheat for 30 minutes or until the green light on the dial blinks that indicate smoker has reached to set temperature.
3. Meanwhile, place a large saucepan over medium-high heat, add oil and butter and when the butter melts, add onion, garlic, and peppers and cook for 3 to 5 minutes or until nicely golden brown.
4. Pour in broth, stir well, let the mixture boil for 5 minutes, then remove pan from the heat and strain the mixture to get just liquid.
5. Inject turkey generously with prepared liquid, then spray the outside of turkey with butter spray and season well with garlic and Italian seasoning.
6. Place turkey on the smoker grill, shut with lid, smoke for 30 minutes, then increase the temperature to 325 degrees F and continue smoking the turkey for 3 hours or until the internal temperature of turkey reach to 165 degrees F.
7. When done, transfer turkey to a cutting board, let rest for 5 minutes, then carve into slices and serve.

Nutrition: Calories: 131 kcal Fat: 7g Protein: 13g Carbs: 3g

247. Turkey Meatballs

Preparation Time: 40 minutes
Cooking Time: 40 minutes
Servings: 8
Ingredients:

- 1 1/4 lb. ground turkey
- 1/2 cup breadcrumbs
- 1 egg, beaten
- 1/4 cup milk
- 1 teaspoon onion powder
- 1/4 cup Worcestershire sauce
- Pinch garlic salt
- Salt and pepper to taste
- 1 cup cranberry jam
- 1/2 cup orange marmalade
- 1/2 cup chicken broth

Directions:

1. In a large bowl, mix the ground turkey, breadcrumbs, egg, milk, onion powder, Worcestershire sauce, garlic salt, salt and pepper.
2. Form meatballs from the mixture.
3. Preheat the Pit Boss grill to 350 degrees F for 15 minutes while the lid is closed.
4. Add the turkey meatballs to a baking pan.
5. Place the baking pan on the grill.
6. Cook for 20 minutes.
7. In a pan over medium heat, simmer the rest of the ingredients for 10 minutes.
8. Add the grilled meatballs to the pan.
9. Coat with the mixture.
10. Cook for 10 minutes.

Nutrition: Calories: 37 kCal Fat: 1.8 g Carbs: 3.1 g Protein: 2.5 g

248. Pit Boss Simple Smoked Turkey

Preparation Time: 1 day and 1 hour
Cooking Time: 4 hours and 30 minutes
Servings: 6
Ingredients:

- 2 gallons of water, divided
- 2 cups of sugar
- 2 cups salt
- Ice cubes
- 1 whole turkey
- ½ cup kosher salt
- ½ cup black pepper
- 3 sticks butter, sliced

Directions:

1. Add one-quart water to a pot over medium heat.
2. Stir in the 2 cups each of sugar and salt.
3. Bring to a boil.
4. Remove from heat and let cool.
5. Add ice and the remaining water.
6. Stir to cool.
7. Add the turkey to the brine.
8. Cover and refrigerate for 24 hours.
9. Rinse the turkey and dry with paper towels.
10. Season with salt and pepper.
11. Preheat the Pit Boss grill to 180 degrees F for 15 minutes while the lid is closed.
12. Smoke the turkey for 2 hours.
13. Increase temperature to 225 degrees. Smoke for another 1 hour.
14. Increase temperature to 325 degrees. Smoke for 30 minutes.
15. Place the turkey on top of a foil sheet.
16. Add butter on top of the turkey.
17. Cover the turkey with foil.
18. Reduce temperature to 165 degrees F.
19. Cook on the grill for 1 hour.

Nutrition: Calories: 48.2 kCal Fat: 1.4 g Carbs: 0 g Protein: 8.3 g

249. Maple Turkey Breast

Preparation Time: 4 hours and 30 minutes
Cooking Time: 2 hours
Servings: 4
Ingredients:

- 3 tablespoons olive oil
- 3 tablespoons dark brown sugar
- 3 tablespoons garlic, minced
- 2 tablespoons Cajun seasoning
- 2 tablespoons Worcestershire sauce
- 6 lb. turkey breast fillets

Directions:

1. Combine olive oil, sugar, garlic, Cajun seasoning and Worcestershire sauce in a bowl.
2. Soak the turkey breast fillets in the marinade.
3. Cover and marinate for 4 hours.
4. Grill the turkey at 180 degrees F for 2 hours.
5. Serving Suggestion: Let rest for 15 minutes before serving.
6. Preparation / Cooking Tips: You can also sprinkle dry rub on the turkey before grilling.

Nutrition: Calories: 416 kCal Fat: 13.3 g Carbs: 0 g Protein: 69.8 g

250. Turkey with Apricot Barbecue Glaze

Preparation Time: 30 minutes
Cooking Time: 30 minutes
Servings: 4
Ingredients:

- 4 turkey breast fillets
- 4 tablespoons chicken rub
- 1 cup apricot barbecue sauce

Directions:

1. Preheat the Pit Boss grill to 365 degrees F for 15 minutes while the lid is closed.
2. Season the turkey fillets with the chicken run.
3. Grill the turkey fillets for 5 minutes per side.
4. Brush both sides with the barbecue sauce and grill for another 5 minutes per side.
5. Serving Suggestion: Serve with buttered cauliflower.
6. Preparation / Cooking Tips: You can sprinkle turkey with chili powder if you want your dish spicy.

Nutrition: Calories: 316 kCal Fat: 12.3 g Carbs: 0 g Protein: 29.8 g

251. Tandoori Chicken Wings

Preparation Time: 20 minutes
Cooking Time: 1 hour 20 minutes
Servings: 4-6
Ingredients:

- ¼ Cup Yogurt
- 1 Whole Scallions, minced
- 1 Tablespoon minced cilantro leaves
- 2 Teaspoon ginger, minced
- 1 Teaspoon Masala
- 1 Teaspoon salt
- 1 Teaspoon ground black pepper
- 1 ½ pound chicken wings
- ¼ cup yogurt
- 2 tablespoon mayonnaises
- 2 tablespoon Cucumber
- 2 teaspoon lemon juice
- ½ teaspoon cumin
- ½ teaspoon salt
- 1/8 cayenne pepper

Directions:

1. Combine yogurt, scallion, ginger, garam masala, salt, cilantro, and pepper ingredients in the jar of a blender and process until smooth.
2. Put chicken and massage the bag to cat all the wings
3. Refrigerate for 4 to 8 hours. Remove the excess marinade from the wings; discard the marinade
4. Set the temperature to 350F and preheat, lid closed, for 10 to 15 minutes. Brush and oil the grill grate
5. Arrange the wings on the grill. Cook for 45 to 50 minutes, or until the skin is brown and crisp and meat is no longer pink at the bone. Turn once or twice during cooking to prevent the wings from sticking to the grill.
6. Meanwhile combine all sauce ingredients; set aside and refrigerate until ready to serve.
7. When wings are cooked through, transfer to a plate or platter. Serve with yogurt sauce

Nutrition: Calories 241 kcal Carbs 11g Protein 12g Fat 16g

252. Asian BBQ Chicken

Preparation Time: 12 to 24 hours
Cooking Time: 1 hour
Servings: 4-6
Ingredients:

- 1 whole chicken
- To taste Asian BBQ Rub
- 1 whole ginger ale

Direction:

1. Rinse chicken in cold water and pat dry with paper towels.
2. Cover the chicken all over with Asian BBQ rub; make sure to drop some in the inside too. Place in large bag or bowl and cover and refrigerate for 12 to 24 hours.
3. When ready to cook, set the Pit Boss grill to 372F and preheat lid closed for 15 minutes.
4. Open can of ginger ale and take a few big gulps. Set the can of soda on a stable surface. Take the chicken out of the fridge and place the bird over top of the soda can. The base of the can and the two legs of the chicken should form a sort of tripod to hold the chicken upright.
5. Stand the chicken in the center of your hot grate and cook the chicken till the skin is golden brown and the internal temperature is about 165F on an instant-read thermometer, approximately 40 minutes to 1 hour.

Nutrition: Calories 140 kcal Carbs 18g Protein 4g Fat 4g

253. Homemade Turkey Gravy

Preparation Time: 20 minutes
Cooking Time: 3 hours 20 minutes
Servings: 8-12
Ingredients:
- 1 turkey, neck
- 2 large Onion, eight
- 4 celeries, stalks
- 4 large carrots, fresh
- 8 clove garlic, smashed
- 8 thyme sprigs
- 4 cup chicken broth
- 1 teaspoon chicken broth
- 1 teaspoon salt
- 1 teaspoon cracked black pepper
- 1 butter, sticks
- 1 cup all-purpose flour

Directions:
1. When ready to cook, set the temperature to 350F and preheat the Pit Boss grill with the lid closed, for 15 minutes.
2. Place turkey neck, celery, carrot (roughly chopped), garlic, onion and thyme on a roasting pan. Add four cups of chicken stock then season with salt and pepper.
3. Move the prepped turkey on the rack into the roasting pan and place in the Pit Boss grill.
4. Cook for about 3-4 hours until the breast reaches 160F. The turkey will continue to cook and it will reach a finished internal temperature of 165F.
5. Strain the drippings into a saucepan and simmer on low.
6. In a saucepan, mix butter (cut into 8 pieces) and flour with a whisk stirring until golden tan. This takes about 8 minutes, stirrings constantly.
7. Whisk the drippings into the roux then cook until it comes to a boil. Season with salt and pepper.

Nutrition: Calories 160 kcal Carbs 27g Protein 55g Fat 23g

254. Bacon Wrapped Turkey Legs

Preparation Time: 10 minutes
Cooking Time: 3 hours
Servings: 4-6
Ingredients:
- Gallon water

To taste Pit Boss rub
- ½ cup pink curing salt
- ½ cup brown sugar
- 6 whole peppercorns
- 2 whole dried bay leaves
- ½ gallon ice water
- 8 whole turkey legs
- 16 sliced bacons

Directions:
1. In a large stockpot, mix one gallon of water, the rub, curing salt, brown sugar, peppercorns and bay leaves.
2. Boil it to over high heat to dissolve the salt and sugar granules. Take off the heat then add in ½ gallon of ice and water.
3. The brine must be at least to room temperature, if not colder.
4. Place the turkey legs, completely submerged in the brine.
5. After 24 hours, drain the turkey legs then remove the brine.
6. Wash the brine off the legs with cold water, then dry thoroughly with paper towels.
7. When ready to cook, start the Pit Boss grill according to grill instructions. Set the heat to 250F and preheat, lid closed for 10 to 15 minutes.
8. Place turkey legs directly on the grill grate.
9. After 2 ½ hours, wrap a piece of bacon around each leg then finish cooking them for 30 to 40 minutes of smoking.
10. The total smoking time for the legs will be 3 hours or until the internal temperature reaches 165F on an instant-read meat thermometer. Serve, Enjoy!

Nutrition: Calories 390 kcal Fat 14g Carbs 44g Protein 60g

255. Smoke Roasted Chicken

Preparation Time: 20 minutes
Cooking Time: 1 hour 20 minutes
Servings: 4-6
Ingredients:

- 8 tablespoon butter, room temperature
- 1 clove garlic, minced
- 1 scallion, minced
- 2 tablespoon fresh herbs such as thyme, rosemary, sage or parsley
- As needed Chicken rub
- Lemon juice
- As needed vegetable oil

Directions:

1. In a small cooking bowl, mix the scallions, garlic, butter, minced fresh herbs, 1-1/2 teaspoon of the rub, and lemon juice. Mix with a spoon.
2. Remove any giblets from the cavity of the chicken. Wash the chicken inside and out with cold running water. Dry thoroughly with paper towels.
3. Sprinkle a generous amount of Chicken Rub inside the cavity of the chicken.
4. Gently loosen the skin around the chicken breast and slide in a few tablespoons of the herb butter under the skin and cover.
5. Cover the outside with the remaining herb butter.
6. Insert the chicken wings behind the back. Tie both legs together with a butcher's string.
7. Powder the outside of the chicken with more Chicken Rub then insert sprigs of fresh herbs inside the cavity of the chicken.
8. Set temperature to High and preheat, lid closed for 15 minutes.
9. Oil the grill with vegetable oil. Move the chicken on the grill grate, breast-side up then close the lid.
10. After chicken has cooked for 1 hour, lift the lid. If chicken is browning too quickly, cover the breast and legs with aluminum foil.
11. Close the lid then continue to roast the chicken until an instant-read meat thermometer inserted into the thickest part registers a temperature of 165F
12. Take off chicken from grill and let rest for 5 minutes. Serve, Enjoy!

Nutrition: Calories 222 kcal Carbs 11g Protein 29g Fat 4g

256. Grilled Asian Chicken Burgers

Preparation Time: 5 minutes
Cooking Time: 50 minutes
Servings: 4-6
Ingredients:

- Pound chicken, ground
- 1 cup panko breadcrumbs
- 1 cup parmesan cheese
- 1 small jalapeno, diced
- 2 whole scallions, minced
- 2 garlic clove
- ¼ cup minced cilantro leaves
- 2 tablespoon mayonnaise
- 2 tablespoon chili sauce
- 1 tablespoon soy sauce
- 1 tablespoon ginger, minced
- 2 teaspoon lemon juice
- 2 teaspoon lemon zest
- 1 teaspoon salt
- 1 teaspoon ground black pepper
- 8 hamburger buns
- 1 tomato, sliced
- Arugula, fresh
- 1 red onion sliced

Directions:

1. Align a rimmed baking sheet with aluminum foil then spray with nonstick cooking spray.
2. In a large bowl, combine the chicken, jalapeno, scallion, garlic, cilantro, panko, Parmesan, chili sauce, soy sauce ginger, mayonnaise, lemon juice and zest, and salt and pepper.
3. Work the mixture with your fingers until the ingredients are well combined. If the mixture looks too wet to form patties and add additional more panko.
4. Wash your hands under cold running water, form the meat into 8 patties, each about an inch larger than the buns and about ¾" thick. Use your thumbs or a tablespoon, make a wide, shallow depression in the top of each
5. Put them on the prepared baking sheet. Spray the tops with nonstick cooking spray. If not cooking right away, cover with plastic wrap and refrigerate.
6. Set the Pit Boss grill to 350F then preheat for 15 minutes, lid closed.
7. Order the burgers, depression-side down, on the grill grate. Remove and discard the foil on the

baking sheet so you'll have an uncontaminated surface to transfer the slider when cooked.

8. Grill the burgers for about 25 to 30 minutes, turning once, or until they release easily from the grill grate when a clean metal spatula is slipped under them. The internal temperature when read on an instant-read meat thermometer should be 160F.

9. Spread mayonnaise and arrange a tomato slice, if desired, and a few arugula leaves on one-half of each bun. Top with a grilled burger and red onions, if using, then replace the top half of the bun. Serve immediately. Enjoy

Nutrition: Calories 329 kcal Carbs 10g Protein 21g Fat 23g

257. Grilled Sweet Cajun Wings

Preparation Time: 10 minutes
Cooking Time: 45 minutes
Servings: 4-6
Ingredients:
- 2-pound chicken wings
- As needed Pork and Poultry rub
- Cajun shake

Directions:
1. Coat wings in Sweet rub and Cajun shake.
2. When ready to cook, set the Pit Boss grill to 350F and preheat, lid closed for 15 minutes.
3. Cook for 30 minutes until skin is brown and center is juicy and an instant-read thermometer reads at least 165F. Serve, Enjoy!

Nutrition: Calories 320 kcal Carbs 3 g Protein 29 g Fat 20 g

258. The Grilled Chicken Challenge

Preparation Time: 15 minutes
Cooking Time: 1 hour and 10 minutes
Servings: 4-6
Ingredients:
- 1 (4-lbs.) whole chicken
- As needed chicken rub

Directions:
1. When ready to cook, set temperature to 375F then preheat, close the lid for 15 minutes.
2. Rinse and dry the whole chicken (remove and discard giblets, if any). Season the entire

chicken, including the inside of the chicken using chicken rub.

3. Place the chicken on the grill and cook for 1 hour and 10 minutes.

4. Remove chicken from grill when internal temperature of breast reaches 160F. Check heat periodically throughout as cook times will vary based on the weight of the chicken.

5. Allow chicken to rest until the internal temperature of breast reaches 165F, 15-20 minutes. Enjoy!

Nutrition: Calories 212 kcal Carbs 42.6g Protein 6.1g Fat 2.4g

Chapter 4: Fish and Seafood Recipes

259. Barbeque Shrimp

Preparation Time: 20 minutes
Cooking Time: 8 minutes
Servings: 6
Ingredients:
- 2-pound raw shrimp (peeled and deveined)
- ¼ cup extra virgin olive oil
- ½ tsp. paprika
- ½ tsp. red pepper flakes
- 2 garlic cloves (minced)
- 1 tsp. cumin
- 1 lemon (juiced)
- 1 tsp. kosher salt
- 1 tbsp. chili paste
- Bamboo or wooden skewers (soaked for 30 minutes, at least)

Directions:
1. Combine the pepper flakes, cumin, lemon, salt, chili, paprika, garlic and olive oil. Add the shrimp and toss to combine.
2. Transfer the shrimp and marinade into a zip-lock bag and refrigerate for 4 hours.
3. Let shrimp rest in room temperature after pulling it out from marinade.
4. Start your grill on smoke, leaving the lid opened for 5 minutes, or until fire starts. Use hickory wood pellet.
5. Keep lid unopened and preheat the grill to "high" for 15 minutes.
6. Thread shrimps onto skewers and arrange the skewers on the grill grate.
7. Smoke shrimps for 8 minutes, 4 minutes per side.
8. Serve and enjoy.

Nutrition: Calories: 267 kCal Fat: 11.6 g Carbs: 4.9 g Protein: 34.9 g

260. Oyster in Shells

Preparation Time: 25 minutes
Cooking Time: 8 minutes
Servings: 4
Ingredients:
- 12 medium oysters
- 1 tsp. oregano
- 1 lemon (juiced)
- 1 tsp. freshly ground black pepper.
- 6 tbsp. unsalted butter (melted)
- 1 tsp. salt or more to taste
- 2 garlic cloves (minced)
- 2 ½ tbsp. grated parmesan cheese
- 2 tbsp. freshly chopped parsley

Directions:
1. Remove dirt.
2. Open the shell completely. Discard the top shell.
3. Gently run the knife under the oyster to loosen the oyster foot from the bottom shell.
4. Repeat step 2 and 3 for the remaining oysters.
5. Combine melted butter, lemon, pepper, salt, garlic, and oregano in a mixing bowl.
6. Pour ½ to 1 teaspoon of the butter mixture on each oyster.
7. Start your wood pellet grill on smoke, leaving the lid opened for 5 minutes, or until fire starts.
8. Keep lid unopened to preheat in the set "HIGH" with lid closed for 15 minutes.
9. Gently arrange the oysters onto the grill grate.
10. Grill oyster for 6 to 8 minutes or until the oyster juice is bubbling and the oyster is plump.
11. Remove oysters from heat. Serve and top with grated parmesan and chopped parsley.

Nutrition: Calories: 200 kCal Fat: 19.2 g Carbs: 3.9 g Protein: 4.6 g

261. Smoked Scallops

Preparation Time: 10 minutes
Cooking Time: 15 minutes
Servings: 6
Ingredients:
- 2 pounds sea scallops
- 4 tbsp. salted butter
- 2 tbsp. lemon juice
- ½ tsp. ground black pepper
- 1 garlic clove (minced)
- 1 kosher tsp. salt
- 1 tsp. freshly chopped tarragon

Directions:
1. Let the scallops dry using paper towels and drizzle all sides with salt and pepper to season.

2. Place you are a cast iron pan in your grill and preheat the grill to 400°F with lid closed for 15 minutes.
3. Combine the butter and garlic in hot cast iron pan. Add the scallops and stir. Close grill lid and cook for 8 minutes.
4. Flip the scallops and cook for an additional 7 minutes.
5. Remove the scallop from heat and let it rest for a few minutes.
6. Stir in the chopped tarragon. Serve and top with lemon juice.

Nutrition: Calories: 204 kCal Fat: 8.9 g Carbs: 4 g Protein: 25.6 g

262. Crab Stuffed Lingcod

Preparation Time: 20 minutes
Cooking Time: 30 minutes
Servings: 6
Ingredients:

- Lemon cream sauce
- Four garlic cloves
- One shallot
- One leek
- 2 tbsp. olive oil
- 1 tbsp. salt
- 1/4 tbsp. black pepper
- 3 tbsp. butter
- 1/4 cup white wine
- 1 cup whipping cream
- 2 tbsp. lemon juice
- 1 tbsp. lemon zest
- Crab mix
- 1 lb. crab meat
- 1/3 cup mayo
- 1/3 cup sour cream
- 1/3 cup lemon cream sauce
- 1/4 green onion, chopped.
- 1/4 tbsp. black pepper
- 1/2 tbsp. old bay seasoning
- Fish
- 2 lb. lingcod
- 1 tbsp. olive oil
- 1 tbsp. salt
- 1 tbsp. paprika
- 1 tbsp. green onion, chopped.
- 1 tbsp. Italian parsley

Directions:
Lemon cream sauce

- Chop garlic, shallot, and leeks, then add to a saucepan with oil, salt, pepper, and butter.
- Sauté over medium heat until the shallot is translucent.
- Deglaze with white wine, then add whipping cream. Bring the sauce to boil, reduce heat, and simmer for 3 minutes.
- Remove from heat and add lemon juice and lemon zest. Transfer the sauce to a blender and blend until smooth.
- Set aside 1/3 cup for the crab mix.

Crab mix

- Add all the fixings to a mixing bowl and mix thoroughly until well combined.
- Set aside.

Fish

1. Fire up your Pit boss to high heat, then slice the fish into 6-ounce portions.
2. Lay the fish on its side on a cutting board and slice it 3/4 way through the middle leaving a 1/2 inch on each end to have a nice pouch.
3. Rub the oil into the fish, then place them on a baking sheet. Sprinkle with salt.
4. Stuff crab mix into each fish, then sprinkle paprika and place it on the grill.
5. Cook for 15 minutes or more if the fillets are more than 2 inches thick.
6. Remove the fish and transfer to serving platters. Pour the remaining lemon cream sauce on each fish and garnish with onions and parsley.

Nutrition: Calories 476 kCal Fat 33g Carbs 6g Protein 38g

263. Pit Boss Smoked Shrimp

Preparation Time: 10 minutes
Cooking Time: 10 minutes
Servings: 6
Ingredients:
- 1 lb. tail-on shrimp, uncooked
- 1/2 tbsp. onion powder
- 1/2 tbsp. garlic powder
- 1/2 tbsp. salt
- 4 tbsp. teriyaki sauce
- 2 tbsp. green onion, minced.
- 4 tbsp. sriracha mayo

Directions:
1. Peel the shrimp shells leaving the tail on, then wash well and rise.
2. Drain well and pat dry with a paper towel.
3. Preheat your Pit boss to 4500F.
4. Season the shrimp with onion powder, garlic powder, and salt. Place the shrimp in the Pit boss and cook for 6 minutes on each side.
5. Remove the shrimp from the Pit boss and toss with teriyaki sauce, then garnish with onions and mayo.

Nutrition: Calories 87 kCal Carbs 2g Protein 16g Fat 2g

264. Grilled Shrimp Kabobs

Preparation Time: 5 minutes
Cooking Time: 10 minutes
Servings: 4
Ingredients:
- 1 lb. colossal shrimp peeled and deveined.
- 2 tbsp. oil
- 1/2 tbsp. garlic salt
- 1/2 tbsp. salt
- 1/8 tbsp. pepper
- Six skewers

Directions:
1. Preheat your Pit boss to 3750F.
2. Pat the shrimp dry with a paper towel.
3. In a mixing bowl, mix oil, garlic salt, salt, and pepper.
4. Toss the shrimp in the mixture until well coated.
5. Skewer the shrimps and cook in the Pit boss with the lid closed for 4 minutes.
6. Open the lid, flip the skewers, cook for another 4 minutes, or wait until the shrimp is pink and the flesh is opaque.
7. Serve.

Nutrition: Calories 130 Protein 7g Carbs 9g Fat 8g

265. Sweet Bacon-Wrapped Shrimp

Preparation Time: 20 minutes
Cooking Time: 10 minutes
Servings: 12
Ingredients:
- 1 lb. raw shrimp
- 1/2 tbsp. salt
- 1/4 tbsp. garlic powder
- 1 lb. bacon cut into halves.

Directions:
1. Preheat your Pit boss to 3500F.
2. Remove the shells and tails from the shrimp, then pat them dry with the paper towels.
3. Sprinkle salt and garlic on the shrimp, then wrap with bacon and secure with a toothpick.
4. Place the shrimps on a baking rack greased with cooking spray.
5. Cook for 10 minutes, flip and cook for another 10 minutes, or until the bacon is crisp enough.
6. Remove from the Pit boss and serve.

Nutrition: Calories 204 kCal Fat 14g Carbs 1g Protein 18g

266. Pit Boss Spot Prawn Skewers

Preparation Time: 10 minutes
Cooking Time: 10 minutes
Servings: 6
Ingredients:
- 2 lb. spot prawns
- 2 tbsp. oil
- Salt and pepper to taste

Directions:
- Preheat your Pit boss to 4000F.
- Skewer your prawns with soaked skewers, then generously sprinkle with oil, salt, and pepper.
- Place the skewers on the grill, then cook with the lid closed for 5 minutes on each side.
- Remove the skewers and serve when hot.

Nutrition: Calories 221 kCal Fat 7g Carbs 2g Protein 34g

267. Pit Boss Bacon-Wrapped Scallops

Preparation Time: 15 minutes
Cooking Time: 20 minutes
Servings: 8
Ingredients:

- 1 lb. sea scallops
- 1/2 lb. bacon
- Sea salt

Directions:

1. Preheat your Pit boss to 3750F.
2. Pat dries the scallops with a towel, then wrap them with a piece of bacon and secure with a toothpick.
3. Lay the scallops on the grill with the bacon side down. Close the lid and cook for 5 minutes on each side.
4. Keep the scallops on the bacon side so that you will not get grill marks on the scallops.
5. Serve and enjoy.

Nutrition: Calories 261 kCal Fat 14g Carbs 5g Protein 28g

268. Pit Boss Lobster Tail

Preparation Time: 10 minutes
Cooking Time: 15 minutes
Servings: 2
Ingredients:

- 10 oz. lobster tail
- 1/4 tbsp. old bay seasoning
- 1/4 tbsp. Himalayan salt
- 2 tbsp. butter, melted.
- 1 tbsp. fresh parsley, chopped.

Directions:

1. Preheat your Pit boss to 4500F.
2. Slice the tail down the middle, then season it with bay seasoning and salt.
3. Place the tails directly on the grill with the meat side down. Grill for 15 minutes or until the internal temperature reaches 1400F.
4. Remove from the Pit boss and drizzle with butter.
5. Serve when hot garnished with parsley.

Nutrition: Calories 305 kCal Fat 14g Carbs 5g Protein 38g

269. Grilled Cajun Shrimp

Preparation Time: 5 minutes
Cooking Time: 25 minutes
Servings: 8
Ingredients:
Dip

- 1/2 cup mayonnaise
- One teaspoon lemon juice
- 1 cup sour cream
- One clove garlic, grated.
- One tablespoon Cajun seasoning
- One tablespoon hickory bacon rub
- One tablespoon hot sauce
- Chopped scallions.

Shrimp

- 1/2 lb. shrimp peeled and deveined.
- Two tablespoons olive oil
- 1/2 tablespoon hickory bacon seasoning
- One tablespoon Cajun seasoning

Directions:

1. Turn on your wood pellet grill.
2. Set it to 350 degrees F.
3. Mix the dip ingredients in a bowl.
4. Transfer to a small pan.
5. Cover with foil.
6. Place on top of the grill.
7. Cook for 10 minutes.
8. Coat the shrimp with the olive oil and sprinkle with the seasonings.
9. Grill for 5 minutes per side.
10. Pour the dip on top or serve with the shrimp.

Nutrition: Calories 87 kCal Carbs 2g Protein 16g Fat 10g

270. Cajun Smoked Shrimp

Preparation Time: 10 minutes
Cooking Time: 10 minutes
Servings: 2
Ingredients:
- 2 tablespoons of virgin olive oil
- 1/2 lemon, juiced.
- 3 cloves garlic, finely minced
- 2 tablespoons of Cajun spice
- Salt, to taste
- 1.5 pounds of shrimp, raw, peeled, deveined.

Directions:
1. Take a zip lock bag and combine olive oil, lemon juice, garlic cloves, Cajun spice, salt, and shrimp.
2. Toss the ingredients well for fine coating.
3. Preheat the smoker grill for 10 minutes until the smoke starts to establish.
4. Put the fish on the grill grate and close lid.
5. Turn the temperature to high and allow the fish to cook the shrimp for 10 minutes, 5 minutes per side.
6. Once done, serve.

Nutrition: Calories 160 kCal Fat 4.8g Protein 19g Carbs 5g

271. Smoked Crab Paprika Garlic with Lemon Butter Flavor

Preparation Time: 5 minutes
Cooking Time: 30 minutes
Servings: 10
Ingredients:
- Fresh Crabs (7-lb., 3.2-kg.)

The Sauce
- Salt – 1 tablespoon
- Cayenne pepper – 1 ½ teaspoon
- Salted butter – 2 cups
- Lemon juice – ½ cup
- Worcestershire sauce – 1 tablespoon
- Garlic powder – 2 teaspoons
- Smoked paprika – 2 teaspoons.

Directions:
1. Preheat a saucepan over low heat then melt the butter. Let it cool.
2. Season the melted butter with salt, cayenne pepper, Worcestershire sauce, garlic powder, and smoked paprika, then pour lemon juice into the melted butter. Stir until incorporated and set aside.
3. Then, plug the wood pellet smoker then fill the hopper with the wood pellet. Turn the switch on.
4. Set the wood pellet smoker for indirect heat then adjust the temperature to 350°F (177°C).
5. Arrange the crabs in a disposable aluminum pan then drizzle the sauce over the crabs.
6. Smoke the crabs for 30 minutes then remove from the wood pellet smoker.
7. Transfer the smoked crabs to a serving dish then serve.
8. Enjoy!

Nutrition: Calories: 455 kCal Fats: 53g Carbs: 3g Protein 8g

272. Cayenne Garlic Smoked Shrimp

Preparation Time: 5 minutes
Cooking Time: 15 minutes
Servings: 10
Ingredients:
- Fresh Shrimps (3-lb., 1.4-kg.)

The Spices
- Olive oil – 2 tablespoons
- Lemon juice – 2 tablespoons
- Salt – ¾ teaspoon
- Smoked paprika – 2 teaspoons.
- Pepper – ½ teaspoon
- Garlic powder – 2 tablespoons
- Onion powder – 2 tablespoons
- Dried thyme – 1 teaspoon
- Cayenne pepper – 2 teaspoons

Directions:
1. Combine salt, smoked paprika, pepper, garlic powder, onion powder, dried thyme, and cayenne pepper then mix well. Set aside. Then, peel the shrimps and discard the head. Place in a disposable aluminum pan. Drizzle olive oil and lemon juice over the shrimps and shake to coat. Let the shrimps rest for approximately 5 minutes. Then, plug the wood pellet smoker then fill the hopper with the wood pellet. Turn the switch on.
2. Set the wood pellet smoker for indirect heat then adjust the temperature to 350°F (177°C).
3. Sprinkle the spice mixture over the shrimps then stir until the shrimps are completely seasoned.

4. Place the disposable aluminum pan with shrimps in the wood pellet smoker and smoke the shrimps for 15 minutes. The shrimps will be opaque and pink. Remove the smoked shrimps from the wood pellet smoker and transfer to a serving dish.
5. Serve and enjoy.

Nutrition: Calories: 233 kCal Fats: 25g Carbs: 7g Protein 12g

273. Cinnamon Ginger Juicy Smoked Crab

Preparation Time: 10 minutes
Cooking Time: 30 minutes
Servings: 10
Ingredients:
- Fresh Crabs (7-lb., 3.2-kg.)

The Spices
- Salt – 1 tablespoon
- Ground celery seeds – 3 tablespoons
- Ground mustard – 2 teaspoons
- Cayenne pepper – ½ teaspoon
- Black pepper – ½ teaspoon
- Smoked paprika – 1 ½ teaspoon.
- Ground clove – A pinch
- Ground allspice – ¾ teaspoon
- Ground ginger – 1 teaspoon
- Ground cardamom – ½ teaspoon
- Ground cinnamon – ½ teaspoon
- Bay leaves - 2

Directions:
1. Combine the entire spices—salt, ground celery seeds, mustard, cayenne pepper, black pepper, smoked paprika, clove, allspice, ginger, cardamom, and cinnamon in a bowl then mix well. Sprinkle the spice mixture over the crabs then wrap the crabs with aluminum foil. Then, plug the wood pellet smoker then fill the hopper with the wood pellet. Turn the switch on. Set the wood pellet smoker for indirect heat then adjust the temperature to 350°F (177°C). Place the wrapped crabs in the wood pellet smoker and smoke for 30 minutes. Once it is done, remove the wrapped smoked carbs from the wood pellet smoker and let it rest for approximately 10 minutes.
2. Unwrap the smoked crabs and transfer it to a serving dish.
3. Serve and enjoy!

Nutrition: Calories: 355 kCal Fats: 22g Carbs: 8g Protein 11g

274. Parsley Prawn Skewers

Preparation Time: 15 minutes
Cooking Time: 8 minutes
Servings: 5
Ingredients:
- ¼ cup fresh parsley leaves, minced.
- 1 tablespoon garlic, crushed.
- 2½ tablespoons olive oil
- 2 tablespoons Thai chili sauce
- 1 tablespoon fresh lime juice
- 1½ pounds prawns peeled and deveined.

Directions:
1. In a large bowl, add all ingredients except for prawns and mix well.
2. In a resealable plastic bag, add marinade and prawns.
3. Seal the bag and shake to coat well.
4. Refrigerate for about 20-30 minutes.
5. Preheat the Z Grills Pit Boss Grill & Smoker on grill setting to 450 degrees F.
6. Remove the prawns from marinade and thread onto metal skewers.
7. Arrange the skewers onto the grill and cook for about 4 minutes per side.
8. Remove the skewers from grill and serve hot.

Nutrition: Calories 234 kCal Fat 9.3 g Carbs 4.9 g Protein 31.2 g

275. Buttered Shrimp

Preparation Time: 15 minutes
Cooking Time: 30 minutes
Servings: 6
Ingredients:
- 8 ounces salted butter, melted.
- ¼ cup Worcestershire sauce
- ¼ cup fresh parsley, chopped.
- 1 lemon, quartered.
- 2 pounds jumbo shrimp peeled and deveined.
- 3 tablespoons BBQ rub

Directions:
1. In a metal baking pan, add all ingredients except for shrimp and BBQ rub and mix well.
2. Season the shrimp with BBQ rub evenly.

3. Add shrimp in the pan with butter mixture and coat well.
4. Set aside for about 20-30 minutes.
5. Preheat the Z Grills Pit Boss Grill & Smoker on grill setting to 250 degrees F.
6. Place the pan onto the grill and cook for about 25-30 minutes.
7. Remove the pan from grill and serve hot.

Nutrition: Calories 462 kCal Fat 33.3 g Carbs 4.7 g Protein 34.9 g

276. Prosciutto Wrapped Scallops

Preparation Time: 15 minutes
Cooking Time: 40 minutes
Servings: 4
Ingredients:
- 8 large scallops shelled and cleaned.
- 8 extra-thin prosciutto slices

Directions:
1. Preheat the Z Grills Pit Boss Grill & Smoker on grill setting to 225-250 degrees F.
2. Arrange the prosciutto slices onto a smooth surface.
3. Place 1 scallop on the edge of 1 prosciutto slice and roll it up tucking in the sides of the prosciutto to cover completely.
4. Repeat with remaining scallops and prosciutto slices.
5. Arrange the wrapped scallops onto a small wire rack.
6. Place the wire rack onto the grill and cook for about 40 minutes.
7. Remove the scallops from grill and serve hot.

Nutrition: Calories 160 kCal Fat 6.7 g Carbs 1.4 g Protein 23.5 g

277. Buttered Clams

Preparation Time: 15 minutes
Cooking Time: 8 minutes
Servings: 6
Ingredients:
- 24 littleneck clams
- ½ cup cold butter, chopped.
- 2 tablespoons fresh parsley, minced.
- 3 garlic cloves, minced.
- 1 teaspoon fresh lemon juice

Directions:
1. Preheat the Z Grills Pit Boss Grill & Smoker on grill setting to 450 degrees F.
2. Scrub the clams under cold running water.
3. In a large casserole dish, mix remaining ingredients.
4. Place the casserole dish onto the grill.
5. Now, arrange the clams directly onto the grill and cook for about 5-8 minutes or until they are opened. (Discard any that fail to open).
6. With tongs, carefully transfer the opened clams into the casserole dish and remove from the grill.
7. Serve immediately.

Nutrition: Calories 306 Fat 17.6 g Carbs 6.4 g Protein 29.3 g

278. Lemony Lobster Tails

Preparation Time: 15 minutes
Cooking Time: 25 hours
Servings: 4
Ingredients:
- ½ cup butter, melted.
- 2 garlic cloves, minced.
- 2 teaspoons fresh lemon juice
- Salt and ground black pepper, as required.
- 4 (8-ounce) lobster tails

Directions:
1. Preheat the Z Grills Pit Boss Grill & Smoker on grill setting to 450 degrees F.
2. In a metal pan, add all ingredients except for lobster tails and mix well.
3. Place the pan onto the grill and cook for about 10 minutes.
4. Meanwhile, cut down the top of the shell and expose lobster meat.
5. Remove pan of butter mixture rom grill.
6. Coat the lobster meat with butter mixture.
7. Place the lobster tails onto the grill and cook for about 15 minutes, coating with butter mixture once halfway through.
8. Remove from the grill and serve hot.

Nutrition: Calories 409 kCal Fat 24.9 g Carbs 0.6 g Protein 43.5 g

279. Blackened Salmon

Preparation Time: 10 minutes
Cooking Time: 30 minutes
Servings: 4
Ingredients:

- 2 lb. salmon, fillet, scaled and deboned
- 2 tablespoons olive oil
- 4 tablespoons sweet dry rub
- 1 tablespoon cayenne pepper
- 2 cloves garlic, minced

Directions:
1. Turn on your wood pellet grill.
2. Set it to 350 degrees F.
3. Brush the salmon with the olive oil.
4. Sprinkle it with the dry rub, cayenne pepper and garlic.
5. Grill for 5 minutes per side.
6. Serving Suggestion: Garnish with chopped parsley.

Nutrition: Calories: 220 kCal Carbs: 1g Fat: 13g Protein: 23g

280. Blackened Catfish

Preparation Time: 10 minutes
Cooking Time: 40 minutes
Servings: 4
Ingredients:
Spice blend

- 1 teaspoon granulated garlic
- 1/4 teaspoon cayenne pepper
- 1/2 cup Cajun seasoning
- 1 teaspoon ground thyme
- 1 teaspoon ground oregano
- 1 teaspoon onion powder
- 1 tablespoon smoked paprika
- 1 teaspoon pepper

Fish

- 4 catfish fillets
- Salt to taste
- 1/2 cup butter

Directions:
1. In a bowl, mix the ingredients for the spice blend.
2. Sprinkle both sides of the fish with the salt and spice blend.
3. Set your wood pellet grill to 450 degrees F.

4. Heat your cast Iron: pan and add the butter. Add the fillets to the pan.
5. Cook for 5 minutes per side.

Nutrition: Calories: 283 kCal Carbs: 1g Fat: 19g Protein: 27g

281. Salmon Cakes

Preparation Time: 10 minutes
Cooking Time: 30 minutes
Servings: 4
Ingredients:

- 1 cup cooked salmon, flaked
- 1/2 red bell pepper, chopped
- 2 eggs, beaten
- 1/4 cup mayonnaise
- 1/2 tablespoon dry sweet rub
- 1 1/2 cups breadcrumbs
- 1 tablespoon mustard
- Olive oil

Directions:
1. Combine all the ingredients except the olive oil in a bowl.
2. Form patties from this mixture.
3. Let sit for 15 minutes
4. Turn on your wood pellet grill.
5. Set it to 350 degrees F.
6. Add a baking pan to the grill.
7. Drizzle a little olive oil on top of the pan.
8. Add the salmon cakes to the pan.
9. Grill for 3 to 4 minutes.

Nutrition: Calories: 459 Carbs: 3g Fat: 37g Protein: 26g

282. Smoked Lemon Salmon

Preparation Time: 10 minutes
Cooking Time: 1 hour and 15 minutes
Servings: 4
Ingredients:

- 2 lb. salmon
- 6 to 8 lemon slices
- Fresh dill

Directions:
1. Set your wood pellet grill to 225 degrees F.
2. Add the salmon on top of a cedar plank.
3. Place the lemon slices on top.
4. Smoke for 1 hour.
5. Add the dill on top before serving.

Tip: You can also brine the salmon before cooking.

Nutrition: Calories: 125 kCal Carbs: 1g Fat: 2g Protein: 26g

283. Smoked Salmon

Preparation Time: 10 minutes
Cooking Time: 1 hour
Servings: 6
Ingredients:
- 1/3 cup olive oil
- 1 teaspoon sesame oil
- 1/3 cup soy sauce
- 1-1/2 tablespoons rice vinegar
- 1 teaspoon garlic, minced
- 2 salmon fillets
- 1 teaspoon onion salt
- 1 teaspoon black pepper

Directions:
1. Combine the olive oil, sesame oil, soy sauce, vinegar and garlic in a bowl.
2. Add the salmon.
3. Marinate for 30 minutes. Turn on your wood pellet grill.
4. Let it fire up for 5 minutes while the lid is open. Set it to 225 degrees F.
5. Add cedar planks on the grill.
6. Take the salmon out of the marinade.
7. Sprinkle both sides with the onion salt and pepper.
8. Add the salmon fillets to the planks.
9. Grill for 30 minutes.
10. Let it rest before serving.

Nutrition: Calories: 132 kCal Carbs: 0g Fat: 8g Protein: 14g

284. Fish Tacos

Preparation Time: 0 minutes
Cooking Time: 30 minutes
Servings: 12
Ingredients:
- 1/4 teaspoon cayenne pepper
- 1/2 teaspoon cumin
- 1 1/2 teaspoon paprika
- 1 teaspoon garlic powder
- 1 teaspoon dried oregano
- Salt and pepper to taste
- 1 1/2 lb. cod fish
- 12 tortillas

Salsa
- Avocado, sliced
- Sour cream

Directions:
1. Preheat your wood pellet grill to 350 degrees F.
2. Combine the salt, pepper, herbs and spices.
3. Sprinkle this mixture on both sides of the fish.
4. Grill the fish for 5 minutes per side.
5. Shred the fish with a fork.
6. Place on top of the tortillas.
7. Top with salsa, sour cream and avocado.
8. Roll up the tortillas and serve.

Nutrition: Calories: 117 kCal Carbs: 2g Fat: 6g Protein: 12g

285. Halibut with Indian Rub and Corn Salsa

Preparation time: 15 minutes
Cooking time: 30 minutes
Servings: 4
Ingredients:
- 2 teaspoons ground cumin
- 1½ teaspoons turmeric
- 1 teaspoon ground coriander
- 1 teaspoons of ground fennel seeds
- Salt and freshly ground black pepper
- 4 hazelnut fillets (Pacific salmon, striped sea bass, hake fillets or their fillets)
- Fish can be substituted), 1 inch thick (2 to 2.5 pounds total) 2 lemons
- 4 tablespoons of ghee (refined at Indian and specialty stores) or refined
- Butter; vegetable oil can be substituted
- 1 tablespoon chopped fresh ginger
- ½ cup finely chopped onions
- 1 cup of cooked fresh corn kernels (about 1 ear of corn)
- Oil for grill
- 1 tablespoon chopped fresh cilantro leaves

Directions:
1. Mix cumin, turmeric, coriander, fennel, ½ tsp. teaspoon black pepper and ½ teaspoon salt or taste Fish fillets on both sides with lemon juice, then rub with all but 2 teaspoons of the spice mixture. Refrigerate for 3 hours
2. While sea fish heat, put 2 tablespoons of ghee in pan, add ginger and onions and simmer until onions are browned.

3. Add the rest of the spice mixture and stew, stirring, until the spices are tender to the toast, then add the corn and lemon and lemon juice. Cook briefly and reserve.
4. Remove the fish from the refrigerator and coat it on both sides with the remaining 2 tablespoons butter or butter Preheat grill and oil grills.
5. When hot, place the fish on the grill over charcoal over medium heat or gas fire and cook for about 5 minutes.
6. Use a spatula. Turn the fish over and grill for 4 minutes until some liquid begins to accumulate. A fish surface and a kitchen knife inserted just at the bone level can hold the meat away.
7. Salmon should be cooked for about 3 minutes on each side.
8. Remove fish on a hot plate or individual dishes.
9. Warm up the corn mixture, add cilantro and a few tablespoons of water.
10. Pour corn over fish, garnish with lemon slices and serve.

Nutrition: Calories: 130 kCal Carbs: 5 g Protein: 79 g Fat 10g

2. Coat the fish with half the oil on both sides. Coat the side of the meat with lemon juice and season with salt and pepper.
3. To process the fish, you will need two large blades; if you don't have them, cut the steak in half or in four.
4. Coat tomato into slices and add the remaining oil.
5. Preheat the grill to very hot grills and oil.
6. Remove to a plate and cover with foil to stay warm.
7. Use the edge of the spatula to clean the grilles. Oil again.
8. Grill the fish, skin side up. Cook for about 5 minutes. Use the blades to rotate. Cook for 3 minutes on the skin until the skeleton inserted horizontally in the middle is hot. (Salmon need less time).
9. Transfer the fish to a hot plate and flatten the meat side with the tomatoes covered.
10. Sprinkle with olives, chopped garlic and basil and serve with aioli in aside, if you like.

Nutrition: Calories: 130 kCal Carbs: 5 g Protein: 23 g Fat 3g

286. Charred Striped Bass Nicoise

Preparation time: 10 minutes
Cooking time: 40 minutes
Servings: 4
Ingredients:
- 3 tablespoons extra virgin olive oil, plus more for grill
- 2 cloves garlic, sliced
- 1 (2-pound) skin-on wild striped bass fillet (Pacific salmon, mahi-mahi or
- Barramundi may be substituted)
- Juice of ½ lemon
- Salt and freshly ground black pepper
- 2 medium-size ripe tomatoes, cut in ¼-inch-thick slices
- 12 pitted oil-cured black olives, coarsely chopped
- 1 tablespoon finely slivered fresh basil leaves
- Aioli (optional)

Directions:
1. In a saucepan, heat the oil, add the garlic and cook over medium heat until golden brown. Remove from heat, strain the garlic and chop.

287. Charcoal-Grilled Striped Bass

Preparation time: 10 minutes
Cooking time: 30 minutes
Servings: 4
Ingredients:
- 1 (3-to 4-pound) striped bass, gutted
- Salt and freshly ground black pepper
- 1 clove garlic, peeled
- 1 large sprig fresh rosemary
- 1 bay leaf
- Oil
- ¼ pound (1 stick) butter, melted and kept hot
- ¼ cup chopped fresh parsley
- Lemon wedges

Directions:
1. Prepare a charcoal fire. When white ash forms on top of coals, they are ready.
2. Meanwhile, prepare fish. Rub it inside and out with salt and pepper.
3. Cut garlic clove into slivers.
4. Using a sharp paring knife, make a few small incisions along backbone of fish.
5. Insert slivers of garlic.

6. Place rosemary sprig and bay leaf in cavity of fish. Tie fish in two or three places with string to secure cavity. Rub fish generously all over with oil. Place fish on hot grill and cook 10 to 15 minutes on one side, brushing occasionally with butter.
7. Using a pancake turner or spatula or both, loosen fish from grill and turn it to other side.
8. Cook 10 to 15 minutes on that side, or until fish is done and flesh flakes easily when tested with a fork. Cooking time will depend on size of fish, intensity of heat and how close fish is to coals.
9. Transfer fish to a hot platter and pour remaining butter over it. Sprinkle with parsley and garnish with lemon wedges.

Nutrition: Calories: 130 kCal Carbs: 5 g Protein: 79 g Fat 3g

288. Greek-Style Fish with Marinated Tomatoes

Preparation time: 10 minutes
Cooking time: 45 minutes
Servings: 4
Ingredients:
- 2 cups of your favorite Sun Gold cherry tomatoes, cut in half
- 4 tablespoons olive oil, or more as needed
- 2 tablespoons white wine vinegar
- 1 tablespoon chopped fresh hot peppers, such as jalapeño, or more to taste
- 1 fresh oregano cooker or 1 coffee stove
- 4 garlic cloves, sliced or more to taste
- Salt and freshly ground black pepper
- 1 large whole fish or 2 small fish (2 to 3 pounds in total), such as striped sea bass, redfish or trout; preferably butter and boneless, or simply emptied lemon sliced into noodles
- 4 to 6 sprigs of fresh thyme

Directions:
1. Prepare the grill; the heat should be medium to high and about 4 inches from the fire.
2. Join in tomatoes, 2 tablespoons olive oil, vinegar, mashed beans, oregano, steam garlic slices and a pinch of salt and pepper in a bowl; let them sit in the room temperature for 30 minutes.

3. Then make a sharp blade of three or four parallel bars on each side of the fish, approximately at the bottom. Season the fish with salt.
4. Also, pepper, at the time, stuffed with garlic residue, a layer of lemon slices, and thyme twigs. On the outside, coat the fish with the remaining 2 tablespoons of oil and sprinkle salt and pepper.
5. Bake until firm enough to rotate, 5 to 8 minutes. Turn and cook the other side 5 to 8 minutes. The fish is cooked when it is cold outside and the paddle is easy to pass through the meat.
6. Try the tomato mixture and change the spice, including more oil if needed. Serve fish garnished with tomatoes and their liquid.

Nutrition: Calories: 130 kCal Carbs: 5 g Protein: 79 g Fat 21g

289. Grilled Fish with Aromatics

Preparation time: 10 minutes
Cooking time: 50 minutes
Servings: 4
Ingredients:
- 4 (1 kilogram) salty guide, cod or snack or 1 (4 to 5 kilograms) salmon, cleaned upside down
- Vegetable oil for baking, scoops and baking.
- 6 tablespoons extra virgin olive oil
- 20 peeled garlic cloves
- 12 twigs of fresh thyme
- 12 sprigs of fresh rosemary
- 2 bay leaves
- Salt and pepper to taste

Directions:
1. Rinse and dry the fish. Make 3 or 4 shallow cuts through the skin of the fish,
2. It may expand during cooking. Refrigerate in cool until ready.
3. Kindle and light a fire on the outdoor grill.
4. Preheat the oven to 300 degrees.
5. When the coals are bright red and evenly dusted with ash, grill and allow to warm for 2 to 3 minutes. Grill well, using vegetable oil and paper toweling, being careful not to use so much oil that it will drip on coals and cause them to flame up.
6. Place the fish on the grill so that the steps below are perpendicular. Cook until fish has golden grill marks, about 3 minutes on each side. Using a

metal spatula, lightly brush the vegetable oil into one or two greased baking dishes, depending on the amount of fish you are preparing.

7. Put them in the oven and bake until they are opaque; it will be about 12 minutes for small fish, 20 to 25 minutes for large fish.
8. About 10 minutes before the end, pour the fish 6 tablespoons of olive oil into a baking pan or mold and place in the oven to warm slightly.
9. On a high heat, boil 2 cups of water at the bottom of the steam. Put the garlic cloves in the garlic, cover and simmer until they are almost soft, about 8 minutes.
10. Add the remaining herbs to the steamer in an even layer, cover and continue cooking for 3 minutes.
11. To serve, pour equal amounts of olive oil into the middle of hot dishes. If small fish are used, put them whole over the oil. If you are using large fish, such as salmon, remove the fillets and place the fillets of the same size in the oil.
12. Season to taste with thick salt and pepper.
13. Put the cooked herbs and garlic on one side of the plate and serve immediately.

Nutrition: Calories: 130 kCal Carbs: 5 g Protein: 79 g Fat 2g

290.   Baked Fresh Wild Sockeye Salmon

Preparation time: 10 minutes
Cooking time: 40 minutes
Servings: 4
Ingredients:
- 2 fresh wild sockeye salmon filets, skin on
- 2 teaspoons Seafood Seasoning
- ¾ teaspoon Old Bay seasoning

Directions:
1. Flush the salmon filets with cold water and pat them dry with a paper towel.
2. Delicately dust the filets with the seasonings.
3. On the wood pellet smoker-grill
4. Arrange the wood pellet smoker-grill for a non-direct cooking and preheat to 400°F utilizing any pellets.
5. Lay the salmon skin-side down on a Teflon-covered fiberglass tangle or directly on the grill grates.
6. Bake the salmon for 15/20 minutes, until the internal temperature arrives at 140°F and

additionally the substance chips effectively with a fork.
7. Rest the salmon for 5-6 minutes before serving.

Nutrition: Calories: 322 kCal Carbs: 2g Fat: 24g Protein: 24g

291.   Alder Creole Wild Pacific Rockfish

Preparation time: 10 minutes
Cooking time: 1 hours
Servings: 4
Ingredients:
- 4 to 8 (4 to 7-ounce) fresh, wild Pacific rockfish filets
- 3 teaspoons roasted garlic–seasoned extra-virgin olive oil
- 2 tablespoons Creole Seafood Seasoning or any Creole seasoning

Directions:
1. Rub the two sides of the filets with the olive oil.
2. Residue the two sides with the seasoning.
3. On the wood pellet smoker-grill
4. Design the wood pellet smoker-grill for a non-direct cooking and preheat to 225°F utilizing birch pellets.
5. Place the filets on a Teflon-coated fiberglass mat to keep them from adhering to the grill grates.
6. Smoke the filets for approximately an hour and a half, until they arrive at an internal temperature of 140°F or potentially the flesh flakes easily with a fork.

Nutrition: Calories: 322 kCal Carbs: 2g Fat: 24g Protein: 24g

292.   Alder Wood-Smoked Boned Trout

Preparation time: 10 minutes
Cooking time: 2 hours
Servings: 4
Ingredients:
- 4 fresh boned entire trout, skin on and pin bones removed
- 5 cups Salmon and Trout Brine

Directions:
1. Put the trout in a 2-liter plastic bag or on a brine rack. Place the bag on a shallow plate in case it spills and refrigerate for 2 hours, turning the trout on wheels to make sure it remains

submerged. In case of spillage, place the bag on a shallow plate

2. Air-dry the brined trout in the refrigerator, revealed, for 2 hours to enable the pellicle to frame.
3. On the wood pellet smoker-grill
4. Configure the wood pellet smoker-grill for a non-direct cooking. On the off chance that your grill has cold-smoking capabilities, at that point configure your pellet smoker-grill for cold-smoking.
5. Preheat the grill to 190°F utilizing alder pellets. A pit temperature of 190°F should result in a cold-smoke temperature of 70°F to 100°F in your smoker box, contingent upon the encompassing temperature.
6. Cold-smoke the trout for 90 minutes.
7. Following 90 minutes, move the cold-smoked boned trout to the wood pellet smoker-grill pit territory and increase the wood pellet smoker-grill temperature to 230°F.
8. Keep cooking the trout until the internal temperature of the trout at the thickest part arrives at 145°F.
9. Remove the trout from the grill and wait 5 minutes before serving.

Notes

- Search for boned trout in the fish department of your nearby supermarket, fish market, or even better, get your very own and remove every one of the bones yourself.
- Boned trout ought to be liberated from bones, yet consistently take care when eating fish.
- Cold-smoking happens at temperatures somewhere in the range of 70°F and 100°F.

Nutrition: Calories: 322 kCal Carbs: 2g Fat: 24g Protein: 24g

293. Garlic Salmon

Preparation time: 10 minutes
Cooking Time: 45 minutes
Servings: 3
Ingredients:

- 2 salmon fillets, 12 ounces each
- 1/3 cup olive oil
- 1 teaspoon of parsley
- 1 teaspoon of garlic powder
- 2 teaspoons of seafood rub

- 5 lemon wedges, for serving

Directions:

1. Preheat the grill on high until smoke established.
2. Line a baking sheet with parchment paper.
3. Put salmon on baking sheet skin side down.
4. Season the fillet with seafood rub.
5. Take a bowl, and combine olive oil, parsley, garlic and set it aside for further use.
6. Brush the salmon with the mixture and transfer it to the baking sheet
7. Cook it over the grill grate for 15 minutes until internal temperature reaches 140 degrees.
8. At the end brush with extra bowl mixture and serve with lemon wedges.

Nutrition: Calories: 322 kCal Carbs: 2g Fat: 24g Protein: 24g

294. Pineapple Maple Glaze Fish

Preparation time: 10 minutes
Cooking Time: 25 minutes
Servings: 3
Ingredients:

- 3 pounds of fresh salmon
- 1/4 cup maple syrup
- 1/2 cup pineapple juice

Brine Ingredients

- 3 cups of water
- Sea salt, to taste
- 2 cups of pineapple juice
- ½ cup of brown sugar
- 5 tablespoons of Worcestershire sauce
- 1 tablespoon of garlic salt

Directions:

1. Combine all the brine ingredients in a large cooking pan.
2. Place the fish into the brine and let it sit for 2 hours for marinating.
3. After 2 hours take out the fish and pat dry with a paper towel and set aside.
4. Preheat the smoker grill to 250 degrees Fahrenheit, until the smoke started to appear.
5. Put salmon on the grill and cook for 15 minutes.
6. Meanwhile, mix pineapple and maple syrup in a bowl and baste fish every 5 minutes.
7. Once the salmon is done, serve and enjoy.

Nutrition: Calories: 322 kCal Carbs: 2g Fat: 24g Protein: 24g

295. Smoked Catfish

Preparation time: 10 minutes
Cooking Time: 15 minutes
Servings: 3
Ingredients:
- 2 tablespoons paprika
- 1/4 teaspoon salt
- 1 tablespoon garlic powder
- 1 tablespoon onion powder
- 1/2 tablespoon dried thyme
- 1/2 tablespoon cayenne

Other Ingredients
- 2 pounds fresh catfish fillets
- 4 tablespoons butter, soften

Directions:
1. Take a mixing bowl, and combine all the rub ingredients in it, including the paprika, salt, garlic powder, onion powder, and thyme and cayenne paper.
2. Rub the fillet with the butter, and then sprinkle a generous amount of rub on top
3. Coat fish well with the rub.
4. Preheat the smoker grill at 200 degrees Fahrenheit for 15 minutes.
5. Cook fish on the grill for 10 minutes, 5minutes per side.
6. Once done, serve and enjoy.

Nutrition: Calories: 222 kCal Carbs: 2g Fat: 14g Protein: 25g

296. Classic Smoked Trout

Preparation time: 10 minutes
Cooking Time: 40 minutes
Servings: 3
Ingredients:
- 4 cups of water
- 1-2 cups dark-brown sugar
- 1 cup of sea salt

Ingredients for The Trout's
- 3 pounds of trout, backbone and pin bones removed
- 4 tablespoons of olive oil

Directions:
1. Preheat the electrical smoker grill, by setting the temperature to 250 degrees F, for 15 minutes by closing the lid.
2. Take a cooking pot, and combine all the brine ingredients, including water, sugar, and salt.

3. Submerged the fish in the brine mixture for a few hours.
4. Afterward, take out the fish, and pat dry with the paper towel.
5. Drizzle olive oil over the fish, and then place it over the grill grate for cooking.
6. Smoke the fish, until the internal temperature reaches 140 degrees Fahrenheit, for 1 hour.
7. Then serve.

Nutrition: Calories: 222 kCal Carbs: 2g Fat: 14g Protein: 25g

297. Smoked Sea Bass

Preparation Time: 10 minutes
Cooking Time: 40 minutes
Servings: 4
Ingredients:
Marinade
- 1 teaspoon Blackened Saskatchewan
- 1 tablespoon. Thyme, fresh
- 1 tablespoon Oregano, fresh
- 8 cloves of Garlic, crushed
- 1 lemon, the juice
- ¼ cup oil

Sea Bass
- 4 Sea bass fillets, skin off
- Chicken Rub Seasoning
- Seafood seasoning (like Old Bay)
- 8 tablespoons. Gold Butter

For garnish
- Thyme
- Lemon

Directions:
1. Make the marinade: In a ziplock bag combine the ingredients and mix. Add the fillets and marinate for 30 min in the fridge. Turn once.
2. Preheat the grill to 325F with closed lid.
3. In a dish for baking add the butter. Remove the fish from marinade and pour it in the baking dish. Season the fish with chicken and seafood rub. Place it in the baking dish and on the grill. Cook 30 minutes. Baste 1 - 2 times.
4. Remove from the grill when the internal temperature is 160F.
5. Garnish with lemon slices and thyme. Enjoy!

Nutrition: Calories: 220 kCal Protein: 32g Carbs: 1g Fat: 8g

298. Simple but Delicious Fish

Preparation Time: 45 minutes
Cooking Time: 10 minutes
Servings: 4 - 6
Ingredients:
- 4 lbs. fish, cut it into pieces (portion size)
- 1 tablespoon Minced Garlic
- 1/3 cup of Olive oil
- 1 cup of Soy Sauce
- Basil, chopped
- 2 Lemons, the juice

Directions:
1. Preheat the grill to 350F with closed lid.
2. Combine the ingredients in a bowl. Stir to combine. Marinade the fish for 45 min.
3. Grill the fish until it reaches 145F internal temperature.
4. Serve with your favorite side dish and enjoy!

Nutrition: Calories: 153 kCal Protein: 25g Carbs: 1g Fat: 4g

299. Baked Cod Au Gratin

Preparation Time: 24 minutes
Cooking Time: 16 minutes
Servings: 4
Ingredients:
- 400 grams of cod fillet
- 3 fennels
- 200 grams of béchamel
- 60 grams of grated Parmesan cheese
- Salt and pepper to taste
- Olive oil to taste

Directions:
1. Remove the beard and the hardest leaves from the fennel and then cut them into 4.
2. Cook them for 7 minutes in boiling salted water, then drain and set aside.
3. Wash and dry the cod fillets, remove skin and bones if present and then cut them into cubes of 3 cm each.
4. As soon as the fennels have cooled, cut them into slices.
5. Brush a baking dish with olive oil and then put the fennel on the bottom.
6. Put the cod on top and then sprinkle with salt and pepper.
7. Sprinkle with the béchamel and then spread over the parmesan.

8. Preheat the Pit Boss to 410 ° F for 15 minutes.
9. Place the grill and then put the pan with the fish on top.
10. Close the lid and cook for 15 minutes.
11. Just cooked, remove the fish from the barbecue and let it rest for 5 minutes.
12. Divide the fennel and fish in serving plates and serve.

Nutrition: Calories 120 kCal Fat 4 g Carbs 6 g Proteins 17 g

300. Crusted Salmon Fillet

Preparation Time: 39 minutes
Cooking Time: 24 minutes
Servings: 4
Ingredients:
- 1 roll of puff pastry
- 300 grams of zucchinis
- 450 grams of salmon fillet
- 8 black olives
- 15 grams of capers
- 20 grams of flaked almonds
- 6 mint leaves
- 3 sprigs of dill
- Salt and pepper to taste
- Olive oil to taste

Directions:
1. Start by preparing the zucchini. Wash and then cut them into thin slices.
2. Heat a drizzle of oil in a pan and then sauté the courgettes for 5 minutes. Season with salt and pepper and set aside.
3. Finely chop the olives and capers.
4. Wash and dry the mint and dill and then chop them.
5. Put all the chopped ingredients in a bowl and mix.
6. Now fillet the salmon, remove the bones, then wash, and dry it.
7. Sprinkle the salmon with salt and pepper and then sprinkle the top surface of the salmon with the chopped herbs and olives.
8. Unroll the sheet of puff pastry; arrange it so that the longest part is facing upright. Then lay the zucchini slices horizontally.
9. Put the almond slices on top and finally the salmon slices.

10. Now close the puff pastry by joining the two ends and then cut the top with a knife. Brush with olive oil.
11. Preheat the Pit Boss at 482 ° F for 15 minutes.
12. Put the pizza stone to heat for 10 minutes, then lay the puff pastry on top, and cook for 20 minutes.
13. After 20 minutes, check the cooking and if the crust is not yet golden enough, continue cooking for another 5 minutes.
14. Just cooked, remove the puff pastry from the barbecue and let it rest for 10 minutes.
15. After 10 minutes, cut the pastry with the sliced salmon, put on serving plates and serve.

Nutrition: Calories 183 kCal Fat 12 g Carbs 8 g Proteins 13 g

Chapter 5:   Vegan and Vegetarian Recipes

301.   Sweet Potato Fries

Preparation Time: 30 Minutes
Cooking Time: 40 Minutes
Servings: 4
Ingredients:
- Three sweet potatoes, sliced into strips
- Four tablespoons olive oil
- Two tablespoons fresh rosemary, chopped
- Salt and pepper to taste

Directions:
1. Set the Pit Boss wood pellet grill to 450 degrees F.
2. Preheat it for 10 minutes.
3. Spread the sweet potato strips in the baking pan.
4. Toss in olive oil and sprinkle with rosemary, salt, and pepper.
5. Cook for 15 minutes.
6. Flip and cook for another 15 minutes.
7. Flip and cook for ten more minutes.

Nutrition: Calories 69 kCal Fat 0.1g Carbs 16g Protein 1.7g

302.   Pit Boss Smoked Potatoes

Preparation Time: 30 minutes
Cooking Time: 1 hour
Servings: 6
Ingredients:
- 2 tbsp. butter
- 1/2 cup milk
- 1 cup heavy cream
- Two clove garlic, crushed and minced
- 2 tbsp. flour
- Four potatoes, sliced thinly
- Salt and pepper to taste
- 1 cup cheddar cheese, grated

Directions:
1. Preheat your wood pellet grill to 375 levels F for 15 minutes at the same time as the lid is closed.
2. Add butter to your forged iron pan.
3. In a bowl, blend the milk, cream, garlic, and flour.
4. Arrange some of the potatoes in a pan.
5. Season with salt and pepper.

6. Pour some of the sauce over the potatoes.
7. Repeat layers till elements were used.
8. Grill for 50 minutes.
9. Sprinkle cheese on top and prepare dinner for 10 minutes.

Nutrition: Calories: 176 kcal Protein: 2.78 g Fat: 12 g Carbs: 15.14 g

303.   Potato Fries with Chipotle Peppers

Preparation Time: 30 Minutes
Cooking Time: 30 Minutes
Servings: 4
Ingredients:
- Four potatoes, sliced into strips
- Three tablespoons olive oil
- Salt and pepper to taste
- 1 cup mayonnaise
- Two chipotle peppers in adobo sauce
- Two tablespoons lime juice

Directions:
1. Set the Pit Boss wood pellet grill to high.
2. Preheat it for 15 minutes while the lid is closed.
3. Coat the potato strips with oil.
4. Sprinkle with salt and pepper.
5. Put a baking pan on the grate.
6. Transfer potato strips to the pan.
7. Cook potatoes until crispy.
8. Mix the remaining ingredients.
9. Pulse in a food processor until pureed.
10. Serve potato fries with chipotle dip.

Nutrition: Calories 153 kCal Fat 7.6g Carbs 19.8g Protein 1.8g

304.   Pit Boss Grilled Zucchini

Preparation Time: 30 Minutes
Cooking Time: 10 Minutes
Servings: 4
Ingredients:
- Four zucchinis, sliced into strips
- One tablespoon sherry vinegar
- Two tablespoons olive oil
- Salt and pepper to taste
- Two fresh thymes, chopped

Directions:

1. Place the zucchini strips in a bowl.
2. Mix the remaining fixings and pour them into the zucchini.
3. Coat evenly.
4. Set the Pit Boss wood pellet grill to 350 degrees F.
5. Preheat for 15 minutes while the lid is closed.
6. Place the zucchini on the grill.
7. Cook for 3 minutes per side.

Nutrition: Calories 74 kCal Fat 5.6g Carbs 6g Protein 2.4g

305. Smoked Potato Salad

Preparation Time: 1 Hour and 15 Minutes
Cooking Time: 40 Minutes
Servings: 4
Ingredients:

- 2 lb. potatoes
- Two tablespoons olive oil
- 2 cups mayonnaise
- One tablespoon white wine vinegar
- One tablespoon dry mustard
- 1/2 onion, chopped
- Two celery stalks, chopped
- Salt and pepper to taste

Directions:

1. Coat the potatoes with oil.
2. Smoke the potatoes in the Pit Boss wood pellet grill at 180 degrees F for 20 minutes.
3. Increase temperature to 450 degrees F and cook for 20 more minutes.
4. Transfer to a bowl and let cool.
5. Peel potatoes.
6. Slice into cubes.
7. Refrigerate for 30 minutes.
8. Stir in the rest of the ingredients.

Nutrition: Calories 162 kCal Fat 1.6g Carbs 18.8g Protein 2.4g

306. Grilled Sweet Potato Planks

Preparation Time: 30 Minutes
Cooking Time: 30 Minutes
Servings: 8
Ingredients:

- Five sweet potatoes, sliced into planks
- One tablespoon olive oil
- One teaspoon onion powder

- Salt and pepper to taste

Directions:

1. Set the Pit Boss wood pellet grill to high.
2. Preheat it for 15 minutes while the lid is closed.
3. Coat the sweet potatoes with oil.
4. Sprinkle with onion powder, salt, and pepper.
5. Grill the sweet potatoes for 15 minutes.

Nutrition: Calories 118 kCal Fat 7.6g Carbs 10.8g Protein 5.4g

307. Roasted Veggies and Hummus

Preparation Time: 30 Minutes
Cooking Time: 20 Minutes
Servings: 4
Ingredients:

- One white onion, sliced into wedges
- 2 cups butternut squash
- 2 cups cauliflower, sliced into florets
- 1 cup mushroom buttons
- Olive oil
- Salt and pepper to taste
- Hummus

Directions:

1. Set the Pit Boss wood pellet grill to high.
2. Preheat it for 10 minutes while the lid is closed.
3. Add the veggies to a baking pan.
4. Roast for 20 minutes.
5. Serve roasted veggies with hummus.

Nutrition: Calories 160 Fat 10.7g Carbs 15.8g Protein 1.1g

308. Pit Boss Smoked Mushrooms

Preparation Time: 15 Minutes
Cooking Time: 45 Minutes
Servings: 2
Ingredients:

- 4 cups whole baby Portobello, cleaned
- 1 tbsp. canola oil
- 1 tbsp. onion powder
- 1 tbsp. garlic, granulated
- 1 tbsp. salt
- 1 tbsp. pepper

Directions:

1. Place all the ingredients in a bowl, mix, and combine.
2. Set your Pit Boss to 180oF.

3. Place the mushrooms on the grill directly and smoke for about 30 minutes.
4. Increase heat to high and cook the mushroom for another 15 minutes.
5. Serve warm and enjoy!

Nutrition: Calories 20 kCal Fat 30g Carbs 10.8g Protein 0g

309. Grilled Zucchini Squash Spears

Preparation Time: 5 Minutes
Cooking Time: 10 Minutes
Servings: 4
Ingredients:
- Four zucchinis, medium
- 2 tbsp. olive oil
- 1 tbsp. sherry vinegar
- Two thyme leaves pulled
- Salt to taste
- Pepper to taste

Directions:
1. Clean zucchini, cut ends off, half each lengthwise, and cut each half into thirds.
2. Combine all the other ingredients in a zip lock bag, medium, then add spears.
3. Toss well and mix to coat the zucchini.
4. Preheat Pit Boss to 350oF with the lid closed for 15 minutes.
5. Remove spears from the zip lock bag and place them directly on your grill grate with the cut side down.
6. Cook for about 3-4 minutes until zucchini is tender and grill marks show.
7. Remove them from the grill and enjoy.

Nutrition: Calories 93 Fat 7.4g Carbs 7.1g Protein 2.4g

310. Grilled Asparagus & Honey-Glazed Carrots

Preparation Time: 15 Minutes
Cooking Time: 35 Minutes
Servings: 4
Ingredients:
- One bunch asparagus, woody ends removed
- 2 tbsp. olive oil
- 1 lb. peeled carrots
- 2 tbsp. honey
- Sea salt to taste
- Lemon zest to taste

Directions:
1. Rinse the vegetables under cold water.
2. Splash the asparagus with oil and generously with a splash of salt.
3. Drizzle carrots generously with honey and splash lightly with salt.
4. Preheat your Pit Boss to 350oF with the lid closed for about 15 minutes.
5. Place the carrots first on the grill and cook for about 10-15 minutes.
6. Now place asparagus on the grill and cook both for about 15-20 minutes or until done to your liking.
7. Top with lemon zest and enjoy.

Nutrition: Calories 184 Total fat 7.3g Total carbs 28.6g Protein 6g

311. Pit Boss Grilled Vegetables

Preparation Time: 5 Minutes
Cooking Time: 15 Minutes
Servings: 12
Ingredients:
- One veggie tray
- 1/4 cup vegetable oil
- 1-2 tbsp. Pit Boss veggie seasoning

Directions:
1. Preheat your Pit Boss to 375oF.
2. Meanwhile, toss the veggies in oil placed on a sheet pan, large, then splash with the seasoning.
3. Place on the Pit Boss and grill for about 10-15 minutes.
4. Remove, serve, and enjoy.

Nutrition: Calories 44 Fat 5g Carbs 10.8g Protein 0g

312. Smoked Acorn Squash

Preparation Time: 10 Minutes
Cooking Time: 2 Hours
Servings: 6
Ingredients:

- Three acorn squashes, seeded and halved
- 3 tbsp. olive oil
- 1/4 cup butter, unsalted
- 1 tbsp. cinnamon, ground
- 1 tbsp. chili powder
- 1 tbsp. nutmeg, ground
- 1/4 cup brown sugar

Directions:

1. Brush the cut sides of your squash with olive oil, then cover with foil poking holes for smoke and steam to get through.
2. Preheat your Pit Boss to 225oF.
3. Place the squash halves on the grill with the cut side down and smoke for about 1½- 2 hours. Remove from the Pit Boss.
4. Let it sit while you prepare spiced butter. Melt butter in a saucepan, then adds spices and sugar, stirring to combine.
5. Remove the foil from the squash halves.
6. Place 1 tbsp. of the butter mixture onto each half.
7. Serve and enjoy!

Nutrition: Calories 149 Fat 10g Carbs 14g Protein 2g

313. Roasted Green Beans with Bacon

Preparation Time: 15 minutes
Cooking Time: 20 minutes
Servings: 6
Ingredients:

- 1-pound green beans
- 4 strips bacon, cut into small pieces
- 4 tablespoons extra virgin olive oil
- 2 cloves garlic, minced
- 1 teaspoon salt

Directions:

1. Fire the Pit Boss Grill to 4000F. Use desired wood pellets when cooking. Keep lid unopened and let it preheat for at most 15 minutes
2. Toss all ingredients on a sheet tray and spread out evenly.
3. Place the tray on the grill grate and roast for 20 minutes.

Nutrition: Cal: 65 kCal Fat: 5.3g Carbs: 3g Protein: 1.3 g

314. Smoked Watermelon

Preparation Time: 15 minutes
Cooking Time: 45-90 minutes
Servings: 5
Ingredients:

- 1 small seedless watermelon
- Balsamic vinegar
- Wooden skewers

Directions:

1. Slice ends of small seedless watermelons
2. Slice the watermelon in 1-inch cubes. Put the cubes in a container and drizzle vinegar on the cubes of watermelon.
3. Preheat the smoker to 225°F. Add wood chips and water to the smoker before starting preheating.
4. Place the cubes on the skewers.
5. Place the skewers on the smoker rack for 50 minutes.
6. Cook
7. Remove the skewers.
8. Serve!

Nutrition: Calories: 20 kCal Fat: 0 g Carbs: 4 g Protein: 1 g

315. Grilled Corn with Honey Butter

Preparation Time: 15 minutes
Cooking Time: 10 minutes
Servings: 6
Ingredients:

- 6 pieces corn, husked
- 2 tablespoons olive oil
- Salt and pepper to taste
- ½ cup butter, room temperature
- ½ cup honey

Directions:

1. Fire the Pit Boss Grill to 3500F. Use desired wood pellets when cooking. Keep lid unopened to preheat until 15 minutes
2. Coat corn with oil and add salt and pepper
3. Place the corn on the grill grate and cook for 10 minutes. Make sure to flip the corn halfway through the cooking time for even cooking.
4. Meanwhile, mix the butter and honey on a small bowl. Set aside.
5. Remove corn from grill and coat with honey butter sauce

Nutrition: Cal: 387 kCal Fat 21.6g Carbs 51.2g Protein 5g

316. Smoky Portobello Mushrooms

Preparation Time: 20 minutes
Cooking Time: 2 hours
Servings: 6
Ingredients:

- 6-12 large Portobello mushrooms
- Sea salt
- Black pepper
- Extra virgin olive oil
- Herbs de Provence

Directions:

1. Preheat the smoker to 200°F while adding water and wood chips to the smoker bowl and tray, respectively.
2. Wash and dry mushrooms
3. Rub the mushrooms with olive oil, salt and pepper seasoning with herbs in a bowl.
4. Place the mushrooms with the cap side down on the smoker rack. Smoke the mushrooms for 2 hours while adding water and wood chips to the smoker after every 60 minutes.
5. Remove the mushrooms and serve

Nutrition: Calories: 106 kCal Fat: 6 g Carbs: 5 g Protein: 8 g

317. Pit Boss Grilled Stuffed Zucchini

Preparation Time: 5 minutes
Cooking Time: 11 minutes
Servings: 8
Ingredients

- 4 zucchinis
- 5 tbsp olive oil
- 2 tbsp red onion, chopped
- 1/4 tbsp garlic, minced
- 1/2 cup bread crumbs
- 1/2 cup mozzarella cheese, shredded
- 1 tbsp fresh mint
- 1/2 tbsp salt
- 3 tbsp parmesan cheese

Directions:

1. Cut the zucchini lengthwise and scoop out the pulp then brush the shells with oil.
2. In a non-stick skillet sauté pulp, onion, and remaining oil. Add garlic and cook for a minute.
3. Add bread crumbs and cook until golden brown. Remove from heat and stir in mozzarella cheese, fresh mint, and salt.

4. Spoon the mixture into the shells and sprinkle parmesan cheese.
5. Place in a grill and grill for 10 minutes or until the zucchini are tender.

Nutrition: Calories 186 kCal, Fat 10g, Carbs 17g, Protein 9g

318. Smoked and Smashed New Potatoes

Preparation Time: 5 minutes
Cooking Time: 8 hours
Servings: 4
Ingredients:

- 1-1/2 pounds small new red potatoes or fingerlings
- Extra virgin olive oil
- Sea salt and black pepper
- 2 tbsp. softened butter

Directions:

1. Let the potatoes dry. Once dried, put in a pan and coat with salt, pepper, and extra virgin olive oil.
2. Place the potatoes on the topmost rack of the smoker.
3. Smoke for 60 minutes.
4. Once done, take them out and smash each one
5. Mix with butter and season

Nutrition: Calories: 258 kCal Fat: 2.0 g Carbs: 15.5 g Protein: 4.1 g

319. Grilled Corn with Honey and Butter

Preparation Time: 30 Minutes
Cooking Time: 10 Minutes
Servings: 4
Ingredients:

- Six pieces of corn
- Two tablespoons olive oil
- 1/2 cup butter
- 1/2 cup honey
- One tablespoon smoked salt
- Pepper to taste

Directions:

1. Preheat the wood pellet grill too high for 15 minutes while the lid is closed.
2. Brush the corn with oil and butter.
3. Grill the corn for 10 minutes, turning from time to time.
4. Mix honey and butter.

5. Brush corn with this mixture and sprinkle with smoked salt and pepper.

Nutrition: Calories 118 kCal Fat 7.6g Carbs 10.8g Protein 5.4g

320. Smoked Mushrooms

Preparation Time: 20 minutes
Cooking Time: 2 hours
Servings: 6
Ingredients:
- 6-12 large Portobello mushrooms
- Sea salt
- black pepper
- Extra virgin olive oil
- Herbs de Provence

Directions:
1. Preheat the smoker to 200°F while adding water and wood chips to the smoker bowl and tray, respectively.
2. Wash and dry mushrooms
3. Rub the mushrooms with olive oil, salt and pepper seasoning with herbs in a bowl.
4. Place the mushrooms with the cap side down on the smoker rack. Smoke the mushrooms for 2 hours while adding water and wood chips to the smoker after every 60 minutes.
5. Remove the mushrooms and serve

Nutrition: Calories: 106 kCal Fat: 6 g Carbs: 5 g Protein: 8 g

321. Smoked Cherry Tomatoes

Preparation Time: 20 minutes
Cooking Time: 1 ½ hours
Servings: 8-10
Ingredients:
- 2 pints of tomatoes

Directions:
1. Preheat the electric smoker to 225°F while adding wood chips and water to the smoker.
2. Clean the tomatoes with clean water and dry them off properly.
3. Place the tomatoes on the pan and place the pan in the smoker.
4. Smoke for 90 minutes while adding water and wood chips to the smoker.

Nutrition: Calories: 16 kCal Fat: 0 g Carbs: 3 g Protein: 1 g

322. Smoked Brussels Sprouts

Preparation Time: 15 minutes
Cooking Time: 45 minutes
Servings: 6
Ingredients:
- 1-1/2 pounds Brussels sprouts
- 2 cloves of garlic minced
- 2 tbsp extra virgin olive oil
- Sea salt and cracked black pepper

Directions:
1. Rinse sprouts
2. Remove the outer leaves and brown bottoms off the sprouts.
3. Place sprouts in a large bowl then coat with olive oil.
4. Add a coat of garlic, salt, and pepper and transfer them to the pan.
5. Add to the top rack of the smoker with water and woodchips.
6. Smoke for 45 minutes or until reaches 250°F temperature.
7. Serve

Nutrition: Calories: 84 kCal Fat: 4.9 g Carbs: 7.2 g Protein: 2.6 g

323. Apple Veggie Burger

Preparation Time: 10 minutes
Cooking Time: 35 minutes
Servings: 6
Ingredients:
- 3 tbsp ground flax or ground chia
- 1/3 cup of warm water
- 1/2 cups rolled oats
- 1 cup chickpeas, drained and rinsed
- 1 tsp cumin
- 1/2 cup onion
- 1 tsp dried basil
- 2 granny smith apples
- 1/3 cup parsley or cilantro, chopped
- 2 tbsp soy sauce
- 2 tsp liquid smoke
- 2 cloves garlic, minced
- 1 tsp chili powder
- 1/4 tsp black pepper

Directions:
1. Preheat the smoker to 225°F while adding wood chips and water to it.

2. In a separate bowl, add chickpeas and mash. Mix together the remaining ingredients along with the dipped flax seeds.
3. Form patties from this mixture.
4. Put the patties on the rack of the smoker and smoke them for 20 minutes on each side.
5. When brown, take them out, and serve.

Nutrition: Calories: 241 kCal Fat: 5 g Carbs: 40 g Protein: 9 g

324. Smoked Tofu

Preparation Time: 10 minutes
Cooking Time: 41 hour and 30 minutes
Servings: 4
Ingredients:
- 400g plain tofu
- Sesame oil

Directions:
1. Preheat the smoker to 225°F while adding wood chips and water to it.
2. Till that time, take the tofu out of the packet and let it rest
3. Slice the tofu in one-inch-thick pieces and apply sesame oil
4. Place the tofu inside the smoker for 45 minutes while adding water and wood chips after one hour.
5. Once cooked, take them out and serve!

Nutrition: Calories: 201 kCal Fat: 13 g Carbs: 1 g Protein: 20 g

325. Easy Smoked Vegetables

Preparation Time: 15 minutes
Cooking Time: 1 ½ hour
Servings: 6
Ingredients:
- 1 cup of pecan wood chips
- 1 ear fresh corn, silk strands removed, and husks, cut corn into 1-inch pieces
- 1 medium yellow squash, 1/2-inch slices
- 1 small red onion, thin wedges
- 1 small green bell pepper, 1-inch strips
- 1 small red bell pepper, 1-inch strips
- 1 small yellow bell pepper, 1-inch strips
- 1 cup mushrooms, halved
- 2 tbsp vegetable oil
- Vegetable seasonings

Directions:
1. Take a large bowl and toss all the vegetables together in it.
2. Sprinkle it with seasoning and coat all the vegetables well with it.
3. Place the wood chips and a bowl of water in the smoker.
4. Preheat the smoker at 100°F or ten minutes.
5. Put the vegetables in a pan and add to the middle rack of the electric smoker.
6. Smoke for thirty minutes until the vegetable becomes tender.
7. When done, serve, and enjoy.

Nutrition: Calories: 97 kCal Fat: 5 g Carbs: 11 g Protein: 2 g

326. Zucchini with Red Potatoes

Preparation Time: 15 minutes
Cooking Time: 4 hours
Servings: 4
Ingredients:
- 2 zucchinis, sliced in 3/4-inch-thick disks
- 1 red pepper, cut into strips
- 2 yellow squashes, sliced in 3/4-inch-thick disks
- 1 medium red onion, cut into wedges
- 6 small red potatoes, cut into chunks

Balsamic Vinaigrette:
- 1/3 cup extra virgin olive oil
- 1/4 teaspoon salt
- 1/4 cup balsamic vinegar
- 2 tsp Dijon mustard
- 1/8 teaspoon pepper

Directions:
1. For Vinaigrette: Take a medium-sized bowl and blend together olive oil, Dijon mustard, salt, pepper, and balsamic vinegar.
2. Place all the veggies into a large bowl and pour the vinaigrette mixture over it and evenly toss.
3. Put the vegetable in a pan and then smoke for 4 hours at a temperature of 225°F.
4. Serve and enjoy the food.

Nutrition: Calories: 381 kCal Fat: 17.6 g Carbs: 49 g Protein: 6.7 g

327. Shiitake Smoked Mushrooms

Preparation Time: 15 minutes
Cooking Time: 45 minutes
Servings: 4-6
Ingredients:

- 4 Cup Shiitake Mushrooms
- 1 tbsp canola oil
- 1 tsp onion powder
- 1 tsp granulated garlic
- 1 tsp salt
- 1 tsp pepper

Directions:

1. Combine all the ingredients together
2. Apply the mix over the mushrooms generously.
3. Preheat the smoker at 180°F. Add wood chips and half a bowl of water in the side tray.
4. Place it in the smoker and smoke for 45 minutes.
5. Serve warm and enjoy.

Nutrition: Calories: 301 kCal Fat: 9 g Carbs: 47.8 g Protein: 7.1 g

328. Garlic and Herb Smoke Potato

Preparation Time: 5 minutes
Cooking Time: 2 hours
Servings: 6
Ingredients:

- 1.5 pounds bag of Gemstone Potatoes
- 1/4 cup Parmesan, fresh grated

For the Marinade

- 2 tbsp olive oil
- 6 garlic cloves, freshly chopped
- 1/2 tsp dried oregano
- 1/2 tsp dried basil
- 1/2 tsp dried dill
- 1/2 tsp salt
- 1/2 tsp dried Italian seasoning
- 1/4 tsp ground pepper

Directions:

1. Preheat the smoker to 225°F.
2. Wash the potatoes thoroughly and add them to a sealable plastic bag.
3. Add garlic cloves, basil, salt, Italian seasoning, dill, oregano, and olive oil to the zip lock bag. Shake.
4. Place in the fridge for 2 hours to marinate.

5. Next, take an Aluminum foil and put 2 tbsp of water along with the coated potatoes. Fold the foil so that the potatoes are sealed in
6. Place in the preheated smoker.
7. Smoke for 2 hours
8. Remove the foil and pour the potatoes into a bowl.
9. Serve with grated Parmesan cheese.

Nutrition: Calories: 146 kCal Fat: 6 g Carbs: 19 g Protein: 4 g

329. Smoked Baked Beans

Preparation Time: 15 minutes
Cooking Time: 3 hours
Servings: 12
Ingredients:

- 1 medium yellow onion diced
- 3 jalapenos
- 56 oz pork and beans
- 3/4 cup barbeque sauce
- 1/2 cup dark brown sugar
- 1/4 cup apple cider vinegar
- 2 tbsp Dijon mustard
- 2 tbsp molasses

Directions:

1. Preheat the smoker to 250°F.
2. Pour the beans along with all the liquid in a pan. Add brown sugar, barbeque sauce, Dijon mustard, apple cider vinegar, and molasses.
3. Stir
4. Place the pan on one of the racks.
5. Smoke for 3 hours until thickened
6. Remove after 3 hours
7. Serve

Nutrition: Calories: 214 kCal Fat: 2 g Carbs: 42 g Protein: 7 g

330. Corn & Cheese Chile Rellenos

Preparation time: 30 minutes
Cooking time: 65 minutes
Servings: 8-12
Ingredients:

- Pellet: hardwood, maple
- 2 lbs. Ripe tomatoes, chopped
- Four cloves' garlic, chopped
- 1/2 cup sweet onion, chopped
- One jalapeno stemmed, seeded, and chopped
- Eight large green new Mexican or poblano chiles
- Three ears sweet corn, husked
- 1/2 tsp. Dry oregano, Mexican, crumbled
- 1 tsp. ground cumin
- 1 tsp. Mild Chile powder
- 1/8 tsp. Ground cinnamon
- Salt and freshly ground pepper
- 3 cups grated Monterey jack
- 1/2 cup Mexican crema
- 1 cup queso fresco, crumbled
- Fresh cilantro leaves

Directions:

1. Place the tomatoes, garlic, onions and jalapeno in a shallow baking dish and place it on the grill grate before starting. This vegetable will expose more wood smoke.
2. When prepared to cook, start the grill on Smoke with the lid open until the fire is established (4 to 5 minutes).
3. Mix the cooled tomato mixture in a blender and liquefy. Put in a pot.
4. Stir in the cumin, oregano, some chile powder, cinnamon, and some salt and pepper to taste.
5. Carefully peel the New Mexican chiles' blistered outer skin: Leave the stem ends intact and try not to tear the flesh.
6. Cut the corn off the cobs and put it in a large mixing bowl.
7. Bake or cook the Rellenos for 25 to 30 minutes or until the filling is bubbling and the cheese has melted.
8. Sprinkle with queso fresco and garnish it with fresh cilantro leaves, if desired. Enjoy!

Nutrition: Calories: 206 kCal Carbs: 5g Fat: 14g Protein: 9g

331. Roasted Tomatoes with Hot Pepper Sauce

Preparation time: 20 minutes
Cooking time: 90 minutes
Servings: 4-6
Ingredients:

- Pellet: hardwood, alder
- 2 lbs. roman fresh tomatoes
- 3 tbsps. parsley, chopped
- 2 tbsps. garlic, chopped
- Black pepper, to taste
- 1/2 cup olive oil
- Hot pepper, to taste
- 1 lb. spaghetti or other pasta

Directions:

1. Prepare and ready to cook, set the temperature to 400degrees F and preheat, lid closed for 15 minutes
2. Rinse with water the tomatoes and cut them in half, length width and then place them in a baking dish cut side up.
3. Sprinkle with chopped parsley, garlic, then add salt and black pepper, and then pour 1/4 cup of olive oil over them.
4. Place on pre-heated and bake for 1 1/2 hours and then tomatoes will shrink, and the skins will be partly blackened.
5. Take the tomatoes from the baking dish and place them in a food processor, leaving the cooking oil and puree them.
6. Put the pasta into boiling salted water and cook until tender. Then drain and mix immediately with the pureed tomatoes.
7. Add the remaining 1/4 cup of raw olive oil and crumbled hot red pepper to taste. Toss and serve. Enjoy!

Nutrition: Calories: 111 kCal Carbs: 5g Fat: 11g Protein: 1g

332. Grilled Fingerling Potato Salad

Preparation time: 15 minutes
Cooking time: 15 minutes
Servings: 6-8
Ingredients:

- Pellet: hardwood, pecan
- 1-1/2 lbs. Fingerling potatoes cut in half lengthwise
- Ten scallions
- 2/3 cup Evo (extra virgin olive oil), divided use
- 2 tbsps. rice vinegar
- 2 tsp. lemon juice
- One small jalapeno, sliced
- 2 tsp. kosher salt

Directions:

1. Prepare and ready to cook, turn temperature to High and preheat, lid closed for 15 minutes.
2. Brush the spring onions with the oil and place them on the grill. Cook for about 2-3 minutes until they are slightly charred. Remove and let cool. Once the spring onions have cooled, slice them and set aside.
3. Brush the Fingerlings with oil (reserving 1/3 cup for later use), then salt and pepper. Place cut side down on the grill cooked through, about 4-5 minutes.
4. In a bowl, mix the remaining 1/3 cup of olive oil, rice vinegar, salt, and lemon juice, then mix the green onions, potatoes and slices jalapeno.
5. Season with salt and pepper and serve. Enjoy!

Nutrition: Calories: 270 kCal Carbs: 18g Fat: 18g Protein: 3g

333. Smoked Jalapeño Poppers

Preparation time: 15 minutes
Cooking time: 60 minutes
Servings: 4-6
Ingredients:

- Pellet: hardwood, mesquite
- 12 medium jalapeños
- Six slices bacon, cut in half
- 8 oz. cream cheese, softened
- 1 cup cheese, grated
- 2 tbsps. pork & poultry rub

Directions:

1. Prepare and ready to cook, turn temperature up to 180 degrees F and preheat, lid closed for 15 minutes.

2. Cut jalapeños in half lengthwise. Remove the seeds and ribs.
3. Combine softened cream cheese with Pork & Poultry rub and grated cheese.
4. Divide the mixture over each jalapeño half. Wrap in bacon and secure with a toothpick.
5. Put the jalapeños on a rimmed baking sheet. Place on the grill and smoke for 30 minutes.
6. Increase the temperature of the grill to 375 encores and cook for another 30 minutes or until the bacon is cooked to the desired doneness. Serve hot, enjoy!

Nutrition: Calories: 280 kCal Carbs: 24g Fat: 19g Protein: 4g

334. Grilled Veggie Sandwich

Preparation time: 30 minutes
Cooking time: 30 minutes
Servings: 4-6
Ingredients:

- Pellet: hardwood, pecan
- Smoked hummus
- 1-1/2 cups chickpeas
- 1/3 cup tahini
- 1 tbsp. minced garlic
- 2 tbsps. olive oil
- 1 tsp. kosher salt
- 4 tbsps. lemon juice
- Grilled veggie sandwich
- One small eggplant, sliced into strips
- One small zucchini, cut into strips
- One small yellow squash, sliced into strips
- Two large Portobello mushrooms
- Olive oil
- Salt and pepper to taste
- Two heirloom tomatoes, sliced
- One bunch of basil leaves pulled
- Four ciabatta buns
- 1/2 cup ricotta
- Juice of 1 lemon
- One garlic clove minced
- Salt and pepper to taste

Directions:

1. Ready to cook, turn temperature to 180 degrees F and preheat, lid closed for 15 minutes.
2. In a prepared bowl of a food processor, combine the smoked chickpeas, tahini, garlic, olive oil,

salt and lemon juice and blend until smooth but not completely smooth. Transfer to a bowl and reserve.
3. Increase grill temp to high (400-500 degrees F).
4. While the vegetables are cooking, mix the ricotta, the lemon juice, garlic, salt and some pepper.
5. Cut the ciabatta buns in half and then open them up—spread the hummus on one side and ricotta on the other. Stack the grilled veggies and top with tomatoes and basil. Enjoy!

Nutrition: Calories: 376 kCal Carbs: 57g Fat: 16g Protein: 10g

335. Smoked Healthy Cabbage

Preparation time: 10 minutes
Cooking time: 2 hours
Servings: 5
Ingredients:
- Pellet: maple pellets
- One head cabbage, cored
- 4 tbsp. butter
- 2 tbsp. rendered bacon fat
- One chicken bouillon cube
- 1 tsp. fresh ground black pepper
- One garlic clove, minced

Directions:
1. Pre-heat your smoker to 240 degrees Fahrenheit using your preferred wood
2. Fill the hole of your cored cabbage with butter, bouillon cube, bacon fat, pepper, and garlic
3. Wrap the cabbage in foil about two-thirds of the way up
4. Make sure to leave the top open
5. Transfer to your smoker rack and smoke for 2 hours
6. Unwrap and enjoy!

Nutrition: Calories: 231 kCal Fats: 10g Carbs: 26g Protein: 1.4g

336. Garlic and Rosemary Potato Wedges

Preparation time: 15 minutes
Cooking time: 1 hour 30 minutes
Servings: 4
Ingredients:
- Pellet: maple pellets
- 4-6 large russet potatoes, cut into wedges

- ¼ cup olive oil
- Two garlic cloves, minced
- 2 tbsp. rosemary leaves, chopped
- 2 tsp. salt
- 1 tsp. fresh ground black pepper
- 1 tsp. sugar
- 1 tsp. onion powder

Directions:
1. Pre-heat your smoker to 250 degrees Fahrenheit using maple wood
2. Take a large bowl and add potatoes and olive oil
3. Toss well
4. Take another small bowl and stir garlic, salt, rosemary, pepper, sugar, onion powder
5. Sprinkle the mix on all sides of the potato wedge
6. Transfer the seasoned wedge to your smoker rack and smoke for one and a ½ hours
7. Serve and enjoy!

Nutrition: Calories: 291 kCal Fats: 10g Carbs: 46g Protein: 2g

337. Smoked Tomato and Mozzarella Dip

Preparation time: 5 minutes
Cooking time: 1 hour
Servings: 4
Ingredients:
- Pellet: mesquite
- 8 ounces smoked mozzarella cheese, shredded
- 8 ounces Colby cheese, shredded
- ½ cup parmesan cheese, grated
- 1 cup sour cream
- 1 cup sun-dried tomatoes
- 1 and ½ tsp. salt
- 1 tsp. fresh ground pepper
- 1 tsp. dried basil
- 1 tsp. dried oregano
- 1 tsp. red pepper flakes
- One garlic clove, minced
- ½ teaspoon onion powder
- French toast, serving

Directions:
1. Pre-heat your smoker to 275 degrees Fahrenheit using your preferred wood
2. Take a large bowl and stir in the cheeses, tomatoes, pepper, salt, basil, oregano, red pepper flakes, garlic, and onion powder and mix well

3. Transfer the mix to a small metal pan and transfer to a smoker
4. Smoke for 1 hour
5. Serve with toasted French Bread Enjoy!

Nutrition: Calories: 174 Fats: 11g Carbs: 15g Protein: 9g

338. Feisty Roasted Cauliflower

Preparation time: 15 minutes
Cooking time: 10 minutes
Servings: 4
Ingredients:
- Pellet: maple
- One cauliflower head, cut into florets
- 1 tbsp. oil
- 1 cup parmesan, grated
- Two garlic cloves, crushed
- ½ teaspoon pepper
- ½ teaspoon salt
- ¼ teaspoon paprika

Directions:
1. Pre-heat your Smoker to 180 degrees F
2. Transfer florets to smoker and smoke for 1 hour
3. Take a bowl and add all ingredients except cheese
4. Once smoking is done, remove florets
5. Increase temperature to 450 degrees F, brush florets with the brush, and transfer to grill
6. Smoke for 10 minutes more
7. Sprinkle cheese on top and let them sit (Lid closed) until cheese melts
8. Serve and enjoy!

Nutrition: Calories: 45 Fats: 2g Carbs: 7g Protein: 2.5g

339. Savory Applesauce on the Grill

Preparation Time: 0 minutes
Cooking Time: 45 minutes
Servings: 2
Ingredients:
- 1½ pounds whole apples
- Salt

Directions:
1. Start the coals or turn a gas grill for medium direct cooking. Just make sure the grates are clean.
2. Put the apples on the grill directly over the fire. Close the lid and cook until the fruit feels soft when gently squeezed with tongs, 10 to 20

minutes total, depending on their size. Move to a cutting board and then let sit until cool enough to touch.
3. Cut the flesh from around the core of each apple; discard the cores. Put the chunks in a blender or food processor and process until smooth, or put them in a bowl and purée with an immersion blender until as chunky or smooth as you like. Add some salt and then taste adjusts the seasoning. Serve or refrigerate in a container for up to 3 days.

Nutrition: Calories: 15 kCal Fat: 0 g Carbs: 3 g Proteins: 0 g

340. Avocado with Lemon

Preparation Time: 5 minutes
Cooking Time: 20 minutes
Servings: 4
Ingredients:
- Two ripe avocados
- Good-quality olive oil for brushing
- One lemon halved
- Salt and pepper

Directions:
1. Start the coals or turn a gas grill for medium direct cooking. Just make sure the grates are clean.
2. Cut the avocados in half lengthwise. Carefully strike a chef's knife into the pit, then wiggle it a bit to lift and remove it. Insert a spoon underneath the flesh against the skin and run it all the way around to separate the entire half of the avocado. Repeat with the other avocado. Brush with oil, and then squeeze one of the lemon halves over them thoroughly on both sides so they don't discolor. Cut the lemon half into four wedges.
3. Put the avocados on the grill directly over the fire, cut side down. Cover with lid and cook, turning once, until browned in places, 5 to 10 minutes total. Serve the halved avocados as is, or slice and fan them for a prettier presentation. Sprinkle with salt and pepper and garnish with the lemon wedges.

Nutrition: Calories: 50.3 kCal Fat: 4.6 g Carbs: 2.8 g Proteins: 0.6 g

341. Simplest Grilled Asparagus

Preparation Time: 0 minutes
Cooking Time: 25 minutes
Servings: 4
Ingredients:

- 1½–2 pounds asparagus
- 1–2 tablespoons good-quality olive oil or melted butter
- Salt

Directions:

1. Start the coals or turn the heat of a gas grill for direct hot cooking. Make sure the grates are clean.
2. Cut the tough bottoms from the asparagus. If they're thick, trim the ends with a vegetable peeler. Mix with the oil and then sprinkle with salt.
3. Put the asparagus on the grill directly over the fire, perpendicular to the grates, so they don't fall through. Cover with the lid and cook, turning once, until the thick part of the stalks can barely be pierced with a skewer or thin knife, 5 to 10 minutes total. Transfer to a platter and serve.

Nutrition: Calories: 225 kCal Fat: 20.6 g Carbs: 9.1 g Proteins: 4.6 g

342. Beets and Greens with Lemon-Dill Vinaigrette

Preparation Time: 0 minutes
Cooking Time: 1 hour
Servings: 4
Ingredients:

- 1½ pounds small beets, with fresh-looking greens still attached if possible
- ½ cup plus 2 tbsp. good-quality olive oil
- Salt and pepper
- 3 tbsp. fresh lemon juice
- 2 tbsp. minced fresh dill

Directions:

1. Start the coals or turn a gas grill for medium to medium-low direct cooking. Make sure the grates are clean.
2. Cut the greens off the beets. Throw away any wilted or discolored leaves; rinse the remainder thoroughly to remove any grit and drain. Trim the root ends of the beets and scrub well under running water. Pat the leaves and beets dry.

Toss the beets with two tablespoons of oil and a sprinkle of salt until evenly coated.

3. Put the beets on the grill directly over the fire. (No need to wash the bowl.) Close the lid and cook, turning them every 5 to 10 minutes, until a knife inserted in the center goes through with no resistance, 30 to 40 minutes total. Transfer to a plate and then let sit until cool enough to handle.
4. Toss the beet greens in the reserved bowl to coat in oil. Put them on the grill directly over the fire. Close the lid and cook, tossing once or twice, until they're bright green and browned in spots, 2 to 5 minutes total. Take a look; if they're on too long, they'll crisp up to the point where they'll shatter. Transfer to a plate.
5. Put the remaining ½ cup oil and the lemon juice in a serving bowl and whisk until thickened. Stir in the dill and some salt and pepper. Peel off the skin from the beets and cut into halves or quarters. Cut the stems from the leaves in 1-inch lengths; cut the leaves across into ribbons. Put the beets, leaves, and stems in the bowl and toss with the vinaigrette until coated. Serve warm or at room temperature. Or makeup to several hours ahead, covers, and refrigerates to serve chilled.

Nutrition: Calories: 73 kCal Fat: 3.8 g Carbs: 9.6 g Proteins: 2.2 g

343. Baby Bok Choy with Lime-Miso Vinaigrette

Preparation Time: 10 minutes
Cooking Time: 25 minutes
Servings: 4
Ingredients:

- ¼ cup good-quality vegetable oil
- Grated zest of 1 lime
- 2 tbsp. fresh lime juice
- 2 tbsp. white or light miso
- 1 tbsp. rice vinegar
- Salt and pepper
- 1½ pounds baby bok choy

Directions:

1. Start the coals or turn a gas grill for medium direct cooking. Make sure the grates are clean.
2. Whisk together the oil, lime zest and juice, miso and vinegar in a small bowl until combined and

thickened. Taste and adjust the seasoning with salt and pepper.

3. Trim the bottoms from the bok choy and cut them into halves or quarters as needed. Pour half of the vinaigrette into a baking dish. Add the bok choy and twist in the vinaigrette until completely coated.

4. Put the bok choy on the grill directly over the fire. Close the lid and cook, turning once, until the leaves brown, and you can insert a knife through the core with no resistance, 5 to 10 minutes per side, depending on their size. Transfer to a platter; drizzle with the reserved vinaigrette and serve warm or at room temperature.

Nutrition: Calories: 209.7 kCal Fats: 9.4 g Carbs: 25.9 g Proteins: 10.1 g

344. Grilled Carrots

Preparation Time: 5 minutes
Cooking Time: 20 minutes
Servings: 6
Ingredients:
- 1 lb. carrots, large
- 1/2 tbsp. salt
- 6 oz. butter
- 1/2 tbsps. black pepper
- Fresh thyme

Directions:
1. Thoroughly wash the carrots and do not peel. Pat them dry and coat with olive oil.
2. Add salt to your carrots.
3. Meanwhile, preheat a pellet grill to 350oF.
4. Now place your carrots directly on the grill or on a raised rack.
5. Close and cook for about 20 minutes.
6. While carrots cook, cook butter in a saucepan, small, over medium heat until browned. Stir frequently to avoid burning. Remove from heat.
7. Remove carrots from the grill onto a plate, and then drizzle with browned butter.
8. Add pepper and splash with thyme.
9. Serve and enjoy.

Nutrition: Calories: 250 kCal Fat: 25 g Carbs: 64g Protein: 1 g

345. Grilled Brussels Sprouts

Preparation Time: 15 minutes
Cooking Time: 20 minutes
Servings: 8
Ingredients:
- 1/2 lb. bacon, grease reserved
- 1 lb. Brussels Sprouts
- 1/2 tbsp. pepper
- 1/2 tbsp. salt

Directions:
1. Cook bacon until crispy on a stovetop, reserve its grease, and then chop into small pieces.
2. Meanwhile, wash the Brussels sprouts, trim off the dry end and remove dried leaves, if any. Half them and set aside.
3. Place 1/4 cup reserved grease in a pan, cast-iron, over medium-high heat.
4. Season the Brussels sprouts with pepper and salt.
5. Brown the sprouts on the pan with the cut side down for about 3-4 minutes.
6. In the meantime, preheat your pellet grill to 350-375oF.
7. Place bacon pieces and browned sprouts into your grill-safe pan.
8. Cook for about 20 minutes.
9. Serve immediately.

Nutrition: Calories: 153 kCal Fat: 10 g Carbs: 5 g Protein: 11 g

346. Smoked Deviled Eggs

Preparation Time: 15 minutes
Cooking Time: 30 minutes
Servings: 5
Ingredients:
- 7 hard-boiled eggs, peeled
- 3 tbsp mayonnaise
- 3 tbsp chives, diced
- 1 tbsp brown mustard
- 1 tbsp apple cider vinegar
- Dash of hot sauce
- Salt and pepper
- 2 tbsp cooked bacon, crumbled
- Paprika to taste

Directions:
1. Preheat the Pit Boss to 180°F for 15 minutes with the lid closed.

2. Place the eggs on the grill grate and smoke the eggs for 30 minutes. Remove the eggs from the grill and let cool.
3. Half the eggs and scoop the egg yolks into a zip lock bag.
4. Add all other ingredients in the zip lock bag except bacon and paprika. Mix until smooth.
5. Pipe the mixture into the egg whites then top with bacon and paprika.
6. Let rest then serve and enjoy.

Nutrition: Calories 140 kCal , Fat 12g, Carbs 1g, Protein 6g

347. Grilled Potato Salad

Preparation Time: 15 minutes
Cooking Time: 10 minutes
Servings: 8
Ingredients:
- 1 ½ pound fingerling potatoes, halved lengthwise
- 1 small jalapeno, sliced
- 10 scallions
- 2 teaspoons salt
- 2 tablespoons rice vinegar
- 2 teaspoons lemon juice
- 2/3 cup olive oil, divided

Directions:
1. Switch on the Pit Boss grill, fill the grill hopper with pecan flavored Pit Bosss, power the grill on by using the control panel, select 'smoke' on the temperature dial, or set the temperature to 450 degrees F and let it preheat for a minimum of 5 minutes.
2. Meanwhile, prepare scallions, and for this, brush them with some oil.
3. When the grill has preheated, open the lid, place scallions on the grill grate, shut the grill and smoke for 3 minutes until lightly charred.
4. Then transfer scallions to a cutting board, let them cool for 5 minutes, then cut into slices and set aside until required.
5. Brush potatoes with some oil, season with some salt and black pepper, place potatoes on the grill grate, shut the grill and smoke for 5 minutes until thoroughly cooked.
6. Then take a large bowl, pour in remaining oil, add salt, lemon juice, and vinegar and stir until combined.

7. Add grilled scallion and potatoes, toss until well mixed, taste to adjust seasoning and then serve.

Nutrition: Calories: 223.7 kCal Fat: 12 g Carbs: 27 g Protein: 1.9 g

348. Cauliflower with Parmesan and Butter

Preparation Time: 15 minutes
Cooking Time: 45 minutes
Servings: 4
Ingredients:
- 1 medium head of cauliflower
- 1 teaspoon minced garlic
- 1 teaspoon salt
- ½ teaspoon ground black pepper
- 1/4 cup olive oil
- 1/2 cup melted butter, unsalted
- 1/2 tablespoon chopped parsley
- 1/4 cup shredded parmesan cheese

Directions:
1. Switch on the Pit Boss grill, fill the grill hopper with flavored Pit Bosss, power the grill on by using the control panel, select 'smoke' on the temperature dial, or set the temperature to 450 degrees F and let it preheat for a minimum of 15 minutes.
2. Meanwhile, brush the cauliflower head with oil, season with salt and black pepper and then place in a skillet pan.
3. When the grill has preheated, open the lid, place prepared skillet pan on the grill grate, shut the grill and smoke for 45 minutes until golden brown and the center has turned tender.
4. Meanwhile, take a small bowl, place melted butter in it, and then stir in garlic, parsley, and cheese until combined.
5. Baste cheese mixture frequently in the last 20 minutes of cooking and, when done, remove the pan from heat and garnish cauliflower with parsley.
6. Cut it into slices and then serve.

Nutrition: Calories: 128 kCal Fat: 7.6 g Carbs: 10.8 g Protein: 7.4 g

349. Smoked Cauliflower

Preparation Time: 15 Minutes
Cooking Time: 10 Minutes
Servings: 3-4
Ingredients:
- 1 Head of cauliflower
- 1 Cup of parmesan cheese
- 1 Tablespoon of olive oil
- 2 Crushed garlic cloves
- ¼ Teaspoon of Paprika
- ½ Teaspoon of salt
- ½ Teaspoon of pepper

Directions:
1. Start your Pit Boss smoker grill with the lid open for about 4 to 5 minutes
2. Set the temperature on about 180°F and preheat with the lid closed for about 10 to 15 minutes
3. Cut the cauliflower into florets of medium-sized; then place the cauliflower right on top of the grate and mix all the ingredients except for the cheese
4. After about 1 hour, remove the cauliflower; then turn the smoker grill on high for about 10 to 15 minutes
5. Brush the cauliflower with the mixture of the ingredients and place it on a sheet tray
6. Place the cauliflower back on the grate for about 10 minutes
7. Sprinkle with the parmesan cheese
8. Serve and enjoy your smoked cauliflower!

Nutrition: Calories: 60 kCal Fat: 3.6g Carbs: 3.1g Protein: 4g

350. Garlic Parmesan Wedges

Preparation Time: 15 minutes
Cooking Time: 45 minutes
Servings: 6
Ingredients:
- 3 large russet potatoes
- ¼ cup extra-virgin olive oil
- 1½ teaspoons salt
- ¾ teaspoon black pepper
- 2 teaspoons garlic powder
- ¾ cup grated Parmesan cheese
- 3 tablespoons chopped fresh cilantro or flat-leaf parsley (optional)

- ½ cup blue cheese or ranch dressing per serving, for dipping (optional)

Directions:
1. Gently scrub the potatoes with cold water using a vegetable brush and allow the potatoes to dry.
2. Cut the potatoes lengthwise in half, then cut those halves into thirds.
3. Use a paper towel to wipe away all the moisture that is released when you cut the potatoes. Moisture prevents the wedges from getting crispy.
4. Place the potato wedges, olive oil, salt, pepper, and garlic powder in a large bowl, and toss lightly with your hands, making sure the oil and spices are distributed evenly.
5. Arrange the wedges in a single layer on a nonstick grilling tray/pan/basket (about 15 × 12 inches).
6. Configure your Pit Boss smoker-grill for indirect cooking and preheat to 425°F using any type of Pit Boss.
7. Place the grilling tray in your preheated smoker-grill and roast the potato wedges for 15 minutes before turning. Roast the potato wedges for an additional 15 to 20 minutes until potatoes are fork tender on the inside and crispy golden brown on the outside.
8. Sprinkle the potato wedges with Parmesan cheese and garnish with cilantro or parsley, if desired. Serve with blue cheese or ranch dressing for dipping, if desired.

Nutrition: Calories: 324 kCal Fat: 11.6g Protein: 8.6g Carbs: 34g

351. Baked Parmesan Mushrooms

Preparation Time: 15 Minutes
Cooking Time: 15 Minutes
Servings: 8
Ingredients:
- Eight mushroom caps
- 1/2 cup Parmesan cheese, grated
- 1/2 teaspoon garlic salt
- 1/4 cup mayonnaise
- Pinch paprika
- Hot sauce

Directions:
1. Place mushroom caps in a baking pan.
2. Mix the remaining ingredients in a bowl.

3. Scoop the mixture onto the mushroom.
4. Place the baking pan on the grill.
5. Cook in the Pit Boss wood pellet grill at 350 degrees F for 15 minutes while the lid is closed.

Nutrition: Calories 118 kCal Fat 7.6g Carbs 10.8g Protein 5.4g

Chapter 6:   Snacks and Appetizers

352.   Pit Boss Bacon-Wrap Asparagus

Preparation Time: 10 minutes
Cooking Time: 25 to 30 minutes
Servings: 3
Ingredients:
- 1-pound fresh thick asparagus (15 to 20 spears)
- extra-virgin olive oil
- 5 slices thinly sliced bacon
- 1 teaspoon Pete's Western Rub (page 169) or salt and pepper

Directions:
1. Snap off the woody ends of asparagus and trim so they are all about the same length.
2. Divide the asparagus into bundles of 3 spears and spritz with olive oil. Wrap each bundle with 1 piece of bacon and then dust with the seasoning or salt and pepper to taste.
3. Configure your Pit Boss smoker-grill for indirect cooking, placing Teflon coated fiberglass mats on top of the grates (to prevent the asparagus from sticking to the grill grates). Preheat to 400°F using any type of Pit Bosss. The grill can be preheated while prepping the asparagus.
4. Grill the bacon-wrapped asparagus for 25 to 30 minutes, until the asparagus is tender and the bacon is cooked and crispy.

Nutrition: Calories: 94 kCal Carbs: 5g Fat: 7g Protein: 4g

353.   Green Beans with Bacon

Preparation Time: 10 minutes
Cooking Time: 20 minutes
Servings: 6
Ingredients:
- 4 strips of bacon, chopped
- 1 1/2 pounds green beans, ends trimmed
- 1 teaspoon minced garlic
- 1 teaspoon salt
- 4 tablespoons olive oil

Directions:
1. Switch on the Pit Boss grill, fill the grill hopper with flavored Pit Boss, power the grill on by using the control panel, select 'smoke' on the temperature dial, or set the temperature to 450

degrees F and let it preheat for a minimum of 15 minutes.
2. Meanwhile, take a sheet tray, place all the ingredients in it and toss until mixed.
3. When the grill has preheated, open the lid, place prepared sheet tray on the grill grate, shut the grill and smoke for 20 minutes until lightly browned and cooked.
4. When done, transfer green beans to a dish and then serve.

Nutrition: Calories: 93 kCal Fat: 4.6 g Carbs: 8.2 g Protein: 5.9 g

354.   Pit Boss Bacon Wrapped Jalapeno Poppers

Preparation Time: 10 minutes
Cooking Time: 20 minutes
Servings: 6
Ingredients:
- 6 jalapenos, fresh
- 4 oz cream cheese
- 1/2 cup cheddar cheese, shredded
- 1 tbsp vegetable rub
- 12 slices cut bacon

Directions:
1. Preheat the Pit Boss smoker and grill to375°F.
2. Slice the jalapenos lengthwise and scrape the seed and membrane. Rinse them with water and set aside.
3. In a mixing bowl, mix cream cheese, cheddar cheese, vegetable rub until well mixed.
4. Fill the jalapeno halves with the mixture then wrap with the bacon pieces.
5. Smoke for 20 minutes or until the bacon crispy.
6. Serve and enjoy.

Nutrition: Calories 280 kCal, Fat 26g, Carbs 5g, Protein 9g

355. Wood Pellet Bacon Wrapped Jalapeno Poppers

Preparation Time: 10 minutes
Cooking Time: 20 minutes
Servings: 6
Ingredients:
- Six jalapenos, fresh
- 4 oz. cream cheese
- 1/2 cup cheddar cheese, shredded
- 1 tbsp. vegetable rub
- 12 slices cut bacon

Directions:
1. Preheat the wood pellet smoker and grill to375°F.
2. Slice the jalapenos lengthwise and scrape the seed and membrane. Rinse them with water and set aside.
3. Mix cream cheese, cheddar cheese, and vegetable rub until well mixed.
4. Fill the jalapeno halves with the mixture, then wrap with the bacon pieces.
5. Smoke for 20 minutes or until the bacon crispy.
6. Serve and enjoy.

Nutrition: Calories 280 kCal, Fat 26g, Carbs 5g, Protein 9g

356. Wood Pellet Grilled Mexican Street Corn

Preparation Time: 5 minutes
Cooking Time: 25 minutes
Servings: 6
Ingredients:
- Six ears of corn on the cob, shucked
- 1 tbsp. olive oil
- Kosher salt and pepper to taste
- 1/4 cup mayo
- 1/4 cup sour cream
- 1 tbsp. garlic paste
- 1/2 tbsp. chili powder
- Pinch of ground red pepper
- 1/2 cup cotija cheese, crumbled
- 1/4 cup cilantro, chopped
- Six lime wedges

Directions:
1. Brush the corn with oil and dash with salt.
2. Place the corn on a wood pellet grill set at 350°F. Cook for 25 minutes as you turn it occasionally.
3. Meanwhile, mix mayo, cream, garlic, chili, and red pepper until well combined.
4. When the corn is cooked, remove from the grill, rest for some minutes, and brush with the mayo mixture.
5. Sprinkle cotija cheese, more chili powder, and cilantro. Serve with lime wedges. Enjoy.

Nutrition: Calories 280 kCal Fat 19g Carbs 24g Protein 7.1g

357. Wood Pellet Grilled Stuffed Zucchini

Preparation Time: 5 minutes
Cooking Time: 11 minutes
Servings: 8
Ingredients:
- Four zucchinis
- 5 tbsp. olive oil
- 2 tbsp. red onion, chopped
- 1/4 tbsp. garlic, minced
- 1/2 cup bread crumbs
- 1/2 cup mozzarella cheese, shredded
- 1 tbsp. fresh mint
- 1/2 tbsp. salt
- 3 tbsp. parmesan cheese

Directions:
1. Slice the zucchini lengthwise and scoop out the pulp, then brush the shells with oil.
2. In a non-stick skillet, sauté pulp, onion, and remaining oil. Add garlic and cook for a minute.
3. Add bread crumbs and cook until golden brown. Remove from heat and stir in mozzarella cheese, fresh mint, and salt.
4. Spoon the mixture into the shells and dash parmesan cheese.
5. Place in a grill and grill for 10 minutes or until the zucchini is tender.

Nutrition: Calories 186 kCal Fat 10g Carbs 17g Protein 9g

358. Wood Pellet Grill Spicy Sweet Potatoes

Preparation Time: 10 minutes
Cooking Time: 35 minutes
Servings: 6
Ingredients:

- 2 lb. sweet potatoes, cut into chunks
- One red onion, chopped
- 2 tbsp. oil
- 2 tbsp. orange juice
- 1 tbsp. roasted cinnamon
- 1 tbsp. salt
- 1/4 tbsp. Chipotle chili pepper

Directions:

1. Preheat the wood pellet grill to 425°F with the lid closed.
2. Toss the sweet potatoes with onion, oil, and juice.
3. In a mixing bowl, mix cinnamon, salt, and pepper, then sprinkle the mixture over the sweet potatoes.
4. Spread the potatoes on a lined baking dish in a single layer.
5. Place the baking dish in the grill and grill for 30 minutes or until the sweet potatoes are tender.
6. Serve and enjoy.

Nutrition: Calories 145 kCal Fat 5g Carbs 23g Protein 2g

359. Wood Pellet Smoked Vegetables

Preparation Time: 5 minutes
Cooking Time: 15 minutes
Servings: 6
Ingredients:

- One ear corn, fresh, husks and silk strands removed
- 1yellow squash, sliced
- One red onion, cut into wedges
- One green pepper, cut into strips
- One red pepper, cut into strips
- One yellow pepper, cut into strips
- 1 cup mushrooms, halved
- 2 tbsp. oil
- 2 tbsp. chicken seasoning

Directions:

1. Soak the pecan wood pellets in water for an hour. Remove the pellets from the water and fill the smoker box with the wet pellets.

2. Place the smoker box under the grill and close the lid. Heat the grill on high heat for 10 minutes or until smoke starts coming out from the wood chips.
3. Meanwhile, toss the veggies in oil and seasonings, then transfer them into a grill basket.
4. Grill for 10 minutes while turning occasionally. Serve and enjoy.

Nutrition: Calories 97 kCal Fat 5g Carbs 11g Protein 2g

360. Wood Pellet Smoked Asparagus

Preparation Time: 5 minutes
Cooking Time: 60 minutes
Servings: 4
Ingredients:

- One bunch of fresh asparagus ends cut
- 2 tbsp. olive oil
- Salt and pepper to taste

Directions:

1. Fire up your wood pellet smoker to 230°F
2. Lay the asparagus in a mixing bowl and drizzle with olive oil. Season with salt and pepper.
3. Place the asparagus in a tinfoil sheet and fold the sides such that you create a basket.
4. Smoke the asparagus for 1 hour or until soft turning after half an hour.
5. Remove from the grill and serve. Enjoy.

Nutrition: Calories 43 kCal Fat 2g Carbs 4g Protein 3g

361. Mexican Street Corn with Chipotle Butter

Preparation Time: 10 minutes
Cooking Time: 14 minutes
Servings: 4
Ingredients:

- Four ears corn
- ½ cup sour cream
- ½ cup mayonnaise
- ¼ cup chopped fresh cilantro,
- Chipotle Butter, for topping
- 1 cup grated Parmesan cheese

Directions:

1. Supply your smoker with wood pellets and follow the manufacturer's specific start-up procedure.
2. Preheat, with the lid closed, to 450°F.

3. Shuck the corn, removing the silks, and cutting off the cores.
4. Tear four squares of aluminum foil large enough to cover an ear of corn completely.
5. In a medium bowl, combine the sour cream, mayonnaise, and cilantro. Slather the mixture all over the ears of corn.
6. Wrap each ear of corn in a piece of foil, sealing tightly. Place on the grill, close the lid, and smoke for 12 to 14 minutes.
7. Get rid of the corn from the foil and place in a shallow baking dish. Top with chipotle butter, Parmesan cheese, and more chopped cilantro.
8. Serve immediately.

Nutrition: Calories: 180 kCal Carbs: 19 g Protein: 5 g Fat: 10g

362. Twice-Smoked Potatoes

Preparation Time: 10 minutes
Cooking Time: 14 minutes
Servings: 4
Ingredients:
- 8 Idaho, Russet, or Yukon Gold potatoes
- 1 (12-ounce) can evaporate milk, heated
- 1 cup (2 sticks) butter, melted
- ½ cup sour cream, at room temperature
- 1 cup grated Parmesan cheese
- ½ pound bacon, cooked and crumbled
- ¼ cup chopped scallions
- Salt
- Freshly ground black pepper
- 1 cup shredded Cheddar cheese

Directions:
1. Supply your smoker with wood pellets and follow the manufacturer's specific start-up procedure.
2. Preheat, with the lid closed, to 400°F.
3. Poke the potatoes all over with a fork. Arrange them directly on the grill grate, close the lid, and smoke for 1 hour and 15 minutes, or until cooked through, and they have some give when pinched.
4. Let the potatoes cool for 10 minutes, then cut in half lengthwise.
5. Into a medium bowl, scoop out the potato flesh, leaving ¼ inch in the shells, place the shells on a baking sheet.

6. Stir in the Parmesan cheese, bacon, and scallions, and season with salt and pepper.
7. Generously stuff each shell with the potato mixture and top with Cheddar cheese.
8. Set the baking sheet on the grill grate, close the lid, and smoke for 20 minutes, or until the cheese is melted.

Nutrition: Calories: 130 kCal Carbs: 21 g Protein: 5 g Fat:: 3.5g

363. Crab-filled Mushrooms

Preparation Time: 20 minutes
Cooking Time: 45 minutes
Servings: 6
Ingredients:
- Six medium-sized Portobello mushrooms
- Extra virgin olive oil
- 1/3 Grated parmesan cheese cup
- Club Beat Staffing:
- 8 ounces' fresh crab meat or canned or imitation crab meat
- Two tablespoons extra virgin olive oil
- 1/3 Chopped celery
- Chopped red peppers
- ½ cup chopped green onion
- ½ cup Italian bread crumbs

Directions:
1. Clean up the mushroom cap with a damp paper towel. Cut off the stem and save it.
2. Remove the brown gills from the bottom of the mushroom cap with a spoon and discard.
3. Prepare crab meat stuffing. If you are a fan of using canned crab meat, drain, rinse, and remove shellfish.
4. Put the crab mixture in each mushroom cap and make a mound in the center.
5. Sprinkle extra virgin olive oil and sprinkle parmesan cheese on each stuffed mushroom cap. Put the mushrooms in a 10 x 15-inch baking dish.
6. Use the pellets to set the wood pellet smoker and grill to indirect heating and preheat to 375 °F.
7. Bake for 30-45 minutes until the filling becomes hot (165 degrees Fahrenheit as measured by an instant-read digital thermometer), and the mushrooms begin to release juice.

Nutrition: Cal:160kCal Carbs:14g Fat:8g Protein: 10g

364. Texas-Style Brisket Beans

Preparation Time: 20 minutes
Cooking Time: 2 hours
Servings: 10
Ingredients:
- Two tablespoons extra virgin olive oil
- One large diced onion
- One diced green pepper
- One red pepper diced
- 2 to 6 jalapeno peppers diced
- Texas-style brisket flat chopped three pieces
- One baked bean, like Bush's country-style baked beans
- One pork and beans
- One red kidney bean, rinse, drain
- 1 cup barbecue sauce like Sweet Baby Ray's barbecue sauce
- ½ cup stuffed brown sugar
- Three garlic, chopped
- Two teaspoons of mustard
- ½ teaspoon kosher salt
- ½ teaspoon black pepper

Directions:
1. Heat the skillet with olive oil over medium heat and add the diced onion, peppers, and jalapeno. Sauté the food for about 8-10 minutes until the onion is translucent.
2. In a 4-quart casserole dish, mix chopped brisket, baked beans, pork beans, kidney beans, cooked onions, peppers, barbecue sauce, brown sugar, garlic, mustard, salt, and black pepper.
3. Using the selected pellets, configure a wood pellet smoking grill for indirect cooking and preheat to 325 ° F. Cook the beans baked in the brisket for 1.5 to 2 hours until they become raw beans. Rest for 15 minutes before eating.

Nutrition: Calories: 199 kCal Carbs: 35g Fat: 2g Protein: 9g

365. Smokey Cheese

Preparation Time: 1 hour and 15 minutes
Cooking Time: 2 hours
Servings: 6
Ingredients:
- Gouda
- Sharp cheddar
- Very sharp 3-year cheddar
- Monterey Jack
- Pepper jack
- Swiss

Directions:
1. According to the cheese block's shape, cut the cheese block into an easy-to-handle size (approximately 4 x 4-inch block) to promote smoke penetration.
2. Leave the cheese on the counter for one hour to form a very thin skin or crust, which acts as a heat barrier but allows smoke to penetrate.
3. Configure the wood pellet smoking grill for indirect heating and install a cold smoke box to prepare for cold smoke. Ensure that the louvers on the smoking box are fully open to allow moisture to escape from the box.
4. Preheat the wood pellet smoker and grill to 180 ° F or use apple pellets and smoke settings, if any, to get a milder smoke flavor.
5. Place the cheese on a Teflon-coated fiberglass non-stick grill mat and let cool for 2 hours.
6. Remove the smoked cheese and cool for 1 hour on the counter using a cooling rack.
7. After labeling the smoked cheese with a vacuum seal, refrigerate for two weeks or more, then smoke will permeate, and the cheese flavor will become milder.

Nutrition: Calories: 102 kCal Carbs: 0g Fat: 9 Protein: 6g

366. Smoked Guacamole

Preparation Time: 15 minutes
Cooking Time: 30 minutes
Servings: 8
Ingredients:
- 1/4 cup chopped Cilantro
- 7 Avocados, peeled and seeded
- ¼ cup chopped Onion, red
- ¼ cup chopped tomato
- Three ears corn
- One teaspoon of Chile Powder
- One teaspoon of Cumin
- Two tablespoons of Lime juice
- One tablespoon minced Garlic
- 1 Chile, poblano
- Black pepper and salt to taste

Directions:
1. Preheat the grill to 180F with a closed lid.
2. Smoke the avocado for 10 min.

3. Set the avocados aside and increase the temperature of the girl to high.
4. Once heated, grill the corn and chili—roast for 20 minutes.
5. Cut the corn. Set aside. Place the chili in a bowl. Cover it with a wrapper and let it sit for about 10 minutes. Peel the chili and dice. Add it to the kernels.
6. In a bowl, mash the avocados, leave few chunks. Add the remaining ingredients and mix.
7. Serve right away because it is best eaten fresh. Enjoy!

Nutrition: Calories: 51 kCal Protein: 1g Carbs: 3g Fat: 4.5g

367. Roasted Cashews

Preparation Time: 15 minutes
Cooking Time: 12 minutes
Servings: 6
Ingredients:
- ¼ cup Rosemary, chopped
- 2 ½ tablespoons Butter, melted
- 2 cups Cashews, raw
- ½ teaspoon of Cayenne pepper
- One teaspoon of salt

Directions:
1. Preheat the grill to 350F with a closed lid.
2. In a baking dish, layer the nuts. Combine the cayenne, salt rosemary, and butter. Add on top. Toss to combine.
3. Grill for 12 minutes.
4. Serve and enjoy.

Nutrition: Calories: 150 kCal Proteins: 5g Carbs: 7g Fat: 15g

368. Flavored Coleslaw

Preparation Time: 15 minutes
Cooking Time: 25 minutes
Servings: 8
Ingredients:
- One shredded Purple Cabbage
- One shredded Green Cabbage
- 2 Scallions, sliced
- 1 cup Carrots, shredded

Dressing
- One tablespoon of Celery Seed
- 1/8 cup of White vinegar

- 1 ½ cups Mayo
- Black pepper and salt to taste

Directions:
1. Preheat the grill to 180F with a closed lid.
2. On a tray, spread the carrots and cabbage. Place the tray on the grate and smoke for about 25 minutes.
3. Transfer to the fridge to cool.
4. In the meantime, make the dressing. In a bowl, combine the ingredients. Mix well.
5. Transfer the veggies to a bowl. Drizzle with the sauce and toss
6. Serve sprinkled with scallions.

Nutrition: Calories: 35 kCal Protein: 1g Carbs: 5g Fat: 5g

369. Mushrooms Stuffed with Crab Meat

Preparation Time: 20 minutes
Cooking Time: 30 to 45 minutes
Servings: 4 to 6
Ingredients:
- 6 medium-sized portobello mushrooms
- Extra virgin olive oil
- 1/3 grated parmesan cheese cup
- Crab meat stuffing:
- 8 ounces fresh crab meat or canned or imitation crab meat
- 2 tablespoons extra virgin olive oil
- 1/3 chopped celery
- Chopped red peppers
- ½ cup chopped green onion
- ½ cup Italian breadcrumbs
- ½ cup mayonnaise
- 8 ounces cream cheese at room temperature
- ½ teaspoon of garlic
- 1 tablespoon dried parsley
- Grated parmesan cheese cup
- 1 teaspoon of Old Bay seasoning
- ¼ teaspoon of kosher salt
- ¼ teaspoon black pepper

Directions:
1. Clean up the mushroom cap with a damp paper towel. Cut off the stem and save it.
2. Remove the brown gills from the bottom of the mushroom cap with a spoon and discard.
3. Prepare crab meat stuffing. If you are a fan of using canned crab meat, drain, rinse, and remove shellfish.

4. Heat the pan with olive oil first over medium-high heat. Add celery, peppers, and green onions and fry for 5 minutes. Set aside for cooling.
5. Gently pour the chilled sautéed vegetables and the remaining ingredients into a large bowl.
6. Cover and refrigerate crab meat stuffing until ready to use.
7. Put the crab mixture in each mushroom cap and make a mound in the center.
8. Sprinkle extra virgin olive oil and sprinkle parmesan cheese on each stuffed mushroom cap. Put the mushrooms in a 10 x 15-inch baking dish.
9. Use the pellets to set the wood pellet smoker and grill to indirect heating and preheat to 375 ° F.
10. Bake for 30-45 minutes until the filling becomes hot (165 degrees Fahrenheit as measured by an instant-read digital thermometer) and the mushrooms begin to release juice.

Nutrition: Calories: 160 kCal Carbs: 14g Fat: 8g Protein: 10g

370. Bacon Wrapped with Asparagus

Preparation Time: 15 minutes
Cooking Time: 25 to 30 minutes
Servings: 4 to 6
Ingredients:
- 1-pound fresh thick asparagus (15-20 spears)
- Extra virgin olive oil
- 5 slices bacon
- 1 teaspoon of salted pepper

Directions:
1. Cut off all the wooden ends of the asparagus and make them all the same length.
2. Divide the asparagus into a bundle of three spears and split with olive oil. Wrap each other's bundle with a piece of bacon, then dust with seasonings or salt pepper for seasoning.
3. Set the wood pellet smoker and grill for indirect cooking and place a Teflon coated fiberglass mat on the grate (to prevent asparagus from sticking to the grate). Preheat to 400 degrees Fahrenheit using all types of pellets. The grill can be preheated during asparagus preparation.

4. Bake the asparagus wrapped in bacon for 25-30 minutes until the asparagus is soft and the bacon is cooked and crispy.

Nutrition: Calories: 71 kCal Carbs: 1g Fat: 4g Protein: 6g

371. Bacon Cheddar Slider

Preparation Time: 30 minutes
Cooking Time: 15 minutes
Servings: 6 to 10
Ingredients:
- 1-pound ground beef (80% lean)
- ½ teaspoon of garlic salt
- ½ teaspoon salt
- ½ teaspoon of garlic
- ½ teaspoon onion
- ½ teaspoon black pepper
- 6 bacon slices, cut in half
- ½ cup mayonnaise
- 2 teaspoons of creamy wasabi (optional)
- 6 sliced sharp Cheddar cheese, cut in half (optional)
- Sliced red onion
- ½ cup sliced kosher dill pickles
- 12 mini-breads sliced horizontally
- Ketchup

Directions:
1. Place ground beef, garlic salt, seasoned salt, garlic powder, onion powder, and black pepper in a medium bowl.
2. Divide in 12 equal parts the meat mixture into shape into small thin round patties (about 2 ounces each) and save.
3. Cook the bacon on medium heat over medium heat for 5-8 minutes until crunchy. Set aside.
4. To make the sauce, mix the mayonnaise and horseradish in a small bowl, if used.
5. Set up a wood pellet smoker and grill for direct cooking to use griddle accessories. Look for the manufacturer to see if there is a griddle accessory that works with the particular wooden pellet smoker and grill.
6. Spray a cooking spray on the griddle cooking surface for best non-stick results.
7. Preheat wood pellet smoker and grill to 350 ° F using selected pellets. The griddle surface should be approximately 400 ° F.
8. Grill the putty for 3-4 minutes each until the internal temperature reaches 160 ° F.

9. If necessary, place a sharp Cheddar cheese slice on each patty while the patty is on the griddle or after the patty is removed from the griddle. Place a small amount of mayonnaise mixture, a slice of red onion, and a hamburger pate in the lower half of each roll. Pickled slices, bacon, and ketchup.

Nutrition: Calories: 80 kCal Carbs: 0g Fat: 5g Protein: 0g

372. Apple Wood Smoked Cheese

Preparation Time: 1 hour 15 minutes
Cooking Time: 2 hours
Servings: 6
Ingredients:
- Gouda
- Sharp Cheddar
- Very sharp 3-year Cheddar
- Monterey Jack
- Pepper Jack
- Swiss

Directions:
1. According to the shape of the cheese block, cut the cheese block into an easy-to-handle size (approximately 4 x 4-inch block) to promote smoke penetration.
2. Leave the cheese on the counter for one hour to form a very thin skin or crust, which acts as a heat barrier, but allows smoke to penetrate.
3. Configure the wood pellet smoking grill for indirect heating and install a cold smoke box to prepare for cold smoke. Make sure that the louvers on the smoking box are fully open to allow moisture to escape from the box.
4. Preheat the wood pellet smoker and grill to 180 ° F or use apple pellets and smoke settings, if any, to get a milder smoke flavor.
5. Place the cheese on a Teflon-coated fiberglass non-stick grill mat and let cool for 2 hours.
6. Remove the smoked cheese and cool for 1 hour on the counter using a cooling rack.
7. After labeling the smoked cheese with a vacuum seal, refrigerate for 2 weeks or more, then smoke will permeate, and the cheese flavor will become milder.

Nutrition: Calories: 102 kCal Carbs: 0g Fat: 9g Protein: 6g

373. Hickory Smoked Moink Ball Skewer

Preparation Time: 30 minutes
Cooking Time: 1 hour 30 minutes
Servings: 9
Ingredients:
- ½ pound ground beef (80% lean)
- ½ pound pork sausage
- 1 large egg
- ½ cup Italian breadcrumbs
- ½ cup chopped red onion
- Grated parmesan cheese cup
- ¼ cup finely chopped parsley
- ¼ cup whole milk
- 2 pieces of garlic, 1 chopped or crushed garlic
- 1 teaspoon oregano
- ½ teaspoon kosher salt
- ½ teaspoon black pepper
- ¼ cup barbecue sauce like Sweet Baby Ray
- ½ pound bacon cut in half, cut in half

Directions:
1. In a container, mix ground beef, ground pork sausage, eggs, crumbs, onions, parmesan cheese, parsley, milk, garlic, salt, oregano, and pepper. Do not overuse the meat.
2. Form a 1½ ounces meatball about 1.5 inches in diameter and place on a Teflon-coated fiberglass mat.
3. Wrap each meatball in half thin bacon. Stab moink balls on 6 skewers (3 balls per skewer).
4. Set up wood pellet smoker and grill for indirect cooking.
5. Preheat wood pellet smoker and grill to 225 ° F using hickory pellets.
6. Tap the moink ball skewer for 30 minutes.
7. Raise the pit temperature to 350 ° F until the meatball internal temperature reaches 175 ° F and the bacon is crisp (about 40-45 minutes).
8. For the last 5 minutes, brush your moink ball with your favorite barbecue sauce.
9. While still hot, offer moink ball skewers.

Nutrition: Calories: 170 kCal Carbs: 2g Fat: 15g Protein: 7g

374. Roasted Vegetables

Preparation Time: 20 minutes
Cooking Time: 20 to 40 minutes
Servings: 4
Ingredients:

- 1 cup cauliflower floret
- 1 cup small mushroom, half
- 1 medium zucchini, sliced in half
- 1 medium yellow squash, sliced in half
- 1 medium-sized red pepper, chopped to 1.5-2 inches
- 1 small red onion, chopped to 1½-2 inch
- 6 ounces small baby carrot
- 6 mid-stem asparagus spears, cut into 1-inch pieces
- 1 cup cherry or grape tomato
- ¼ Extra virgin olive oil with cup roasted garlic flavor
- 2 tablespoons of balsamic vinegar
- 3 garlic cloves, chopped
- 1 teaspoon dry thyme
- 1 teaspoon dried oregano
- 1 teaspoon of garlic salt
- ½ teaspoon black pepper

Directions:

1. Put cauliflower florets, mushrooms, zucchini, yellow pumpkin, red peppers, red onions, carrots, asparagus, and tomatoes in a large bowl.
2. Add olive oil, balsamic vinegar, garlic, thyme, oregano, garlic salt, and black pepper to add to the vegetables.
3. Gently throw the vegetables by hand until completely covered with olive oil, herbs, and spices.
4. Spread the seasoned vegetables evenly on a non-stick grill tray/bread/basket (about 15 x 12 inches).
5. Set the wood pellet smoker and grill for indirect cooking and preheat to 425 degrees Fahrenheit using all types of wood pellets.
6. Transfer the grill tray to a preheated smoker and grill and roast the vegetables for 20-40 minutes or until the vegetables are perfectly cooked. Please put it out immediately.

Nutrition: Calories: 114 kCal Carbs: 17g Fat: 4g Protein: 3g

375. Atomic Buffalo Turds

Preparation Time: 45 minutes
Cooking Time: 2 hours
Servings: 6
Ingredients:

- 10 medium jalapeno peppers
- 8 ounces regular cream cheese at room temperature
- ¾ cup Monterey Jack and Cheddar cheese blend shred (optional)
- 1 teaspoon smoked paprika
- 1 teaspoon garlic powder
- ½ teaspoon cayenne pepper
- Teaspoon red pepper flakes (optional)
- 20 sausages
- 10 slices bacon, cut in half

Directions:

1. Wear food service gloves when using. Jalapeno peppers are washed vertically and sliced. Carefully remove seeds and veins using a spoon or paring knife and discard. Place Jalapeno on a grilled vegetable tray and set aside.
2. In a small bowl, mix cream cheese, shredded cheese, paprika, garlic powder, cayenne pepper if used, and red pepper flakes if used, until thoroughly mixed.
3. Mix cream cheese with half of the jalapeno pepper.
4. Place the smoked sausage on half of the filled jalapeno pepper.
5. Wrap half of the thin bacon around half of each jalapeno pepper.
6. Fix the bacon to the sausage with a toothpick so that the pepper does not pierce. Place the ABT on the grill tray or pan.
7. Set the wood pellet smoker and grill for indirect cooking and preheat to 250 degrees Fahrenheit using hickory pellets or blends.
8. Cook jalapeno peppers at 250 ° F for about 1.5 to 2 hours until the bacon is cooked and crisp.
9. Remove the ABT from the grill and let it rest for 5 minutes before hors d'oeuvres.

Nutrition: Calories: 131 kCal Carbs: 1g Fat: 12g Protein: 5g

376. Grilled Corn

Preparation Time: 15 minutes
Cooking Time: 25 minutes
Servings: 6
Ingredients:

- 6 fresh ears corn
- Salt
- Black pepper
- Olive oil
- Vegetable seasoning
- Butter for serving

Directions:

1. Preheat the grill to high with a closed lid.
2. Peel the husks. Remove the corn's silk. Rub with black pepper, salt, vegetable seasoning, and oil.
3. Close the husks and grill for 25 minutes. Turn them occasionally.
4. Serve topped with butter and enjoy.

Nutrition: Calories: 70 Protein: 3g Carbs: 18g Fat: 2g

377. Thyme and Rosemary Mash Potatoes

Preparation Time: 20 minutes
Cooking Time: 1 hour
Servings: 6
Ingredients:

- 4 ½ lbs. potatoes, russet
- Salt
- 1 pint of heavy cream
- 3 thyme sprigs + 2 tablespoons for garnish
- 2 rosemary sprigs
- 6-7 sage leaves
- 6-7 black peppercorns
- Black pepper to taste
- 2 sticks butter, softened
- 2 garlic cloves, chopped

Directions:

1. Preheat the grill to 350F with a closed lid.
2. Peel the russet potatoes. Cut into small pieces and place them in a baking dish. Fill it with water (1 ½ cups). Place on the grill and cook with a closed lid for about 1 hour.
3. In the meantime, in a saucepan combine the garlic, peppercorns, herbs, and cream. Place on the grate and cook covered for about 15 minutes. Once done, strain to remove the garlic and herbs. Keep warm.
4. Take out the water of the potatoes and place them in a stockpot. Rice them with a fork and pour 2/3 of the mixture. Add 1 stick softened butter and salt.
5. Serve right away.

Nutrition: Calories: 180 kCal Protein: 4g Carbs: 28g Fat: 10g

378. Grilled Broccoli

Preparation Time: 15 minutes
Cooking Time: 10 minutes
Servings: 4 to 6
Ingredients:

- 4 bunches of broccoli
- 4 tablespoons olive oil
- Black pepper and salt to taste
- ½ lemon, the juice
- ½ lemon cut into wedges

Directions:

1. Preheat the grill to high with a closed lid.
2. In a bowl add the broccoli and drizzle with oil. Coat well. Season with salt.
3. Grill for 5 minutes and then flip. Cook for 3 minutes more.
4. Once done transfer on a plate. Squeeze lemon on top and serve with lemon wedges. Enjoy!

Nutrition: Calories: 144 kCal Protein: 1.5g Carbs: 2g Fat: 15g

379. Smoked Coleslaw

Preparation Time: 15 minutes
Cooking Time: 25 minutes
Servings: 8
Ingredients:

- 1 shredded purple cabbage
- 1 shredded green cabbage
- 2 scallions, sliced
- 1 cup carrots, shredded

Dressing

- 1 tablespoon of celery Seed
- 1/8 cup of white vinegar
- 1 ½ cups mayo
- Black pepper and salt to taste

Directions:

1. Preheat the grill to 180F with a closed lid.

2. On a tray spread the carrots and cabbage. Place the tray on the grate and smoke for about 25 minutes.
3. Transfer to the fridge to cool.
4. In the meantime, make the dressing. In a bowl combine the ingredients. Mix well.
5. Transfer the veggies to a bowl. Drizzle with the sauce and toss
6. Serve sprinkled with scallions.

Nutrition: Calories: 35g Protein: 16g Carbs: 41g Fat: 15g

380. The Best Potato Roast

Preparation Time: 15 minutes
Cooking Time: 35 minutes
Servings: 6
Ingredients:
- 4 potatoes, large (scrubbed)
- 1 ½ cups gravy (beef or chicken)
- Rib seasoning to taste
- 1 ½ cups Cheddar cheese
- Black pepper and salt to taste
- 2 tablespoons sliced scallions

Directions:
1. Preheat the grill to high with a closed lid.
2. Slice each potato into wedges or fries. Transfer into a bowl and drizzle with oil. Season with Rib seasoning.
3. Spread the wedges/fries on a baking sheet (rimmed). Roast for about 20 minutes. Turn the wedges/fries and cook for 15 minutes more.
4. In the meantime, in a saucepan warm the chicken/beef gravy. Cut the cheese into small cubes.
5. Once done cooking place the potatoes on a plate or into a bowl. Distribute the cut cheese and pour hot gravy on top.
6. Serve garnished with scallion. Season with pepper. Enjoy!

Nutrition: Calories: 220 kCal Protein: 3g Carbs: 38g Fat: 15g

381. Corn Salsa

Preparation Time: 10 minutes
Cooking Time: 15 minutes
Servings: 4
Ingredients:
- 4 ears corn, large with the husk on

- 4 tomatoes (Roma) diced and seeded
- 1 teaspoon of onion powder
- 1 teaspoon of garlic powder
- 1 Onion, diced
- ½ cup chopped cilantro
- Black pepper and salt to taste
- 1 lime, the juice
- 1 grille jalapeno, diced

Directions:
1. Preheat the grill to 450F.
2. Place the ears of corn on the grate and cook until charred. Remove husk. Cut into kernels.
3. Combine all ingredients, plus the corn, and mix well. Refrigerate before serving.

Nutrition: Calories: 120 kCal Protein: 2g Carbs: 4g Fat: 1g

382. Grilled Nut Mix

Preparation Time: 10 minutes
Cooking Time: 20 minutes
Servings: 8
Ingredients:
- 3 cups mixed nuts, salted
- 1 teaspoon thyme, dried
- 1 ½ tablespoon brown sugar, packed
- 1 tablespoon olive oil
- ¼ teaspoon of mustard powder
- ¼ teaspoon cayenne pepper

Directions:
1. Preheat the grill to 250F with a closed lid.
2. In a bowl combine the ingredients and place the nuts on a baking tray lined with parchment paper. Place the try on the grill. Cook 20 minutes.
3. Serve and enjoy.

Nutrition: Calories: 65 kCal Protein: 23g Carbs: 4g Fat: 52g

383. Wood pellet Spicy Brisket

Preparation Time: 20 minutes
Cooking Time: 9 hours
Servings: 10
Ingredients:

- 2 tbsps. garlic powder
- 2 tbsps. onion powder
- 2 tbsps. paprika
- 2 tbsps. chili powder
- 1/3 cup salt
- 1/3 cup black pepper
- 12 lb. whole packer brisket, trimmed
- 1-1/2 cup beef broth

Directions:

1. Set your wood pellet temperature to 225degrees F. Let preheat for 15 minutes with the lid closed.
2. Meanwhile, mix garlic, onion, paprika, chili, salt, and pepper in a mixing bowl.
3. The brisket generously on all sides.
4. Place the meat on the grill with the fat side down and let it cool until the internal temperature reaches 160degrees F.
5. Remove the meat from the grill and double wrap it with foil. Return it to the grill and cook until the internal temperature reaches 204degrees F.
6. Remove from grill, unwrap the brisket and let rest for 15 minutes.
7. Slice and serve.

Nutrition: Calories: 270 kCal Fat: 8 g Carbs: 3 g Protein: 20 g

384. Pellet Grill Funeral Potatoes

Preparation Time: 10 minutes
Cooking Time: 1 hour
Servings: 8
Ingredients:

- 32 oz., package frozen hash browns
- 1/2 cup cheddar cheese, grated
- One can cream of chicken soup
- 1 cup sour cream
- 1 cup Mayonnaise
- 3 cups corn flakes, whole or crushed
- 1/4 cup melted butter

Directions:

1. Preheat your pellet grill to 350oF.

2. Spray a 13 x 9 baking pan, aluminum, using a cooking spray, non-stick.
3. Mix hash browns, cheddar cheese, chicken soup cream, sour cream, and mayonnaise in a large bowl.
4. Spoon the mixture into a baking pan gently.
5. Mix corn flakes and melted butter, then sprinkle over the casserole.
6. Grill for about 1-1/2 hours until potatoes become tender. If the top browns too much, cover using a foil until potatoes are done.
7. Remove from the grill and serve hot.

Nutrition: Calories: 403 kCal Fat: 37 g Carbs: 14 g Protein: 4 g

385. Smoky Caramelized Onions on the Pellet Grill

Preparation Time: 5 minutes
Cooking Time: 1 hour
Servings: 4
Ingredients:

- Five large sliced onions
- 1/2 cup fat of your choice
- Pinch of Sea salt

Directions:

1. Place all the ingredients into a pan. For a deep rich brown, caramelized onion, cook them off for about 1hour on a stovetop.
2. Keep the grill temperatures not higher than 250 - 275oF.
3. Now transfer the pan into the grill.
4. Cook for about 1-1½ hours until brown. Check and stir with a spoon, wooden, after every 15 minutes. Make sure not to run out of pellets.
5. Now remove from the grill and season with more salt if necessary.
6. Serve immediately or place in a refrigerator for up to 1 week.

Nutrition: Calories: 286 kCal Fat: 10.3 Carbs: 12.8 g Protein: 1.5 g

386. Hickory Smoked Green Beans

Preparation Time: 15 minutes
Cooking Time: 3 hours
Servings: 10
Ingredients:
- 6 cups fresh green beans, halved and ends cut off
- 2 cups chicken broth
- 1 tbsp. pepper, ground
- 1/4 tbsp. salt
- 2 tbsps. apple cider vinegar
- 1/4 cup diced onion
- 6-8 bite-size bacon slices
- Optional: sliced almonds

Directions:
1. Add green beans to a colander, then rinse thoroughly. Set aside.
2. Place chicken broth, pepper, salt, and apple cider in a large pan. Add green beans.
3. Blanch over medium heat for about 3-4 minutes, and then remove from heat.
4. Transfer the mixture into an aluminum pan, disposable. Make sure all of them go into the pan, so do not drain them.
5. Place bacon slices over the beans and place the pan into the wood pellet smoker,
6. Smoke for about 3 hours uncovered.
7. Remove from the smoker and top with almond slices.
8. Serve immediately.

Nutrition: Calories: 57 kCal Fat: 3 g Carbs: 4 g Protein: 4 g

387. Vegetable Sandwich

Preparation Time: 30 minutes
Cooking Time: 45 minutes
Servings: 4
Ingredients:
For the Smoked Hummus
- 1 1/2 cups cooked chickpeas
- 1 tablespoon minced garlic
- 1 teaspoon salt
- 4 tablespoons lemon juice
- 2 tablespoon olive oil
- 1/3 cup tahini

For the Vegetables
- 2 large portobello mushrooms
- 1 small eggplant, destemmed, sliced into strips
- 1 teaspoon salt
- 1 small zucchini, trimmed, sliced into strips
- ½ teaspoon ground black pepper
- 1 small yellow squash, peeled, sliced into strips
- ¼ cup olive oil

For the Cheese
- 1 lemon, juiced
- ½ teaspoon minced garlic
- ¼ teaspoon ground black pepper
- ¼ teaspoon salt
- 1/2 cup ricotta cheese

To Assemble
- 1 bunch basil, leaves chopped
- 2 heirloom tomatoes, sliced
- 4 ciabatta buns, halved

Directions:
1. Switch on the Pit Boss grill, fill the grill hopper with pecan flavored Pit Boss, power the grill on by using the control panel, select 'smoke' on the temperature dial, or set the temperature to 180 degrees F and let it preheat for a minimum of 15 minutes.
2. Meanwhile, prepare the hummus, and for this, take a sheet tray and spread chickpeas on it.
3. When the grill has preheated, open the lid, place sheet tray on the grill grate, shut the grill and smoke for 20 minutes.
4. When done, transfer chickpeas to a food processor, add remaining ingredients for the hummus in it, and pulse for 2 minutes until smooth, set aside until required.
5. Change the smoking temperature to 500 degrees F, shut with lid, and let it preheat for 10 minutes.
6. Meanwhile, prepare vegetables and for this, take a large bowl, place all the vegetables in it, add salt and black pepper, drizzle with oil and lemon juice and toss until coated.
7. Place vegetables on the grill grate, shut with lid and then smoke for eggplant, zucchini, and squash for 15 minutes and mushrooms for 25 minutes.
8. Meanwhile, prepare the cheese and for this, take a small bowl, place all of its ingredients in it and stir until well combined.
9. Assemble the sandwich for this, cut buns in half lengthwise, spread prepared hummus on one side, spread cheese on the other side, then stuff

with grilled vegetables and top with tomatoes and basil.

10. Serve straight away.

Nutrition: Calories: 560 kCal Fat: 40 g Carbs: 45 g Protein: 8.3 g

388. Grilled Zucchini

Preparation Time: 5 minutes
Cooking Time: 10 minutes
Servings: 6
Ingredients:

- 4 medium zucchinis
- 2 tablespoons olive oil
- 1 tablespoon sherry vinegar
- 2 sprigs of thyme, leaves chopped
- ½ teaspoon salt
- 1/3 teaspoon ground black pepper

Directions:

1. Switch on the Pit Boss grill, fill the grill hopper with oak flavored Pit Bosss, power the grill on by using the control panel, select 'smoke' on the temperature dial, or set the temperature to 350 degrees F and let it preheat for a minimum of 5 minutes.
2. Meanwhile, cut the ends of each zucchini, cut each in half and then into thirds and place in a plastic bag.
3. Add remaining ingredients, seal the bag, and shake well to coat zucchini pieces.
4. When the grill has preheated, open the lid, place zucchini on the grill grate, shut the grill and smoke for 4 minutes per side.
5. When done, transfer zucchini to a dish, garnish with more thyme and then serve.

Nutrition: Calories: 74 kCal Fat: 5.4 g Carbs: 6.1 g Protein: 2.6 g

389. Grilled Sugar Snap Peas

Preparation Time: 15 minutes
Cooking Time: 10 minutes
Servings: 4
Ingredients:

- 2-pound sugar snap peas, ends trimmed
- ½ teaspoon garlic powder
- 1 teaspoon salt
- 2/3 teaspoon ground black pepper
- 2 tablespoons olive oil

Directions:

1. Switch on the Pit Boss grill, fill the grill hopper with apple-flavored Pit Bosss, power the grill on by using the control panel, select 'smoke' on the temperature dial, or set the temperature to 450 degrees F and let it preheat for a minimum of 15 minutes.
2. Meanwhile, take a medium bowl, place peas in it, add garlic powder and oil, season with salt and black pepper, toss until mixed and then spread on the sheet pan.
3. When the grill has preheated, open the lid, place the prepared sheet pan on the grill grate, shut the grill and smoke for 10 minutes until slightly charred.
4. Serve straight away.

Nutrition: Calories: 91 kCal Fat: 5 g Carbs: 9 g Protein: 4 g

390. Grilled Asparagus

Preparation Time: 5 minutes
Cooking Time: 20 minutes
Servings: 4
Ingredients:

- 3 cups of vegetables sliced
- 2 tbsp. of olive oil
- 2 tbsp. of garlic & herb seasoning

Directions:

1. Preheat your Pit Boss grill to a temperature of about 350°F
2. While your Pit Boss is heating, slice the vegetables. Cut the spears from the Broccoli and the Zucchini; then wash the outsides and slice into spears; cut the peppers into wide strips. You can also grill carrots, corn, asparagus, and potatoes -grill at a temperature of about 350°F for about 20 minutes. Serve and enjoy!

Nutrition Calories: 47 kCal, Fat: 3g, Carbs: 1g, Protein: 2.2g

391. Grill Eggplants

Preparation Time: 5 minutes
Cooking Time: 12 minutes
Servings: 6

Ingredients:

- 1 to 2 large eggplants
- 3 tablespoons of extra virgin olive oil
- 2 tablespoons of balsamic vinegar
- 2 finely minced garlic cloves
- 1 pinch of each thyme, dill; oregano, and basil

Directions:

1. Gather your ingredients.
2. Heat your Pit Boss grill to a medium-high
3. When the Pit Boss grill becomes hot; slice the eggplant into slices of about 1/2-inch of thickness
4. In a bowl, whisk the olive oil with the balsamic vinegar, the garlic, the herbs, the salt, and the pepper.
5. Brush both sides of the sliced eggplant with oil and with the vinegar mixture.
6. Place the eggplant over the preheated grill
7. Grill the eggplant for about 12 minutes
8. Serve and enjoy!

Nutrition Calories: 56 kCal, Fat: 0.8g, Carbs: 11g, Protein: 4g

392. Roasted Fall Vegetables

Preparation Time: 10 minutes
Cooking Time: 35 minutes
Servings: 8

Ingredients:

- Potatoes – ½ pound
- Brussels sprouts, halved – ½ pound
- Butternut squash, dice – ½ pound
- Cremini mushrooms, halved – 1 pint
- Salt – 1 tablespoon
- Ground black pepper – ¾ tablespoon
- Olive oil – 2 tablespoons

Directions:

1. In the meantime, take a large bowl, place potatoes in it, add salt and black pepper, drizzle with oil and then toss until coated.
2. Take a sheet tray and then spread seasoned potatoes on it.
3. When the grill has preheated, place sheet pan containing potatoes on the grilling rack and then grill for 15 minutes.

4. Then add mushrooms and sprouts into the pan, toss to coat and then continue grilling for 20 minutes until all the vegetables have turned nicely browned and thoroughly cooked.
5. Serve immediately.

Nutrition: Calories: 80 kCal Carbs: 7g Fat: 6g Protein: 1g

393. Cinnamon Almonds

Preparation Time: 15 minutes
Cooking Time: 1 hour and 30 minutes
Servings: 4

Ingredients:

- Almonds – 1 pound
- Granulated sugar – ½ cup
- Brown sugar – ½ cup
- Cinnamon – 1 tablespoon
- Salt – 1/8 teaspoon
- Egg white – 1

Directions:

1. In the meantime, take a small bowl, place egg white in it, and then whisk until frothy.
2. Add remaining ingredients for the seasoning in it, whisk until blended, then add almonds and toss until well coated.
3. Take a sheet pan and then spread almonds mixture in it.
4. When the grill has preheated, place sheet pan containing almonds mixture on the grilling rack and grill for 90 minutes until almonds have roasted, stirring every 10 minutes.
5. Check the fire after one hour of smoking and add more wood pallets if required.
6. When done, remove sheet pan from grill, let it cool slightly and then serve.

Nutrition: Calories 136.9 kCal Carbs: 15g Fat: 8g Protein: 3g

394. Roasted Pumpkin Seeds

Preparation Time: 10 minutes
Cooking Time: 40 minutes
Servings: 8
Ingredients:

- Pumpkin seeds – 1 pound
- Salt – 1 tablespoon
- Olive oil – 1 tablespoon

Directions:

1. In the meantime, take a baking sheet, grease it with oil, spread pumpkin seeds on it and then stir until coated.
2. When the grill has preheated, place baking sheet containing pumpkin sees on the grilling rack and let grill for 20 minutes.
3. Season pumpkin seeds with salt, switch temperature of the grill to 325 degrees F, and continue grilling for 20 minutes until roasted.
4. When done, let pumpkin seeds cool slightly and then serve.

Nutrition: Calories: 130 kCal Carbs: 13g Fat: 5g Protein 8g

395. Crispy Garlic Potatoes

Preparation Time: 15 minutes
Cooking Time: 40 minutes
Servings: 4
Ingredients:

- Baby potatoes, scrubbed – 1 pound
- Large white onion, peeled, sliced – 1
- Garlic, peeled, sliced – 3
- Chopped parsley – 1 teaspoon
- Butter, unsalted, sliced – 3 tablespoons

Directions:

1. In the meantime, cut potatoes in slices and then arrange them on a large piece of foil or baking sheet, separating potatoes by onion slices and butter.
2. Sprinkle garlic slices over vegetables, and then season with salt, black pepper, and parsley.
3. When the grill has preheated, place a baking sheet containing potato mixture on the grilling rack and grill for 40 minutes until potato slices have turned tender.
4. Serve immediately.

Nutrition: Calories: 150 kCal Carbs: 15g Fat: 10g Protein: 1g

396. Stuffed Avocados

Preparation Time: 5 minutes
Cooking Time: 10 to 15 minutes
Servings: 3 to 4
Ingredients:

- 4 Avocados, Halved, Pit Removed
- 8 Eggs
- 2 Cups Shredded Cheddar Cheese
- 4 Slices Bacon, Cooked and Chopped
- 1/4 Cup Cherry Tomatoes, Halved
- Green Onions, Sliced Thin
- Salt and Pepper, To Taste

Directions:

1. When ready to cook, set the temperature to High and preheat, lid closed for 15 minutes.
2. After removing the pit from the avocado, scoop out a little of the flesh to make enough room to fit 1 egg per half.
3. Fill the bottom of a cast iron pan with kosher salt and nestle the avocado halves into the salt, cut side up. The salt helps to keep them in place while cooking, like ice with oysters.
4. Crack egg into each half, top with a hand full of shredded cheddar cheese, some cherry tomatoes and bacon. Season with salt and pepper to taste.
5. Place the cast iron pan directly on the grill grate and bake the avocados for 12-15 minutes until the cheese is melted and the egg is just set.
6. Remove from the grill and let rest 5-10 minutes. Enjoy!

Nutrition: Calories: 120 kCal Carbs: 12g Fat: 18g Protein: 2g

397. Smoked Tomatoes

Preparation Time: 5 minutes
Cooking Time: 45 minutes
Servings: 3
Ingredients:

- Tomatoes, cut in half
- Dried lovage (optional)
- Sea salt
- Black pepper
- Olive oil (enough to coat the tomatoes)

Directions:

1. Set your grill to the Smoke setting.
2. Slice tomatoes in half and coat with olive oil in a bowl large enough to hold them. Add a liberal

pinch of sea salt, freshly cracked black pepper, and dried lovage to taste (if using). Use your hands and mix the tomatoes until evenly coated in the mixture.

3. Place tomatoes on a baking sheet and then on the grill.
4. Increase temperature to about 180-200.
5. Tomatoes will be done in approximately 45 minutes. The edges will begin to curl and insides to bubble.

Nutrition: Calories: 35 kCal Carbs: 2g Fat: 2g Protein: 1g

398. Smoked Olives

Preparation Time: 5 minutes
Cooking Time: 30 to 50 minutes
Servings: 4
Ingredients:
- 1 cup black olives such as Greek Kalamata or Atalante, drained lightly
- 1 cup green olives, drained lightly
- 2 tbsp. extra-virgin olive oil
- 2 tbsp. white wine - vermouth works great
- 2 garlic cloves minced
- 3/4 tsp dried rosemary We have also used oregano with some great success but the rosemary has a better all-around taste.
- fresh ground black pepper to taste
- Perfect Mix Pit Bosss

Directions:
1. Set Pit Boss grill at 220 with perfect mix Pit Bosss.
2. Arrange the olives in a shallow piece of heavy-duty foil molded into a small tray.
3. Add the remaining Ingredients:
4. Place the olives in the smoker and cook until the olives absorb half of the liquid and take on a light but identifiable smoke flavor, 30-50 minutes. Time depends on your grill!! Taste test after about 15-20 minutes.
5. The olives can be served immediately with some asiago grated cheese over them or can sit for several hours to develop the flavor further.
6. Refrigerate any leftovers. Be sure to save the leftover olive oil for bread dipping.

Nutrition: Calories: 40 Carbs: 1g Fat: 4g

399. Smoked Jalapeno Poppers

Preparation Time: 10 minutes
Cooking Time: 20 to 25 minutes
Servings: 4
Ingredients:
- 12 jalapeño peppers
- 8-ounces cream cheese, room temperature
- 10 pieces of bacon

Directions:
1. Preheat your grill or another wood-Pit Boss grill to 350°.
2. Wash and cut the tops off of the peppers, and then slice them in half the long way. Scrape the seeds and the membranes out, and set aside.
3. Spoon softened cream cheese into the popper, and wrap with bacon and secure with a toothpick.
4. Place on wire racks that are non-stick or have been sprayed with non-stick spray, and grill for 20-25 minutes, or until the bacon is cooked.

Nutrition: Calories: 94 Carbs: 5g Fat: 7g

400. Heirloom Tomato Tart

Preparation Time: 20 minutes
Cooking Time: 1 hour and 40 minutes
Servings: 6
Ingredients:
- 1 Sheet Puff Pastry
- 2 Lbs. Heirloom Tomatoes, Various Shapes and Sizes
- 1/2 Cup Ricotta
- 5 Eggs
- 1/2 Tbsp. Kosher Salt
- 1/2 Tsp Thyme Leaves
- 1/2 Tsp Red Pepper Flakes
- Pinch of Black Pepper
- 4 Sprigs Thyme
- Salt and Pepper, To Taste

Directions:
1. When ready to cook, set temperature to 350°F and preheat, lid closed for 15 minutes.
2. Place the puff pastry on a parchment lined sheet tray, and make a cut ¾ of the way through the pastry, ½" from the edge.
3. Slice the tomatoes and season with salt. Place on a sheet tray lined with paper towels.
4. In a small bowl combine the ricotta, 4 of the eggs, salt, thyme leaves, red pepper flakes and

black pepper. Whisk together until combined. Spread the ricotta mixture over the puff pastry, staying within ½" from the edge.

5. Lay the tomatoes out on top of the ricotta, and sprinkle with salt, pepper and thyme sprigs.
6. In a small bowl whisk the last egg. Brush the egg wash onto the exposed edges of the pastry.
7. Place the sheet tray directly on the grill grate and bake for 45 minutes, rotating half-way through.
8. When the edges are browned and the moisture from the tomatoes has evaporated, remove from the grill and let cool 5-7 minutes before serving. Enjoy!

Nutrition: Calories: 290 kCal Protein: 7g Carbs: 20g Fat: 17g

401.   Smoked Pickled Green Beans

Preparation Time: 5 minutes
Cooking Time: 15 to 20 minutes
Servings: 2
Ingredients:
- 1 Lb. Green Beans, Blanched
- 1/2 Cup Salt
- 1/2 Cup Sugar
- 1 Tbsp. Red Pepper Flake
- 2 Cups White Wine Vinegar
- 2 Cups Ice Water

Directions:
1. When ready to cook, set temperature to 180°F and preheat, lid closed for 15 minutes.
2. Place the blanched green beans on a mesh grill mat and place mat directly on the grill grate. Smoke the green beans for 30-45 minutes until they've picked up the desired amount of smoke. Remove from grill and set aside until the brine is ready.
3. In a medium sized saucepan, bring all remaining Ingredients: except ice water, to a boil over medium high heat on the stove. Simmer for 5-10 minutes then remove from heat and steep 20 minutes more. Pour brine over ice water to cool.
4. Once brine has cooled, pour over the green beans and weigh them down with a few plates to ensure they are completely submerged. Let sit 24 hours before use.

Nutrition: Calories: 8 kCal Fat: 0g Carbs: 3g Protein: 1g

402.   Baked Asparagus Pancetta Cheese Tart

Preparation Time: 10 minutes
Cooking Time: 20 to 30 minutes
Servings: 5
Ingredients:
- 1 Sheet Puff Pastry
- 8 Oz Asparagus, Pencil Spears
- 8 Oz Pancetta, Cooked and Drained
- 1 Cup Cream
- 4 Eggs
- 1/4 Cup Goat Cheese
- 4 Tbsp. Grated Parmesan
- 1 Tbsp. Chopped Chives
- Black Pepper

Directions:
1. When ready to cook, set the temperature to 375°F and preheat, lid closed for 15 minutes.
2. Place the puff pastry on a half sheet tray and score around the perimeter 1-inch in from the edges making sure not to cut all the way through. Prick the center of the puff pastry with a fork.
3. Place the sheet tray directly on the grill grate and bake for 15-20 minutes until the pastry has puffed and browned a little bit.
4. While the pastry bakes combine the cream, 3 eggs, both cheeses and chives in a small bowl. Whisk to mix well.
5. Remove the sheet tray from the grill and pour the egg mixture into the puff pastry. Lay the asparagus spears on top of the egg mixture and sprinkle with cooked pancetta.
6. Whisk remaining egg in a small bowl and brush the top of the pastry with the egg wash.
7. Place back on the grill grate and cook for another 15-20 minutes until the egg mixture is just set.
8. Finish tart with lemon zest, more chopped chives and shaved parmesan.

Nutrition: Calories: 450 kCal Carbs: 5g Fat: 40g Protein: 9g

403. Georgia Sweet Onion Bake

Preparation Time: 10 Minutes
Cooking Time: 30 Minutes
Servings: 4

Ingredients:

- 4 large Vidalia or other sweet onions
- 8 tablespoons (1 stick) unsalted butter, melted
- 4 chicken bouillon cubes
- 1 cup grated Parmesan cheese

Directions:

1. Supply your smoker with Pit Boss and follow the manufacturer's specific start-up procedure. Preheat, with the lid closed, to 350°F.
2. Coat a high-sided baking pan with cooking spray or butter.
3. Peel the onions and cut into quarters, separating into individual petals.
4. Spread the onions out in the prepared pan and pour the melted butter over them.
5. Crush the bouillon cubes and sprinkle over the buttery onion pieces, then top with the cheese.
6. Transfer the pan to the grill, close the lid, and smoke for 30 minutes.
7. Remove the pan from the grill, cover tightly with aluminum foil, and poke several holes all over to vent.
8. Place the pan back on the grill, close the lid, and smoke for an additional 30 to 45 minutes.
9. Uncover the onions, stir, and serve hot.

Nutrition: Calories: 150 kCal Carbs: 14g Fat: 9g Protein: 2g

404. Roasted Okra

Preparation Time: 10 Minutes
Cooking Time: 30 Minutes
Servings: 4

Ingredients:

- 1-pound whole okra
- 2 tablespoons extra-virgin olive oil
- 2 teaspoons seasoned salt
- 2 teaspoons freshly ground black pepper

Directions:

1. Supply your smoker with Pit Boss and follow the manufacturer's specific start-up procedure. Preheat, with the lid closed, to 400°F. Alternatively, preheat your oven to 400°F.
2. Line a shallow rimmed baking pan with aluminum foil and coat with cooking spray.
3. Arrange the okra on the pan in a single layer. Drizzle with the olive oil, turning to coat. Season on all sides with the salt and pepper.
4. Place the baking pan on the grill grate, close the lid, and smoke for 30 minutes, or until crisp and slightly charred. Alternatively, roast in the oven for 30 minutes.
5. Serve hot.
6. Smoking Tip: Whether you make this okra in the oven or in your Pit Boss grill, be sure to fully preheat the oven or cook chamber for the best results.

Nutrition: Calories: 65 kCal Carbs: 10 g Protein: 1g Fat: 1g

405. Sweet Potato Chips

Preparation Time: 10 Minutes
Cooking Time: 12 to 15 Minutes
Servings: 4

Ingredients:

- 2 sweet potatoes
- 1-quart warm water
- 1 tablespoon cornstarch, plus 2 teaspoons
- ¼ cup extra-virgin olive oil
- 1 tablespoon salt
- 1 tablespoon packed brown sugar
- 1 teaspoon ground cinnamon
- 1 teaspoon freshly ground black pepper
- ½ teaspoon cayenne pepper

Directions:

1. Using a mandolin, thinly slice the sweet potatoes.
2. Pour the warm water into a large bowl and add 1 tablespoon of cornstarch and the potato slices. Let soak for 15 to 20 minutes.
3. Supply your smoker with Pit Boss and follow the manufacturer's specific start-up procedure. Preheat, with the lid closed, to 375°F.
4. Drain the potato slices, then arrange in a single layer on a perforated pizza pan or a baking sheet lined with aluminum foil. Brush the potato slices on both sides with the olive oil.
5. In a small bowl, whisk together the salt, brown sugar, cinnamon, black pepper, cayenne pepper, and the remaining 2 teaspoons of cornstarch. Sprinkle this seasoning blend on both sides of the potatoes.

6. Place the pan or baking sheet on the grill grate, close the lid, and smoke for 35 to 45 minutes, flipping after 20 minutes, until the chips curl up and become crispy.
7. Store in an airtight container.

Ingredient Tip: Avoid storing your sweet potatoes in the refrigerator's produce bin, which tends to give them a hard center and an unpleasant flavor. What, you don't have a root cellar? Just keep them in a cool, dry area of your kitchen.

Nutrition: Calories: 80 kCal Carbs: 20 g Protein: 2 g Fat: 0g

406. Pit Boss Grilled Zucchini Squash Spears

Preparation Time: 5 minutes,
Cooking Time: 10 minutes.
Servings: 5
Ingredients:
1. 4 zucchinis, cleaned and ends cut
2. 2 tbsp. olive oil
3. 1 tbsp. sherry vinegar
4. 2 thyme leaves pulled
5. Salt and pepper to taste

Directions:
1. Cut the zucchini into halves then cut each half thirds.
2. Add the rest of the ingredients in a zip lock bag with the zucchini pieces. Toss to mix well.
3. Preheat the Pit Boss temperature to 350°F with the lid closed for 15 minutes.
4. Remove the zucchini from the bag and place them on the grill grate with the cut side down.
5. Cook for 4 minutes until the zucchini are tender
6. Remove from grill and serve with thyme leaves. Enjoy.

Nutrition: Calories: 74 kCal Fat: 5.4g Carbs: 6.1g Protein: 2.6g

407. Whole Roasted Cauliflower with Garlic Parmesan Butter

Preparation Time: 15 minutes
Cooking Time: 45 minutes
Servings: 5
Ingredients:
- 1/4 cup olive oil
- Salt and pepper to taste
- 1 cauliflower, fresh
- 1/2 cup butter, melted
- 1/4 cup parmesan cheese, grated
- 2 garlic cloves, minced
- 1/2 tbsp. parsley, chopped

Directions:
1. Preheat the Pit Boss grill with the lid closed for 15 minutes.
2. Meanwhile, brush the cauliflower with oil then season with salt and pepper.
3. Place the cauliflower in a cast Iron: and place it on a grill grate.
4. Cook for 45 minutes or until the cauliflower is golden brown and tender
5. Meanwhile, mix butter, cheese, garlic, and parsley in a mixing bowl.
6. In the last 20 minutes of cooking, add the butter mixture.
7. Remove the cauliflower and top with more cheese and parsley if you desire. Enjoy.

Nutrition: Calories: 156 kCal Fat: 11.1g Carbs: 8.8g Protein: 8.2g

408. Pit Boss Cold Smoked Cheese

Preparation Time: 5 minutes
Cooking Time: 2 minutes
Servings: 10
Ingredients:
- Ice
- 1 aluminum pan, full-size and disposable
- 1 aluminum pan, half-size, and disposable
- Toothpicks
- A block of cheese

Directions:
1. Preheat the Pit Boss to 165°F with the lid closed for 15 minutes.
2. Place the small pan in the large pan. Fill the surrounding of the small pan with ice.
3. Place the cheese in the small pan on top of toothpicks then place the pan on the grill and close the lid.
4. Smoke cheese for 1 hour, flip the cheese, and smoke for 1 more hour with the lid closed.
5. Remove the cheese from the grill and wrap it in parchment paper. Store in the fridge for 2 3 days for the smoke flavor to mellow.
6. Remove from the fridge and serve. Enjoy.

Nutrition: Calories: 1910 kCal Fat: 7g Carbs: 2g Protein: 6g

409. Pit Boss Grilled Asparagus and Honey Glazed Carrots

Preparation Time: 15 minutes
Cooking Time: 35 minutes
Servings: 5
Ingredients:

- 1 bunch asparagus, trimmed ends
- 1 lb. carrots, peeled
- 2 tbsp. olive oil
- Sea salt to taste
- 2 tbsp. honey
- Lemon zest

Directions:

1. Sprinkle the asparagus with oil and sea salt. Drizzle the carrots with honey and salt.
2. Preheat the Pit Boss to 165°F with the lid closed for 15 minutes.
3. Place the carrots in the Pit Boss and cook for 15 minutes. Add asparagus and cook for 20 more minutes or until cooked through.
4. Top the carrots and asparagus with lemon zest. Enjoy.

Nutrition: Calories: 1680 kCal Fat: 30g Carbs: 10g Protein: 4g

410. Pit Boss Smoked Asparagus

Preparation Time: 5 minutes
Cooking Time: 1 hour
Servings: 4
Ingredients:

- 1 bunch fresh asparagus ends cut
- 2 tbsp. olive oil
- Salt and pepper to taste

Directions:

1. Fire up your Pit Boss smoker to 230°F
2. Place the asparagus in a mixing bowl and drizzle with olive oil. Season with salt and pepper.
3. Place the asparagus in a tinfoil sheet and fold the sides such that you create a basket.
4. Smoke the asparagus for 1 hour or until soft turning after half an hour.
5. Remove from the grill and serve. Enjoy.

Nutrition: Calories: 43 kCal Fat: 2g Carbs: 4g Protein: 3g

411. Pit Boss Smoked Acorn Squash

Preparation Time: 10 minutes
Cooking Time: 2 hours
Servings: 6
Ingredients:

- 3 tbsp. olive oil
- 3 acorn squashes, halved and seeded
- 1/4 cup unsalted butter
- 1/4 cup brown Sugar:
- 1 tbsp. cinnamon, ground
- 1 tbsp. chili powder
- 1 tbsp. nutmeg, ground

Directions:

1. Brush olive oil on the acorn squash cut sides then covers the halves with foil. Poke holes on the foil to allow steam and smoke through.
2. Fire up the Pit Boss to 225°F and smoke the squash for 1 ½-2 hours.
3. Remove the squash from the smoker and allow it to sit.
4. Meanwhile, melt butter, Sugar: and spices in a saucepan. Stir well to combine.
5. Remove the foil from the squash and spoon the butter mixture in each squash half. Enjoy.

Nutrition: Calories: 149 kCal Fat: 10g Carbs: 14g Protein: 2g

412. Vegan Smoked Carrot Dogs

Preparation Time: 25 minutes
Cooking Time: 35 minutes
Servings: 4
Ingredients:

- 4 thick carrots
- 2 tbsp. avocado oil
- 1 tbsp. liquid smoke
- 1/2 tbsp. garlic powder
- Salt and pepper to taste

Directions:

1. Preheat the Pit Boss grill to 425°F and line a baking sheet with parchment paper.
2. Peel the carrots and round the edges.
3. In a mixing bowl, mix oil, liquid smoke, garlic, salt, and pepper. Place the carrots on the baking dish then pour the mixture over.
4. Roll the carrots to coat evenly with the mixture and use fingertips to massage the mixture into the carrots.

5. Place in the grill and grill for 35 minutes or until the carrots are fork-tender ensuring to turn and brush the carrots every 5 minutes with the marinade.

6. Remove from the grill and place the carrots in hot dog bun. Serve with your favorite toppings and enjoy.

Nutrition: Calories: 149 kCal Fat: 1.6g Carbs: 27.9g Protein: 5.4g

413. Pit Boss Grill Smoked Vegetables

Preparation Time: 5 minutes
Cooking Time: 15 minutes
Servings: 6
Ingredients:
- 1 ear corn, fresh, husks and silk strands removed
- 1yellow squash, sliced
- 1 red onion, cut into wedges
- 1 green pepper, cut into strips
- 1 red pepper, cut into strips
- 1 yellow pepper, cut into strips
- 1 cup mushrooms, halved
- 2 tbsp. oil
- 2 tbsp. chicken seasoning

Directions:
1. Soak the pecan Pit Boss in water for an hour. Remove the Pit Bosss from water and fill the smoker box with the wet Pit Bosss.
2. Place the smoker box under the grill and close the lid. Heat the grill on high heat for 10 minutes or until smoke starts coming out from the wood chips.
3. Meanwhile, toss the veggies in oil and seasonings then transfer them into a grill basket.
4. Grill for 10 minutes while turning occasionally. Serve and enjoy.

Nutrition: Calories: 97 kCal Fat: 5g Carbs: 11g Protein: 2g

414. Pit Boss Grill Spicy Sweet Potatoes

Preparation Time: 10 minutes
Cooking Time: 35 minutes
Servings: 6
Ingredients:
- 2 lb. sweet potatoes, cut into chunks

- 1 red onion, chopped
- 2 tbsp. oil
- 2 tbsp. orange juice
- 1 tbsp. roasted cinnamon
- 1 tbsp. salt
- 1/4 tbsp. Chipotle chili pepper

Directions:
1. Preheat the Pit Boss grill to 425°F with the lid closed.
2. Toss the sweet potatoes with onion, oil, and juice.
3. In a mixing bowl, mix cinnamon, salt, and pepper then sprinkle the mixture over the sweet potatoes.
4. Spread the potatoes on a lined baking dish in a single layer.
5. Place the baking dish in the grill and grill for 30 minutes or until the sweet potatoes are tender.
6. Serve and enjoy.

Nutrition: Calories: 145 kCal Fat: 5g Carbs: 23g Protein: 2g

415. Pit Boss Grilled Mexican Street Corn

Preparation Time: 5 minutes
Cooking Time: 25 minutes
Servings: 6
Ingredients:
- 6 ears of corn on the cob
- 1 tbsp. olive oil
- Kosher salt and pepper to taste
- 1/4 cup mayo
- 1/4 cup sour cream
- 1 tbsp. garlic paste
- 1/2 tbsp. chili powder
- Pinch of ground red pepper
- 1/2 cup coria cheese, crumbled
- 1/4 cup cilantro, chopped
- 6 lime wedges

Directions:
1. Brush the corn with oil.
2. Sprinkle with salt.
3. Place the corn on a Pit Boss grill set at 350°F. Cook for 25 minutes as you turn it occasionally.
4. Meanwhile mix mayo, cream, garlic, chili, and red pepper until well combined.
5. Let it rest for some minutes then brush with the mayo mixture.

6. Sprinkle cottage cheese, more chili powder, and cilantro. Serve with lime wedges. Enjoy.

Nutrition: Calories: 144 kCal Fat: 5g Carbs: 10g Protein: 0g

416. Smoked Broccoli

Preparation Time: 10 minutes
Cooking Time: 30 minutes
Servings: 4
Ingredients:
- 2 heads broccoli
- Kosher salt
- 2 tablespoons vegetable oil
- Fresh Pepper (ground)

Directions:
1. Preheat your smoker to 350F.
2. Separate the florets from the heads.
3. Coat the broccoli with vegetable oil by tossing. Thereafter, season with salt and pepper.
4. Using a grilling basket, put the broccoli on the grate of the smoker and smoke for 30 minutes or till crisp.
5. Enjoy!

Nutrition: Calories 76 kCal Fat 7g Protein 1.3g Carbs 3.1g

417. Smoked Mushrooms 2 -

Preparation Time: 10 minutes
Cooking Time: 1 hour
Servings: 4
Ingredients:
- 2 lb. mushrooms (Button or Portabella)
- 2 cups Italian dressing
- Pepper
- Salt

Directions:
1. In a gallon zip lock bag, add in the mushrooms.
2. Pour in the Italian dressing in the zip lock bag and some pepper and salt to taste.
3. Refrigerate for 1 hour.
4. Once ready to cook, preheat your smoker to 250F.
5. Smoke mushrooms for an hour or till much soft and a bit smaller in size.

Note: mushrooms will smoke well at any temperature so long as they don't burn.

Nutrition: Calories 392 kCal Fat 34g Carbs 19.8g Protein 7.6g

418. Smoked Butternut Squash

Preparation Time: 15 minutes
Cooking Time: 1 hour 30 minutes
Servings: 5
Ingredients:
- 1 whole butternut squash
- 2 tablespoons olive oil
- 1 tablespoon brown sugar
- 1/2 tablespoon chili powder
- 1 teaspoon black pepper
- 1 teaspoon kosher salt
- 1/2 teaspoon garlic powder

Directions:
1. Preheat your smoker to 325F.
2. Half the squash lengthwise with a knife. Make lines to its flesh as shown above.
3. In a bowl, add the olive oil, garlic pepper, chili powder and brown sugar and combine. Brush this mixture on the expose top part.
4. Put the butternut squash on the smoker and smoke for 1.5 hours or till your preferred tenderness. Brush the squash with the mixture once more on the last 30 minutes of smoking.
5. Remove from the smoker.

Nutrition: Calories 110 kCal Fat 5.9g Carbs 15.7g Protein 1.3g

419. Smoke-Grilled Eggplant

Preparation Time: 10 minutes
Cooking Time: 10 minutes
Servings: 4
Ingredients:
- 1 eggplant (large in size)
- 4 tablespoons coconut aminos
- 2 tablespoons avocado oil
- 2 teaspoons cumin (ground)
- 2 teaspoons smoked paprika
- 2 teaspoons coriander (ground)
- 2 teaspoons cumin (ground)
- 1/2 teaspoon cayenne pepper
- 1/2 teaspoon garlic powder
- 1/2 teaspoon sea salt

Directions:
1. Cut the eggplant lengthwise to 1/4-inch slices. Drizzle and brush the eggplant slices with the coconut aminos and avocado oil.

2. In a small mixing bowl, combine the spices. Sprinkle the mix on the slices on both sides, ensuring they are full coated.
3. Preheat your grill to medium high heat and place the slices. Grill each side for 3 minutes till they become tender.
4. Remove from the grill and enjoy.

Nutrition: Calories 62 kCal Fat 1.5g Carbs 11.6g Protein 1.6g

420. Smoked Vegetables

Preparation Time: 15 minutes
Cooking Time: 45 minutes
Servings: 4
Ingredients:
- Summer squash (sliced)
- Olive oil
- Balsamic vinegar
- Red onion
- Zucchini (sliced)
- Red pepper
- Black pepper
- Garlic (sliced)
- Sea salt

Directions:
1. Add all ingredients in a mixing bowl and combine.
2. Preheat smoker to 350F.
3. Smoked for 30 to 45 minutes or till well cooked through.

Nutrition: Calories 120 kCal Fat 7g Carbs 12g Protein 2g

421. Kale Chips

Preparation Time: 30 Minutes
Cooking Time: 20 Minutes
Servings: 4
Ingredients:
- 4 cups kale leaves
- Olive oil
- Salt to taste

Directions:
1. Drizzle kale with oil and sprinkle it with salt.
2. Set the Pit Boss wood pellet grill to 250 degrees F.
3. Preheat it for 15 minutes while the lid is closed.
4. Add the kale leaves to a baking pan.
5. Place the pan on the grill.

6. Cook the kale for 20 minutes or until crispy.

Nutrition: Calories 118 kCal Fat 7.6g Carbs 10.8g Protein 5.4g

422. Roasted Spicy Tomatoes

Preparation Time: 30 Minutes
Cooking Time: 1 Hour and 30 Minutes
Servings: 4
Ingredients:
- 2 lb. large tomatoes, sliced in half
- Olive oil
- Two tablespoon garlic, chopped
- Three tablespoons parsley, chopped
- Salt and pepper to taste
- Hot pepper sauce

Directions:
1. Set the temperature to 400 degrees F.
2. Preheat it for 15 minutes while the lid is closed.
3. Add tomatoes to a baking pan.
4. Drizzle with oil and sprinkle with garlic, parsley, salt, and pepper.
5. Roast for 1 hour and 30 minutes.
6. Drizzle with hot pepper sauce and serve.

Nutrition: Calories 118 kCal Fat 7.6g Carbs 10.8g Protein 5.4g

423. Quiche with Mushrooms, Bacon and Mozzarella

Preparation Time: 25 minutes
Cooking Time: 32 minutes
Servings: 8
Ingredients:
- 1 roll of puff pastry
- 300 grams of mushrooms
- 2 mozzarellas
- 100 grams of bacon cut into cubes
- 1 clove of garlic
- 100 ml of cooking cream
- 40 grams of grated Parmesan cheese
- 1 egg
- Salt and pepper to taste
- Olive oil to taste

Directions:
1. Start by washing and drying the mushrooms and then cut them into slices.
2. Peel and wash the garlic and then chop it.

3. Put a tablespoon of oil in a non-stick pan, and as soon as it is hot, put the garlic to brown.
4. Add the pancetta and brown it for 3 minutes.
5. Add the mushrooms, season with salt and pepper and cook for 10 minutes.
6. Turn off and let them cool.
7. Put the egg, the cooking cream and the Parmesan in a bowl.
8. Mix with a whisk until you get a homogeneous mixture.
9. Put the mixture of mushrooms and bacon and mix again.
10. Put the puff pastry in a round baking pan, brushed with olive oil.
11. Prick the bottom of the puff pastry with a fork and then put the filling inside.
12. Preheat the Pit Boss with the lid closed for 15 minutes at 482 ° F.
13. Insert the grill into the barbecue, place the baking pan in the center, close the lid and cook for 30 minutes.
14. Just cooked, remove it from the barbecue and let it rest for 10 minutes.
15. After 10 minutes, cut it into slices, put it on plates and serve.

Nutrition Calories 299 kCal Fat 12 g Carbs 17 g Proteins 11 g

424. Quiche with Tomatoes, Olives and Walnuts

Preparation Time: 13 minutes
Cooking Time: 28 minutes
Servings: 4
Ingredients:
- 1 roll of puff pastry
- 250 grams of feta
- 170 grams of Greek yogurt
- 12 pitted olives
- 1 shallot
- 100 grams of cherry tomatoes
- 2 eggs
- 1 teaspoon of dried oregano
- 4 chopped walnut kernels
- Olive oil to taste
- Salt and pepper to taste

Directions:
1. Peel and wash the shallot and then chop it.
2. Wash and dry the cherry tomatoes and then cut them in half.

3. Put the yogurt, the feta cut into small pieces, the shallot, the eggs, the oregano and the olives in a bowl. Mix well and then season with salt and pepper.
4. Brush a baking pan with olive oil and line it with the puff pastry.
5. Prick the bottom with a fork and put the filling inside.
6. Now put the tomatoes and chopped walnut kernels on top.
7. Preheat the Pit Boss at 500 ° F for 15 minutes.
8. Preheat a pizza stone for 10 minutes.
9. Put the baking pan on the stone and let it cook for 20 minutes.
10. When cooked, remove the quiche from the barbecue and let it rest for 10 minutes.
11. Remove the quiche from the baking dish, cut it into slices, put it on plates and serve.

Nutrition Calories 322 kCal Fat 21 g Carbs 18 g Protein 14g

425. Quiche with Salmon and Shallots

Preparation Time: 15 minutes
Cooking Time: 26 minutes
Servings: 4
Ingredients:
- 1 roll of short crust pastry
- 2 shallots
- 3 eggs
- 200 ml of cooking cream
- 100 grams of smoked salmon
- Olive oil to taste
- Salt and pepper to taste

Directions:
1. Start by peeling and washing the shallots, and then cut them into thin slices.
2. Heat a tablespoon of oil in a pan and then sauté the shallots for two minutes. Season with salt and pepper and turn off.
3. Put the eggs in a bowl and beat them with a fork.
4. Add the cooking cream, salt and pepper and mix well.
5. Now put the shallots in the bowl and mix everything together.
6. Take a round baking pan and put the short crust pastry inside.
7. Put the shallots mixture inside and then the salmon cut into thin slices.

8. Preheat the Pit Boss at 482 ° F for 15 minutes.
9. Put on the pizza stone and let it heat for 10 minutes.
10. Put the baking pan on top of the stone and cook, with the lid closed, for 25 minutes.
11. Just cooked, remove the quiche from the Pit Boss and let it rest for 10 minutes.
12. After 10 minutes, cut it into slices, put it on plates and serve.

Nutrition: Calories 283 kCal Fat 17 g Carbs 21 g Proteins 9 g

426. Quiche with Blue Cheese, Peas and Onions

Preparation Time: 14 minutes
Cooking Time: 22 minutes
Servings: 4
Ingredients:
- 1 roll of short crust pastry
- 2 eggs
- 240 grams of peas
- 2 red onions
- 150 grams of blue cheese
- Salt and pepper to taste
- Olive oil to taste

Directions:
1. Peel and wash the onions and then cut them into slices.
2. Rinse the peas under running water and let them drain.
3. Heat a tablespoon of olive in a pan and when hot, sauté the onions for 2 minutes.
4. Now add the peas and brown them for 5 minutes.
5. Season with salt and pepper, then turn off and let them cool.
6. Meanwhile, beat the eggs in a bowl with salt and pepper.
7. Add the blue cheese cut into cubes and mix.
8. Now add the onion, peas, and mix.
9. Brush a baking pan with olive oil and then line it with the short crust pastry.
10. Put the filling inside and set aside.
11. Preheat the Pit Boss at 500° F for 15 minutes with the lid closed.
12. Place the grid and then place the baking dish in the center of the grid.
13. Close the lid and cook for 20 minutes.

14. Just cooked, remove the quiche from the barbecue and let it rest for 10 minutes.
15. After 10 minutes, cut it into slices, put it on plates and serve.

Nutrition: Calories 355 kCalFat 21 g Carbs 17 g Proteins 8 g

427. Leeks and Baked Eggs

Preparation Time: 5 minutes
Cooking Time: 31 minutes
Servings: 4
Ingredients:
- 400 grams of leeks already cleaned
- 4 eggs
- 50 grams of breadcrumbs
- 100 grams of gruyere
- 20 grams of grated Parmesan cheese
- Salt and pepper to taste
- Olive oil to taste

Directions:
1. First cut off the base of leeks, then cut them sideways and leaf them through. Wash them under running water and then cook them in boiling salted water for 10 minutes.
2. Drain and let them cool.
3. Take a baking dish, brush it with olive oil and then sprinkle it with breadcrumbs.
4. Now put a layer of leeks and then put a layer of gruyere cut into slices on top.
5. Continue like this until you have used up all the ingredients.
6. Now season with oil, salt and pepper.
7. Preheat the Pit Boss at 446 ° F for 15 minutes.
8. Place the grill, and put the baking dish in the center of the grill and cook for 10 minutes.
9. after 10 minutes, place the eggs on top of the leeks, sprinkle with Parmesan cheese and continue cooking for another 6 minutes.
10. Remove the pan from the barbecue and let it rest for 5 minutes.
11. Divide the leeks and eggs into four parts, put it on plates and serve.

Nutrition: Calories 326 kCal Fat 20 g Carbs 16 g Proteins 19 g

428. Pit Boss Smoked Devil Eggs

Preparation Time: 30 minutes
Cooking Time: 45 minutes
Servings: 8
Ingredients:

- 12 hard-boiled eggs, peeled and sliced in half
- Two jalapeño peppers
- Two slices bacon, cooked crisp and chopped
- 1/2 cup mayonnaise
- 2 tsp. white vinegar
- 2 tsp. mustard
- 1/2 teaspoon chili powder
- 1/2 teaspoon paprika
- Salt to taste
- Pinch paprika
- Chopped chives

Directions:

1. With the roasted peppers, Serving Set the wood pellet grill to 180 ranges F.
2. Preheat for 15 minutes while the lid is closed.
3. Smoke the eggs and peppers for forty-five minutes.
4. Transfer to a plate.
5. Scoop out the egg yolks and location in a bowl.
6. Stir in the rest of the substances.
7. Mash the eggs and blend well.
8. Scoop the egg combination on top of the egg whites.

Nutrition: Calories: 182 kcal Protein: 10.94 g Fat: 14.1 g Carbs: 2.12 g

429. Flan of Zucchini and Ham

Preparation Time: 32 minutes
Cooking Time: 31 minutes
Servings: 4
Ingredients:

- 800 grams of zucchinis
- 10 slices of raw ham
- 1 onion
- 5 eggs
- 300 ml of cooking cream
- 120 grams of grated Parmesan cheese
- Olive oil to taste
- Salt and pepper to taste

Directions:

1. Peel the courgettes, wash them and then cut them into cubes.
2. Peel and wash the onion and then chop it.
3. Put two tablespoons of oil to heat in a pan. As soon as it is hot, fry the onion for a couple of minutes.
4. Now add the zucchinis and two glasses of water and cook for 10 minutes. Season with salt and pepper and turn off.
5. In a bowl put the eggs, salt and pepper and whip them with an electric whisk.
6. Then add the Parmesan and cream and mix well.
7. Now put the zucchini cubes and mix again.
8. Brush a loaf pan with oil. Put under a layer of raw ham and then pour half of the egg and courgette mixture.
9. Put another layer of ham and pour the other half of the mixture.
10. Preheat the Pit Boss at 446 ° F for 15 minutes.
11. Place the grill inside the barbecue and then place the mold in the center.
12. Cook with the lid closed for 30 minutes.
13. As soon as the flan is ready, remove it from the grill and let it cool completely.
14. Then cut it into slices and serve.

Nutrition: Calories 340 g Fat 26 g Carbs 26 g Proteins 13g

430. Baked Pumpkin Seeds

Preparation Time: 15 minutes
Cooking Time: 45 minutes
Servings: 10
Ingredients:

- 10 cups pumpkin seeds
- 4 teaspoons melted butter
- Java steak dry rub

Directions:

1. Set your wood pellet grill to smoke.
2. Preheat it to 300 degrees F.
3. Toss the seeds in steak rub and butter.
4. Place seeds
5. Cook for 45 minutes, stirring occasionally.

Nutrition: Calories: 170 kCal Fat: 15g Carbs: 4 g   Protein: 9 g

431. Cinnamon Pumpkin Seeds

Preparation Time: 5 minutes
Cooking Time: 20-25 minutes
Servings: 8
Ingredients:
- 8 cups pumpkin seeds
- 2 tablespoons melted butter
- 2 tablespoons sugar
- 1 teaspoon ground cinnamon

Directions:
1. Set your wood pellet grill to smoke.
2. Preheat it to 350 degrees F.
3. Toss the pumpkin seeds in the butter, sugar and cinnamon.
4. Spread in a baking pan.
5. Roast for 20 to 25 minutes.

Nutrition: Calories: 285 kCal Fat: 12 g Carbs: 34 g Protein: 12 g

432. Roasted Trail Mix

Preparation Time: 10 minutes
Cooking Time: 15 minutes
Servings: 6
Ingredients:
- 1 cup pretzels
- 1 cup crackers
- 1 cup mixed nuts and seed
- 3 tablespoons butter
- 1 teaspoon smoked paprika

Directions:
1. Start your wood pellet grill.
2. Preheat it to 225 degrees F.
3. Toss all the ingredients in a roasting pan.
4. Smoke for 15 minutes.
5. Let cool and serve.

Nutrition: Calories: 150 kCal Fat: 11 g Carbs: 11 g Protein: 5 g

433. Grilled Watermelon

Preparation Time: 5 minutes
Cooking Time: 6 minutes
Servings: 8
Ingredients:
- 1 watermelon, sliced
- Feta cheese
- Mint leaves, chopped

Directions:
1. Preheat your wood pellet grill to 450 degrees F.
2. Grill the watermelon for 3 minutes per side.
3. Slice into cubes.
4. Transfer to a bowl.
5. Top with the cheese and mint leaves.

Nutrition: Calories: 14 kCal Fat: 0 g Carbs: 3 g Protein: 0g

434. Grilled Peaches

Preparation Time: 5 minutes
Cooking Time: 10 minutes
Servings: 6
Ingredients:
- 1/2 tablespoon ground cinnamon
- 3 tablespoons brown sugar
- 3 peaches, sliced in half and pitted
- 1 tablespoon melted butter

Directions:
1. Turn on your wood pellet grill.
2. Set it to smoke.
3. Establish fire in the burn pot for 5 minutes.
4. Set it to 400 degrees F.
5. In a bowl, mix the cinnamon and brown sugar.
6. Coat the peaches with the butter.
7. Grill for 6 minutes.
8. Flip and sprinkle with the sugar mixture.
9. Grill for 2 minutes.

Nutrition: Calories: 98 Cal Fat: 6 g Carbs: 12 g Protein: 1 g Fiber: 1 g

435. Grilled Strawberries

Preparation Time: 5 minutes
Cooking Time: 5 minutes
Servings: 4
Ingredients:
- 1 tablespoon lemon juice
- 4 tablespoons honey
- 16 strawberries

Directions:
1. Turn on your wood pellet grill.
2. Set it to 450 degrees F.
3. Thread the strawberries into skewers.
4. Brush with the honey and lemon juice.
5. Grill for 5 minutes.

Nutrition: Calories: 53 kCal Fat: 0 g Carbs: 12 g Protein: 1 g

436. Cilantro and Lime Corn

Preparation Time: 15 minutes
Cooking Time: 15 minutes
Servings: 4
Ingredients:
- 4 corn cobs
- 1 tablespoon lime juice
- 2 tablespoons melted butter
- Smoked paprika
- 1 cup cilantro, chopped

Directions:
1. Preheat your wood pellet grill to 400 degrees F.
2. Grill for 15 minutes, rotating every 5 minutes.
3. Brush the corn cobs with a mixture of lime juice and butter.
4. Season with the paprika.

Nutrition: Calories: 100 kCal Fat: 2 g Carbs: 19 g Protein: 3 g

Chapter 7: Pizza and Bread Recipes

437. Basic Pizza Dough

Preparation Time: 18 minutes
Cooking Time: 3 hours
Servings: 2
Ingredients:
- 500 grams of flour
- 300 ml of warm water
- 2 tablespoons of olive oil
- 5 grams of brewer's yeast
- 1 teaspoon of salt

Directions:
1. Start by pouring the yeast into the water at room temperature and let it melt well.
2. Put the flour in a bowl.
3. Start pouring a little water at a time and knead with your hands.
4. As soon as you have poured half the water, add the salt to the dough.
5. Continue to knead always pouring a little water at a time.
6. Knead well until you have obtained a homogeneous mixture.
7. At this point, you can add the oil, also poured a little at a time while you continue to knead.
8. Finally, transfer the dough to the work surface and knead it with your hands.
9. Once you have a nice smooth dough, let it rest on the work surface for about ten minutes, covering the bowl with a kitchen towel.
10. After 10 minutes, take the dough and knead it again, stretching it and then reassembling it to form a ball.
11. Transfer the resulting dough back to the bowl. Put the bowl in a warm place, cover with cling film and let it rise for 2 hours.
12. After the rising time, transfer the dough to the work surface and divide it in half.
13. Transfer the two doughs to a tray and let them rest for another half hour, always covered with plastic wrap or a cloth before you can roll the pizza dough and season it to your liking.

Nutrition: Calories 207 kCal Fat 4g Carbs 37g Proteins 6g

438. Pizza with Olives and Capers

Preparation Time: 16 minutes
Cooking Time: 16 minutes
Servings: 4
Ingredients:
- 850 grams of pizza dough
- 400 grams of tomato pulp
- 130 grams of black olives
- 200 grams of buffalo mozzarella
- 30 grams of capers
- Salt and pepper to taste
- Olive oil to taste

Directions:
1. Start by preparing the dressing.
2. Cut the mozzarella into thin slices and set aside.
3. Rinse and dry the capers.
4. Now take 4 loaves of pizza dough and stretch them until you get a thin disc.
5. Preheat the Pit Boss for indirect cooking at 500 ° F for 10 minutes.
6. Place the pizza stone in the center of the grill and let it heat for 10 minutes.
7. In the meantime, season the pizza bases. First, put the tomato pulp, helping to distribute it evenly with a spoon.
8. Put the mozzarella on top, then the olives and finally the capers.
9. Season with a drizzle of oil and with the help of the pizza shovel, place the pizza on the stone.
10. Close the lid and cook for 15 minutes.
11. As soon as the pizza is cooked, proceed to cooking the others.
12. Cut the pizzas into four slices each and serve.

Nutrition: Calories 346 kCal Fat 13g Carbs 49 g Proteins 11g

439. Whole Meal Bread

Preparation Time: 61 minutes
Cooking Time: 16 minutes
Servings: 8

Ingredients:
- 750 grams of whole meal flour
- 2 teaspoons of salt
- A sachet of yeast
- 2 tablespoons of oil
- 1 teaspoon of brown sugar
- 500 ml of warm water
- 1 beaten egg

Directions:
1. Put flour, yeast and salt in a bowl and mix.
2. Put the water, sugar and oil in another bowl and mix well, then add them to the bowl with the flour.
3. Start kneading with your hands and continue until you get a soft and malleable dough.
4. Now put the dough on a lightly floured work surface, and knead for another 10 minutes.
5. Divide the dough into 3 parts and place them in three bread molds brushed with olive oil.
6. Cover the molds with cling film and let them rise for 40 minutes.
7. After the 40 minutes, preheat the Pit Boss at 482 ° F for 15 minutes with the lid closed.
8. Brush the surface of the bread with the beaten egg and then place it inside the Pit Boss, one at a time to cook for 15 minutes, indirectly and with the lid closed.
9. After 15 minutes, remove the mold with the bread and continue cooking the other.
10. Let the bread rest for 10 minutes, then cut it into slices and serve.

Nutrition: Calories 247 kCal Fat 4g Carbs 41g Proteins 13g

440. Potato Focaccia with Rosemary

Preparation Time: 3 hours
Cooking Time: 22 minutes
Servings: 8

Ingredients:
- 300 grams of flour
- 200 grams of potatoes
- 140 ml of warm water
- 1 teaspoon of brown sugar
- 7 grams of brewer's yeast
- Olive oil to taste
- Salt and pepper to taste
- 1 tablespoon of rosemary needles

Directions:
1. Start with the potatoes; wash them thoroughly under running water without peeling them.
2. Cook them for 25 minutes in plenty of boiling salted water.
3. Just cooked, drain, pass them under cold water and peel them.
4. Mash them with a potato masher and collect them in a bowl.
5. Add the flour, baking powder, 2 teaspoons of salt, sugar and water.
6. Knead vigorously for at least 15 minutes until the mixture is soft.
7. Compact it with your hands and give it the usual shape of a ball. Cover with cling film and let it rise for 2 hours.
8. Preheat the Pit Boss at 464 ° F for 15 minutes.
9. Put on the pizza stone and let it heat up for 15 minutes.
10. Brush a round baking pan with olive oil and put the dough inside.
11. Roll it out with your hands and brush the surface with olive oil.
12. Sprinkle with a little salt and rosemary needles and put the baking pan on the pizza stone.
13. Close the lid and cook for 20 minutes.
14. Check the cooking and if the focaccia is golden brown, remove it from the barbecue otherwise continue cooking for another 5 minutes.
15. Just cooked, remove it from the barbecue and let it rest for 5 minutes.
16. After 5 minutes, cut it into 8 slices and serve.

Nutrition: Calories 343 kCal Fat 6g Carbs 40g Proteins 5g

441. Salty Donut

Preparation Time: 35 minutes
Cooking Time: 31 minutes
Servings: 4
Ingredients:

- 200 grams of diced cooked ham
- 150 grams of smoked provolone
- 180 grams of flour
- 100 grams of whole meal flour
- 100 ml of seed oil
- 100 ml of cooking cream
- 80 grams of grated Parmesan cheese
- 3 eggs
- 30 grams of rocket
- 10 pitted black olives
- 1 sachet of yeast for pizza
- Salt and pepper to taste
- Olive oil to taste

Directions:

1. Start by cutting the provolone into cubes.
2. Now chop the olives very coarsely.
3. Wash and dry the rocket.
4. Put the eggs in a bowl and whisk them with an electric whisk.
5. Add the cooking cream and oil and continue mixing.
6. In another bowl, mix together the Parmesan, flour, yeast, provolone, ham, rocket and olives.
7. Mix well and then add the mixture to the eggs.
8. Salt, pepper, and finish mixing the mixture.
9. Now take a Bundt cake mold and brush it with olive oil,
10. Put the mixture inside the mold and preheat the Pit Boss at 446 ° F for 15 minutes.
11. Place the grill on the barbecue and then place the mold in the center.
12. Cook with the lid closed for 30 minutes.
13. After 30 minutes, check the cooking with a toothpick.
14. If the donut is still undercooked, continue cooking for another 5 minutes, otherwise remove the mold from the barbecue.
15. Let the donut rest for 15 minutes, then cut it into thick slices and serve.

Nutrition: Calories 357 kCal Fat 18 g Carbs 26 g Protein 20g

442. Rustic Pie with Zucchini and Ricotta

Preparation Time: 26 minutes
Cooking Time: 28 minutes
Servings: 4
Ingredients:

- 1 roll of puff pastry
- 300 grams of zucchini
- 4 zucchini flowers
- 100 grams of Taleggio
- 300 grams of cottage cheese
- 2 eggs
- 50 grams of grated Parmesan cheese
- Olive oil to taste
- Salt and pepper to taste

Directions:

1. Wash the zucchinis, and then cut them into thin slices.
2. Put a tablespoon of oil in a pan and as soon as it is hot, sauté the courgettes for 5 minutes. Season with salt and pepper and turn off.
3. Wash and dry the zucchinis flowers and then cut them into thin slices.
4. Put the ricotta in a bowl. Add the parmesan, eggs, salt, pepper, and mix. Put the zucchinis flowers and mix again.
5. Brush a round baking pan with olive oil and line it with the puff pastry.
6. Prick the bottom of the puff pastry with a fork and put the zucchinis on the bottom. Pour over the ricotta mixture and then put the Taleggio cheese cut into cubes on top.
7. Preheat the Pit Boss at 500 ° F for 15 minutes.
8. Place the pizza stone and let it heat for 10 minutes.
9. Now put the baking pan on the stone and cook, with the lid closed, for 25 minutes.
10. As soon as it is ready, remove the pie from the barbecue and let it rest for 10 minutes, then cut it into slices and serve.

Nutrition: Calories 354 kCal Fat 25 g Carbs 21 g Protein 11 g

443. Potato Pie with Cheese and Herbs

Preparation Time: 22 minutes
Cooking Time: 21 minutes
Servings: 4

Ingredients:

- 600 grams of potatoes
- 200 grams of emmenthal
- 200 ml of milk
- 40 grams of shelled walnuts
- 1 small piece of thyme
- 1 sprig of rosemary
- 6 sage leaves
- 1 sprig of chopped parsley
- 1 egg
- Butter to taste
- Breadcrumbs to taste
- Salt and pepper to taste
- Olive oil to taste

Directions:

1. Bring a saucepan with plenty of salted water to a boil.
2. In the meantime, peel the potatoes, wash them and then cut them into thin slices.
3. Put the potato slices to cook for 5 minutes, then drain and let them cool.
4. Wash and dry thyme, sage and rosemary. Remove the sprigs of thyme and rosemary and then put everything in the glass of the blender.
5. Add the walnuts, milk, egg, salt and pepper and blend until the mixture is liquid and homogeneous.
6. Brush a baking dish with olive oil and put a layer of potatoes at the bottom.
7. Put a little herb sauce on top and then a few slices of Emmenthal and repeat the same operation until all the ingredients are used up.
8. Sprinkle the surface with breadcrumbs and a few tufts of butter and then cover the pan with aluminum foil.
9. Preheat the Pit Boss at 446 ° F for 15 minutes.
10. Place the grill and place the pan with the potatoes in the center.
11. Cook for 10 minutes, and then remove the aluminum foil.
12. Continue cooking for another 10 minutes and then remove from the grill.
13. Let it rest for 10 minutes, then divide the portions and serve.

Nutrition: Calories 165 kCal Fat 10 g Carbs 10 g Proteins 9 g

444. Focaccia with Onion and Bacon

Preparation Time: 70 minutes
Cooking Time: 17 minutes
Servings: 4

Ingredients:

- 250 grams of flour
- 5 grams of brewer's yeast
- 160 ml of water
- 1 small onion
- 100 grams of bacon cut into cubes
- 30 grams of grated Emmenthal
- Olive oil to taste
- Salt and pepper to taste

Directions:

1. Put the flour and salt in a bowl and mix.
2. Add water, oil and yeast. Start kneading with your hands and knead the mixture until you get a smooth and lump-free dough.
3. Cover the bowl with a kitchen towel and let it rise for 60 minutes.
4. In the meantime, peel and wash the onion and then cut it into slices.
5. Heat a tablespoon of oil in a pan and brown the onion for 2 minutes.
6. Add the bacon and continue cooking for another 3 minutes. Season with salt and pepper and turn off.
7. After 60 minutes, take the dough and place it on a lightly floured work surface.
8. Roll out the dough with a rolling pin, until you get a thin sheet.
9. Arrange the onion and bacon on one-half of the dough, taking care to leave a little margin from the edge.
10. Fold the unseasoned pasta over the seasoned one and close the edges.
11. Put the grated Emmenthal on the surface of the focaccia then let it rest for another 20 minutes at room temperature
12. Preheat the Pit Boss at 482 ° F for 15 minutes.
13. Put the pizza stone to heat 10 minutes.
14. With the help of a pizza shovel, place the focaccia on the stone.
15. Cook with the lid closed for 15 minutes.

16. After 15 minutes, remove the focaccia from the barbecue and let it rest for 5 minutes.
17. Now cut it into slices and serve.

Nutrition: Calories 274 kCal Fat 15 g Carbs 27 g Proteins 9 g

445. Pizza with Gorgonzola, Pears and Walnuts

Preparation Time: 15 minutes
Cooking Time: 12 minutes
Servings: 4
Ingredients:
- 800 grams of pizza dough
- 4 mozzarellas
- 2 pears
- 200 grams of gorgonzola
- 4 chopped walnut kernels
- Salt and pepper to taste
- Olive oil to taste

Directions:
1. Divide the pizza dough into 4 loaves.
2. Put them on a lightly floured work surface and roll them out with your hands until you have 4 circles of dough.
3. Lightly brush the surface of the pizza with oil.
4. Cut the mozzarella into slices and place them on top of each pizza.
5. Wash and dry the pears, remove the seeds and then cut them into slices. Divide the slices of pears in each pizza.
6. Now cut the gorgonzola into cubes and place it on top of the pizzas.
7. Season with salt, pepper and olive oil, and sprinkle with chopped walnuts.
8. Preheat the Pit Boss for 15 minutes at 482 ° F.
9. Put the pizza stone to heat for 10 minutes.
10. After 10 minutes, put the first pizza to cook for 12 minutes, with the lid closed.
11. Repeat the same operation for the other pizzas.
12. As soon as they are ready, cut the pizzas into four parts and serve.

Nutrition: Calories 247 kCal Fat 10 g Carbs 28 g Proteins 11 g

446. Salty Plum Cake with Spinach, Cherry Tomatoes and Feta

Preparation Time: 41 minutes
Cooking Time: 36 minutes
Servings: 6
Ingredients:
- 4 eggs
- 30 grams of brown sugar
- 120 ml of seed oil
- 180 ml of milk
- 460 grams of flour
- 150 grams of cooked spinach
- 16 grams of yeast
- 100 grams of feta
- 80 grams of cherry tomatoes
- 2 shallots
- Olive oil to taste
- Salt and pepper to taste

Directions:
1. Peel and wash the shallots and then cut them into slices.
2. Finely chop the spinach.
3. In a large bowl, break 4 eggs, start beating them with a whisk.
4. Add the salt, sugar, seed oil, milk and half of the flour and mix everything well.
5. Proceed by combining the boiled spinach and baking powder and continue stirring.
6. Add the remaining flour and mix until the mixture is smooth and free of lumps.
7. Wash and dry the cherry tomatoes and then cut them into small pieces.
8. Finally add the crumbled feta, cherry tomatoes, black olives and shallots. Mix again and add everything to the dough.
9. Season with salt and pepper and then pour the mixture into an earlier oiled and floured plum cake mold.
10. Preheat the Pit Boss at 482 ° F for 15 minutes.
11. Preheat the pizza stone for 10 minutes.
12. Put the mold on the stone and cook for 30 minutes.
13. After 30 minutes, check the cooking with a toothpick and if it is cooked then remove it from the barbecue, otherwise continue cooking for another 5 minutes.
14. Just cooked, remove the plum cake from the Pit Boss and let it rest for 15 minutes.

15. Remove the plum cake from the mold, cut it into slices and serve.

Nutrition: Calories 300 kCal Fat 13 g Carbs 18 g Proteins 7 g

447. Pretzel

Preparation Time: 30 minutes
Cooking Time: 1 hour and 30 minutes
Servings: 6
Ingredients:
- 1 packet active instant dry yeast
- 1 tablespoon sugar
- 1 1/2 cups warm water
- 2 oz. melted butter
- 4 ½ cups all-purpose flour

Cooking spray
- 1/2 cups baking soda
- 10 cups boiling water
- Egg yolks, beaten
- Sea salt

Directions:
1. In a bowl, add the yeast, sugar and warm water.
2. Combine using a mixer.
3. Let sit for 10 minutes.
4. Once it bubbles, stir in the butter and flour.
5. Mix for 3 minutes.
6. Transfer to a bowl.
7. Spray with oil.
8. Add a clean towel on top of the bowl.
9. Let it rise for 1 hour.
10. Roll the dough into long strips.
11. Form a knot to create a pretzel shape.
12. Start your wood pellet grill.
13. Set it to 350 degrees F.
14. Add the baking soda to the boiling water.
15. Drop the pretzels into the boiling water.
16. Transfer to a baking sheet.
17. Brush the top with the egg yolk and sprinkle with the salt.
18. Bake in the wood pellet grill for 20 minutes.

Nutrition: Calories: 110 kCal Fat: 1g Carbs: 23 g Protein: 3 g

448. Salty Plum Cake with Bacon and Gruyere

Preparation Time: 15 minutes
Cooking Time: 31 minutes
Servings: 6
Ingredients:
- 200 grams of flour
- 150 grams of bacon
- 100 ml of milk
- 16 grams of yeast
- 100 grams of grated gruyere
- 3 eggs
- 100 ml of cooking cream
- 60 ml of olive oil
- 100 grams of grated Parmesan
- Salt and pepper to taste

Directions:
1. Put the flour and baking powder in a bowl and mix them.
2. Add the parmesan and gruyere. Mix the ingredients well and then add the diced bacon.
3. Mix and finally add the olive oil slowly.
4. In another bowl, put the eggs, cream and milk.
5. Mix everything with a whisk until you get a homogeneous mixture. Add salt and pepper and then pour the mixture into the bowl with the flour.
6. Stir with a wooden spoon until the ingredients are well blended.
7. Brush with oil and then flour a plum cake mold.
8. Pour the mixture into the mold and level it with a spoon.
9. Preheat the Pit Boss at 482 ° F for 15 minutes.
10. Put the grill on and then put the mold in the center.
11. Cook, with the lid closed, for 30 minutes.
12. After 30 minutes, check the cooking with a toothpick.
13. If it is cooked remove from the barbecue, otherwise continue cooking for another 5 minutes.
14. As soon as it is cooked, remove the plum cake from the barbecue and let it rest for 15 minutes.
15. Remove the plum cake from the mold, cut it into slices and serve.

Nutrition: Calories 477 kCal Fat 30 g Carbs 28 g Proteins 23 g

449. Pizza with Raw Ham, Buffalo Mozzarella and Pistachios

Preparation Time: 14 minutes
Cooking Time: 18 minutes
Servings: 4
Ingredients:
- 800 grams of pizza dough
- 250 grams of tomato pulp
- 2 mozzarellas
- 4 buffalo mozzarellas
- 100 grams of raw ham
- 40 grams of chopped pistachios
- Salt and pepper to taste
- Olive oil to taste

Directions:
1. Divide the pizza dough into 4 loaves of 200 grams each.
2. Put them on a lightly floured work surface and spread them with your hands until you get 4 thin circles.
3. Place the tomato pulp and the sliced mozzarella on each pizza.
4. Preheat the Pit Boss at 500 ° F for 15 minutes with the lid closed.
5. Put the pizza stone to heat for 10 minutes.
6. After 10 minutes, place the pizza on the stone, using a pizza shovel.
7. Cook for 15 minutes and then remove from the barbecue.
8. Repeat the same operation also with the other 3 pizzas.
9. Let the pizza rest for 5 minutes and in the meantime put the buffalo mozzarella cut into pieces, the raw ham and finally the pistachio on top of the pizza.
10. Season with oil, salt and pepper, cut into slices and serve.

Nutrition: Calories 301 kCal Fat 6 g Carbs 36 g Proteins 8 g

450. Quick Yeast Dinner Rolls

Preparation Time: 5 minutes
Cooking Time: 30 minutes
Servings 8
Ingredients:
- 2 tablespoons yeast, quick rise
- 1 cup water, lukewarm
- 3 cups flour
- ¼ cup sugar
- 1 teaspoon salt
- ¼ cup unsalted butter, softened
- 1 egg
- Cooking spray, as needed
- 1 egg, for egg wash

Directions:
1. Combine the yeast and warm water in a small bowl to activate the yeast. Let sit for about 5 to 10 minutes, or until foamy.
2. Combine the flour, sugar, and salt in the bowl of a stand mixer fitted with the dough hook. Pour the water and yeast into the dry ingredients with the machine running on low speed.
3. Add the butter and egg and mix for 10 minutes, gradually increasing the speed from low to high.
4. Form the dough into a ball and place in a buttered bowl. Cover with a cloth and let the dough rise for approximately 40 minutes.
5. Transfer the risen dough to a lightly floured work surface and divide into 8 pieces, forming a ball with each.
6. Lightly spritz a cast iron pan with cooking spray and arrange the balls in the pan. Cover with a cloth and let rise for 20 minutes.
7. When ready to cook, set Pit Boss temperature to 375 F (191 C) and preheat, lid closed for 15 minutes.
8. Brush the rolls with the egg wash. Place the pan on the grill and bake for 30 minutes, or until lightly browned.
9. Remove from the grill. Serve hot.

Nutrition: Calories 140 kCal Fat 4 g Carbs 23 g Proteins 3 g

451. Baked Cornbread with Honey Butter

Preparation Time: 10 minutes
Cooking Time: 35 to 45 minutes
Servings 6

Ingredients:

- 4 ears whole corn
- 1 cup all-purpose flour
- 1 cup cornmeal
- 2/3 cup white sugar
- 1½ teaspoons baking powder
- ½ teaspoon baking soda
- ½ teaspoon salt
- 1 cup buttermilk
- ½ cup butter, softened
- 2 eggs
- ½ cup butter, softened
- ¼ cup honey

Directions:

1. When ready to cook, set Pit Boss temperature to High and preheat, lid closed for 15 minutes.
2. Peel back the outer layer of the corn husk, keeping it attached to the cob. Remove the silk from the corn and place the husk back into place. Soak the corn in cold water for 10 minutes.
3. Place the corn directly on the grill grate and cook for 15 to 20 minutes, or until the kernels are tender, stirring occasionally. Remove from the grill and set aside.
4. In a large bowl, stir together the flour, cornmeal, sugar, baking powder, baking soda and salt.
5. In a separate bowl, whisk together the buttermilk, butter, and eggs. Pour the wet mixture into the cornmeal mixture and fold together until there are no dry spots. Pour the batter into a greased baking dish.
6. Cut the kernels from the corn and sprinkle over the top of the batter, pressing the kernels down with a spoon to submerge.
7. Turn Pit Boss temperature down to 350 F (177 C). Place the baking dish on the grill. Bake for about 20 to 25 minutes, or until the top is golden brown and a toothpick inserted into the middle of the cornbread comes out clean.
8. Remove the cornbread from the grill and let cool for 10 minutes before serving.
9. To make the honey butter, mix the butter and honey until combined. Serve the cornbread with the honey butter.

Nutrition: Calories 160 kCal Fat 8 g Carbs 19 g Proteins 3 g

452. Brown Sugared Bacon Cinnamon Rolls

Preparation Time: 5 minutes
Cooking Time: 25 to 35 minutes
Servings 6

Ingredients:

- 12 slices bacon, sliced
- 1/3 cup brown sugar
- 8 cinnamon rolls, store-brought
- 2 ounces (57 g) cream cheese, softened

Directions:

1. When ready to cook, set Pit Boss temperature to 350 F (177 C) and preheat, lid closed for 15 minutes.
2. Dredge 8 slices of the bacon in the brown sugar, making sure to cover both sides of the bacon.
3. Place the coated bacon slices along with the other bacon slices on a cooling rack placed on top of a large baking sheet.
4. Place the sheet on the grill and cook for 15 to 20 minutes, or until the fat is rendered, but the bacon is still pliable.
5. Open and unroll the cinnamon rolls. While bacon is still warm, place 1 slice of the brown sugared bacon on top of 1 of the unrolled rolls and roll back up. Repeat with the remaining rolls.
6. Turn Pit Boss temperature down to 325 F (163 C). Place the cinnamon rolls in a greased baking dish and cook for 10 to 15 minutes, or until golden. Rotate the pan a half turn halfway through cooking time.
7. Meanwhile, crumble the cooked 4 bacon slices and add into the cream cheese.
8. Spread the cream cheese frosting over the warm cinnamon rolls. Serve warm.

Nutrition: Calories 380 kCal Fat 13 g Carbs 55 g Proteins 10 g

453. Pit Boss Soft Gingerbread Cookie

Preparation Time: 10 minutes
Cooking Time: 10 minutes
Servings 8
Ingredients:
- 1¾ cups all-purpose flour
- 1½ teaspoons ground ginger
- ½ teaspoon ground cinnamon
- ½ teaspoon baking soda
- ¼ teaspoon ground cloves
- ¼ teaspoon kosher salt
- 1/3 cup brown sugar
- ¾ cup butter
- ½ cup plus 4 tablespoons granulated sugar, divided
- ¼ cup molasses
- 1 egg

Directions:
1. When ready to cook, set Pit Boss temperature to 325 F (163 C) and preheat, lid closed for 15 minutes.
2. In a medium bowl, stir together the flour, ginger, cinnamon, baking soda, cloves, and salt. Set aside.
3. In the bowl of a stand mixer, cream together the brown sugar, butter and ½ cup of the granulated sugar until light and fluffy. Stir in the molasses and egg and mix on medium speed until combined, scraping down the sides of the bowl.
4. Add the flour mixture to the bowl and mix on low speed until combined. Scrape the sides again and mix for 30 seconds longer.
5. Roll the dough into balls, 1 tablespoon at a time, and then roll the balls in the remaining 4 tablespoons of the sugar.
6. Place the dough balls on a baking sheet lined with parchment paper, leaving a couple inches between each cookie.
7. Place the sheet directly on the grill grate and cook for about 10 minutes, or until lightly browned but still soft in the center.
8. Remove from the grill and let cool on a wire rack. Serve.

Nutrition: Calories 133 kCal Fat 5 g Carbs 21 g Proteins 2 g

454. Sweet Pull-Apart Rolls

Preparation Time: 5 minutes
Cooking Time: 10 to 12 minutes
Servings 8
Ingredients:
- 1/3 cup vegetable oil
- ¼ cup warm water
- ¼ cup sugar
- 2 tablespoons active dry yeast
- 1 egg
- 3 1/2 cups all-purpose flour, divided
- ½ teaspoon salt
- Cooking spray, as needed

Directions:
1. When ready to cook, set Pit Boss temperature to 400 F (204 C) and preheat, lid closed for 15 minutes.
2. Spritz a cast iron pan with cooking spray and set aside.
3. In the bowl of a stand mixer, combine the oil, warm water, sugar, and yeast. Let sit for 5 to 10 minutes, or until frothy and bubbly.
4. With a dough hook, mix in the egg, 2 cups of the flour and salt until combined. Add the remaining flour, ½ cup at a time.
5. Spritz your hands with cooking spray and shape the dough into 12 balls.
6. Arrange the balls in the prepared cast iron pan and let rest for 10 minutes. Place the pan in the grill and bake for about 10 to 12 minutes, or until the tops are lightly golden.
7. Serve immediately.

Nutrition: Calories: 120 kCal Fat: 2 g Carbs: 21 g Protein: 4 g

455. Chocolate-Hazelnut and Strawberry Grilled Dessert Pizza

Preparation time: 10 minutes
Total cooking time: 6 minutes
Servings: 4
Ingredients:
- 2 tbsp. all-purpose flour, plus more as needed
- ½ store-bought pizza dough (about 8 ounces)
- 1 tbsp. canola oil
- 1 cup sliced fresh strawberries
- 1 tbsp. sugar
- ½ cup chocolate-hazelnut spread

Directions:
1. Insert the Grill Grate and cover the hood. Select GRILL, then set the temperature to MAX, and set the time to 6 minutes. Select START/STOP to begin preheating.
2. While the unit is preheating, dust a clean work surface with the flour, place the dough on the floured surface and roll it out to a 9-inch round of even thickness. Sprinkle the roller and work surface with additional flour, as needed, to ensure the dough does not stick.
3. Brush the surface of the rolled-out dough evenly with half the oil. Flip the dough over, and brush with the remaining oil. Poke the dough with a fork 5 or 6 times across its surface to prevent air pockets from forming during cooking.
4. When the unit beeps to signify it has preheated, place the dough on the Grill Grate. Close the hood and cook for 3 minutes.
5. After 3 minutes, flip the dough. Close the hood and continue cooking for the remaining 3 minutes.
6. Meanwhile, in a medium mixing bowl, combine the strawberries and sugar.
7. Move the pizza to a cutting board and let cool. Top with the chocolate-hazelnut spread and strawberries. Cut into pieces and serve.

Nutrition: Calories: 377 kCal Fat: 4g Carbs: 53g Protein: 7g

456. Ice Cream Bread

Preparation Time: 30 minutes.
Cooking Time: 1 hour
Servings: 12-16
Ingredients:
- 1 ½ quart full-fat butter pecan ice cream, softened
- One t. salt
- Two c. semisweet chocolate chips
- One c. sugar
- One stick melted butter
- Butter, for greasing
- 4 c. self-rising flour

Directions:
1. Add Preferred Wood Pellet pellets to your smoker and follow your cooker's startup procedure. Preheat your smoker, with your lid closed, until it reaches 350.
2. Mix the salt, sugar, flour, and ice cream with an electric mixer set to medium for two minutes.
3. As the mixer is still running, add in the chocolate chips, beating until everything is blended.
4. Spray a Bundt pan or tube pan with cooking spray. If you choose to use a pan that is solid, the center will take too long to cook. That is why a tube or Bundt pan works best.
5. Add the batter to your prepared pan.
6. Set the cake on the grill, cover, and smoke for 50 minutes to an hour. A toothpick should come out clean.
7. Take the pan off the grill. For 10 minutes, cool the bread. Carefully remove the bread from the pan and then drizzle it with some melted butter.

Nutrition: Calories 279 kCal Fat 29g Carbs 38g Protein 20g

457. Peanut Butter Cookies

Preparation Time: 5 minutes
Cooking Time: 25 minutes
Servings: 24
Ingredients:
- 1 egg
- 1 cup sugar
- 1 cup peanut butter

Directions:
1. Set your wood pellet grill to smoke.
2. Preheat to high.

3. Mix all the ingredients in one bowl
4. Form cookies from the mixture.
5. Place in a baking pan.
6. Bake in the grill for 20 minutes.
7. Let cool for 5 minutes before serving.

Nutrition: Calories: 166 kCal Fat: 8 g Carbs: 20 g Protein: 3 g

458. Smoked Crepes

Preparation Time: 10 minutes
Cooking Time: 2 hours
Servings: 6
Ingredients:
- 2-pound apples, sliced into wedges
- Apple butter seasoning
- 1/2 cup apple juice
- 2 teaspoon lemon juice
- 5 tablespoon butter
- 3/4 teaspoon cinnamon, ground
- 2 tablespoon brown sugar
- 3/4 teaspoon cornstarch
- 6 crepes

Directions:
1. Preheat your wood pellet grill to 225 degrees F.
2. Season the apples with the apple butter seasoning.
3. Add to the grill.
4. Smoke for 1 hour.
5. Let cool and slice thinly.
6. Add to a baking pan.
7. Stir in the rest of the ingredients except the crepes. Roast for 15 minutes.
8. Add the apple mixture on top of the crepes. Roll and serve.

Nutrition: Calories: 130 kCal Fat: 5 g Carbs: 14 g Protein: 7 g

459. Apple Crumble

Preparation Time: 30 minutes
Cooking Time: 1 hour and 30 minutes
Servings: 8
Ingredients:
- 2 cups and 2 tablespoons flour, divided
- 1/2 cup shortening
- Pinch salt
- 1/4 cup cold water
- 8 cups apples, sliced into cubes

- 3 teaspoons lemon juice
- 1/2 teaspoon ground nutmeg
- 1 teaspoon apple butter seasoning
- 1/8 teaspoon ground cloves
- 1 teaspoon cinnamon
- 1/4 cup butter

Directions:
1. Set your wood pellet grill to smoke.
2. Preheat it to 350 degrees F.
3. Mix 1 1/2 cups flour, shortening and salt in a bowl until crumbly.
4. Slowly add cold water. Mix gently.
5. Wrap the dough in plastic and refrigerate for 20 to 30 minutes.
6. Place the apples in a bowl.
7. Toss in lemon juice. Take the dough out.
8. Press into a pan.
9. In a bowl, combine the 2 tablespoons flour, nutmeg, apple butter seasoning, ground cloves and cinnamon.
10. Add this to the bowl with apples.
11. Add the butter and mix with a mixer until crumbly.
12. Spread this on top of the dough.
13. Bake for 1 hour.

Nutrition: Calories: 283 kCal Fat: 6 g Carbs: 55 g Protein: 1 g

460. Fruits on Bread

Preparation Time: 30 minutes
Cooking Time: 1 hour and 30 minutes
Servings: 8
Ingredients:
- 1/2 cup milk
- 1 teaspoon sugar
- 1/4 cup warm water
- 2 1/2 teaspoon active yeast, instant
- 2 1/2 cups all-purpose flour
- 2 tablespoon melted butter
- 1 egg
- 1/2 teaspoon vanilla
- 1/2 teaspoon salt
- Vegetable oil
- 1 tablespoon ground cinnamon
- Chocolate spread
- Fruits, sliced

Directions:
1. Add the milk, sugar, water and yeast in a bowl. Let sit for 10 minutes.
2. In another bowl, add the flour.
3. Create a well in the center.
4. Add the sugar mixture, butter, egg, vanilla and salt.
5. Mix and knead.
6. Place in a bowl.
7. Cover with clean towel.
8. Let rise for 1 hour.
9. Start your wood pellet grill.
10. Set it to 450 degrees F.
11. Grease a cast iron skillet with the oil.
12. Create balls from the mixture.
13. Press and sprinkle with the cinnamon.
14. Fry for 1 minute per side.
15. Spread with chocolate and top with sliced fruits.

Nutrition: Calories: 110 kCal Fat: 2 g Carbs: 21 g Protein: 5 g

461. Grilled Steak with American Cheese Sandwich

Preparation Time: 10 minutes
Cooking Time: 55 minutes
Servings: 4
Ingredients:
- 1 pound of beef steak.
- 1/2 teaspoon of salt to taste.
- 1/2 teaspoon of pepper to taste.
- 1 tablespoon of Worcestershire sauce.
- 2 tablespoons of butter.
- 1 chopped onion.
- 1/2 chopped green bell pepper.
- Salt and pepper to taste.
- 8 slices of American Cheese.
- 8 slices of white bread.
- 4 tablespoons of butter.

Directions:
1. Turn your Pit Boss Smoker and Grill to smoke and fire up for about four to five minutes. Set the temperature of the grill to 450 degrees F and let it preheat for about ten to fifteen minutes with its lid closed.
2. Next, place a non-stick skillet on the griddle and preheat for about fifteen minutes until it becomes hot. Once hot, add in the butter and let melt. Once the butter melts, add in the onions and green bell pepper then cook for about five minutes until they become brown in color, set aside.
3. Next, still using the same pan on the griddle, add in the steak, Worcestershire sauce, salt, and pepper to taste then cook for about five to six minutes until it is cooked through. Add in the cooked bell pepper mixture; stir to combine then heat for another three minutes, set aside.
4. Use a sharp knife to slice the bread in half, butter each side then grill for about three to four minutes with its sides down. To assemble, add slices of cheese on each bread slice, top with the steak mixture then your favorite toppings, close the sandwich with another bread slice then serve.

Nutrition: Calories 589 kCal Carbs 28g Protein 24g Fat 41g

462. Ground Turkey Burgers

Preparation Time: 15 minutes
Cooking Time: 50 minutes
Servings: 6
Ingredients:

- beaten egg
- 2/3 cup of bread crumbs.
- 1/2 cup of chopped celery
- 1/4 cup of chopped onion
- 1 tablespoon of minced parsley
- 1 teaspoon of Worcestershire sauce
- 1 teaspoon of dried oregano
- 1/2 teaspoon of salt to taste
- 1/4 teaspoon of pepper
- 1-1/4 pounds of lean ground turkey
- 6 hamburger buns
- Optional topping
- 1 sliced tomato
- 1 sliced onion
- Lettuce leaves

Directions:

1. Using a small mixing bowl, add in all the ingredients on the list aside from the turkey and buns then mix properly to combine.
2. Add in the ground turkey then mix everything to combine. Feel free to use clean hands for this. Make about six patties of the mixture then set aside.
3. Preheat your Pit Boss Smoker and Grill to 375 degrees F, place the turkey patties on the grill and grill for about forty-five minutes until its internal temperature reads 165 degrees F. to assemble, use a knife to split the bun into two, top with the prepared burger and your favorite topping then close with another half of the buns, serve.

Nutrition: Calories 293 kCal Fat 11g Carbs 27g Protein 22g

463. BBQ Shredded Beef Burger

Preparation Time: 10 minutes
Cooking Time: 5 hours 10 minutes
Servings: 4
Ingredients:

- 3 pounds of boneless chuck roast.
- Salt to taste
- Pepper to taste
- 2 tablespoons of minced garlic
- 1 cup of chopped onion
- 28 oz. of barbeque sauce
- 6 buns

Directions:

1. Set the temperature of the Pit Boss Smoker and Grill to 250 degrees F then preheat for about fifteen minutes with its lid closed.
2. Use a knife to trim off the excess fat present on the roast then place the meat on the preheated grill.
3. Grill the roast for about three and a half hours until it attains an internal temperature of 160 degrees F.
4. Next, place the chuck roast in an aluminum foil, add in the garlic, onion, barbeque sauce, salt, and pepper then stir to coat.
5. Place the roast bake on the grill and cook for another one and a half hour until an inserted thermometer reads 204 degrees F.
6. Once cooked, let the meat cool for a few minutes then shred with a fork. Fill the buns with the shredded beef then serve.

Nutrition: Calories 593 kCal Fat 31g Carbs 34g Protein 44g

464. Grilled Pork Burgers

Prearation Time: 15 minutes
Cooking Time: 1 hour
Servings: 4 – 6
Ingredients:

- 1 beaten egg
- 3/4 cup of soft breadcrumbs
- 3/4 cup of grated parmesan cheese
- 1 tablespoon of dried parsley
- 1 teaspoons of dried basil
- 1/2 teaspoon of salt to taste
- 1/2 teaspoon of garlic powder
- 1/4 teaspoon of pepper to taste
- 2 pounds of ground pork
- 6 hamburger buns
- Toppings
- Lettuce leaves
- Sliced tomato
- Sliced sweet onion

Directions:

1. Using a large mixing bowl, add in the egg, bread crumbs, cheese, parsley, basil, garlic powder,

salt, and pepper to taste then mix properly to combine.

2. Add in the ground pork then mix properly to combine using clean hands. Form about six patties out the mixture then set aside.

3. Next, set a Pit Boss smoker and grill to smoke (250 degrees F) then let it fire up for about five minutes. Place the patties on the grill and smoke for about thirty minutes.

4. Flip the patties over, increase the temperature of the grill to 300 degrees F then grill the patties for a few minutes until an inserted thermometer reads 160 degrees F.

5. Serve the pork burgers on the buns, lettuce, tomato, and onion.

Nutrition: Calories 522 kCal Fat 28g Carbs 28g Protein 38g

465. Delicious BLT Sandwich

Preparation Time: 15 minutes
Cooking Time: 35 minutes
Servings: 4-6
Ingredients:
- 8 slices of bacon
- 1/2 romaine heart
- 1sliced tomato
- 4 slices of sandwich bread
- 3 tablespoons of mayonnaise
- Salted butter
- Sea salt to taste
- Pepper to taste

Directions:
1. Preheat a Pit Boss Smoker and Grill to 350 degrees F for about fifteen minutes with its lid closed.

2. Place the bacon slices on the preheated grill and cook for about fifteen to twenty minutes until they become crispy.

3. Next, butter both sides of the bread, place a grill pan on the griddle of the Pit Boss, and toast the bread for a few minutes until they become brown on both sides, set aside.

4. Using a small mixing bowl, add in the sliced tomatoes, season with salt and pepper to taste then mix to coat.

5. Next, spread mayo on both sides of the toasted bread, top with the lettuce, tomato, and bacon then enjoy.

Nutrition: Calories 284 kCal Protein 19g Fat 19g Carbs 11g

466. Delicious Grilled Chicken Sandwich

Preparation Time: 15 minutes
Cooking Time: 50 minutes
Servings: 4
Ingredients:
- 1/4 cup of mayonnaise
- 1 tablespoon of Dijon mustard
- 1 tablespoon of honey
- 4 boneless and skinless chicken breasts
- 1/2 teaspoon of steak seasoning
- 4 slices of American Swiss cheese
- 4 hamburger buns
- 2 bacon strips
- Lettuce leaves and tomato slices

Directions:
1. Using a small mixing bowl, add in the mayonnaise, mustard, and honey then mix properly to combine.

2. Use a meat mallet to pound the chicken into even thickness then slice into four parts. Season the chicken with the steak seasoning then set aside.

3. Preheat a Pit Boss Smoker and Grill to 350 degrees F for about ten to fifteen minutes with its lid closed.

4. Place the seasoned chicken on the grill and grill for about twenty-five to thirty minutes until it reads an internal temperature of 165 degrees F. Grill the bacon until crispy then crumble.

5. Add the cheese on the chicken and cook for about one minute until it melts completely. At the same time, grill the buns for about one to two minutes until it is toasted as desired.

6. Place the chicken on the buns, top with the grilled bacon, mayonnaise mixture, lettuce, and tomato then serve.

Nutrition: Calories 410 kCal Fat 17g Carbs 29g Protein 34g

467. Bacon, Egg, And Cheese Sandwich

Preparation Time: 15 minutes
Cooking Time: 20 minutes
Servings: 4
Ingredients:

- 2 large eggs
- 2 tablespoons of milk or water
- A pinch of salt to taste
- A pinch of pepper to taste
- 3 teaspoons of butter
- 4 slices of white bread
- 2 slices of Jack cheese
- 4 slices of bacon

Directions:

1. Using a small mixing bowl, add in the eggs, milk, salt, and pepper to taste then mix properly to combine.
2. Preheat a Pit Boss Smoker and Grill to 400 degrees F for about ten to fifteen minutes with its lid closed.
3. Place the bacon slices on the preheated grill and grill for about eight to ten minutes, flipping once until it becomes crispy. Set the bacon aside on a paper-lined towel.
4. Decrease the temperature of the grill to 350 degrees F, place a grill pan on the grill, and let it heat for about ten minutes.
5. Spread two tablespoons of butter on the cut side of the bread, place the bread on the skillet pan and toast for about two minutes until brown in color.
6. Place the cheese on the toasted bread, close the lid of the grill then cook for about one minute until the cheese melts completely, set aside. Still using the same grill pan, add in the rest of the butter then let melt. Pour in the egg mixture and cook for a few minutes until it is cooked as desired.
7. Assemble the sandwich as desired then serve.

Nutrition: Calories 401 kCal Fat 23g Carbs 26g Protein 23g

468. Fajita Sandwiches

Preparation time: 25 minutes
Cooking time: 15 minutes
Servings: 4 - 6
Ingredients:

- 2 pounds skirt steak (trimmed)
- 4 limes (juiced. Add extra lime wedges to serve)
- ¼ cup soy sauce
- 2 tablespoons tequila (optional)
- 2 teaspoons Worcestershire sauce
- 2 cloves garlic (minced)
- 1 ½ teaspoon cumin (ground)
- 1 ½ teaspoon chili powder
- 1 teaspoon salt
- ½ cup + 1 tablespoon vegetable oil
- 1 teaspoon black pepper (freshly ground)
- 3 bell peppers (trimmed, seeded, cut into strips)
- 1 red or white onion (large, peeled, trimmed, thin wedge slices)
- 6 ciabatta (or another sandwich rolls you like, may be toasted or grilled)
- 1/3 cup cilantro leaves (fresh, to garnish)
- Pico de Gallo, guacamole, pickled sliced jalapenos, sour cream, grated cheese, and/or hot sauce for serving.

Directions:
Grill Prep

1. Cut your steak into four even pieces, and then put them in a resealable plastic baggie. Set that aside as you prepare the marinade.
2. Grab a jar that is nice and airtight. Add in your lime juice from the four limes, your tequila, soy sauce, and Worcestershire sauce, if you are using it. Also add in your cumin, rub, salt, garlic, and ½ cup of vegetable oil. Shake it all up as vigorously as you can, and then pour all of that over your meat.
3. Massage the bag as well as you can, so that the meat is properly coated. Then seal the bag and keep it in your fridge for 4 to 8 hours. Do not go any longer than 8 hours, or the texture of the meat will get weird.

On the Grill

1. Grab a cast iron skillet and set it on one side of your Smoker grill.
2. Preheat your Smoker grill on high, with the lid open. Once the fire gets going — which should

take 4 to 5 minutes, tops — close the lid for 10 to 15 minutes.

3. Drain the marinade from the steak, and then pat your stake dry with some paper towels, so that your meat can sear better.
4. Season the marinated meat with freshly ground black pepper.
5. Toss the rest of your oil (the tablespoon) onto your skillet.
6. Now, place your steak on the grill gate.
7. Toss half of your bell peppers, and your onions onto the skillet which should be hot by now.
8. Grill your steaks, making sure you turn them once, cooking each side for 2 to 3 minutes, or until it is done the way you like it.
9. Stir your vegetables a bit, to give them a nice char, for 10 to 12 minutes.
10. Move the steaks to a large platter and tent them with some aluminum foil.
11. As the steaks rest, sauté the rest of your veggies in the skillet, and then toast your ciabatta rolls on the grill, if you want. Make sure the cut sides of your ciabatta rolls are down.
12. Slice the steak as thinly as you can, going against the grain, and then arrange them on one side of the platter.
13. You can now pile the onions and peppers on the other side. You could also serve some of the sliced steak and veggies right of the skillet.
14. Garnish with some cilantro.
15. Wrap up your ciabatta rolls with a cloth napkin, and serve them in a basket, as well as your veggies and meat, and the condiments to accompany them.

Nutrition: Calories 145 kCal Fat 18g Carbs 14g Protein 11g

469. Low Carb Almond Flour Bread

Preparation Time: 10 minutes
Cooking Time: 1 hour 15 minutes
Servings: 12
Ingredients:
- 1 tsp. sea salt or to taste
- 1 tbsp. apple cider vinegar
- ½ cup of warm water
- ¼ cup of coconut oil
- 4 large eggs (beaten)
- 1 tbsp. gluten-free baking powder

- 2 cup blanched almond flour
- ¼ cup Psyllium husk powder
- 1 tsp. ginger (optional)

Directions:
1. Preheat the grill to 350°F with the lid closed for 15 minutes.
2. Line a 9 by 5 inch loaf pan with parchment paper. Set aside.
3. Combine the ginger, Psyllium husk powder, almond flour, salt, baking powder in a large mixing bowl.
4. In another mixing bowl, mix the coconut oil, apple cider vinegar, eggs and warm water. Mix thoroughly.
5. Gradually pour the flour mixture into the egg mixture, stirring as you pour. Stir until it forms a smooth batter.
6. Fill the lined loaf pan with the batter and cover the batter with aluminum foil.
7. Place the loaf pan directly on the grill and bake for about 1 hour or until a toothpick or knife inserted in the middle of the bread comes out clean.

Nutrition: Calories: 93 kCal Fat: 7.5 g Carbs: 3.6 g Protein: 3.1 g

470. Rosemary Cheese Bread

Preparation Time: 10 minutes
Cooking Time: 12 minutes
Servings: 10
Ingredients:
- 1½ cup sunflower seeds
- ½ tsp. sea salt
- 1 egg
- 1 tsp. fresh rosemary (finely chopped)
- 2 tsp. xanthan gum
- 2 tbsp. cream cheese
- 2 cups grated mozzarella

Directions:
1. Preheat the grill to 400°F with the lid closed for 15 minutes.
2. Toss the sunflower seeds into a powerful blender and blend until it smooth and flour-like.
3. Transfer the sunflower seed flour into a mixing bowl and add the rosemary and xanthan gum. Mix and set aside.

4. Melt the cheese in a microwave. To do this, combine the cream cheese and mozzarella cheese in a microwave-safe dish.
5. Place the microwave-safe dish in the grill and heat the cheese on high for 1 minute.
6. Bring out the dish and stir. Place the dish in the grill and heat for 30 seconds. Bring out the dish and stir until smooth.
7. Pour the melted cheese into a large mixing bowl.
8. Add the sunflower flour mixture to the melted cheese and stir the ingredients are well combined.
9. Add the salt and egg and mix thoroughly to form a smooth dough.
10. Measure out equal pieces of the dough and roll into sticks.
11. Grease a baking sheet with oil and arrange the breadsticks into the baking sheet in a single layer.
12. Use the back of a knife or metal spoon to make lines on the breadsticks.
13. Place the baking sheet on the grill and make for about 12 minutes or until the breadsticks turn golden brown.
14. Remove the baking sheet from the grill and let the breadsticks cool for a few minutes.
15. Serve.

Nutrition: Calories: 23 kCal Fat: 1.9g Carbs: 0.6 g Protein: 1.2 g

471. Cinnamon Almond Shortbread

Preparation Time: 20 minutes
Cooking Time: 20 minutes
Servings: 5
Ingredients:

- 2 tsp. cinnamon
- ½ cup unsalted butter (softened)
- 1 large egg (beaten)
- ½ tsp. salt or to taste
- 2 cups almond flour
- ¼ cup sugar
- 1 tsp. ginger (optional)

Directions:

1. Preheat the grill to 300°F with the lid closed for 5 minutes.
2. Grease a cookie sheet with oil.

3. In a large bowl, combine the cinnamon, almond flour, sugar, ginger, and salt. Mix thoroughly to combine.
4. In another mixing bowl, whisk the egg and softened butter together.
5. Pour the egg mixture into the flour mixture and mix until the mixture forms a smooth batter.
6. Use a tablespoon to measure out equal amounts of the mixture and roll into balls.
7. Arrange the balls into the cookie sheet in a single layer.
8. Now, use the flat bottom of a clean glass cup to press each ball into a flat round cookie. Grease the bottom of the cup before using it to press the balls.
9. Place the cookie sheet on the grill and bake until browned. This will take about 20 to 25 minutes.
10. Remove the cookie sheet from the grill and let the shortbreads cool for a few minutes.
11. Serve and enjoy.

Nutrition: Calories: 152 kCal Fat: 12.7g Carbs: 6.5 g Protein: 3.5 g

472. Marshmallow Donut

Preparation Time: 10 minutes
Cooking Time: 35 minutes
Servings: 8-12
Ingredients:
For the donuts

- 1 cup all-purpose flour
- Cooking spray
- ¼ teaspoon baking soda
- 1/3 cup of sugar
- ¾ cup buttermilk
- 2 tbsp. butter (unsalted)
- One egg
- ½ tsp. vanilla extract
- Four chocolate bars (whatever kind you want)
- 24 marshmallows (sliced in half)

For the Glaze

- ¼ cup whole milk
- 1 tsp. vanilla extract
- 2 cups confectioners' sugar

Directions:
Grill Prep:

1. Spray the donut pans with some cooking spray.
2. Mix sugar, flour, and baking soda

3. Grab a different bowl; whisk your egg, melted butter, buttermilk, and vanilla.
4. Mix the dry and wet ingredients using a spatula, blending them perfectly.
5. Pipe your batter onto your greased donut pans.

On the Grill:

1. Set up your wood pellet smoker grill for indirect cooking.
2. Preheat your wood pellet smoker grill for 10 to 15 minutes at 350 degrees Fahrenheit.
3. Bake your batter for 25 minutes, till your donuts are nice and puffy, and the toothpick you insert to check it comes out nice and clean. Then let it cool in the pan.
4. Mix your vanilla and milk in a saucepan and heat it over low heat till it's a bit warm.
5. Sift your confectioner's sugar into your milk and vanilla mix till it's wonderfully combined.
6. Take your glaze off the fire, and let it set on a bowl of warm water.
7. Take your delicious donuts and dip them right into your glaze, then set your cooling rack over some foil, and then put your donuts on the shelf, letting them rest for 5 minutes.
8. Halve your donuts, and then place your halved marshmallows in between, as well as some chocolate.
9. Grill these sandwiches for 4 to 5 minutes. You want the chocolate and marshmallows to melt.
10. Take them off the grill, serve, and enjoy!

Nutrition: Calories: 217 kCal Fat: 5 g Carbs: 32 g Protein: 11 g

Chapter 8:   Dessert Recipes

473. S'mores Dip with Candied Pecans

Preparation Time: 10 minutes
Cooking Time: 37 to 45 minutes
Servings 4
Ingredients:
Candied Smoked Pecans
- ½ cup sugar
- ½ cup brown sugar
- 1 tablespoon ground cinnamon
- 1 teaspoon salt
- ¼ teaspoon cayenne pepper
- 1 egg white
- 1 teaspoon water
- 1-pound (454 g) pecans

S'mores Dip
- 1 tablespoon butter
- 2 cups milk chocolate chips
- 10 large marshmallows, cut in half
- Graham crackers, for serving

Directions:
1. When ready to cook, set Pit Boss temperature to 300 F (149 C) and preheat, lid closed for 15 minutes.
2. In a small bowl, stir together the sugars, cinnamon, salt, and cayenne pepper. In a medium bowl, whisk together the egg white and water until frothy.
3. Pour the pecans into a large bowl. Pour in the egg white mixture and sugar mixture and toss to coat well.
4. Spread the coated pecans on a sheet tray lined with parchment paper. Place the tray directly on the grill grate. Smoke for 30 to 35 minutes, stirring often.
5. Remove from the grill and let cool. Break apart and roughly chop. Set aside.
6. When ready to cook, set Pit Boss temperature to 400 F (204 C) and preheat, lid closed for 15 minutes.
7. Place a cast iron skillet directly on the grill grate while the grill heats up.
8. When the cast iron skillet is hot, melt the butter in the skillet and swirl around the skillet to coat.
9. Add the chocolate chips to the skillet, then top with the marshmallows. Cook for 7 to 10 minutes, or until the chocolate is melted and marshmallows are lightly browned. Remove from the grill.
10. Spread a handful of the candied pecans over the top and serve with the dip with the graham crackers.

Nutrition: Calories: 357 kCal Carbs: 64 g Fat: 12 g Protein: 4 g

474. S'mores Dip

Preparation Time: 0 Minutes
Cooking Time: 15 Minutes
Servings: 6-8
Ingredients:
- 12 ounces semisweet chocolate chips
- ¼ c. milk
- Two T. melted salted butter
- 16 ounces marshmallows
- Apple wedges
- Graham crackers

Directions:
1. Add wood pellets to your smoker and get your cooker's startup procedure. Preheat your smoker, with your lid closed, until it reaches 450.
2. Put a cast-iron skillet on your grill and add in the milk and melted butter. Stir together for a minute.
3. Cover, and let it smoke for five to seven minutes. The marshmallows should be toasted lightly.
4. Take the skillet off the heat and serve with apple wedges and graham crackers.

Nutrition: Calories: 90 kCal Carbs: 15g Fat: 3g Protein: 1g

475. Sweet Pumpkin Seeds

Preparation Time: 12 Minutes
Cooking Time: 30 Minutes
Servings: 8-12
Ingredients:
- Two T. sugar
- seeds from a pumpkin
- One t. cinnamon
- Two T. melted butter

Directions:
1. Add wood pellets to your smoker and follow your cooker's startup operation. Preheat your smoker, with your lid closed, until it reaches 350.
2. Clean the seeds and toss them in the melted butter. Add them to the sugar and cinnamon. Spread them out on a baking sheet, place on the grill, and smoke for 25 minutes.
3. Serve.

Nutrition: Calories: 160 Carbs: 5g Fat: 12g Protein: 7g

476. Feta Cheese Stuffed Meatballs

Preparation Time: 12 Minutes
Cooking Time: 35 Minutes
Servings: 6
Ingredients:
- Pepper
- Salt
- ¾ c. Feta cheese
- ½ t. thyme
- Two t. chopped oregano
- Zest of one lemon
- One-pound ground pork
- One-pound ground beef
- One T. olive oil

Directions:
1. Place the pepper, salt, thyme, oregano, olive oil, lemon zest, and ground meats into a large bowl.
2. Combine the ingredients thoroughly using your hands.
3. Cut the Feta into little cubes and begin making the meatballs. Take a half tablespoon of the meat mixture and roll it around a piece of cheese. Continue until all meat has been used.
4. Add wood pellets to your smoker and follow your cooker's startup procedure.
5. Preheat your smoker, with your lid closed, until it reaches 350.

6. Brush the meatballs with more olive oil and put onto the grill. Grill for ten minutes until browned.

Nutrition: Calories: 390 kCal Carbs: 8g Fat: 31g Protein: 20g

477. Smoked Carolina Pulled Pork Sandwiches

Preparation time: 10 minutes
Cooking time: 8 hours
Servings: 6 - 8
Ingredients:
- 1 bone-in Boston butt (6 - 7 pounds)
- Pork and poultry rub
- 1 cup apple cider vinegar
- 1 cup beer
- 2 tablespoons fresh lemon juice
- 1 tablespoon Worcestershire sauce
- 1 teaspoon red pepper flakes
- Buns

For the sauce and slaw
- 2 cups apple cider vinegar
- 1 ½ cups water
- ½ cup ketchup
- ¼ cup brown sugar
- 5 teaspoons salt
- 2 - 4 teaspoons red pepper flakes
- 1 teaspoon black pepper (freshly ground)
- 1 teaspoon white pepper (freshly ground)
- ½ cabbage (large, cored, shredded)

Directions:
1. Season your pork butt with the rub, and make sure the rub gets on every inch.
2. Wrap up your seasoned butt in some plastic and keep in your fridge for 8 hours.
3. To make your mop sauce, grab a nonreactive bowl, and mix your lemon juice, beer, Worcestershire sauce, apple cider vinegar, and red pepper flakes in it. Then set aside.

On the Grill
1. Set up your Smoker grill for indirect cooking.
2. Preheat your Smoker grill for 15 minutes at 180 degrees Fahrenheit, with the lid shut.
3. Take the plastic off your pork butt, and then set the meat right on your grill grates. Smoke your meat for 3 hours, making sure you mop with the mop sauce with each new hour.
4. Crank up the head so it is now at 250 degrees Fahrenheit, and then keep roasting your pork

until the internal Smoke Temperature is 160 degrees Fahrenheit. This should take 3 more hours. Keep mopping with the mop sauce every hour on the hour.

5. Wrap up your pork butt in some foil, and then keep cooking until the internal Smoke Temperature hits 204 degrees Fahrenheit.
6. Leaving your pork in foil, wrap it all up with some heavy bath towels, and then set them in an insulated cooler for one hour, max.
7. To make your vinegar sauce, grab a mixing brown and add the apple cider vinegar, ketchup, water, brown sugar, salt, red pepper flakes, white pepper, and black pepper. Stir it all up until all the crystals from the salt and sugar are fully dissolved.
8. Taste it for seasoning and add some more sugar or red pepper flakes to suit your taste. Then let it sit for an hour, so that the flavors can mingle fully.
9. To make the Carolina coleslaw, mix the shredded cabbage with 1 cup of the vinegar sauce in a bowl, and then add ¼ of red onion (diced) as well as some shredded carrots.
10. For the pulled pork, chunk your pork into bits, making sure you get rid of the bone and any pieces of gristle or fat. Pull your pork by shredding it, and then put the shreds into a disposable roasting pan.
11. Keep the meat moist with the juices in the foil, and some of your vinegar sauce.
12. Serve your meat on your buns, along with coleslaw. Have a mean meal!

Nutrition: Calories 150 kCal Fat 15g Carbs 12g Protein 10g

478. Baked S'mores Donut

Preparation time: 10 minutes
Cooking time: 35 minutes
Servings: 8 - 12
Ingredients:
For the donuts
- 1 cup all-purpose flour
- Cooking spray
- ¼ teaspoon baking soda
- 1/3 cup sugar
- ¾ cup buttermilk
- 2 tablespoons butter (unsalted)

- 1 egg
- ½ teaspoon vanilla extract
- 4 chocolate bars (whatever kind you want)
- 24 marshmallows (sliced in half)

For the Glaze
- ¼ cup whole milk
- 1 teaspoon vanilla extract
- 2 cups confectioners' sugar

Directions:
Grill Prep
1. Spray the donut pans with some cooking spray.
2. Grab a large mixing bowl, and whisk your sugar, flour, and baking soda together.
3. Grab a different bowl; whisk your egg, melted butter, buttermilk, and vanilla.
4. Mix the dry and wet ingredients using a spatula, blending them perfectly.
5. Pipe your batter onto your greased donut pans.

On the Grill
1. Set up your Smoker grill for indirect cooking.
2. Preheat your Smoker grill for 10 to 15 minutes at 350 degrees Fahrenheit.
3. Bake your batter for 25 minutes, till your donuts are nice and puffy, and the toothpick you insert to check it comes out nice and clean. Then let it cool in the pan.
4. Mix your vanilla and milk in a saucepan and heat it up over low heat till it is a bit warm.
5. Sift your confectioner's sugar into your milk and vanilla mix, till it is wonderfully combined.
6. Take your glaze off the fire, and let it set on a bowl of warm water.
7. Take your delicious donuts and dip them right into your glaze, then set your cooling rack over some foil, and then set your donuts on the rack, letting them rest for 5 minutes.
8. Halve your donuts, and then place your halved marshmallows in between, as well as some chocolate.
9. Grill these sandwiches for 4 to 5 minutes. You want the chocolate and marshmallows to melt.
10. Take them off the grill, serve, and enjoy!

Nutrition: Calories 213 kCal Fat 22g Carbs 52g Protein 20g

479. Baked Cherry Cheesecake Galette

Preparation time: 10 minutes
Cooking time: 20 minutes
Servings: 6 - 8

Ingredients:

For the cherry filling
- 1-pound cherries (thawed, drained)
- ¼ cup sugar
- 1 teaspoon cornstarch
- 1 teaspoon coriander
- A pinch of salt
- 1 tablespoon orange zest
- ½ tablespoon lemon zest

For the cream cheese filling
- 8 ounces cream cheese (softened)
- 1 teaspoon vanilla
- ¼ cup sugar
- 1 egg

For the galette
- 1 refrigerated pie crust
- Egg washes (1 egg, 1 tablespoon water, cream, or milk)
- Granulated sugar
- Vanilla ice cream to serve

Directions:

Grill Prep
1. Grab a medium bowl, and mix you cherries, orange zest, lemon zest, coriander, half of the sugar, cornstarch, and a pinch of salt.
2. Grab another bowl, and in it, mix your egg, vanilla, and cream cheese. Whip them up.
3. Get your pie dough onto a sheet tray, and then stretch it out with a rolling pin. Get it to about 1 inch in diameter.
4. Spread out your cream cheese filling in the middle of the pie dough. Be careful to leave a border of an inch around the edge. Then pile on your cherry mix on the cream cheese.
5. Now, you are going to fold in the edges of the pie dough into little parts, over the filling.
6. Next, brush the edges of the pie dough with egg wash, and then sprinkle on some granulated sugar.

On the Grill
1. Set up your Smoker grill for indirect cooking.
2. Preheat your Smoker grill at a Smoke Temperature of 350 degrees Fahrenheit, keeping it closed, for 15 minutes.
3. Set your sheet try right on the grill grate, and then bake that yummy goodness for 15 to 20 minutes. You want the crust to become nice and golden brown, and for the cheesecake filling to be completely set.
4. Dish the galette while warm with some ice cream. And then enjoy.

Nutrition: Calories 174 kCal Fat 14g Carbs 16g Protein 16g

480. Apple Pie on the Grill

Preparation Time: 20 minutes
Cooking Time: 30 minutes
Servings: 4 - 6

Ingredients:
- ¼ cup of Sugar
- 4 Apples, sliced
- 1 tbsp. of Cornstarch
- 1 tsp. Cinnamon, ground
- 1 Pie Crust, refrigerated, softens in according to the Directions: on the box
- ½ cup of Peach preserves

Directions:
1. Preheat the grill to 375F with closed lid.
2. In a bowl combine the cinnamon, cornstarch, sugar, and apples. Set aside.
3. Place the piecrust in a pie pan. Spread the preserves and then place the apples. Fold the crust slightly.
4. Place a pan on the grill (upside - down) so that you do not brill/bake the pie directly on Preferred Wood Pellet.
5. Cook 30 - 40 minutes. Once done, set aside to rest.
6. Serve and enjoy!

Nutrition: Calories 148 kCal Fat 10g Carbs 16g Protein 11g

481. Grilled Layered Cake

Preparation Time: 10 minutes
Cooking Time: 14 minutes
Servings: 6
Ingredients:

- 2 x pound cake
- 3 cups of whipped cream
- ¼ cup melted butter
- 1 cup of blueberries
- 1 cup of raspberries
- 1 cup sliced strawberries

Directions:

1. Preheat the grill to high with closed lid.
2. Slice the cake loaf (3/4 inch), about 10 per loaf. Brush both sides with butter.
3. Grill for 7 minutes on each side. Set aside.
4. Once cooled completely start layering your cake. Place cake, berries then cream.
5. Sprinkle with berries and serve.

Nutrition: Calories 186 kCal Fat 10g Carbs 19g Protein 16g

482. Coconut Chocolate Simple Brownies

Preparation Time: 15 minutes
Cooking Time: 25 minutes
Servings: 4 - 6
Ingredients:

- 4 eggs
- 1 cup Cane Sugar
- ¾ cup of Coconut oil
- 4 oz. chocolate, chopped
- ½ tsp. of Sea salt
- ¼ cup cocoa powder, unsweetened
- ½ cup flour
- 4 oz. Chocolate chips
- 1 tsp. of Vanilla

Directions:

1. Preheat the grill to 350F with closed lid.
2. Take a baking pan (9x9), grease it and line a parchment paper.
3. In a bowl combine the salt, cocoa powder, and flour. Stir and set aside.
4. In the microwave or double boiler melt the coconut oil and chopped chocolate. Let it cool a bit.
5. Add the vanilla, eggs, and sugar. Whisk to combine.

6. Add into the flour and add chocolate chips. Pour the mixture into a pan.
7. Place the pan on the grate. Bake for 20 minutes. If you want dryer brownies to bake for 5 - 10 minutes more.
8. Let them cool before cutting.
9. Cut the brownies into squares and serve.

Nutrition: Calories 161 kCal Fat 17g Carbs 53g Protein 0g

483. Seasonal Fruit on the Grill

Preparation Time: 5 minutes
Cooking Time: 5 minutes
Servings: 2 - 4
Ingredients:

- 2 plums, peaches apricots, etc. (choose seasonally)
- 3 tbsp. Sugar, turbinado
- ¼ cup of Honey
- Gelato, as desired

Directions:

1. Preheat the grill to 450F with closed lid.
2. Slice each fruit in halves and remove pits. Brush with honey. Sprinkle with some sugar.
3. Grill on the grate until you see that there are grill marks. Set aside.
4. Serve each with a scoop of gelato. Enjoy!

Nutrition: Calories 192 kCal Fat 12g Carbs 32g Protein 22g

484. Cinnamon Sugar Pumpkin Seeds

Preparation Time: 30 minutes
Cooking Time: 30 minutes
Servings: 8-12
Ingredients:

- 2 tbsp. sugar
- 2 cups seeds from a pumpkin
- 1 tsp. cinnamon
- 2 tbsp. melted butter

Directions:

1. Add Preferred Wood Pellet pellets to your smoker and follow your cooker's startup procedure. Preheat your smoker, with your lid closed, until it reaches 350.
2. Clean the seeds and toss them in the melted butter. Add them to the sugar and cinnamon. Spread them out on a baking sheet, place on the grill, and smoke for 25 minutes.

3. Serve.

Nutrition: Calories 145 kCal Fat 18g Carbs 11g Protein 19g

485. Smoked Berry Pie

Preparation Time: 30 minutes
Cooking Time: 40 minutes
Servings: 8
Ingredients:

- Butter, for greasing
- ½ c. all-purpose flour
- ½ c. milk
- 2 pints blackberries
- 2 c. sugar, divided
- 1 box refrigerated piecrusts
- 1 stick melted butter
- 1 stick of butter
- Vanilla ice cream

Directions:

1. Add Preferred Wood Pellet to your smoker and follow your cooker's startup procedure. Preheat your smoker, with your lid closed, until it reaches 375.
2. Butter a cast iron skillet.
3. Unroll a piecrust and lay it in the bottom and up the sides of the skillet. Use a fork to poke holes in the crust.
4. Lay the skillet on the grill and smoke for five minutes, or until the crust is browned. Set off the grill.
5. Mix 1 ½ c. of sugar, the flour, and the melted butter together. Add in the blackberries and toss everything together.
6. The berry mixture should be added to the skillet. The milk should be added on the top afterward. Sprinkle on half of the diced butter.
7. Unroll the second pie crust and lay it over the skillet. You can also slice it into strips and weave it on top to make it look like a lattice. Place the rest of the diced butter over the top. Sprinkle the rest of the sugar over the crust and place it skillet back on the grill.
8. Lower the lid and smoke for 15 to 20 minutes or until it is browned and bubbly. You may want to cover with some foil to keep it from burning during the last few minutes of cooking. Serve the hot pie with some vanilla ice cream.

Nutrition: Cal 244kCal Fat 13g Carbs 12g Protein 10g

486. Melted Marshmallow Dip

Preparation Time: 30 minutes
Cooking Time: 20 minutes
Servings: 6-8
Ingredients:

- 12 ounces semisweet chocolate chips
- ¼ c. milk
- 2 tbsp. melted salted butter
- 16 ounces marshmallows
- Apple wedges
- Graham crackers

Directions:

1. Add Preferred Wood Pellet pellets to your smoker and follow your cooker's startup procedure. Preheat your smoker, with your lid closed, until it reaches 450.
2. Put a cast iron skillet on your grill and add in the milk and melted butter. Stir together for a minute.
3. Once it has heated up, top with the chocolate chips, making sure it makes a single layer. Place the marshmallows on top, standing them on their end and covering the chocolate.
4. Cover, and let it smoke for five to seven minutes. The marshmallows should be toasted lightly.
5. Take the skillet off Preferred Wood Pellet and serve with apple wedges and graham crackers.

Nutrition: Calories 114 kCal Fat 16g Carbs 24g Protein 11g

487. Savory-Sweet Cookies

Preparation Time: 30 minutes.
Cooking Time: 30 minutes
Servings: 12
Ingredients:

- 8 slices cooked and crumbled bacon
- 2 ½ t. apple cider vinegar
- One t. vanilla
- Two c. semisweet chocolate chips
- Two room temp eggs
- 1 ½ t. baking soda
- One c. granulated sugar
- ½ t. salt
- 2 ¾ c. all-purpose flour
- One c. light brown sugar
- 1 ½ stick softened butter

Directions:

1. Mix salt, baking soda and flour.
2. Cream the sugar and the butter together. Lower the speed. Add in the eggs, vinegar, and vanilla.
3. Still on low, slowly add in the flour mixture, bacon pieces, and chocolate chips.
4. Add Preferred Wood Pellet pellets to your smoker and follow your cooker's startup procedure. Preheat your smoker, with your lid closed, until it reaches 375.
5. Place some parchment on a baking sheet and drop a teaspoonful of cookie batter on the baking sheet. Let them cook on the grill, covered, for approximately 12 minutes or until they are browned. Enjoy.

Nutrition: Calories 344 kCal Fat 17g Carbs 83g Protein 0 g

488. Chocolate Chip Cookies

Preparation Time: 30 minutes.
Cooking Time: 30 minutes
Servings: 12
Ingredients:

- 1 ½ c. chopped walnuts
- One t. vanilla
- Two c. chocolate chips
- One t. baking soda
- 2 ½ c. plain flour
- ½ t. salt
- 1 ½ stick softened butter
- Two eggs
- One c. brown sugar
- ½ c. sugar

Directions:

1. Add Preferred Wood Pellet pellets to your smoker and follow your cooker's startup procedure. Preheat your smoker, with your lid closed, until it reaches 350.
2. Mix the baking soda, salt, and flour.
3. Cream the brown sugar, sugar, and butter. Mix in the vanilla and eggs until it comes together.
4. Slowly add in the flour while continuing to beat. Once all flour has been incorporated, add in the chocolate chips and walnuts. Using a spoon, fold into batter.
5. Place an aluminum foil onto grill. In an aluminum foil, drop spoonful of dough and bake for 17 minutes

Nutrition: Calories 356 kCal Fat 115g Carbs 122g Protein 0g

489. Cherry Cream Cheese Galette

Preparation Time: 10 minutes
Cooking Time: 20 minutes
Servings: 6-8
Ingredients:
For the cherry filling

- 1-pound cherries (thawed, drained)
- ¼ cup of sugar
- 1 tsp. cornstarch
- 1 tsp. coriander
- A pinch of salt
- 1 tbsp. orange zest
- ½ tablespoon lemon zest

For the cream cheese filling

- 8 ounces of cream cheese (softened)
- 1 tsp. vanilla
- ¼ cup of sugar
- One egg

For the Galette

- One refrigerated pie crust
- 1 egg, 1 tbsp. water, cream, or milk
- Granulated sugar
- Vanilla ice cream to serve

Directions:

1. Grab a medium bowl; mix your cherries, orange zest, lemon zest, and coriander, half of the sugar, cornstarch, and a pinch of salt.

2. Grab another bowl, and in it, mix your egg, vanilla, and cream cheese. Whip it up.
3. Get your pie dough onto a sheet tray, and then stretch it out with a rolling pin. Get it to about 1 inch in diameter.
4. Spread out your cream cheese filling in the middle of the pie dough. Be careful to leave a border of an inch around the edge. Then pile your cherry mix on the cream cheese.
5. Now, you're going to fold in the pie dough's edges into little parts over the filling.
6. Next, brush the edges of the pie dough with egg wash, and then sprinkle on some granulated sugar.

On the Grill:
1. Set up your wood pellet smoker grill for indirect cooking.
2. Preheat your wood pellet smoker grill at a temperature of 350 degrees Fahrenheit, keeping it closed for 15 minutes.
3. Set your sheet to try right on the grill grate, and then bake that yummy goodness for 15 to 20 minutes. You want the crust to become nice and golden brown and for the cheesecake filling to be completely set.
4. Dish the Galette while warm with some ice cream. And then enjoy.

Nutrition: Calories: 400 kCal Fat: 51 g Carbs: 18 g Protein: 5 g

490. Nectarine and Nutella Sundae

Preparation Time: 10 Minutes
Cooking Time: 25 Minutes
Servings: 4
Ingredients:
- 2nectarines halved and pitted
- 2tsp honey
- 4tbsp Nutella
- 4scoops vanilla ice cream
- 1/4 cup pecans, chopped
- Whipped cream, to top
- 4cherries, to top

Directions:
1. Preheat pellet grill to 400°F.
2. Slice nectarines in half and remove the pits.
3. Brush the inside (cut side) of each nectarine half with honey.

4. Place nectarines directly on the grill grate, cut side down—Cook for 5-6 minutes, or until grill marks develop.
5. Flip nectarines and cook on the other side for about 2 minutes.
6. Remove nectarines from the grill and allow it to cool.
7. Fill the pit cavity on each nectarine half with 1 tbsp Nutella.
8. Place one scoop of ice cream on top of Nutella. Top with whipped cream, cherries, and sprinkle chopped pecans. Serve and enjoy!

Nutrition: Calories: 90 kCal Fat: 3g Carbs: 15g Protein: 2g

491. Cinnamon Sugar Donut Holes

Preparation Time: 10 Minutes
Cooking Time: 35 Minutes
Servings: 4
Ingredients:
- 1/2 cup flour
- 1tbsp cornstarch
- 1/2 tsp baking powder
- 1/8 tsp baking soda
- 1/8 tsp ground cinnamon
- 1/2 tsp kosher salt
- 1/4 cup buttermilk
- 1/4 cup sugar
- 11/2 tbsp butter, melted
- 1egg
- 1/2 tsp vanilla
- Topping
- 2tbsp sugar
- 1tbsp sugar
- 1tsp ground cinnamon

Directions:
1. Preheat pellet grill to 350°F.
2. In a medium bowl, combine flour, cornstarch, baking powder, baking soda, ground cinnamon, and kosher salt. Whisk to combine.
3. In a separate bowl, combine buttermilk, sugar, melted butter, egg, and vanilla. Whisk until the egg is thoroughly combined.
4. Pour wet mixture into the flour mixture and stir. Stir just until combined, careful not to overwork the mixture.
5. Spray mini muffin tin with cooking spray.
6. Spoon 1 tbsp of donut mixture into each mini muffin hole.

7. Place the tin on the pellet grill grate and bake for about 18 minutes, or until a toothpick can come out clean.
8. Remove muffin tin from the grill and let rest for about 5 minutes.
9. In a small bowl, combine 1 tbsp sugar and 1 tsp ground cinnamon.
10. Melt 2 tbsp of butter in a glass dish. Dip each donut hole in the melted butter, then mix and toss with cinnamon sugar. Place completed donut holes on a plate to serve.

Nutrition: Calories: 190 kCal Fat: 17g Carbs: 21g Protein: 3 g

492. Pellet Grill Chocolate Chip Cookies

Preparation Time: 20 Minutes
Cooking Time: 45 Minutes
Servings: 12
Ingredients:
- 1cup salted butter softened
- 1cup of sugar
- 1cup light brown sugar
- 2tsp vanilla extract
- 2large eggs
- 3cups all-purpose flour
- 1tsp baking soda
- 1/2 tsp baking powder
- 1tsp natural sea salt
- 2cups semi-sweet chocolate chips or chunks

Directions:
1. Preheat pellet grill to 375°F.
2. Line a large baking sheet with parchment paper and set aside.
3. In a medium bowl, mix flour, baking soda, salt, and baking powder. Once combined, set aside.
4. In stand mixer bowl, combine butter, white sugar, and brown sugar until combined. Beat in eggs and vanilla. Beat until fluffy.
5. Mix in dry ingredients, continue to stir until combined.
6. Add chocolate chips and mix thoroughly.
7. Roll 3 tbsp of dough at a time into balls and place them on your cookie sheet. Evenly space them apart, with about 2-3 inches in between each ball.
8. Place cookie sheet directly on the grill grate and bake for 20-25 minutes until the cookies' outside is slightly browned.

9. Remove from grill and allow to rest for 10 minutes. Serve d enjoy!

Nutrition: Calories: 120 kCal Fat: 4g Carbs: 22.8 g Protein: 1.4 g

493. Delicious Donuts on a Grill

Preparation Time: 5 Minutes
Cooking Time: 10 Minutes
Servings: 6
Ingredients:
- 1-1/2 cups sugar, powdered
- 1/3 cup whole milk
- 1/2 teaspoon vanilla extract
- 16 ounces of biscuit dough, prepared
- Oil spray, for greasing
- 1cup chocolate sprinkles, for sprinkling

Directions:
1. Take a medium bowl and mix sugar, milk, and vanilla extract.
2. Combine well to create a glaze.
3. Set the glaze aside for further use.
4. Place the dough onto the flat, clean surface.
5. Flat the dough with a rolling pin.
6. Use a ring mold, about an inch, and cut the hole in each round dough's center.
7. Place the dough on a plate and refrigerate for 10 minutes.
8. Open the grill and install the grill grate inside it.
9. Close the hood.
10. Now, select the grill from the menu, and set the temperature to medium.
11. Set the time to 6 minutes.
12. Select start and begin preheating.
13. Remove the dough from the refrigerator and coat it with cooking spray from both sides.
14. When the unit beeps, the grill is preheated; place the adjustable amount of dough on the grill grate.
15. Close the hood, and cook for 3 minutes.
16. After 3 minutes, remove donuts and place the remaining dough inside.
17. Cook for 3 minutes.
18. Once all the donuts are ready, sprinkle chocolate sprinkles on top.
19. Enjoy.

Nutrition: Calories: 400 kCal Fat: 11g Carbs: 71.3g Protein: 5.7g

494. Smoked Pumpkin Pie

Preparation Time: 10 Minutes
Cooking Time: 50 Minutes
Servings: 8
Ingredients:

- 1tbsp cinnamon
- 1-1/2 tbsp pumpkin
- 14oz can sweetened condensed milk
- 2beaten eggs
- pumpkin pie spice
- 15oz can
- 1unbaked pie shell
- Topping: whipped cream

Directions:

1. Preheat your smoker to 325oF.
2. Place a baking sheet, rimmed, on the smoker upside down, or use a cake pan.
3. Combine all your ingredients in a bowl, large, except the pie shell, then pour the mixture into a pie crust.
4. Place the pie on the baking sheet and smoke for about 50-60 minutes until a knife comes out clean when inserted. Make sure the center is set.
5. Remove and cool for about 2 hours or refrigerate overnight.
6. Serve with a whipped cream dollop and enjoy it!

Nutrition: Calories: 292 kCal Fat: 11g Carbs: 42g Protein: 7g

495. Wood Pellet Smoked Nut Mix

Preparation Time: 15 Minutes
Cooking Time: 20 Minutes
Servings: 12
Ingredients:

- 3cups mixed nuts (pecans, peanuts, almonds, etc.)
- 1/2 tbsp brown sugar
- 1tbsp thyme, dried
- 1/4 tbsp mustard powder
- 1tbsp olive oil, extra-virgin

Directions:

1. Preheat your pellet grill to 250oF with the lid closed for about 15 minutes.
2. Combine all ingredients in a bowl, large, then transfer into a cookie sheet lined with parchment paper.

3. Place the cookie sheet on a grill and grill for about 20 minutes.
4. Remove the nuts from the grill and let cool.
5. Serve and enjoy.

Nutrition: Calories: 249 kCal Fat: 21.5g Carbs: 12.3g Protein: 5.7g

496. Grilled Peaches and Cream

Preparation Time: 15 Minutes
Cooking Time: 8 Minutes
Servings: 8
Ingredients:

- 4halved and pitted peaches
- 1tbsp vegetable oil
- 2tbsp clover honey
- 1cup cream cheese, soft with honey and nuts

Directions:

1. Preheat your pellet grill to medium-high heat.
2. Coat the peaches lightly with oil and place on the grill pit side down.
3. Grill for about 5 minutes until nice grill marks on the surfaces.
4. Turn over the peaches, then drizzle with honey.
5. Spread and cream cheese dollop where the pit was and grill for additional 2-3 minutes until the filling becomes warm.
6. Serve immediately.

Nutrition: Calories: 139 kCal Fat: 10.2g Carbs: 11.6g Protein: 1.1g

497. Berry Cobbler on a Pellet Grill

Preparation Time: 15 Minutes
Cooking Time: 35 Minutes
Servings: 8

Ingredients:

For fruit filling

- 3cups frozen mixed berries
- 1lemon juice
- 1cup brown sugar
- 1tbsp vanilla extract
- 1bsp lemon zest, finely grated
- A pinch of salt

For cobbler topping

- 1-1/2 cups all-purpose flour
- 1-1/2 tbsp baking powder
- 3tbsp sugar, granulated
- 1/2 tbsp salt
- 8tbsp cold butter
- 1/2 cup sour cream
- 2tbsp raw sugar

Directions:

1. Set your pellet grill on "smoke" for about 4-5 minutes with the lid open until fire establishes, and your grill starts smoking.
2. Preheat your grill to 350 for about 10-15 minutes with the grill lid closed.
3. Meanwhile, combine frozen mixed berries, Lemon juice, brown sugar, vanilla, lemon zest, and salt pinch. Transfer into a skillet and let the fruit sit and thaw.
4. Mix flour, baking powder, sugar, and salt in a bowl, medium. Cut cold butter into peas sizes using a pastry blender, then add to the mixture. Stir to mix everything.
5. Stir in sour cream until dough starts coming together.
6. Pinch small pieces of dough and place over the fruit until fully covered. Splash the top with raw sugar.
7. Now place the skillet directly on the grill grate, close the lid, cook for about 35 minutes until juices bubble, and a golden-brown dough topping.
8. Remove the skillet from the pellet grill and cool for several minutes.
9. Scoop and serve warm.

Nutrition: Calories: 371 kCal Fat: 13g Carbs: 60g Protein: 3g

498. Pellet Grill Apple Crisp

Preparation Time: 20 Minutes
Cooking Time: 60 Minutes
Servings: 15

Ingredients:

- Apples
- Ten large apples
- 1/2 cup flour
- 1cup sugar, dark brown
- 1/2 tbsp cinnamon
- 1/2 cup butter slices
- Crisp
- 3cups oatmeal, old-fashioned
- 1-1/2 cups softened butter, salted
- 1-1/2 tbsp cinnamon
- 2cups brown sugar

Directions:

1. Preheat your grill to 350.
2. Wash, peel, core, and dice the apples into cubes, medium-size
3. Mix flour, dark brown sugar, and cinnamon, then toss with your apple cubes.
4. Spray a baking pan, 10x13", with cooking spray, then place apples inside. Top with butter slices.
5. Mix all crisp ingredients in a medium bowl until well combined. Place the mixture over the apples.
6. Place on the grill and cook for about 1-hour checking after every 15-20 minutes to ensure cooking is even. Do not place it on the hottest grill part.
7. Remove and let sit for about 20-25 minutes
8. It's very warm.

Nutrition: Calories: 528 kCal Fat: 26g Carbs: 75g Protein: 4g

499. Fromage Macaroni and Cheese

Preparation Time: 30 Minutes
Cooking Time: 1 Hour
Servings: 8
Ingredients:

- ¼ c. all-purpose flour
- ½ stick butter
- Butter, for greasing
- One-pound cooked elbow macaroni
- One c. grated Parmesan
- 8 ounces cream cheese
- Two c. shredded Monterey Jack
- 3 t. garlic powder
- Two t. salt
- One t. pepper
- Two c. shredded Cheddar, divided
- Three c. milk

Directions:

1. Add the butter to a pot and melt. Mix in the flour. Stir constantly for a minute. Mix in the pepper, salt, garlic powder, and milk. Let it boil.
2. After lowering the heat, let it simmer for about 5 mins, or until it has thickened. Remove from the heat.
3. Mix in the cream cheese, parmesan, Monterey Jack, and 1 ½ c. of cheddar. Stir everything until melted. Fold in the pasta.
4. Add wood pellets to your smoker and keep your cooker's startup procedure. Preheat your smoker, with your lid closed, until it reaches 225.
5. Butter a 9" x 13" baking pan. Pour the macaroni mixture into the pan and lay on the grill. Cover and allow it to smoke for an hour, or until it has become bubbly. Top the macaroni with the rest of the cheddar during the last
6. Serve.

Nutrition: Calories: 180 kCal Carbs: 19g Fat: 8g Protein: 8g

500. Spicy Barbecue Pecans

Preparation Time: 15 Minutes
Cooking Time: 1 Hour
Servings: 2
Ingredients:

- 2 ½ t. garlic powder
- 16 ounces raw pecan halves
- One t. onion powder
- One t. pepper
- Two t. salt
- One t. dried thyme
- Butter, for greasing
- 3 T. melted butter

Directions:

1. Add wood pellets to your smoker and follow your cooker's startup method.
2. Preheat your smoker, with your lid closed, until it reaches 225.
3. Cover and smoke for an hour, flipping the nuts one. Make sure the nuts are toasted and heated. They should be removed from the grill.
4. Set aside to cool and dry.

Nutrition: Calories: 150 kCal Carbs: 16g Fat: 9g Protein: 1g

501. Pit Boss Blackberry Pie

Preparation Time: 10 Minutes
Cooking Time: 40 Minutes
Servings: 8
Ingredients:

- Butter, for greasing
- ½ c. all-purpose flour
- ½ c. milk
- Two pints blackberries
- Two c. sugar, divided
- One box of refrigerated piecrusts
- One stick melted butter
- One stick of butter
- Vanilla ice cream

Directions:

1. Add wood pellets to your smoker and follow your cooker's startup method.
2. Preheat your smoker, with your lid closed, until it reaches 375.
3. Unroll the second pie crust and lay it over the skillet.
4. Lower the lid, then smoke for 15 to 20 minutes or until it is browned and bubbly.
5. Serve the hot pie with some vanilla ice cream.

Nutrition: Calories: 100 kCal Carbs: 10g Fat: 0g Protein: 15g

502. Bacon Chocolate Chip Cookies

Preparation Time: 10 Minutes
Cooking Time: 30 Minutes
Servings: 24
Ingredients:

- Eight slices of cooked and crumbled bacon
- 2 ½ t. apple cider vinegar
- One t. vanilla
- Two c. semisweet chocolate chips
- Two-room temp eggs
- 1 ½ t. baking soda
- One c. granulated sugar
- ½ t. salt
- Two ¾ c. all-purpose flour
- One c. light brown sugar
- 1 ½ stick softened butter

Directions:

1. Mix the flour, baking soda, and salt.
2. Cream the sugar and the butter together. Then lower the speed. Add in the eggs, vinegar, and vanilla.
3. Still on low, slowly add in the flour mixture, bacon pieces, and chocolate chips.
4. Add wood pellets to your smoker and follow your cooker's startup method.
5. Preheat your smoker, with your lid closed, until it reaches 375.
6. Place some parchment on a baking sheet and drop a teaspoonful of cookie batter on the baking sheet. Let them cook on the grill,
7. covered, for approximately 12 minutes or until they are browned. Enjoy.

Nutrition: Calories: 167 kCal Carbs: 21g Fat: 9g Protein: 2g

503. Pineapple Cake

Preparation Time: 20 Minutes
Cooking Time: 60 Minutes
Servings: 8
Ingredients:

- One c. sugar
- One T. baking powder
- One c. buttermilk
- Two eggs
- ½ t. salt
- One jar maraschino cherry
- One stick butter, divided
- ¾ c. brown sugar
- One can pineapple slice
- 1 ½ c. flour

Directions:

1. Add wood pellets to your smoker and observe your cooker's startup procedure. Preheat your smoker, with your lid closed, until it reaches 350.
2. Take a medium-sized cast-iron skillet and melt one half stick butter. Be sure to coat the entire skillet. Sprinkle brown sugar into a cast-iron skillet.
3. Lay the sliced pineapple on top of the brown sugar. Place a cherry into the middle of each pineapple ring.
4. Mix the salt, baking powder, flour, and sugar. Add in the eggs; one-half stick melted butter and buttermilk. Whisk to combine.
5. Put the cake on the grill and cook for an hour.
6. Take off from the grill and let it sit for ten minutes. Flip onto a serving platter.

Nutrition: Calories: 165 kCal Carbs: 40g Fat: 0g Protein: 1g

504. Banana Boats

Preparation Time: 30 minutes
Cooking time: 10 minutes
Servings: 4
Ingredients:

- Four green bananas
- Chocolate chips
- Miniature marshmallows
- Peanut butter chips
- Crushed cookies

Directions:

1. Split a banana lengthwise from end to end, leaving the peel intact on the opposite side.
2. Top with desired toppings.
3. Wrap the banana in heavy-duty aluminum foil.

Grilling:

1. Place the bananas on a 400F grill and close the dome for 10 minutes.
2. Unwrap and serve topped with vanilla ice cream, whipped cream, or by them.

Nutrition: Calories: 310 kCal Fat: 17 g Carbs: 40 g Protein: 4 g

505. Grilled Pineapple Sundaes

Preparation Time: 30 minutes
Cooking time: 5 minutes
Servings: 4
Ingredients:
- 4 fresh pineapple spears
- Vanilla Ice Cream
- Jarred Caramel Sauce
- Toasted Coconut

Directions:
1. Place pineapple spears on a 400F grill and close the dome for 2 minutes.
2. Turn the pineapple and close the dome for another 2 minutes.
3. Turn the pineapple once more and close the dome for another minute.
4. Serve pineapple topped with ice cream, caramel sauce, and toasted coconut.

Nutrition: Calories: 112 kCal Fat: 1 g Carbs: 29 g Protein: 0.4g

Chapter 9:   Sauces and Rubs

506. Charred Peaches with Bourbon Butter Sauce

Preparation time: 10 minutes
Cooking time: 12 minutes
Servings: 4

Ingredients:
- Four tablespoons salted butter
- ¼ cup bourbon
- ½ cup brown sugar
- Four ripe peaches halved and pitted
- ¼ cup candied pecans

Directions:
1. Insert the Grill Grate and cover the hood. Select GRILL, then set the temperature to MAX, and set the time to 12 minutes. Select START/STOP to begin preheating.
2. While the unit is preheating, in a saucepan over medium heat, melt the butter for about 5 minutes. Once the butter is browned, remove the pan from the heat and carefully add the bourbon.
3. Return the saucepan into medium-high heat and add the brown sugar. Bring to a boil and let the sugar dissolve for 5 minutes, stirring occasionally.
4. Pour the bourbon butter sauce into a medium shallow bowl and arrange the peaches cut side down to coat in the sauce.
5. When the unit beeps a sign that it has preheated, place the fruit on the Grill Grate in a single layer (you may need to do this in multiple batches). Gently press the fruit down to maximize grill marks. Close the hood and grill for 10 to 12 minutes without flipping. If working in batches, repeat this step for all the peaches.
6. When cooking is complete, remove the peaches and top each with the pecans. Drizzle with the remaining bourbon butter sauce and serve immediately.

Nutrition: Calories: 309 kCal Fat: 8g Carbs: 34g Protein: 2g

507. Grilled Pineapple with Chocolate Sauce

Preparation Time: 10 Minutes
Cooking Time: 25 Minutes
Servings: 8

Ingredients:
- 1pineapple
- 8 oz bittersweet chocolate chips
- 1/2 cup spiced rum
- 1/2 cup whipping cream
- 2tbsp light brown sugar

Directions:
1. Preheat pellet grill to 400°F.
2. De-skin, the pineapple, then slice the pineapple into 1 in cubes.
3. In a saucepan, combine chocolate chips. When chips begin to melt, add rum to the saucepan. Continue to stir until combined, then add a splash of the pineapple's juice.
4. Add in whipping cream and continue to stir the mixture. Once the sauce is smooth and thickening, lower heat to simmer to keep warm.
5. Thread pineapple cubes onto skewers. Sprinkle skewers with brown sugar.
6. Place skewers on the grill grate. Grill for about 5 minutes per side, or until grill marks begin to develop.
7. Remove skewers from grill and allow to rest on a plate for about 5 minutes. Serve alongside warm chocolate sauce for dipping.

Nutrition: Calories: 112.6 kCal Fat: 0.5 g Carbs: 28.8 g Protein: 0.4 g

508. Smoked Tomato Cream Sauce

Preparation Time: 15 minutes
Cooking Time: 1 hour 20 minutes
Servings: 1
Ingredients:

- 1 lbs. beefsteak tomatoes, fresh and quartered
- 1-1/2 tbsp. olive oil
- Black pepper, freshly ground
- Salt, kosher
- 1/2 cup yellow onions, chopped
- 1 tbsp. tomato paste
- 2 tbsp. minced garlic
- Pinch cayenne
- 1/2 cup chicken stock
- 1/2 cup heavy cream

Directions:

1. Prepare your smoker using directions from the manufacturer. Toss tomatoes and 1 tbsp. oil in a bowl, mixing, then season with pepper and salt. Smoke the tomatoes placed on a smoker rack for about 30 minutes. Remove and set aside reserving tomato juices. Heat 1/2 tbsp. oil in a saucepan over high-medium heat.
2. Add onion and cook for about 3-4 minutes. Add tomato paste and garlic then cook for an additional 1 minute. Add smoked tomatoes, cayenne, tomato juices, pepper, and salt then cook for about 3-4 minutes. Stir often.
3. Add chicken stock and boil for about 25-30 minutes under a gentle simmer. Stir often. Place the mixture in a blender and puree until smooth. Now squeeze the mixture through a sieve, fine-mesh, discard solids, release the juices, Transfer the sauce in a saucepan, small, and add the cream.
4. Simmer for close to 6 minutes over low-medium heat until thickened slightly. Season with pepper and salt. Serve warm with risotto cakes.

Nutrition: Calories 50 kCal Fat 5g Carbs 2g Protein 0g

509. Smoked Mushroom Sauce

Preparation Time: 30 minutes
Cooking Time: 1 hour
Servings: 4
Ingredients:

- 1-quart chef mix mushrooms
- 2 tbsp. canola oil
- 1/4 cup julienned shallots
- 2 tbsp. chopped garlic
- Salt and pepper to taste
- 1/4 cup alfasi cabernet sauvignon
- 1 cup beef stock
- 2 tbsp. margarine

Directions:

1. Crumple four foil sheets into balls. Puncture multiple places in the foil pan then place mushrooms in the foil pan. Smoke in a pellet grill for about 30 minutes. Remove and cool.
2. Heat canola oil in a pan, sauté, add shallots and sauté until translucent. Add mushrooms and cook until supple and rendered down. Add garlic and season with pepper and salt. Cook until fragrant.
3. Add beef stock and wine then cook for about 6-8 minutes over low heat. Adjust seasoning. Add margarine and stir until sauce is thickened and a nice sheen. Serve and enjoy!

Nutrition: Calories 300 kCal Fat 30g Carbs 10g Protein 4g

510. Choran Sauce

Preparation Time: 10 minutes
Cooking Time: 30 minutes
Servings: 4
Ingredients:

- 1 cup béarnaise sauce
- ¼ cup tomato coulis
- 2 tablespoons red wine vinegar

Directions:

1. In a blender place all ingredients and blend until smooth
2. Pour smoothie in a glass and serve

Nutrition: Calories 30 kCal Fat 0g Carbs 7g Protein 0g

511. Chimichurri Sauce

Preparation Time: 10 minutes
Cooking Time: 30 minutes
Servings: 4
Ingredients:

- 1 cup parsley
- 2 garlic cloves
- 1 tablespoon oregano leaves
- ¼ cup olive oil
- ¼ cup red wine vinegar
- ½ tsp. red pepper flakes

Directions:

1. In a blender place all ingredients and blend until smooth
2. Pour smoothie in a glass and serve

Nutrition: Calories 49 kCal Fat 1.8 g Carbs 7.7 g Protein 1.1 g

512. Bourbon Barbecue Sauce

Preparation Time: 5 minutes
Cooking Time: 40 minutes
Servings: 8 to 12
Ingredients:

- ½ onion (minced)
- ¾ cup bourbon whiskey
- 4 cloves garlic (minced)
- ½ teaspoon black pepper (ground)
- 2 cups ketchup
- 1/3 Cup cider vinegar
- ½ tablespoon salt
- ¼ cup tomato paste
- ½ cup packed brown sugar
- ¼ cup Worcestershire sauce
- 1/3 Teaspoons hot pepper sauce (or add as you see fit)

Directions:

1. Set your wood pellet smoker grill for indirect cooking.
2. Let the grill heat at 350 degrees Fahrenheit for 15 minutes, with the lid closed.
3. Grab a large skillet, and add your garlic, whiskey, and onion. Let it all simmer for 20 minutes on your smoker grill. You're waiting for the onions to get translucent.
4. Toss in the salt, ground black pepper, tomato paste, ketchup, Worcestershire sauce, vinegar, brown sugar, and hot pepper sauce. Mix it all up.

5. Bring it all to a boil, then drop the heat to 225 degrees Fahrenheit and then let it simmer for 20 minutes more.
6. If you like your sauce smooth, then use a strainer to extract it from the onions and stuff.
7. Enjoy this sauce with your barbecue meals!

Nutrition: Calories: 20 kCal Protein: 1g Carbs: 35g Fat : 0g

513. Texas Style Coffee Mop Sauce

Preparation Time: 5 minutes
Cooking Time: 25 minutes
Servings: 8 to 12
Ingredients:

- 1 tablespoon sugar
- 1 cup Catsup
- ¼ cup butter
- ½ cup Worcestershire sauce
- 1 cup dark or strong coffee
- 1 tablespoon black pepper (fresh, coarse, ground)
- 1 tablespoon kosher salt

Directions:

1. Mix all your ingredients in a pot large enough to allow you to work without it spilling over
2. Set up your smoker grill for direct cooking
3. Preheat your smoker grill to 350 degrees Fahrenheit for 15 minutes, with the lid closed.
4. Now simmer your ingredients on your smoker grill for 20 minutes. Allow it to thicken. Enjoy!

Nutrition: Calories:40 kCal Protein: 0g Carbs: 7g Fat: 0g

514. Beer Mopping Sauce

Preparation Time: 5 minutes
Cooking Time: 20 minutes
Servings: 8 to 12
Ingredients:

- 12 ounces of beer
- ½ cup water
- ½ cup cider vinegar
- ½ cup canola or corn oil
- ½ onion (medium, chopped)
- 2 garlic cloves (minced)
- 1 tablespoon Worcestershire sauce
- 1 tablespoon brisket seasoning

Directions:

1. Whisk your ingredients all together in a saucepan.
2. Set up the grill for direct cooking
3. Let the grill heat at 350 degrees Fahrenheit for 15 minutes, with the lid closed.
4. Let your ingredients simmer on the grates until they come to a boil, lower the heat.
5. Let it get nice and thick, and then take it off the grill, and let it cool
6. Best pellets: hickory

Nutrition: Calories: 40 kCal Protein: 0g Carbs: 5g Fat: 0g

515. Carolina Mopping Sauce

Preparation Time: 5 minutes
Cooking Time: 5 minutes
Servings: 8 to 12
Ingredients:

- 1 cup cider vinegar
- 1 tablespoon hot sauce
- 1 tablespoon red pepper flakes
- 1 cup distilled white
- 1 teaspoon onion powder
- 1 teaspoon garlic powder
- 2 tablespoons brown sugar (packed)
- 1 teaspoon dry mustard
- ½ teaspoon salt
- ¼ teaspoon black pepper (ground)

Directions:

1. Simply mix all your ingredients, and then store in an air-tight fridge for a month.
2. If you need more heat, just add some more red pepper flakes.

Nutrition: Cal: 90 kCal Protein: 0g Carbs: 22g Fat: 0g

516. Pulled Pork Mop Recipe

Preparation Time: 5 minutes
Cooking Time: 5 minutes
Servings: 8 to 12
Ingredients:

- 16 ounces cider vinegar
- 16 ounces vegetable oil
- 32 ounces water
- 1 cup ultra-dry rub
- 2 tablespoons Worcestershire sauce
- 2 tablespoons soy sauce

Directions:

1. Simply whisk all the ingredients together, after dissolving your dry rub with some hot water.

Nutrition: Calories: 45 kCal Protein: 0g Carbs: 10g Fat: 0g

517. Apple Butter and Fireball BBQ Sauce

Preparation Time: 10 minutes
Cooking Time: 60 minutes
Servings: 3
Ingredients:

- 1 tablespoon olive oil
- ½ yellow onion, diced
- 3 garlic cloves, minced
- 1 ½ cups apple butter
- ½ cup cinnamon whiskey, such as Fireball
- ½ cup ketchup
- 1/3 cup apple cider vinegar
- ½ cup brown sugar, packed
- 2 tablespoons Worcestershire sauce
- 1 teaspoon cayenne pepper flakes
- 1 teaspoon ground mustard
- 1 teaspoon ground black pepper
- 1 teaspoon salt

Directions:

2. Coat the bottom of a saucepan with the oil.
3. Add the garlic and onion and place on the stove over medium heat, sautéing the onions until they become translucent.
4. Pour the cinnamon whiskey into the saucepan with the tender vegetables and stir until well combined.
5. Bring the mixture to a boil before reducing the heat and simmering for 10 minutes, while stirring frequently.
6. While the mixture is simmering, combine the ketchup, apple butter, Worcestershire sauce,

vinegar, mustard, brown sugar, salt, black pepper, and cayenne pepper in a mixing bowl.

7. Combine the mixture from Step 3 into the mix from Step 2.
8. Turn the heat up and bring the mixture back to a boil, while stirring regularly. Once it boils, reduce the heat again and let it simmer for 25 to 30 minutes.
9. Take the saucepan off the heat and let it cool down. Use immediately or pour into mason jars and store in the fridge until ready to use.

Nutrition: Calories: 66 kCal Protein:0g Carbs: 16g Fat: 0g

518. Mixed Herb Sauce

Preparation Time: 9 minutes
Cooking Time: 0 minute
Serving: 2
Ingredients:
- ½ cup extra-virgin olive oil
- 1 bunch fresh parsley, stems removed
- 1 bunch fresh cilantro, stems removed
- 1 small red onion, chopped
- 3 tablespoons dried oregano
- 1 tablespoon minced garlic
- Juice of 1 lemon
- 2 tablespoons red wine vinegar
- 1 teaspoon salt
- 1 teaspoon freshly ground black pepper
- 1 teaspoon cayenne pepper

Directions:
1. Using a food processor or blender, combine all of the ingredients and pulse several times until finely chopped.
2. The chimichurri sauce will keep in an airtight container in the refrigerator for up to 5 days.

Nutrition: Calories 24 kCal Fat 0 g Protein 1 g Carbs: 5g

519. Chipotle Butter

Preparation Time: 9 minutes
Cooking Time: 4 minutes
Serving: 1
Ingredients:
- 1 cup (2 sticks) salted butter
- 2 chipotle chilies in adobo sauce, finely chopped
- 2 teaspoons adobo sauce
- 2 teaspoons salt
- Juice of 1 lime

Directions:
1. On the stove top, in a small saucepan over medium heat, melt the butter. Stir in the chopped chilies, adobo sauce, salt, and lime juice, continuing to stir until the salt is dissolved, about 5 minutes. Remove from the heat.
2. Serve the chipotle butter hot or cold. It will keep in an airtight container in the refrigerator for up to 2 weeks.

Nutrition: Calories 110 kCal Fat 11g Protein 0g Carbs: 1g

520. Cilantro-Balsamic Drizzle

Preparation Time: 7 minutes
Cooking Time: 0 minute
Serving: 2
Ingredients:
- ½ cup balsamic vinegar
- ½ cup dry white wine
- ¼ cup extra-virgin olive oil
- ½ cup chopped fresh cilantro
- 2 teaspoons garlic powder
- 1 teaspoon salt
- 1 teaspoon freshly ground black pepper
- 1 teaspoon red pepper flakes
- Splash of Sriracha

Directions:
1. In a medium bowl, whisk together the balsamic vinegar, wine, olive oil, cilantro, garlic powder, salt, pepper, and red pepper flakes until well combined.
2. Add a dash of Sriracha and stir.
3. Store in an airtight container in the refrigerator for up to 2 weeks.

Nutrition Calories 77 kCal Fat 11g Protein 4g Carbs:

521. Sweet Potato Mustard

Preparation Time: 74 minutes
Cooking Time: 23 minutes
Serving: 1
Ingredients:

- ½ cup apple cider vinegar
- 1/3 cup yellow mustard seeds
- 1 bay leaf
- 1 cup water
- 1 tablespoon molasses
- 1 tablespoon bourbon
- 2/3 cup sweet potato purée
- ¼ cup packed brown sugar
- 2 tablespoons ground mustard
- ½ teaspoon smoked paprika
- 1 teaspoon salt
- ½ teaspoon ground cinnamon
- ½ teaspoon ground allspice
- ½ teaspoon cayenne pepper

Directions:

1. On the stove top, in a saucepan over medium-high heat, bring the apple cider vinegar to a boil.
2. Remove from the heat, stir in the mustard seeds and bay leaf, and let steep, uncovered, for 1 hour. Discard the bay leaf after steeping.
3. Pour the liquid into a food processor or blender, making sure to scrape in the mustard seeds as well. Add the water, molasses, and bourbon, and pulse until smooth.
4. Pour the mixture back into the saucepan over medium heat and stir in the sweet potato purée. Bring to a boil, then reduce the heat to low and cook, stirring occasionally, for 5 minutes.
5. Whisk in the brown sugar, ground mustard, smoked paprika, salt, cinnamon, allspice, and cayenne, and simmer until thickened, about 10 minutes.
6. Remove from the heat and let cool completely before refrigerating.
7. The sweet potato mustard is best served cold. It will keep in an airtight container in the refrigerator for up to 2 weeks.

Nutrition: Calories 10 kCal Fat 0g Protein 0g Carbs: 2g

522. Mandarin Glaze

Preparation Time: 9 minutes
Cooking Time: 0 minute
Serving: 2
Ingredients:

- 1 (11-ounce) can mandarin oranges, with their juices
- ½ cup ketchup
- 3 tablespoons brown sugar
- 1 tablespoon apple cider vinegar
- 1 tablespoon yellow mustard
- 1 teaspoon ground cloves
- 1 teaspoon ground cinnamon
- 1 teaspoon garlic powder
- 1 teaspoon onion powder
- 1 teaspoon salt
- 1 teaspoon freshly ground black pepper

Directions:

1. Using a food processor or blender, combine the mandarin oranges and juice, the ketchup, brown sugar, apple cider vinegar, mustard, cloves, cinnamon, garlic powder, onion powder, salt, and pepper, and pulse until the oranges are in tiny pieces.
2. Transfer the mixture to a small saucepan on the stove top and bring to a boil over medium heat, stirring occasionally.
3. Reduce the heat to low and simmer for 15 minutes.
4. Remove from the heat and strain out the orange pieces if desired. Serve the glaze hot.
5. The glaze will keep in an airtight container in the refrigerator for up to 5 days.

Nutrition: Calories 35 kCal Fat 0g Protein 0g Carbs: 9g

523. Heavenly Rabbit Smoke

Preparation Time: 10 minutes
Cooking Time: Nil
Serving: 5
Ingredients:
- 1 teaspoon dried thyme
- 1 teaspoon dried parsley
- 2 teaspoons dried oregano
- ½ teaspoon dried marjoram
- ½ teaspoon ground nutmeg
- ½ teaspoon ground cinnamon
- 1 teaspoon chicken bouillon granules
- 1 and ½ teaspoons garlic powder
- 1 teaspoon cracked pepper
- ½ teaspoon salt
- 1 and ½ teaspoon onion powder

Directions:
1. Mix the ingredients mentioned above to prepare the seasoning and use it as needed.

Nutrition: Calories: 20 kCal Carbs: 5g Protein: 1g Fat :

524. Uncle Johnny's Rub

Preparation Time: 10 minutes
Cooking Time: Nil
Serving: 4
Ingredients:
- ½ teaspoon oregano
- 4 tablespoons ground paprika
- 1 tablespoon brown sugar
- 1 tablespoon ground cumin
- 1 tablespoon chili powder
- 1 tablespoon mustard powder
- 1 tablespoon salt
- 2 tablespoons pepper
- 1 tablespoon garlic powder

Directions:
1. Mix the ingredients mentioned above to prepare the seasoning and use it as needed.

Nutrition: Calories: 20 kCal Carbs: 5g Protein: 1g Fat :

525. Fajita Seasoning

Preparation Time: 10 minutes
Cooking Time: Nil
Serving: 4
Ingredients:
- ¼ cup of chili powder
- 2 tablespoon of ground cumin
- 1 tablespoon of salt
- 4 teaspoons of black pepper
- 3 teaspoons of dried oregano
- 2 teaspoons of paprika
- 1 teaspoon of onion powder
- 1 teaspoon of parsley

Directions:
1. Mix the ingredients mentioned above to prepare the seasoning and use it as needed.

Nutrition: Calories: 23 kCal Carbs: 5g Protein: 1g Fat: 0g

526. Herbed Mixed Salt

Preparation Time: 10 minutes
Cooking Time: Nil
Serving: 4
Ingredients:
- ½ cup coarse salt
- ¼ cup packed fresh rosemary leaves
- ¼ cup packed fresh lemon thyme
- 1 cup of salt

Directions:
1. Mix the ingredients mentioned above
2. Let it sit and Air Dry for 2 hours
3. Use as needed

Nutrition: Calories: 3 kCal Carbs: 2g Protein: 1g Fat: 2g

527. Classic BBQ Rub

Preparation Time: 10 minutes
Cooking Time: Nil
Serving: 4
Ingredients:
- 1 teaspoon salt
- 1/8 teaspoon ground cumin
- ¾ teaspoon ground white pepper
- ¾ teaspoon ground black pepper
- ¾ teaspoon dried thyme
- ¾ teaspoon ground savory
- ¾ teaspoon ground coriander seeds
- 1 teaspoon ground bay leaves
- 1 and ½ teaspoon dried basil
- 2 teaspoons garlic powder

Directions:
1. Mix the ingredients mentioned above to prepare the seasoning and use it as needed.

Nutrition: Calories: 360 kCal Carbs: 78g Protein: 4g Fat: 2g

528. Garlic and Rosemary Meat Rub

Preparation Time: 10 minutes
Cooking Time: Nil
Serving: 4
Ingredients:
- 1 tablespoon pepper
- 1 tablespoon salt
- 3 tablespoons fresh rosemary, chopped
- 1 tablespoon dried rosemary
- 8 garlic cloves, diced
- ½ cup olive oil

Directions:
1. Mix the ingredients mentioned above to prepare the seasoning and use it as needed.

Nutrition: Calories: 2 kCal Fat : 2 g Carbs: 0 g Protein: 0 g

529. A Viking Mix

Preparation Time: 10 minutes
Cooking Time: Nil
Serving: 4
Ingredients:
- 5 teaspoons paprika
- 2 teaspoons salt
- 2 teaspoons onion powder
- 1 teaspoon cayenne
- 2 teaspoons ground pepper
- 1 teaspoon dry mustard

Directions:
1. Mix the ingredients mentioned above to prepare the seasoning and use it as needed.

Nutrition: Calories: 280 kCal Carbs: 22g Protein: 15g Fat: 14g

530. Fancy Taco Seasoning

Preparation Time: 10 minutes
Cooking Time: Nil
Serving: 4
Ingredients:
- 1 tablespoon of Chili powder
- ½ a teaspoon of Garlic powder
- ½ a teaspoon of Onion powder
- 1 and a ½ teaspoon of ground cumin
- 1 teaspoon of salt
- 1 teaspoon of pepper
- ¼ teaspoon of crushed red pepper flakes
- ¼ teaspoon of dried oregano

- ½ a teaspoon of paprika

Directions:
1. Mix the ingredients mentioned above to prepare the Taco seasoning and use it as needed.

Nutrition: Calories: 10 kCal Carbs: 7g Protein: 2g Fat: 1g

531. Special BBQ Sauce

Preparation Time: 10 minutes
Cooking Time: Nil
Serving: 4
Ingredients:
- ½ a cup of apple cider vinegar
- 2 tablespoons of water
- 2 tablespoon of coconut aminos
- ¼ teaspoon of mustard seeds
- ¼ teaspoon of onion powder
- ¼ teaspoon of garlic powder
- 1/8 teaspoon of cinnamon
- 1/8 teaspoon of black pepper

Directions:
1. Add all the listed ingredients to your saucepan
2. Bring it to a boil and stir well
3. Simmer for a few minutes
4. Remove the heat and allow it to cool
5. Use as needed!

Nutrition: Calories: 20 kCal Carbs: 4g Protein: 2g Fat: 1.5g

532. Classic Home-Made Worcestershire Sauce

Preparation Time: 10 minutes
Cooking Time: 15 minutes
Serving: 4
Ingredients:
- ½ a cup of apple cider vinegar
- 2 tablespoons of water
- 2 tablespoon of coconut aminos
- ¼ teaspoon of mustard seeds
- ¼ teaspoon of onion powder
- ¼ teaspoon of garlic powder
- 1/8 teaspoon of cinnamon
- 1/8 teaspoon of black pepper

Directions:
1. Add all the listed ingredients to your saucepan
2. Bring it to a boil and stir well
3. Simmer for a few minutes
4. Remove the heat and allow it to cool
5. Use as needed!

Nutrition: Calories: 10 kCal Carbs: 1g Protein: 0g Fat: 0g

533. Original Ketchup

Preparation Time: 10 minutes
Cooking Time: 20 minutes
Serving: 4
Ingredients:

- ½ a cup of chopped pitted dates
- 1 can of 6-ounce tomato paste
- 1 can of 14-ounce diced tomatoes
- 2 tablespoon of coconut vinegar
- ½ a cup of bone broth
- 1 teaspoon of garlic powder
- 1 teaspoon of onion powder
- 1 teaspoon of salt
- ½ a teaspoon of cayenne pepper

Directions:
1. Add the ingredients to a small-sized saucepan
2. Cook on medium-low for 20 minutes
3. Remove the heat
4. Take an immersion blender and blend the mixture until smooth
5. Remove the mixer and simmer on low for 10 minutes
6. Use as needed

Nutrition: Calories: 110 kCal Carbs: 27g Protein: 1g Fat: 0g

534. Lovely Mayonnaise

Preparation Time: 10 minutes
Cooking Time: Nil
Serving: 4
Ingredients:

- 1 whole egg
- ½ a teaspoon of sea salt
- ½ a teaspoon of ground mustard
- 1 and a ¼ cup of extra light olive oil
- 1 tablespoon of lemon juice

Directions:
1. Place the egg, ground mustard, salt and ¼ cup of olive oil into a food processor
2. Whirl on low until mixed
3. While the processor is running, drizzle remaining olive oil and keep whirling for 3 minutes
4. Add lemon juice and pulse on low until thoroughly mixed
5. Chill for 30 minutes

6. Use as needed
Nutrition: Calories: 680 kCal Carbs: 1g Protein: 2g Fat: 75g

535. Mouthwatering Sour Cream

Preparation Time: 10 minutes
Cooking Time: Nil
Serving: 4
Ingredients:
1. 1 can of thick unsweetened coconut milk
2. 1 and a ½ tablespoon of lemon juice
3. ½ a tablespoon of apple cider vinegar
4. 1/8 teaspoon of salt

Directions:
1. Chill the coconut milk in the can overnight
2. Flip the can upside and open, pour off the liquid
3. Scrape out the thick cream and add lemon juice, salt, and vinegar
4. Whisk until smooth
5. Use it when needed!

Nutrition: Calories: 343 kCal Carbs: 2g Protein: 2g Fat: 37g

536. Regular Everyday Breadcrumbs

Preparation Time: 10 minutes
Cooking Time: Nil
Serving: 4
Ingredients:

- 1 cup of almond flour/meal
- ½ a teaspoon of sea salt
- ½ a teaspoon of black pepper
- ½ a teaspoon of garlic powder
- ½ a teaspoon of dried parsley
- ¼ teaspoon of onion powder
- ¼ teaspoon of dried oregano

Directions:
1. Take a small-sized bowl and add all the listed ingredients and whisk them well
2. Use as needed

Nutrition: Calories: 360 kCal Carbs: 66g Protein: 12g Fat: 4g

537. Salted Raw Caramel Dip

Preparation Time: 5 minutes
Cooking Time: 0 minute
Serving: 2
Ingredients:
- 1 cup soft Medjool date, pitted
- 1 teaspoon vanilla extract
- ¼ cup almond milk
- 1 teaspoon fresh lemon juice
- 1 tablespoon coconut oil
- ¼ teaspoon salt

Directions:
1. Add all ingredients in your blender
2. Pulse until you get a smooth mixture
3. Serve chilled and enjoy!

Nutrition: Calories: 160 kCal Carbs: 40g Protein: 2g Fat: 2g

538. Hot Sauce with Cilantro

Preparation Time: 10 Minutes
Cooking Time: 30 Minutes
Servings: 4
Ingredients:
- ½ tsp coriander
- ½ tsp cumin seeds
- ¼ tsp black pepper
- 2 green cardamom pods
- 2 garlic cloves
- 1 tsp salt
- 1 oz. parsley
- 2 tablespoons olive oil

Directions:
1. In a blender place all ingredients and blend until smooth
2. Pour smoothie in a glass and serve

Nutrition: Calories: 60 kCal Carbs: 2g Fat: 5g Protein: 2g

539. Pit Boss Chimichurri Sauce

Preparation Time: 10 Minutes
Cooking Time: 30 Minutes
Servings: 4
Ingredients:
- 1 cup parsley
- 2 garlic cloves
- 1 tablespoon oregano leaves
- ¼ cup olive oil

- ¼ cup red wine vinegar
- ½ tsp red pepper flakes

Directions:
1. In a blender place all ingredients and blend until smooth
2. Pour smoothie in a glass and serve

Nutrition: Calories: 160 kCal Carbs: 4g Fat: 10g Protein: 0g

540. Basil Pesto Sauce

Preparation Time: 10 Minutes
Cooking Time: 30 Minutes
Servings: 4
Ingredients:
- 2 cloves garlic
- 2 oz. basil leaves
- 1 tablespoon pine nuts
- 1 oz. parmesan cheese
- ½ cup olive oil

Directions:
1. In a blender place all ingredients and blend until smooth
2. Pour smoothie in a glass and serve

Nutrition: Calories: 460 kCal Carbs: 7g Fat: 46g Protein: 6g

541. Vegan Pesto

Preparation Time: 10 Minutes
Cooking Time: 30 Minutes
Servings: 4
Ingredients:
- 1 cup cilantro leaves
- 1 cup basil leaves
- 1 cup parsley leaves
- ½ cup mint leaves
- ½ cup walnuts
- 1 tsp miso
- 1 tsp lemon juice
- ¼ cup olive oil

Directions:
1. In a blender place all ingredients and blend until smooth
2. Pour smoothie in a glass and serve

Nutrition: Calories: 500 kCal Carbs: 5g Fat: 51g Protein: 5g

542. Fennel and Almonds Sauce

Preparation Time: 10 Minutes
Cooking Time: 30 Minutes
Servings: 4
Ingredients:

- 1 cup fennel bulb
- 1 cup olive oil
- 1 cup almonds
- 1 cup fennel fronds

Directions:

1. In a blender place all ingredients and blend until smooth
2. Pour smoothie in a glass and serve

Nutrition: Calories: 100 kCal Carbs: 15g Fat: 18g Protein: 3g

543. Honey Dipping Sauce

Preparation Time: 10 Minutes
Cooking Time: 30 Minutes
Servings: 4
Ingredients:

- 5 tablespoons unsalted butter
- 8 tablespoons kimchi paste
- 2 tablespoons honey
- 1 tsp sesame seeds

Directions:

1. In a blender place all ingredients and blend until smooth
2. Pour smoothie in a glass and serve

Nutrition: Calories: 220 kCal Carbs: 33g Fat: 50g Protein: 0g

544. Ginger Dipping Sauce

Preparation Time: 10 Minutes
Cooking Time: 30 Minutes
Servings: 4
Ingredients:

- 6 tablespoons ponzu sauce
- 2 tablespoons scallions
- 2 tsp ginger
- 2 tsp mirin
- 1 tsp sesame oil
- ¼ tsp salt

Directions:

1. In a blender place all ingredients and blend until smooth
2. Pour smoothie in a glass and serve

Nutrition: Calories: 160 kCal Carbs: 43g Fat: 1g Protein: 4g

545. Thai Dipping Sauce

Preparation Time: 10 Minutes
Cooking Time: 30 Minutes
Servings: 4
Ingredients:

- 6 tsp garlic sauce
- 2 tablespoons fish sauce
- 2 tablespoons lime juice
- 1 tablespoon brown sugar
- 1 tsp chili flakes

Directions:

1. In a blender place all ingredients and blend until smooth
2. Pour smoothie in a glass and serve

Nutrition: Calories: 60 kCal Carbs: 13g Fat: 1g Protein: 0g

546. Coconut Dipping Sauce

Preparation Time: 10 Minutes
Cooking Time: 30 Minutes
Servings: 4
Ingredients:

- 4 tablespoons coconut milk
- 1 tablespoon curry paste
- 2 tablespoons lime juice
- 2 tsp soy sauce
- 1 tsp fish sauce
- 1 tsp honey

Directions:

1. In a blender place all ingredients and blend until smooth
2. Pour smoothie in a glass and serve

Nutrition: Calories: 30 kCal Carbs: 12g Fat: 1g Protein: 0g

547. Black Bean Dipping Sauce

Preparation Time: 10 Minutes
Cooking Time: 30 Minutes
Servings: 4
Ingredients:
- 2 tablespoons black bean paste
- 2 tablespoons peanut butter
- 1 tablespoon maple syrup
- 2 tablespoons olive oil

Directions:
1. In a blender place all ingredients and blend until smooth
2. Pour smoothie in a glass and serve

Nutrition: Calories: 20 kCal Carbs: 13g Fat: 1g Protein: 0g

548. Maple Syrup Dipping Sauce

Preparation Time: 10 Minutes
Cooking Time: 30 Minutes
Servings: 4
Ingredients:
- 2 tablespoons peanut butter
- 2 tablespoons maple syrup
- 2 tsp olive oil
- 2 tablespoon Korean black bean paste

Directions:
1. In a blender place all ingredients and blend until smooth
2. Pour smoothie in a glass and serve

Nutrition: Calories: 60 kCal Carbs: 13g Fat: 1g Protein: 0g

549. Soy Dipping Sauce

Preparation Time: 10 Minutes
Cooking Time: 30 Minutes
Servings: 4
Ingredients:
- ¼ cup soy sauce
- ¼ cup sugar
- ¼ cup rice vinegar
- ½ cup scallions
- ½ cup cilantro

Directions:
1. In a blender place all ingredients and blend until smooth
2. Pour smoothie in a glass and serve

Nutrition: Calories: 9 kCal Carbs: 0.8 g Fat: 0.1 g Protein: 1.3 g

550. Avocado Salsa

Preparation Time: 10 Minutes
Cooking Time: 30 Minutes
Servings: 4
Ingredients:
- 2 avocados
- 1 onion
- 1 jalapeno
- 2 garlic cloves
- ¼ cup red wine vinegar
- 1 tablespoon lime juice
- ¼ cup parsley leaves

Directions:
1. In a blender place all ingredients and blend until smooth
2. Pour smoothie in a glass and serve

Nutrition: Calories: 60 kCal Carbs: 13g Fat: 1g Protein: 0g

551. Barbeque Sauce

Preparation Time: 10 Minutes
Cooking Time: 30 Minutes
Servings: 4
Ingredients:
- ¼ cup ketchup
- 1 tablespoon brown sugar
- 1 tsp molasses
- 1 tsp hot sauce
- 1 tsp mustard   1 tsp onion powder

Directions:
1. In a blender place all ingredients and blend until smooth
2. Pour smoothie in a glass and serve

Nutrition: Calories: Calories: 116 kCal Carbs: 30g Fat: 1g Protein: 0g

Chapter 10:   Smoking Recipes

552.   Aromatic Smoked Duck Breast

Preparation Time: 15 minutes + marinate time
Cooking Time: 3 hours 10 minutes
Servings: 5
Ingredients:
- Duck breast, 3 pounds

For Marinade
- 3 cups apple juice
- One tablespoon salt
- One and ½ tablespoon sugar
- 2 tbsp. soy sauce
- ¾ teaspoon paprika
- ¾ teaspoon garlic powder
- 1 tsp. dried basils
- ¾ teaspoon pepper

Directions:
1. Add apple juice into a container and season with salt, sugar, soy sauce, paprika, garlic powder, dried basil, pepper, and stir well
2. Score duck breast at several places and put breast into the marinade, marinate for 4 hours
3. Pre-heat your smoker to 325 degrees F, remove the breast from marinade, and place in smoker
4. Smoke until the internal temperature reaches 325 degrees F
5. Remove and cut smoked duck breast into thick slices, serve and enjoy!

Nutrition: Calories: 136 kCal Protein: 7.48 g Fat: 2.82 g Carbs: 20.42 g

553.   Smoked Quails

Preparation Time: 15minutes + marinate time
Cook Time: 1 hour 10 minutes
Servings: 4
Ingredients:
- 5 pounds quails

For Marinade
- 2 cups orange juice
- 1 cup of soy sauce
- 2 tbsp. garlic, minced
- ½ cup brown sugar
- ¼ cup olive oil
- 1 tbsp. pepper
- 1 cup onion, chopped

Directions:
1. Add orange juice into a container and add soy sauce, garlic, brown sugar, olive oil, pepper, onion, and stir well
2. Add quails to container and toss well to coat
3. Cover the container with id and marinate quail for 3 hours
4. Marinate quails overnight
5. Pre-heat your Smoker to 225 degrees F
6. Add quails (breast side up) and smoke for 1 hour until internal temperature reaches 145 degrees F
7. Once done, remove and serve
8. Enjoy!

Nutrition: Calories: 417 kCal Protein: 43.2 g Fat: 16.98 g Carbs: 20.78 g

554.   Smoked Whole Turkey

Preparation Time: 20 Minutes
Cooking Time: 8 Hours
Servings: 6
Ingredients:
- 1 Whole Turkey of about 12 to 16 lb.
- 1 Cup of your Favorite Rub
- 1 Cup of Sugar
- 1 Tablespoon of minced garlic
- ½ Cup of Worcestershire sauce
- 2 Tablespoons of Canola Oil

Directions:
1. Thaw the Turkey and remove the giblets
2. Pour in 3 gallons of water in a non-metal bucket of about 5 gallons
3. Add the BBQ rub and mix very well
4. Add the garlic, the sugar and the Worcestershire sauce; then submerge the turkey into the bucket.
5. Refrigerate the turkey in the bucket for an overnight.
6. Place the Grill on a High Smoke and smoke the Turkey for about 3 hours
7. Switch the grilling temp to about 350 degrees F; then push a metal meat thermometer into the thickest part of the turkey breast
8. Cook for about 4 hours; then take off the Pit Boss grill and let rest for about 15 minutes

9. Slice the turkey, then serve and enjoy your dish!
Nutrition: Calories: 165 kCal Fat: 14g Carbs: 0.5g Protein: 15.2g

555. Smoked Rabbit

Preparation Time: 15 minutes + 60 minutes marinate time
Cooking Time: 2 hours
Servings: 5
Ingredients:
- One cottontail skinned and gutted
- 2 tbsp. salt
- ½ cup white vinegar
- Water as needed

For Rub
- 1 tbsp. garlic powder
- 1 tbsp. cayenne pepper
- 1 tbsp. salt
- One bottle BBQ sauce

Directions:
1. Take a bowl and add in your kosher salt alongside the white vinegar to make your brine
2. Pour the brine over your rabbit using a shallow dish and add just enough water to cover up the whole of your rabbit
3. Let it sit for an hour
4. Pre-heat your smoker to a temperature of 200 degree
5. Take a bowl and whisk in the garlic powder, salt, pepper, and cayenne pepper to make the rubbing
6. Season the rabbit nicely
7. Toss your rabbit in your smoker and add the hickory wood to your wood chamber
8. Let it smoke for two hours and keep adding wood pellets after every 15 minutes
9. Remove the rabbit from your smoker and serve hot

Nutrition: Calories 93 kCal Protein: 3.31 g Fat: 0.3 g Carbs: 19.44 g

556. Smoked Whole Duck

Preparation Time: 15 minutes
Cooking Time: 2 hours 30 minutes
Servings: 4
Ingredients:
- 2 Tablespoons of baking soda
- 1 Tablespoon of Chinese five spices
- 1 Thawed duck
- 1 Granny smith cored and diced apple
- 1 Quartered sliced orange
- 2 Tablespoons of chicken seasoning, divided

Directions:
1. Start by washing the duck under cool running water from the inside and out; then pat the meat dry with clean paper towels
2. Combine the Chicken seasoning and the Chinese Five spice; then combine with the baking soda for extra crispy skin
3. Season the duck from the inside and out
4. Tuck the apple and the orange and apple slices into the cavity.
5. Turn your Wood Pellet Smoker Grill to smoke model; then let the fire catch and set it to about 300°F to preheat
6. Place the duck on the grill grate or in a pan. Roast for about 2 ½ hours at a temperature of about 160°F
7. Place the foil loosely on top of the duck and let rest for about 15 minutes.
8. Serve and enjoy your delicious dish!

Nutrition: Calories 310 kCal Protein: 23.8 g Fat: 20.62 g Carbs: 5.92 g

557. Smoked Venison

Preparation Time: 10 minutes
Cooking Time: 2 hours
Servings: 4
Ingredients:
- 1 lb. of venison tenderloin
- ¼ Cup of lemon juice
- ¼ Cup of olive oil
- 5 Minced garlic cloves
- 1 tsp. of salt
- 1 tsp. of ground black pepper

Directions:
1. Start by putting the whole venison tenderloin in a zip-style bag or a large bowl.

2. Add the lemon juice, the olive oil, the garlic, the salt, and the pepper into a food processor
3. Process your ingredients until they are very well incorporated
4. Pour the marinade on top of the venison; then massage it in very well
5. Refrigerate and let marinate for about 4 hours or an overnight
6. When you are ready to cook, just remove your marinade's venison and rinse it off very well.
7. Pat the meat dry and let it come to room temperature for about 30 minutes before cooking it
8. In the meantime, preheat your smoker to a temperature of about 225°F
9. Smoke the tenderloin for about 2 hours
10. Let the meat rest for about 10 minutes before slicing it
11. Top with black pepper; then serve and enjoy your dish!

Nutrition: Calories: 302 kCal Protein: 34.42 g Fat: 16.24 g Carbs: 3.36 g

558. Venison Meatloaf

Preparation Time: 20 minutes
Cooking Time: 1hour 30 minutes
Servings: 7
Ingredients:
- 2 lbs. of ground venison
- 1 Diced onion
- 1 beaten egg
- 1 Pinch of salt
- 1 Pinch of pepper
- 1 tbsp. of Worcestershire sauce
- 1 Cup of bread crumbs
- 1 Oz of packet onion soup mix
- 1 Cup of milk

For the Glaze Topping
- ¼ Cup of ketchup
- ¼ Cup of brown sugar
- ¼ Cup of apple cider vinegar

Directions:
1. When you are ready to cook, start your wood pellet grill on smoke with the lid open for about 4 to 5 minutes
2. Set the temperature to about 350°F and preheat with the lid close for about 10 to 15 minutes

3. Spray a loaf pan with cooking spray; then, in a large bowl, combine the ground venison altogether with the onion, the egg, the salt, the pepper, and the breadcrumbs
4. Add the Worcestershire sauce, the milk, and the onion soup packet, and be careful not to over mix.
5. In a small bowl, mix the ketchup, the brown sugar, and the apple cider vinegar.
6. Spread half of the glaze on the bottom and sides of a pan.
7. Add the meatloaf and spread the remaining quantity on top of the meatloaf
8. Directly place on the smoker grill grate and smoke for about 1 hour and 15 minutes
9. Let the meatloaf cool for several minutes before slicing it
10. Serve and enjoy your dish!

Nutrition: Calories: 323 kCal Protein: 29.33 g Fat: 12.7 g Carbs: 23.61 g

559. Wood Pellet Elk Jerky

Preparation Time: 10 minutes
Cooking Time: 6 hours
Servings: 10
Ingredients:
- 4 Pounds of elk hamburger
- ¼ Cup of soy sauce
- ¼ Cup of Teriyaki sauce
- ¼ Cup of Worcestershire sauce
- 1 Tablespoon of paprika
- 1 Tablespoon of chili powder
- 1 Tablespoon of crushed red pepper
- 3 Tablespoons of hot sauce
- 1 Tablespoon of pepper
- 1 Tablespoon of garlic powder
- 1 Tablespoon of onion salt
- 1 Tablespoon of salt

Directions:
1. Start by mixing all of the ingredients and seasoning and the elk hamburger in a large bowl; then let sit in the refrigerator for about 12 hours
2. Light your wood pellet smoker to a low temperature of about 160°F
3. Take the elk meat out of your refrigerator and start making strips of the meat manually or with a rolling pin

4. Add smoker wood chips to your wood pellet smoker grill and rub some quantity of olive oil over the smoker grate; layout the strips in one row

5. Warm a dehydrator up about halfway during the smoking process

6. Remove the elk jerky meat off your smoker at about 3 hours

7. Line it into the kitchen.

8. Line your dehydrator with the elk jerky meat and keep it in for about 5 to 6 additional hours. Serve and enjoy!

Nutrition: Calories: 41 kCal Protein: 1.39 g Fat: 1.39 g Carbs: 6.23 g

---

560. Spiced Smoked Venison Tender

Preparation Time: 20 minutes
Cooking Time: 7 hours 10 minutes
Servings: 10
Ingredients:
- Venison (5-lb., 2.3-kg.)

The Rub
- Black pepper – 3 tablespoons
- Paprika – 2 tablespoons
- Kosher salt – 1 ½ tablespoon
- Garlic powder – 1 tablespoon
- Onion powder – 1 tablespoon
- Cayenne pepper – ¾ tablespoon
- Coriander – ¾ tablespoon
- Dill – ½ tablespoon

The Heat
- Use charcoal and Alder wood chunks for indirect smokes.
- The Water Pan
- Beef broth – 2 cups
- Ginger – ½ teaspoon
- Lemongrass - 1

Directions:
1. Rub the venison with black pepper, paprika, kosher salt, garlic powder, onion powder, cayenne pepper, coriander, and dill.

2. Prepare the grill and set it for indirect heat.

3. Place charcoal and starters in a grill, then ignite the starters. Put the burning charcoal on one side of the grill.

4. Place a heavy-duty aluminum pan, then place it on the other side of the grill.

5. Pour beef broth into the aluminum pan, then add ginger and lemongrass to the broth.

6. Place wood chunks on top of the burning charcoal, then set the grill grate.

7. Cover the grill with the lid and set the temperature to 200°F (93°C).

8. Wait until the grill reaches the desired temperature, then place the seasoned venison on the grate inside the grill.

9. Maintain the heat and control the temperature. Add more charcoal and wood chunks if it is necessary.

10. Once the smoked venison's internal temperature has reached 160°F (71°C), remove it from the grill and transfer it to a serving dish. Serve and enjoy.

Nutrition: Calories: 30 kCal Protein: 3.28 g Fat: 0.6 g Carbs: 3.72 g

---

561. Cinnamon Smoked Quails Orange Tea

Preparation Time: 10 minutes
Cooking Time: 1 hour 10 minutes
Servings: 10
Ingredients:
- Quails (6-lb., 2.7-kg.)

The Rub
- Sichuan peppercorns – ¼ cup
- Kosher salt – 2 tablespoons
- grated orange zest – 1 teaspoon
- Ginger – 1 teaspoon
- Tea leaves – 1 cup
- Brown sugar – 1 cup
- Cinnamon – 1 teaspoon
- Cloves – 2
- Olive oil – ¼ cup
- Lemon juice – 3 tablespoons

The Heat
- Use charcoal and Applewood chunks for indirect smokes.
- The Water Pan
- Orange juice – 2 cups

Directions:
1. Combine Sichuan peppercorns with kosher salt, grated orange zest, ginger, tea leaves, brown sugar, cinnamon, and cloves

2. Pour olive oil and lemon juice over the spice mixture, then stir until incorporated.

3. Rub the quails with the spice mixture and marinate for at least 3 hours. Store in the fridge to keep the quails fresh.
4. Prepare the grill and set it for indirect heat.
5. Place charcoal and starters in a grill, then ignite the starters. Put the burning charcoal on one side of the grill. Place a heavy-duty aluminum pan, then place it on the other side of the grill. Pour orange juice into the aluminum pan, then place wood chunks on top of the burning charcoal. Set the grill grate.
6. Cover the grill with the lid and set the temperature to 200°F (93°C).
7. Place the seasoned quails on the grate inside the grill, then smoke for 2 hours.
8. Once the smoked quails are done, or the smoked quails' internal temperature has reached 160°F (71°C), remove from the grill and transfer to a serving dish. Serve and enjoy.

Nutrition: Calories: 175 kCal Protein: 2.12 g Fat: 9.03 g Carbs: 22.45 g

562. Spicy and Hot Smoked Rabbit Barbecue

Preparation Time: 20 minutes
Cooking Time: 3 hours 10 minutes
Servings: 10
Ingredients:
- Rabbit (6-lb., 2.7-kg.)

The Brine
- Kosher salt – 2 tablespoons
- White vinegar – ½ cup
- Water – 1 quart

The Rub
- Garlic powder – 2 tablespoons
- Cayenne pepper – 1 tablespoon
- Kosher salt – 1 tablespoon
- Black pepper – 1 tablespoon

The Glaze
- Garlic powder – 2 tablespoons
- Diced jalapeno pepper – 2 teaspoons
- Cayenne pepper – 1 teaspoon
- Olive oil – 2 tablespoons
- Ketchup – 2 cups
- Brown sugar – 1 cup
- Apple cider vinegar – 1 cup
- Apple juice – ½ cup
- Honey – ½ cup
- Worcestershire sauce – 1 tablespoon

- Kosher salt – 1 teaspoon
- Black pepper – 1 teaspoon

The Heat
- Use charcoal and Hickory wood chunks for indirect smokes.
- The Water Pan
- Apple juice – 2 cups

Directions:
1. Pour water into a container, then stir in kosher salt and white vinegar.
2. Score the rabbit at several places, then put the rabbit into the brine. Soak the rabbit for at least an hour.
3. After an hour, take the rabbit out of the brine, then wash and rinse it. Pat the rabbit dry.
4. Prepare the grill and set it for indirect heat.
5. Place charcoal and starters in a grill, then ignite the starters. Put the burning charcoal on one side of the grill.
6. Place a heavy-duty aluminum pan, then place it on the other side of the grill.
7. Pour apple juice into the aluminum pan, then place wood chunks on top of the burning charcoal. Set the grill grate.
8. Cover the grill with the lid and set the temperature to 200°F (93°C).
9. Combine the rub ingredients—garlic powder, cayenne pepper, kosher salt, and black pepper in a bowl, then mix well.
10. Rub the rabbit with the spice mixture, then place it on the grate inside the grill. Smoke the seasoned rabbit for 3 hours.
11. Maintain the heat and control the temperature. Add more charcoal and wood chunks if it is needed.
12. Next, pour olive oil, ketchup, apple juice, apple cider vinegar, and honey into a bowl, then season with garlic powder, diced jalapeno pepper, cayenne pepper, and brown sugar, Worcestershire sauce, and salt, and pepper, then stir until incorporated.
13. After 15 minutes of smoking, baste the rabbit with the glaze mixture and repeat once every 30 minutes.
14. Once the smoked rabbit is tender, and the smoked rabbit's internal temperature has reached 170°F (77°C), remove it from the grill.
15. Place the smoked rabbit on a serving dish and serve. Enjoy!

Nutrition: Calories: 247 kCal Protein: 1.47 g Fat: 2.99 g Carbs: 57.38 g

563. Roasted Venison Tenderloin

Preparation Time: 10 minutes
Cooking Time: 28 minutes
Servings: 6
Ingredients:
The Meat
- Venison tenderloin – 2, each about 1 ½ pound

The Marinade
- Dry red wine – ¼ cup
- Minced garlic – 1 teaspoon
- Soy sauce – 2 tablespoons
- Chopped rosemary – 1 tablespoon
- Ground black pepper – 1 teaspoon
- Olive oil – ½ cup

The Seasoning
- Salt – 1 tablespoon
- Ground black pepper – ½ tablespoon

Directions:
- Before preheating the grill, marinate the venison.
- For this, prepare the marinade; take a small mixing bowl and whisk garlic, wine, and soy sauce until combined.
- Add black pepper and rosemary, stir until mixed, and then whisk in oil until emulsified.
- Place venison in a large plastic bag, pour in prepared marinade, seal the bag, turn it upside down to coat venison and let it marinate in the refrigerator for a minimum of 8 hours.
- Then remove the venison from the marinade, pat dry and then season with salt and black pepper.
- When the grill has preheated, place venison on the grilling rack, grill for 4 minutes per side until nicely browned, and then continue cooking for 20 minutes until the venison's internal temperature reaches 135 degrees F.
- When done, let venison rest for 5 minutes, then cut into slices and serve immediately.

Nutrition: Calories: 182 kCal Protein: 0.65 g Fat: 19 g Carbs: 2.63 g

564. Cornish Game Hens

Preparation Time: 20 minutes
Cooking Time: 60minutes
Servings: 4
Ingredients:
The Meat
- Game hens, giblets removed – 4

The Rub
- Melted butter, unsalted – 4 tablespoons
- Chicken rub – 4 teaspoons
- Other Ingredients
- Rosemary sprig – 4

Directions:
1. In the meantime, prepare hens and for this, rinse well, pat dry, then tuck their wings and tie their legs by using a kitchen string.
2. Then rub melted butter outside of hens, sprinkle with chicken rub, and then place a sprig of rosemary into the cavity of each hen.
3. When the grill has preheated, place hens on the grilling rack and grill for 1 hour or until the control panel shows 165 degrees F's internal temperature, turning halfway.
4. When done, remove hens from the grill and let it rest for 5 minutes.
5. Serve immediately.

Nutrition: Calories: 276 kCal Protein: 30.09 g Fat: 16.66 g Carbs: 0.05 g

565. Duck Breasts

Preparation Time: 10 minutes
Cooking Time: 8 minutes
Servings: 3
Ingredients:
The Meat
- Duck breasts – 3

The Rub
- Game rub – 3 ounces

Directions:
1. In the meantime, prepare the duck, and for this, season the bottom of each breast with the rub.
2. Score the top of each breast, season it with the remaining rub, and rest for 10 minutes.
3. When the grill has preheated, place duck breast on the grilling rack and grill for 4 minutes per side or until the control panel shows the internal temperature of 130 degrees F, turning halfway.

4. When done, remove the duck from the grill and let it rest for 10 minutes.
5. Then cut the duck breasts into slices and serve immediately.

Nutrition: Calories: 205 kCal Protein: 33.08 g Fat: 7.08 g Carbs: 0 g

566. Venison Steaks

Preparation Time: 10 minutes
Cooking Time: 26 minutes
Servings: 4
Ingredients:
The Meat
- Venison steaks – 10, 6 ounces

The Marinade
- Sprite, diet – 1 liter
- Game rub – 6 ounces
- Other Ingredients
- Asparagus – 2 pounds

Directions:
1. Before preheating the grill, marinate the venison steaks and for this, take a container, pour in the sprite, and then stir in the game rub.
2. Add venison steaks and then let it marinate in the refrigerator for a minimum of 6 hours.
3. Then remove venison steaks from the marinade and pat dry.
4. When the grill has preheated, place steaks on the grilling rack and let smoke for 8 minutes per side or until the control panel shows the internal temperature of 125 degrees F.
5. When done, remove the steak from the grill and let it rest for 10 minutes.
6. Meanwhile, add asparagus to the grilling rack and cook for 10 minutes, turning halfway.
7. Then cut the steak into slices and serve with asparagus.

Nutrition: Calories: 156 kCal Protein: 27.42 g Fat: 2 g Carbs: 8.8 g

567. Mandarin Glazed Hens

Preparation Time: 20 minutes
Cooking Time: 40minutes
Servings: 4
Ingredients:
The Meat
- Cornish game hens, giblets removed – 5

The Rub
- Onion powder – 2 tablespoons
- Garlic powder – 1 tablespoon
- Ginger powder – 1 tablespoon
- Salt – 1 tablespoon
- Olive oil – 2 tablespoons

The Stuffing
- Sprigs of thyme – 16
- Orange, cut into quarters – 2

The Glaze
- Mandarin glaze – 1 cup

Directions:
1. In the meantime, prepare hens.
2. Prepare the rub. Take a small bowl, place all of its ingredients in it, and stir until mixed.
3. Stuff each hen's cavity with four thyme sprigs and one wedge of orange, then sprinkle the exterior with the prepared rub.
4. Rub hens with oil and then tie the legs of hens with a kitchen string.
5. When the grill has preheated, place hens on the grilling rack and grill for 20 minutes.
6. Then brush hens with mandarin glaze, continue grilling for 20 minutes and then brush again with mandarin glaze.
7. Serve immediately.

Nutrition: Calories: 226 kCal Protein: 25.84 g Fat: 10.98 g Carbs: 4.76 g

568. Cajun Crab Stuffed Shrimp and Jicama Corn Salad

Preparation Time: 20 minutes
Cooking Time: 0 minute
Servings: 4
Ingredients:
- Stuffed shrimp
- Lump crab meat
- Red onion
- Minced garlic seasoning
- Lime juice
- Lime zest
- Jalapeno
- Ritz Crackers
- Bacon
- Grilled red onion and jalapeno

Directions:
1. Pick cartilage from the crab. Combine ingredients wrap with bacon. Grill till browned.
2. Remoulade Mayo, Chili sauce, Tiger sauce, Creole mustard, Lemon juice, Lemon zest, Scallions, Parsley, minced celery, minced garlic, Salt, Capers chopped, Salt, Black pepper. Combine all ingredients and chill Jicama corn salad.
3. We diced the corn on the cob, black beans, carrot, scallions, cilantro, basil, Lime juice, Lime zest, Cumin Red bell pepper, Grill red peppercorn on the cob.
4. Rinse black beans. Combine ingredients and chill.

Nutrition: Calories: 94 kCal Protein: 13.51 g Fat: 1.13 g Carbs: 7.48 g

569. Char Siu Baby Back Ribs

Preparation Time: 120 minutes
Cooking Time: 60minutes
Servings: 6
Ingredients:
Marinade
- 1/3 c hoisin sauce - 1/3 c soy sauce
- 2 Tbsps. mirin - 2 Tbsps. honey
- 2 Tbsps. light brown sugar
- 1 Tbsp. Sambal Chili Paste
- 1/2 tbsp. Sesame Oil
- 1/2 Tbsp. Chili Oil
- 1/2 tsp. Chinese 5 spice seasoning

- 3/4 tsp. red food coloring
- Three cloves garlic, minced fine

Basting Liquid
- 1/4 c hoisin
- 1/4 c soy sauce
- 3 Tbsp. honey
- 1 Tbsp. sesame oil
- 1 Tbsp. mirin
- 1 tsp. red miso paste
- 1 tsp. Sambal chili paste

Garnish
- Toasted Sesame Seeds - Scallions

Directions:
4. Combine all marinade fixings, and race to join.
5. Slice child back ribs into two bone areas. That builds the surface territory for the marinade to give more flavor Spot ribs and marinade in a hurdle to top back, evacuating however much air as could be expected, and marinate for in any event 4Hrs. Marinate medium-term if conceivable.
6. Evacuate ribs and hold marinade.
7. Spot ribs on smoker at 250F. Try not to contact the principal 2Hrs.
8. Join saved marinade and extra treating fluid fixings into a sauce skillet. Bring to a stew, mixing once in a while, for 10mins. Take out from the heat.
9. At the 2hrs mark, treat ribs with seasoning fluid, and rehash each 30mins, until ribs are delicate, roughly 4Hrs. Cut ribs segments into singular ribs, embellish with sesame seeds and scallions.

Nutrition: Calories: 123 kCal Protein: 3.24 g Fat: 5.31 g Carbs: 17.29 g

570. Smoked Bacon

Preparation Time: 20 minutes
Cooking Time: 3 hours
Servings: 12
Ingredients:
- Pork belly, fat trimmed – 2 pounds
- Salt – ½ cup
- Brown sugar – ½ cup
- Ground black pepper – 1 tablespoon

Directions:
1. Before preheating the grill, cure the pork and for this, stir together all of the ingredients for it and then rub it well on the pork belly.

2. Place pork belly into a large plastic bag, seal it, and let it rest for 8 days in the refrigerator.
3. Then remove pork belly from the refrigerator, rinse well and pat dry.
4. When the grill has preheated, place the pork belly on the grilling rack and let smoke for 3 hours or until the control panel shows the internal temperature of 150 degrees F, turning halfway.
5. Check the fire after one hour of smoking and add more wood pallets if required.
6. When done, remove pork from the grill, wrap it in plastic wrap, and rest for 1 hour in the freezer until pork is firm and nearly frozen.
7. When ready to eat, cut pork into slices and then serve.

Nutrition: Calories: 688 kCal; Protein: 58.9g; Carbs: 2.7g; Fat: 47.3g

571. Corned Beef Pastrami

Preparation Time: 5 days
Cooking Time: 3 hours
Servings: 6
Ingredients:
- 1.5lb coarse ground pepper
- 2 tbsp. granulated garlic
- 2 tbsp. onion flakes
- 2 tbsp. ancho chili powder
- Ancho espresso rub

Directions:
1. Rinse the meat in chilly water and afterward absorb cold water for 24hrs, changing the water each 6 hours to pull a more incredible amount of the salt and fix it from the meat.
2. Remove from the water and pat dry with a towel. Apply the rub fixings and put them in a safe spot while the smoker heats up. Cook at 250F until the inward temperature hits 150F. That should take 3 to 4 hours.
3. Wrap in either foil or butcher paper and keep cooking until the inner temp arrives 185 to 195F. That should take another 2 hours around.

Nutrition: Calories: 276 kCal Protein: 20.39 g Fat: 19.76 g Carbs: 3.65 g

572. Marinated Smoked Turkey Breast

Preparation Time: 15 minutes
Cooking Time: 4 hours
Servings: 6
Ingredients:
- 1 (5 pounds) boneless chicken breast
- 4 cups water
- 2 tablespoons kosher salt
- 1 teaspoon Italian seasoning
- 2 tablespoons honey
- 1 tablespoon cider vinegar

Rub
- ½ teaspoon onion powder
- 1 teaspoon paprika
- 1 teaspoon salt
- 1 teaspoon ground black pepper
- 1 tablespoon brown sugar
- ½ teaspoon garlic powder
- 1 teaspoon oregano

Directions:
1. In a huge container, combine the water, honey, cider vinegar, Italian seasoning and salt.
2. Add the chicken breast and toss to combine. Cover the bowl and place it in the refrigerator and chill for 4 hours.
3. Rinse the chicken breast with water and pat dry with paper towels.
4. In another mixing bowl, combine the brown sugar, salt, paprika, onion powder, pepper, oregano and garlic.
5. Generously season the chicken breasts with the rub mix.
6. Preheat the grill to 225°F with lid closed for 15 minutes. Use cherry Pit Bosss.
7. Arrange the turkey breast into a grill rack. Place the grill rack on the grill.
8. Smoke for about 3 to 4 hours or until the internal temperature of the turkey breast reaches 165°F.
9. Remove the chicken breast from heat and let them rest for a few minutes. Serve.

Nutrition: Calories 903 kCal Fat: 34g Carbs: 9.9g Protein 131.5g

573. Spatchcock Smoked Turkey

Preparation Time: 15 minutes
Cooking Time: 4 hours 3 minutes
Servings: 6

Ingredients:
- 1 (18 pounds) turkey
- 2 tablespoons finely chopped fresh parsley
- 1 tablespoon finely chopped fresh rosemary
- 2 tablespoons finely chopped fresh thyme
- ½ cup melted butter
- 1 teaspoon garlic powder
- 1 teaspoon onion powder
- 1 teaspoon ground black pepper
- 2 teaspoons salt or to taste
- 2 tablespoons finely chopped scallions

Directions:
1. Remove the turkey giblets and rinse turkey, in and out, under cold running water.
2. Place the turkey on a working surface, breast side down. Use a poultry shear to cut the turkey along both sides of the backbone to remove the turkey back bone.
3. Flip the turkey over, back side down. Now, press the turkey down to flatten it.
4. In a mixing bowl, combine the parsley, rosemary, scallions, thyme, butter, pepper, salt, and garlic and onion powder.
5. Rub butter mixture over all sides of the turkey.
6. Preheat your grill to HIGH (450°F) with lid closed for 15 minutes.
7. Place the turkey directly on the grill grate and cook for 30 minutes. Reduce the heat to 300°F and cook for an additional 4 hours, or until the internal temperature of the thickest part of the thigh reaches 165°F.
8. Take out the turkey meat from the grill and let it rest for a few minutes. Cut into sizes and serve.

Nutrition: Calories: 780 kCal Fat: 19g Carbs: 29.7g Protein 116.4g

574. Smoked Whole Chicken with Honey Glaze

Preparation Time: 30 minutes
Cooking Time: 3 Hours
Servings: 1

Ingredients:
- 1 4 pounds of chicken with the giblets thoroughly removed and patted dry
- 1 ½ lemon
- 1 tablespoon of honey
- 4 tablespoons of unsalted butter
- 4 tablespoon of chicken seasoning

Directions:
1. Fire up your smoker and set the temperature to 225 degrees F
2. Take a small saucepan and melt the butter along with honey over a low flame
3. Now squeeze ½ lemon in this mixture and then move it from the heat source
4. Take the chicken and smoke by keeping the skin side down. Do so until the chicken turns light brown and the skin starts to release from the grate.
5. Turn the chicken over and apply the honey butter mixture to it
6. Continue to smoke it making sure to taste it every 45 minutes until the thickest core reaches a temperature of 160 degrees F
7. Now remove the chicken from the grill and let it rest for 5 minutes
8. Serve with the leftover sliced lemon and enjoy

Nutrition: Calories: 320 kCal Carbs: 29 g Protein: 36 g Fat: 14

575. Smoked Bananas Foster Bread Pudding

Preparation Time: 1 hour
Cooking Time: 2 hours 15 minutes
Servings: 8 to 10

Ingredients:
- 1loaf (about 4 cups) brioche or challah, cubed into 1-inch cubes
- 3eggs, lightly beaten
- 2cups of milk
- 2/3 cups sugar
- 2large bananas, peeled and smashed
- 1tbsp vanilla extract
- 1tbsp cinnamon
- 1/4 tsp. nutmeg
- 1/2 cup pecans

Rum Sauce Ingredients
- 1/2 cup spiced rum
- 1/4 cup unsalted butter
- 1cup dark brown sugar
- 1tsp cinnamon
- 5large bananas, peeled and quartered

Directions:

1. Place pecans on a skillet over medium heat and lightly toast for about 5 minutes, until you can smell them.
2. Remove from heat and allow cooling. Once cooled, chop pecans.
3. Lightly butter a 9" x 13" baking dish and evenly layer bread cubes in the container.
4. In a large bowl, whisk eggs, milk, sugar, mashed bananas, vanilla extract, cinnamon, and nutmeg.
5. Whip the egg mixture over the bread in the baking dish evenly. Sprinkle with chopped pecans. Cover with aluminum foil and refrigerate for about 30 minutes.
6. Preheat pellet grill to 180degrees F. Turn your smoke setting to high, if applicable.
7. Remove foil from dish and place on the smoker for 5 minutes with the lid closed, allowing bread to absorb smoky flavor.
8. Remove the dish from the grill and cover with foil again. Increase your pellet grill's temperature to 350degrees F.
9. Place dish on the grill grate and cook for 50-60 minutes until everything is cooked through and the bread pudding is bubbling.
10. In a saucepan, while pudding cooks, heat butter for rum sauce over medium heat. If the butter begins to melt, add the brown sugar, cinnamon, and bananas. Sauté until bananas start to soften.
11. Add rum and watch. When the liquid begins to bubble, light a match, and tilt the pan. Slowly and carefully move the game towards the fluid until the sauce lights. When the flames go away, remove the skillet from heat.
12. If you're uncomfortable lighting the liquid with a match, just cook it for 3-4 minutes over medium heat after the rum has been added.
13. Keep rum sauce on a simmer or reheat once it's time to serve.
14. Remove bread pudding from the grill and allow it to cool for about 5 minutes.
15. Cut into squares, put each square on a plate, add a banana piece, and then drizzle rum sauce over the top. Serve on its own or a la mode and enjoy it!

Nutrition: Calories: 274.7 kCal Fat: 7.9 g Carbs: 35.5 g Protein: 4 g

576. Smoked Cheesecake

Preparation Time: 30 minutes
Cooking Time: 2 hours
Servings: 8-10
Ingredients:

- 12-ounces graham crackers
- 3 tablespoons brown sugar
- 6 tablespoons melted butter
- 32-ounces room-temp cream cheese
- 1 packed cup light brown sugar
- 2 teaspoons pure vanilla extract
- 1 teaspoon orange zest
- 5 eggs
- 1 tablespoon fresh orange juice
- 2 tablespoons melted butter

Directions:

1. Preheat oven to 400-degrees. Grease a springform pan and line inside with foil. Begin by making the crust. Put graham crackers in a food processor and pulse into a fine powder with brown sugar.
2. Pulse in melted butter to get a crumbly dough that you can press into the pan, and it sticks.
3. Bake in the oven within 5-8 minutes, until golden. Move to a rack and cool. Warm your smoker to 300-degrees.
4. For the filling, mix cream cheese, 1 cup of sugar, vanilla, and orange zest in a mixer until smooth. Add eggs - one at a time - and orange juice until smooth.
5. Pour batter into the pan. Put the cheesecake in the smoker, uncovered, and smoke within 1 ½- 2 hours.
6. Cheesecake is done when the filling jiggles but is firm, like jello. Move cheesecake to the counter and cool to room temperature. Cover with saran wrap, then chill in the fridge for at least 4 hours, or serve warm!

Nutrition: Calories: 838 kCal Protein: 15g Carbs: 66g Fat: 57g

577. Smoked Peach Parfait

Preparation Time: 20 minutes
Cooking Time: 35-45 minutes
Servings: 4
Ingredients:
- 4barely ripe peaches halved and pitted
- 1tablespoon firmly packed brown sugar
- 1-pint vanilla ice cream
- 3tablespoons honey

Directions:
1. Preheat your smoker to 200 degrees Fahrenheit
2. Sprinkle cut peach halves with brown sugar
3. Transfer them to smoker and smoke for 33-45 minutes
4. Transfer the peach halves to dessert plates and top with vanilla ice cream
5. Drizzle honey and serve!

Nutrition: Calories: 309 kCal Fat: 12g Carbs: 37g Protein: 0g

578. Smoked Peaches

Preparation Time: 5 minutes
Cooking Time: 30 minutes
Servings: 4
Ingredients:
- 4 halved peaches
- 2 cups vanilla ice cream

Directions:
1. Preheat smoker to 200-degrees with wood chips in the container. Put peaches in a foil pan, with the cut-side facing up.
2. Put in the smoker for 20 minutes, and then flip the peaches. Smoke for another 10 minutes. Serve with ice cream!

Nutrition: Calories: 128 kCal Protein: 2.6g Carbs: 22g Fat: 3.9g

579. Smoked Ice Cream

Preparation Time: 15 minutes
Cooking Time: 1 hour & 40 minutes
Servings: 4
Ingredients:
- Ice chips
- Coldwater
- 1-quart heavy cream
- 1 ½ cups heavy cream
- 8 egg yolks
- ¾ cups dark brown sugar
- 1 cup whole milk
- 1 ½ teaspoon pure vanilla extract
- ½ teaspoon of sea salt

Directions:
1. Preheat your smoker to 150-degrees with the chips. Fill a foil pan halfway with ice and then add water, so ice is covered.
2. Put another, smaller foil pan in the ice bath, and pour in 1 quart of cream. Smoke for 1 hour and 40 minutes, stirring.
3. When time is up, put the smoked cream in a container and stick it in the fridge. When it's cooled, mix ½ cup smoked cream with ½ cup fresh cream.
4. Taste and add until you get 2 cups total and the ratio to your liking. Keep leftovers for another use.
5. In a saucepan, mix egg yolks and brown sugar. Add cream mixture and milk, and combine. Heat on medium-low, stirring, until the liquid hits 170-degrees.
6. Pour liquid through a strainer into a container, add vanilla and salt, and put in an ice bath until it hits 45-degrees or lower.
7. When ready, churn according to your ice cream maker's directions. Chill in the freezer for 4-5 hours.

Nutrition: Calories: 434 kCal Protein: 8.5g Carbs: 32g Fat: 30.5g

580. Smoked Pineapple

Preparation Time: 15 minutes
Cooking Time: 2 hours & 30 minutes
Servings: 8-10
Ingredients:
- 1 whole sliced pineapple
- Generous sprinkle of brown sugar
- Vanilla ice cream (for serving)

Directions:
1. Preheat your smoker to 250-degrees with the wood chips. Put pineapple in a foil pan. Sprinkle with brown sugar. Smoke for 2 ½ hours. Serve with vanilla ice cream!

Nutrition: Calories: 127 kCal Protein: 1.7g Carbs: 23.5g Fat: 3.6g

581. Smoked Banana Pudding

Preparation Time: 10 minutes
Cooking Time: 30 minutes
Servings: 6
Ingredients:
- 4 bananas
- ¼ cup brown sugar
- ¼ cup melted butter
- Sprinkle of cinnamon
- 10 egg yolks
- 1-quart whole milk
- ½ cup white sugar
- 1 cup heavy cream
- Splash of light rum
- 1 teaspoon pure vanilla extract
- 2 tablespoons unflavored powdered gelatin
- 1 cup crushed nilla wafers (for serving)

Directions:
1. Leave the peel on, and cut bananas in half. Preheat your smoker to 200-degrees with the wood chips in the container.
2. When the smoker is ready, put the banana halves on the top rack. Smoke for just 30 minutes. Remove from the smoker and unpeel.
3. Mix brown sugar, melted butter, and cinnamon. Put bananas in an oven-safe skillet and pour over brown sugar/butter mixture. Broil for just 5 minutes or so, until caramelizing.
4. In a blender, mix smoked bananas with yolks, milk, and white sugar. When smooth, add in 1

cup cream, rum, and vanilla, and mix. Move this puree into a saucepan.
5. Whisk in the gelatin. Heat on medium-high until pudding is 135-degrees. Cook at this temp for 5 minutes, then strain. Chill in the fridge until firm, then serve with crushed nilla wafers on top!

Nutrition: Calories: 587 kCal Protein: 15.4g Carbs: 63.5g Fat: 32g

582. Smoked Apple Pie

Preparation Time: 15 minutes
Cooking Time: 60 minutes
Servings: 6-8
Ingredients:
- 8 cups cored, peeled, and sliced apples
- 1 tablespoon fresh lemon juice
- ½ cup white sugar
- 2 tablespoons all-purpose flour
- 1 teaspoon ground cinnamon
- ¼ teaspoon ground nutmeg
- A dough of 2 pie crusts (store-bought)
- ¼ cup melted butter
- 1 tablespoon apple cider
- 2 tablespoons heavy whipping cream

Directions:
1. Preheat your smoker to 400-degrees, adding chips to the container. Mix apples, lemon, sugar, flour, cinnamon, and nutmeg in a bowl.
2. Roll out your pie crust into two 11-inch circles. Put one dough circle on a 9-inch pie plate. Brush with melted butter, then add the apple filling.
3. With apple cider, moisten the crust's edges, then cover with the second dough circle. Seal the edges with your fingers.
4. With a knife, make some slits in the top crust and brush with heavy cream. Assuming the smoker is ready now, add the pie and smoke for 50-60 minutes. Cool on a wire rack before serving!

Nutrition: Calories: 529 kCal Protein: 3.1g Carbs: 81g Fat: 23.9g

583. Smoky Lemon Bars

Preparation Time: 15 minutes
Cooking Time: 1 hour & 20 minutes
Servings: 6-8
Ingredients:

- ¾ cup fresh lemon juice
- 1 ½ cups white sugar
- 2 eggs
- 3 egg yolks
- 1 ½ teaspoons cornstarch
- Pinch of salt
- 4 tablespoons cold butter
- ¼ cup olive oil
- ½ tablespoon lemon zest
- 1 ¼ cups flour
- ¼ cup white sugar
- ½ cup powdered sugar
- 1 teaspoon lemon zest
- Pinch of salt
- 10 tablespoons cubed butter
- 3 tablespoons powdered sugar (for serving)

Directions:

1. Preheat your smoker to 350-degrees with wood chips in their container. For now, we're looking at the first list of ingredients.
2. While the smoker heats up, mix lemon juice, sugar, eggs, yolk, cornstarch, and a bit of salt. Pour into a cake pan and smoke for 15 minutes.
3. Stir, then smoke for another 15 minutes. Remove from the smoker. Pour into a saucepan and boil on medium-high.
4. Boil for 60 seconds, then strains into a bowl. Mix in 4 tablespoons butter, oil, and lemon zest.
5. Now for the crust. In a food processor, mix flour, sugar, powdered sugar, lemon zest, and salt. Add in the butter and pulse until you get crumbly dough.
6. Line a 9x9 baking dish using parchment paper and press in the dough. Bake crust for 30 minutes or so until the crust is just turning golden.
7. Pour in the filling and smoke for another 20 minutes. Remove from the smoker and cool to room temperature before sticking in the fridge to chill. Serve with powdered sugar!

Nutrition: Calories: 736 kCal Protein: 6.4g Carbs: 100g Fat: 39.5g

584. Smoked Chocolate

Preparation Time: 15 minutes
Cooking Time: 45 minutes
Servings: 1
Ingredients:

- 2 pounds milk chocolate (at least 1-inch thick)

Directions:

1. Fill a deep cookie sheet with ice and put a grate lined with foil over it. Put your chocolate on it and stick it in the fridge for now.
2. Preheat your smoker to 110-degrees, with wood inside. If it doesn't get that low, preheat it to its lowest temperature.
3. Fill water tray (if you have one) with ice water. When the smoker is smoking, turn it off and put the cookie sheet, grate, and chocolate inside.
4. Smoke for 35-45 minutes, checking on it frequently. It lasts 1 month in the fridge in an airtight container and can also be frozen for 3 months.

Nutrition: Calories: 303 kCal Protein: 4.3g Carbs: 33.7g Fat: 16.8g

585. Smoked Cinnamon Coffee Pie

Preparation Time: 15 minutes
Cooking Time: 35 minutes
Servings: 10
Ingredients:

- 1 lb. vanilla biscuits
- 25 Oreo without filling
- 6 1/2 tbsp butter

The Filling

- 2 ¼ cup unsweetened heavy cream
- ¾ cup granulated sugar
- ½ cup coffee
- 3 tbsp flour
- 7 organic egg yolks

The Topping

- 2/12 cup fluffy whipped cream

Directions:

1. Turn an electric smoker on, set the temperature to 325°F (163°C), and coat a medium pie pan with cooking spray. Place vanilla biscuits, Oreo, and butter in a food processor, then process until combined.
2. Transfer the crust mixture to the prepared pie pan, then press on the pie pan's bottom and

sides. Set aside. Pour heavy cream into a saucepan, then bring to a simmer.

3. Add sugar to the saucepan, then stir until the sugar is completely dissolved. Remove from heat, then let it cool.
4. Place egg yolks in a mixing bowl, then beat until incorporated. Add coffee powder, cinnamon powder, and the cool heavy cream mixture to the mixing bowl, then beat until combined.
5. Strain the filling and pour into the piecrust. Once the smoker has reached the desired temperature, place the pie on the smoker's rack.
6. Smoke the pie and set the time to 35 minutes. Once the filling is set, remove the pie from the smoker and let it cool. Top with whipped cream, then serve.

Nutrition: Calories: 90 kCal Carbs: 18g Fat: 3g Protein: 1g

586. Sweet Smoked Apple

Preparation Time: 15 minutes
Cooking Time: 60 minutes
Servings: 10
Ingredients:

- 2 lb. fresh apples
- ½ cup diced butter
- ½ cup white wine
- ½ cup milk
- ½ tsp pepper
- ¼ tsp nutmeg

Directions:

1. Cut the apples into wedges, then discard the seeds. Turn an electric smoker on and set the temperature to 225°F (107°C).
2. Once the smoker is ready, arrange the apple wedges on the smoker's rack. Close the smoker and set the time to 60 minutes.
3. Once the smoked apples are done, remove them from the smoker and transfer them to a food processor. Add diced apple to the food processor, then season with salt and pepper.
4. Pour white wine and milk into the food processor, then process until incorporated. Transfer to a serving dish, then serve.

Nutrition: Calories: 100 kCal Carbs: 0g Fat: 8g Protein: 7g

587. Smoked Ice Cream with Caramel Sauce

Preparation Time: 15 minutes
Cooking Time: 40 minutes
Servings: 10
Ingredients:

- 1 ½ liter Vanilla ice cream

The Sauce

- 1 cup Double cream
- 1 cup Maple syrup
- 1 cup of sugar

Directions:

1. Turn an electric smoker on and set the temperature to 225°F (107°C). Combine double cream, maple syrup, and sugar in a disposable aluminum pan, then mix well.
2. Place the sauce mixture in the smoker, then set the time to 30 minutes. Smoke the caramel sauce. Once the sauce is done, remove it from the smoker, then let it cool.
3. Set the temperature of the smoker to 400°F (204°C). Place the ice cream in an aluminum pan, and once the smoker has reached the desired temperature, place the ice cream in the smoker.
4. Set the time to 10 minutes and smoke the ice cream.
5. Remove the smoked ice cream from the smoker, then scoop it out and place it on serving cups. Drizzle caramel sauce on top, then serve.

Nutrition: Calories: 193 kCal Carbs: 27g Fat: 8g Protein: 3g

588. Smoked Pears with Buttery Sweet Filling

Preparation Time: 15 minutes
Cooking Time: 0 minutes
Servings: 10
Ingredients:

- 10 fresh pears

The Spice

- 3 tbsp lemon juice

The Filling

- ½ cup butter
- ½ cup brown sugar
- ¼ cup crackers crumbs
- 2 tsp cinnamon
- ½ tsp nutmeg
- ¼ tsp grated lemon zest
- 1 tbsp rum
- 1 tsp vanilla extract

The Topping
- ¾ cup Whipped cream

Directions:
1. Turn an electric smoker on and set the time to 225°F (107°C). Cut the pears into halves lengthwise, then discard the seeds.
2. Brush each halved peach with lemon juice arrange on a baking tray. Place butter in a bowl then melts in a microwave.
3. Once the butter is melted, add brown sugar, and cracker crumbs to the bowl. Season with cinnamon, nutmeg, grated lemon zest, rum, and vanilla extract. Mix until combined.
4. Fill each halved pear with the filling mixture and once the smoker is ready, place the filled pears on the smoker's rack.
5. Set the time to an hour and smoke the pears until the filling is melted. Once the smoked pears are done, remove them from the smoker and let them cool. Garnish each pear with whipped cream, then serve.

Nutrition: Calories: 200 kCal Carbs: 34g Fat: 7g Protein: 2g

589. Smoked Chocolate Bacon Pecan Pie

Preparation Time: 1hr 45 minutes
Cooking Time: 45 minutes
Servings: 8

Ingredients:
- 4 eggs
- 1 cup chopped pecans
- 1 tablespoon of vanilla
- ½ cup semi to sweet chocolate chips
- ½ cup dark corn syrup
- ½ cup light corn syrup
- ¾ cup bacon (crumbled)
- ¼ cup bourbon
- 4 tablespoons or ¼ cup of butter
- ½ cup brown sugar
- ½ cup white sugar
- 1 tablespoon cornstarch
- 1 package refrigerated pie dough
- 16 ounces heavy cream
- ¾ cup white sugar
- ¼ cup bacon
- 1 tablespoon vanilla

Directions:
Pie:
1. Carry Smoker to 350 degrees.
2. Blend 4 tablespoons spread, ½ cup darker sugar, and ½ cup white sugar in a blending bowl.
3. In a different bowl, blend 4 eggs and 1 tablespoon cornstarch and add to blender.
4. Include ½ cup dull corn syrup, ½ cup light corn syrup, ¼ cup whiskey, 1 cup slashed walnuts, 1 cup bacon, and 1 tablespoon vanilla to blend.
5. Spot pie batter in a 9-inch pie skillet.
6. Daintily flour mixture.
7. Uniformly place ½ cup chocolate contributes pie dish.
8. Take blend into the pie dish.
9. Smoke at 350 degrees for 40mins or until the focus is firm.
10. Cool and top with bacon whipped cream.

Bacon whipped Cream:
1. Consolidate fixings (16 ounces substantial cream, ¾ cup white sugar, ¼ cup bacon to finely cleaved, and 1 tablespoon vanilla) and mix at rapid until blend thickens. This formula can be separated into 6mins pie container or custard dishes or filled in as one entire pie.

Nutrition: Calories: 200 kCal Carbs: 18g Fat: 0g Protein: 3g

590. Grilled Smoked Bananas with Dark Chocolate & Toasted Hazelnuts

Preparation Time: 15 minutes
Cooking Time: 5 minutes
Servings: 2-4

Ingredients:
- 4 small bananas, semi-ripe
- ½ tsp. sea salt
- 2-3 tbsp. dark chocolate, chopped fine
- 4-6 tsp. hazelnuts, chopped, toasted
- vanilla ice cream, to serve

Directions:
1. Warm your smoker to 250°F/120°C and soak your woodchips for an hour. Remove the woodchips from the liquid, then pat dry before using.
2. Peel the banana in half so that the top part of the banana is exposed, but the bottom is still sitting in its skin. Make a few slits in the banana, then place them into your smoker for 5 minutes.

3. Remove the bananas from the smoker, then sprinkle with salt, chocolate, and topped nuts. Serve with ice cream and enjoy.

Nutrition: Calories: 185 kCal Carbs: 48g Fat: 1g Protein: 2g

Chapter 11:   Additional Recipes

591. Roasted Turkey with Herb

Preparation Time: 15 Minutes
Cooking Time: 3 Hours 30 Minutes
Servings: 12
Ingredients:

- 14 pounds turkey, cleaned
- 2 tablespoons chopped mixed herbs
- Pork and poultry rub as needed
- ¼ teaspoon ground black pepper
- 3 tablespoons butter, unsalted, melted
- 8 tablespoons butter, unsalted, softened
- 2 cups chicken broth

Directions:

1. Clean the turkey by removing the giblets, wash it inside out, pat dry with paper towels, then place it on a roasting pan and tuck the turkey wings by tiring with butcher's string.
2. Switch on the grill, fill the grill hopper with hickory flavored Pit Boss, power the grill on by using the control panel, select 'smoke' on the temperature dial, or set the temperature to 325 degrees F and let it preheat for a minimum of 15 minutes.
3. Meanwhile, prepared herb butter and for this, take a small bowl, place the softened butter in it, add black pepper and mixed herbs and beat until fluffy.
4. Place some of the prepared herb butter underneath the skin of turkey by using a handle of a wooden spoon, and massage the skin to distribute butter evenly.
5. Then rub the exterior of the turkey with melted butter, season with pork and poultry rub, and pour the broth in the roasting pan.
6. When the grill has preheated, open the lid, place roasting pan containing turkey on the grill grate, shut the grill and smoke for 3 hours and 30 minutes until the internal temperature reaches 165 degrees F and the top has turned golden brown.
7. When done, transfer turkey to a cutting board, let it rest for 30 minutes, then carve it into slices and serve.

Nutrition: Calories: 154.6 kCal Fat: 3.1 g Carbs: 8.4 g Protein: 28.8 g

592. Maple Bourbon Turkey

Preparation Time: 15 minutes
Cooking Time: 3 hours
Servings: 8
Ingredients:

- 1 (12 pounds) turkey
- 8 cup chicken broth
- 1 stick butter (softened)
- 1 teaspoon thyme
- 2 garlic clove (minced)
- 1 teaspoon dried basil
- 1 teaspoon pepper
- 1 teaspoon salt
- 1 tablespoon minced rosemary
- 1 teaspoon paprika
- 1 lemon (wedged)
- 1 onion
- 1 orange (wedged)
- 1 apple (wedged)
- Maple Bourbon Glaze:
- ¾ cup bourbon
- 1/2 cup maple syrup
- 1 stick butter (melted)
- 1 tablespoon lime

Directions:

1. Wash the turkey meat inside and out under cold running water.
2. Insert the onion, lemon, orange and apple into the turkey cavity.
3. In a mixing bowl, combine the butter, paprika, thyme, garlic, basil, pepper, salt, basil and rosemary.
4. Brush the turkey generously with the herb butter mixture.
5. Set a rack into a roasting pan and place the turkey on the rack. Put a 5 cups of chicken broth into the bottom of the roasting pan.
6. Preheat the grill to 350°F with lid closed for 15 minutes, using maple Pit Bosss.
7. Place the roasting pan in the grill and cook for 1 hour.
8. Meanwhile, combine all the maple bourbon glaze ingredients in a mixing bowl. Mix until well combined.

9. Baste the turkey with glaze mixture. Continue cooking, basting turkey every 30 minutes and adding more broth as needed for 2 hours, or until the internal temperature of the turkey reaches 165°F.
10. Take off the turkey from the grill and let it rest for a few minutes. Cut into slices and serve.

Nutrition: Calories 1536 kCal Fat 58.6g Carbs: 24g Protein 20.1g

593.   Thanksgiving Turkey

Preparation Time: 15 minutes
Cooking Time: 4 hours
Servings: 6
Ingredients:
- 2 cups butter (softened)
- 1 tablespoon cracked black pepper
- 2 teaspoons kosher salt
- 2 tablespoons freshly chopped rosemary
- 2 tablespoons freshly chopped parsley
- 2 tablespoons freshly chopped sage
- 2 teaspoons dried thyme
- 6 garlic cloves (minced)
- 1 (18 pound) turkey

Directions:
1. In a mixing bowl, combine the butter, sage, rosemary, 1 teaspoon black pepper, 1 teaspoon salt, thyme, parsley and garlic.
2. Use your fingers to loosen the skin from the turkey.
3. Generously, Rub butter mixture under the turkey skin and all over the turkey as well. 4. Season turkey generously with herb mix. 5. Preheat the grill to 300°F with lid closed for 15 minutes.
4. Place the turkey on the grill and roast for about 4 hours, or until the turkey thigh temperature reaches 160°F.
5. Take out the turkey meat from the grill and let it rest for a few minutes. Cut into sizes and serve.

Nutrition: Calories 278 kCal Fat 30.8g Carbs: 1.6g Protein 0.6g

594.   Pit Boss Turkey Jerky

Preparation Time: 15 minutes
Cooking Time: 4 hours
Servings: 6
Ingredients:
Marinade
- 1 cup pineapple juice
- ½ cup brown sugar
- 2 tablespoons Sirach
- 2 teaspoons onion powder
- 2 tablespoons minced garlic
- 2 tablespoons rice wine vinegar
- 2 tablespoons hoisin
- 1 tablespoon red pepper flakes
- 1 tablespoon coarsely ground black pepper flakes
- 2 cups coconut amino
- 2 jalapenos (thinly sliced)

Meat
- 3 pounds turkey boneless skinless breasts (sliced to ¼ inch thick)

Directions:
1. Pour the marinade mixture ingredients in a container and mix until the ingredients are well combined.
2. Put the turkey slices in a gallon sized zip lock bag and pour the marinade into the bag. Massage the marinade into the turkey. Seal the bag and refrigerate for 8 hours.
3. Remove the turkey slices from the marinade.
4. Activate the Pit Boss grill for smoking and leave lip opened for 5 minutes until fire starts.
5. Close the lid and preheat your Pit Boss grill to 180°F, using hickory Pit Boss.
6. Remove the turkey slices from the marinade and pat them dry with a paper towel.
7. Arrange the turkey slices on the grill in a single layer. Smoke the turkey for about 3 to 4 hours, turning often after the first 2 hours of smoking. The jerky should be dark and dry when it is done.
8. Remove the jerky from the grill and let it sit for about 1 hour to cool. Serve immediately or store in refrigerator.

Nutrition: Calories: 109 kCal Carbs: 12g Fat: 1g Protein: 14g

595. Slow Roasted Shawarma

Preparation Time: 30 minutes
Cooking Time: 4 Hours
Servings: 1
Ingredients:

- 5 ½ lbs. of chicken thighs; boneless, skinless
- 4 ½ lbs. of lamb fat
- Pita bread
- 5 ½ lbs. of top sirloin
- 2 yellow onions; large
- 4 tablespoons of rub
- Desired toppings like pickles, tomatoes, fries, salad and more

Directions:

1. Slice the meat and fat into ½" slices and place then in 3 separate bowls
2. Season each of the bowls with the rub and massage the rub into the meat to make sure it seeps well
3. Now place half of the onion at the base of each half skewer. This will make for a firm base
4. Add 2 layers from each of the bowls at a time
5. Make the track as symmetrical as you can
6. Now, put the other 2 half onions at the top of this
7. Wrap it in a plastic wrap and let it refrigerate overnight
8. Set the grill to preheat keeping the temperature to 275 degrees F
9. Lay the shawarma on the grill grate and let it cook for approx. 4 hours. Make sure to turn it at least once
10. Remove from the grill and shoot the temperature to 445 degrees F
11. Now place a cast iron griddle on the grill grate and pour it with olive oil
12. When the griddle has turned hot, place the whole shawarma on the cast iron and smoke it for 5 to 10 minutes per side
13. Remove from the grill and slice off the edges
14. Repeat the same with the leftover shawarma
15. Serve in pita bread and add the chosen toppings
16. Enjoy

Nutrition: Calories: 171 kCal Carbs: 10 g Protein: 29 g Fat: 15g

596. Duck Poppers

Preparation Time: 30 minutes
Cooking Time: 4 Hours
Servings: 1
Ingredients:

- 8 – 10 pieces of bacon, cut event into same-sized pieces measuring 4 inches each
- 3 duck breasts; boneless and with skin removed and sliced into strips measuring ½ inches
- Sriracha sauce
- 6 de-seeded jalapenos, with the top cut off and sliced into strips

Directions:

1. Wrap the bacon around one trip of pepper and one slice of duck
2. Secure it firmly with the help of a toothpick
3. Fire the grill on low flame and keep this wrap and grill it for half an hour until the bacon turns crisp
4. Rotate often to ensure even cooking
5. Serve with sriracha sauce

Nutrition: Calories: 164 kCal Carbs: 2 g Protein: 9 g Fat: 15g

597. Baked Garlic Parmesan Wings

Preparation Time: 30 minutes
Cooking Time: 3 Hours
Servings: 1
Ingredients:
For the chicken wings

- 5lbs. of chicken wings
- ½ cup of chicken rub

For the garnish

- 1 cup of shredded parmesan cheese
- 3 tablespoons of chopped parsley

For the sauce

- 10 cloves of finely diced garlic
- 1 cup of butter
- 2 tablespoon of chicken rub

Directions:

1. Set the grill on preheat by keeping the temperature to high
2. Take a large bowl and toss the wings in it along with the chicken rub
3. Now place the wings directly on the grill grate and cook it for 10 minutes
4. Flip it and cook for the ten minutes

5. Check the internal temperature and it needs to reach in the range of 165 to 180 degrees F

For the garlic sauce

1. Take a midsized saucepan and mix garlic, butter, and the leftover rub.
2. Cook it over medium heat on a stovetop
3. Cook for 10 minutes while stirring in between to avoid the making of lumps
4. Now when the wings have been cooked, remove them from the grill and place in a large bowl
5. Toss the wings with garlic sauce along with parsley and parmesan cheese
6. Serve and enjoy

Nutrition: Calories: 330 kCal Carbs: 10g Protein: 23g Fat: 22g

598. Grilled Chicken in Pit Boss

Preparation Time: 10 minutes
Cooking Time: 30 minutes
Servings: 8
Ingredients:

- Whole chicken - 4-5 lbs.
- Grilled chicken mix

Directions:

1. Preheat the Pit Boss grill with the 'smoke' option for 5 minutes.
2. Preheat another 10 minutes and keep the temperature on high until it reaches 450 degrees.
3. Use baker's twine to tie the chicken's legs together.
4. Keep the breast side up when you place the chicken in the grill.
5. Grill for 70 minutes. Do not open the grill during this process.
6. Check the temperature of your grilled chicken. Make sure it is 165 degrees. If not, leave the chicken in for longer.
7. Carefully take the chicken out of the grill.
8. Set aside for 15 minutes.
9. Cut and serve.

Nutrition: Calories: 284 kCal Carbs: 0 g Protein: 57 g Fat: 6 g

599. Chicken Wings in Pit Boss

Preparation Time: 10 minutes
Cooking Time: 50 minutes
Servings: 1
Ingredients:

- Chicken wings - 6-8 lbs.
- Canola oil – 1/3 cup
- Barbeque seasoning mix - 1 tablespoon

Directions:

1. Combine the seasonings and oil in one large bowl.
2. Put the chicken wings in the bowl and mix well.
3. Turn your Pit Boss to the 'smoke' setting and leave it on for 4-5 minutes.
4. Set the heat to 350 degrees and leave it to preheat for 15 minutes with the lid closed.
5. Place the wings on the grill with enough space between the pieces.
6. Let it cook for 45 minutes or until the skin looks crispy.
7. Remove from the grill and serve with your choice of sides.

Nutrition: Calories: 95 kCal Protein: 5 g Fat: 8 g Carbs: 3g

600. Orange Bread Pudding

Preparation Time: 15 minutes
Cooking Time: 1 hour & 40 minutes
Servings: 6-8
Ingredients:

- 8 cups cubed brioche bread
- 3 cups heavy whipping cream
- 2 cups whole milk
- 1 ½ cups white sugar
- Pinch of salt
- Zest of 2 oranges
- 4 eggs
- 2 egg yolks
- 1 teaspoon orange extract

Directions:

1. Preheat your smoker to 230-degrees with the wood chips in the container. In a foil pan, arrange bread cubes in a single layer.
2. When the smoker is ready, add pan and smoke for 40 minutes. While that smokes, put the cream, milk, sugar, and salt in a saucepan.
3. Boil, whisking, to dissolve the sugar. Remove the pan from the hot stovetop. Add orange zest. Put

eggs, egg yolks, and orange extract in a bowl and mix.

4. Slowly and carefully whisk in the hot mixture. Add your smoked bread cubes and let them soak for 10 minutes or so on the counter.
5. Grease a smoker-safe skillet and pour in the bread pudding. Smoke for 40 minutes, then check to see if the bread is puffy and golden and the custard has set. Serve warm!

Nutrition: Calories: 533 kCal Protein: 9g Carbs: 59g Fat: 30.9g

601. Grilled Apple Pie

Preparation Time: 15 minutes
Cooking Time: 30-40 minutes
Servings: 6
Ingredients:

- 4-5 apples, thinly sliced
- 1/4 cup (50g) sugar
- 1 tbsp. cornstarch
- flour
- 1 refrigerated pie crust, softened as directed on box
- 1/4 cup (80g) peach preserve

Directions:

1. Preheat your smoker to 375°F/190°C and soak your woodchips for an hour. Remove the woodchips from the liquid, then pat dry before using.
2. Then take a medium bowl and add the apples, sugar, and cornstarch, then stir well until combined. Pop to one side.
3. Now dust your work surface with flour and roll out the pie crust. Place the pie crust into a pie pan without greasing it first.
4. Spread the preserve into the bottom of the pie, then top with apple slices. Pop into the smoker and cook for 30-40 minutes until bubbly and brown.
5. Remove from the smoker, let it rest for 10 minutes, then serve and enjoy!

Nutrition: Calories: 270 kCal Carbs: 34g Fat: 14g Protein: 3g

602. Pear and Fig Upside Down Cake

Preparation Time: 15 minutes
Cooking Time: 35-45 minutes
Servings: 8
Ingredients:
For the cake

- 1 tbsp. unsalted butter, for greasing
- 9 tbsp unsalted butter, room temperature
- ¾ cup (150g) granulated sugar
- 3 free-range eggs
- 1 tsp. vanilla
- 1 ½ cups (190g) cake flour, sifted
- ¾ tsp. baking powder
- ¼ tsp. baking soda
- 8 tbsp. sour cream
- ¼ tsp. salt

For the fruit and glaze

- 1 pear, cut into slices, lengthwise
- 4 grapes, cut in half
- 4 tbsp. unsalted butter, room temperature
- ½ cup (100g) brown sugar

Directions:

1. Preheat your smoker to 350°F/175°C and soak your woodchips for an hour. Remove the woodchips from the liquid, then pat dry before using.
2. Grab a 10" (25cm) cake pan and grease well with butter. Take a medium bowl and cream the butter and sugar together.
3. Put the fruit into the bottom of the cake pan, then put the sugar and butter mixture (from the fruit and glaze ingredients) over the top. Pop to one side.
4. Take another bowl and add the butter and sugar, then beat until light and fluffy. Add the eggs and the vanilla, then beat for another minute.
5. Lastly, add the flour, baking powder, baking soda, sour cream, and salt, then stir well to combine. Pour this cake batter over the fruit, then pop it into the smoker.
6. Cook for 35-45 minutes until cooked through. Remove from the smoker, rest for 10 minutes, then serve and enjoy.

Nutrition: Calories: 260 kCal Carbs: 34g Fat: 13g Protein: 3g

603. Baked Lemon Meringue Pie

Preparation Time: 15 minutes
Cooking Time: 0 minutes
Servings: 6-8
Ingredients:
For filling

- 1 ½ cups (300g) sugar
- 2/3 cup (160ml) lemon juice
- 1 tbsp. lemon zest
- pinch of salt
- 4 tbsp. unsalted butter
- 3 free-range eggs + 3 egg yolks

For Pie

- 1 pie dough
- 1 tbsp. heavy cream
- 1 free-range egg

For meringue

- 3 egg whites
- 4-5 tbsp. sugar
- 1 tsp. vanilla extract

Directions:

1. Warm your smoker to 250°F/120°C and soak your woodchips for an hour. Remove the woodchips from the liquid, then pat dry before using.
2. Take a medium bowl and add the sugar, lemon juice, lemon zest, and salt. Stir well to combine. Pour this mixture onto a greased baking sheet, then place it into your smoker for 30 minutes. Remove from the smoker and set to one side.
3. Turn up the temperature of your smoker to 350°F/175°C and grease your pie dish. Lightly flour your work surface and start to roll out the pie dough until it's approximately 1/8" (1/4 cm).
4. Place into the pie dish, then push down well. Pop into the freezer for 30 minutes. Meanwhile, take a small bowl and add the cream and one of the eggs.
5. Stir well to combine, then brush over the edges of the pie. Transfer the pie to the smoker and cook for 10 minutes. Remove and allow it to cool.
6. For the filling, put 3 eggs and 3 egg yolks (keep hold of whites), whisk, and stir in the lemon mixture in a large bowl. Mix well.
7. Using a Bain Marie or double boiler, warm the lemon mixture for 10 minutes until it thickens nicely. Keep stirring. Remove this filling from the heat and whisk in the butter.
8. Pour the lemon mixture into the pie crust and place back into the smoker for 20 minutes until the filling has been set. Cool overnight in the fridge.
9. Put the egg whites into a bowl with the sugar for your meringue, then place in a Bain Marie or double boiler to warm through. Keep stirring until the sugar has dissolved.
10. Remove from the heat, then beat with a whisk until the egg whites are white and fluffy. Add the vanilla, then beat again.
11. Pipe the meringue mixture onto the top of the pie, then use a kitchen torch to brown the top. Serve and enjoy!

Nutrition: Calories: 310 kCal Carbs: 51g Fat: 12g Protein: 2g

604. Molten Lava Chocolate Cake

Preparation Time: 15 minutes
Cooking Time: 0 minutes
Servings: 4-6
Ingredients:

- melted butter, for greasing
- extra flour, for coating the ramekins
- ½ cup (115g) butter
- 1 cup (170g) bittersweet chocolate
- 2 free-range eggs plus 2 yolks
- ½ cup (110g) sugar
- pinch of salt
- 2 tbsp. all-purpose flour

Directions:

1. Preheat your smoker to 450°F/230°C and soak your woodchips for an hour. Remove the woodchips from the liquid, then pat dry before using.
2. Then take four ramekins and butter and flour them well. Place them onto a baking sheet and pop to one side.
3. Using a Bain Marie or double boiler, melt the butter and the chocolate together over simmering heat, stirring well to combine. Remove and allow it to cool.
4. Take a medium bowl and beat the eggs and egg yolks with the sugar and salt until thick. Pour in the cooled chocolate and stir well, then stir through the flour.

5. Spoon the butter into your pre-prepared ramekins, then place it into the smoker. Cook for 20 minutes until the edges are firm.
6. Remove from the smoker, leave to rest for a minute, then serve and enjoy!

Nutrition: Calories: 250 kCal Carbs: 32g Fat: 13g Protein: 6g

605. Spicy Sausage & Cheese Balls

Preparation Time: 20 minutes
Cooking Time: 40 minutes
Servings: 4
Ingredients:
- 1lb Hot Breakfast Sausage
- 2 cups Bisquick Baking Mix
- 8 ounces Cream Cheese
- 8 ounces Extra Sharp Cheddar Cheese
- 1/4 cup Fresno Peppers
- 1 tablespoon Dried Parsley
- 1 teaspoon Killer Hogs AP Rub
- 1/2 teaspoon Onion Powder

Directions:
1. Get ready smoker or flame broil for roundabout cooking at 400 degrees F.
2. Blend Sausage, Baking Mix, destroyed cheddar, cream cheddar, and remaining fixings in a huge bowl until all-around fused.
3. Utilize a little scoop to parcel blend into chomp to estimate balls and roll tenderly fit as a fiddle.
4. Spot wiener and cheddar balls on a cast-iron container and cook for 15mins.
5. Present with your most loved plunging sauces.

Nutrition: Calories: 95 kCal Carbs: 4g Fat: 7g Protein: 5g

606. White Chocolate Bread Pudding

Preparation Time: 20 minutes
Cooking Time: 1hr 15 minutes
Servings: 12
Ingredients:
- 1 loaf of French bread
- 4 cups Heavy Cream
- 3 Large Eggs
- 2 cups White Sugar
- 1 package White Chocolate morsels
- ¼ cup Melted Butter
- 2 teaspoons Vanilla
- 1 teaspoon Ground Nutmeg

- 1 teaspoon Salt
- Bourbon White Chocolate Sauce
- 1 package White Chocolate morsels
- 1 cup Heavy Cream
- 2 tablespoons Melted Butter
- 2 tablespoons Bourbon
- ½ teaspoon Salt

Directions:
1. Get ready pellet smoker or any flame broil/smoker for backhanded cooking at 350 degrees F.
2. Tear French bread into little portions and spot it in a massive bowl. Pour four cups of Heavy Cream over Bread and douse for 30mins.
3. Join eggs, sugar, softened spread, and vanilla in a medium to estimate bowl. Include a package of white chocolate pieces and a delicate blend. Season with Nutmeg and Salt.
4. Pour egg combo over the splashed French bread and blend to sign up for.
5. Pour the combination right into a properly to buttered nine X 13 to inchmeal dish and spot it at the smoker.
6. Cook for 60Secs or until bread pudding has set and the top is darker.
7. For the sauce: Melt margarine in a saucepot over medium warm temperature. Add whiskey and hold on cooking for three to 4mins until liquor vanished and margarine begins to darkish-colored.
8. Include vast cream and heat till a mild stew. Take from the warmth and consist of white chocolate pieces a bit at a time continuously blending until the complete percent has softened. Season with a hint of salt and serve over bread pudding.

Nutrition: Calories: 372 kCal Carbs: 31g Fat: 25g Protein: 5g

607. Cheesy Jalapeño Skillet Dip

Preparation Time: 10 minutes
Cooking Time: 15 minutes
Servings: 8
Ingredients:

- 8 ounces cream cheese
- 16 ounces shredded cheese
- 1/3 cup mayonnaise
- 4 ounces diced green chilies
- 3 fresh jalapeños
- 2 teaspoons Killer Hogs AP Rub
- 2 teaspoons Mexican Style Seasoning

For the topping

- ¼ cup Mexican Blend Shredded Cheese
- Sliced jalapeños
- Mexican Style Seasoning
- 3 tablespoons Killer Hogs AP Rub
- 2 tablespoons Chili Powder
- 2 tablespoons Paprika
- 2 teaspoons Cumin
- ½ teaspoon Granulated Onion
- ¼ teaspoon Cayenne Pepper
- ¼ teaspoon Chipotle Chili Pepper ground
- ¼ teaspoon Oregano

Directions:

1. Preheat smoker or flame broil for roundabout cooking at 350 degree
2. Join fixings in a big bowl and spot in a cast to press skillet
3. Top with Mexican Blend destroyed cheddar and cuts of jalapeno's
4. Spot iron skillet on flame broil mesh and cook until cheddar hot and bubbly and the top has seared
5. Marginally about 25mins.
6. Serve warm with enormous corn chips (scoops), tortilla chips, or your preferred vegetables for plunging.

Nutrition: Calories: 150 kCal Carbs: 22g Fat: 6g Protein: 3g

608. Cajun Turkey Club

Preparation Time: 5 Minutes
Cooking Time: 10 Minutes
Servings: 3
Ingredients:

- 1 3lbs Turkey Breast
- 1 stick Butter (melted)
- 8 ounces Chicken Broth
- 1 tablespoon Killer Hogs Hot Sauce
- 1/4 cup Malcolm's King Craw Seasoning
- 8 Pieces to Thick Sliced Bacon
- 1 cup Brown Sugar
- 1 head Green Leaf Lettuce
- 1 Tomato (sliced)
- 6 slices Toasted Bread
- ½ cup Cajun Mayo
- 1 cup Mayo
- 1 tablespoon Dijon Mustard
- 1 tablespoon Killer Hogs Sweet Fire Pickles (chopped)
- 1 tablespoon Horseradish
- ½ teaspoon Malcolm's King Craw Seasoning
- 1 teaspoon Killer Hogs Hot Sauce
- Pinch of Salt & Black Pepper to taste

Directions:

1. Get ready pellet smoker for backhanded cooking at 325 degrees F utilizing your preferred wood pellets for enhancing.
2. Join dissolved margarine, chicken stock, hot sauce, and 1 tbsp of Cajun Seasoning in a blending bowl. Infuse the blend into the turkey bosom scattering the infusion destinations for even inclusion.
3. Shower the outside of the turkey bosom with a Vegetable cooking splash and season with Malcolm's King Craw Seasoning.
4. Spot the turkey bosom on the smoker and cook until the inside temperature arrives at 165 degrees. Utilize a moment-read thermometer to screen temp during the cooking procedure.
5. Consolidate darker sugar and 1 teaspoon of King Craw in a little bowl. Spread the bacon with the sugar blend and spot it on a cooling rack.
6. Cook the bacon for 12 to 15mins or until darker. Make certain to turn the bacon part of the way through for cooking.
7. Toast the bread, cut the tomatoes dainty, and wash/dry the lettuce leaves.
8. At the point when the turkey bosom arrives at 165 take it from the flame broil and rest for 15mins. Take the netting out from around the bosom and cut into slender cuts.
9. To cause the sandwich: To slather Cajun Mayo* on the toast, stack on a few cuts of turkey bosom, lettuce, tomato, and bacon. Include

another bit of toast and rehash a similar procedure. Include the top bit of toast slathered with more Cajun mayo, cut the sandwich into equal parts and appreciate.

Nutrition: Calories: 130 kCal Carbs: 1g Fat: 4g Protein: 21g

609. Juicy Cheeseburger

Preparation Time: 10 minutes
Cooking Time: 10 minutes
Servings: 6
Ingredients:
- 2 lbs. ground beef
- 1 egg beaten
- 1 Cup dry bread crumbs
- 3 tablespoons evaporated milk
- 2 tablespoons Worcestershire sauce
- 1 tablespoon Grilla Grills All Purpose Rub
- 4 slices of cheddar cheese
- 4 buns

Directions:
1. Start by consolidating the hamburger, egg, dissipated milk, Worcestershire and focus on a bowl. Utilize your hands to blend well. Partition this blend into 4 equivalent parts. At that point take every one of the 4 pieces and partition them into equal parts. Take every one of these little parts and smooth them. The objective is to have 8 equivalent level patties that you will at that point join into 4 burgers.
2. When you have your patties smoothed, place your cheddar in the center and afterward place the other patty over this and firmly squeeze the sides to seal. You may even need to push the meat back towards the inside a piece to shape a marginally thicker patty. The patties ought to be marginally bigger than a standard burger bun as they will recoil a bit during cooking.
3. Preheat your Kong to 300 degrees.
4. Keep in mind during flame broiling that you fundamentally have two meager patties, one on each side, so the Cooking Time ought not to have a place. You will cook these for 5 to 8mins per side—closer to 5mins on the off chance that you favor an uncommon burger or more towards 8mins if you like a well-to-done burger.
5. At the point when you flip the burgers, take a toothpick and penetrate the focal point of the

burger to permit steam to get away. This will shield you from having a hit to out or having a visitor who gets a jaw consume from liquid cheddar as they take their first nibble.
6. Toss these on a pleasant roll and top with fixings that supplement whatever your burgers are loaded down with.

Nutrition: Calories: 300 kCal Carbs: 33g Fat: 12g Protein: 15g

610. No-Flip Burgers

Preparation Time: 30 minutes
Cooking Time: 30 minutes
Servings: 2
Ingredients:
- Ground Beef Patties
- Grilla Grills Beef Rub
- Choice of Cheese
- Choice of Toppings
- Pretzel Buns

Directions:
1. To start, you'll need to begin with freezing yet not solidified meat patties. This will help guarantee that you don't overcook your burgers. Liberally sprinkle on our Beef Rub or All to Purpose Rub and delicately knead into the two sides of the patty. As another option, you can likewise season with salt and pepper and some garlic salt.
2. Preheat your wood pellet to 250 degrees Fahrenheit and cook for about 45mins. Contingent upon the thickness of your burgers you will need to keep an eye on them after around 30 to 45mins, yet there's no compelling reason to flip. For a medium to uncommon burger, we recommend cooking to about 155 degrees.
3. After the initial 30 to 40mins, if you like loose cheddar on your burger feel free to leave it up. Close your barbecue back up and let them up for another 10mins before taking it up. For an additional punch of flavor, finish your burger off with a sprinkle of Grilla Grill's Gold 'N Bold sauce. Appreciate.

Nutrition: Calories: 190 kCal Carbs: 17g Fat: 9g Protein: 13g

611. Juicy Smokey Burger

Preparation Time: 30 minutes
Cooking Time: 30 minutes
Servings: 2
Ingredients:

- 1 pound Beef
- 1/3 pound per burger
- Cheddar cheese
- Grilla AP Rub
- Salt
- Freshly Ground Black Pepper
- Hamburger Bun
- BBQ Sauce

Directions:

1. Split every 1/3 pound of meat, which is 2.66 ounces per half.
2. Level out one half to roughly six inches plate. Put wrecked of American cheddar, leaving 1/2 inch clear.
3. Put another portion of the meat on top, and seal edges. Rehash for all burgers.
4. Sprinkle with Grilla AP rub, salt, and pepper flame broil seasonings.
5. Smoke at 250 for 50mins. No compelling reason to turn.
6. Apply Smokey Dokey BBQ sauce, ideally a mustard-based sauce like Grilla Gold and Bold, or Sticky Fingers Carolina Classic. Cook for an extra 10 minutes, or to favored doneness.

Nutrition: Calories: 264 Carbs: 57g Fat: 2g Protein: 4g

612. Grilled Fruit with Cream

Preparation Time: 15 minutes
Cooking Time: 10 minutes
Servings: 6
Ingredients:

- 2 halved Apricot
- 1 halved Nectarine
- 2 halved peaches
- ¼ cup of Blueberries
- ½ cup of Raspberries
- 2 tablespoons of Honey
- 1 orange, the peel
- 2 cups of Cream
- ½ cup of Balsamic Vinegar

Directions:

1. Preheat the grill to 400F with a closed lid.
2. Grill the peaches, nectarines, and apricots for 4 minutes on each side.
3. Place a pan over the stove and turn on medium heat. Add 2 tablespoons of honey, vinegar, and orange peel. Simmer until medium thick.
4. In the meantime, add honey and cream in a bowl. Whip until it reaches a soft form.
5. Place the fruits on a serving plate. Sprinkle with berries. Drizzle with balsamic reduction. Serve with cream and enjoy!

Nutrition: Calories: 230 Protein: 3g Carbs: 35g Fat: 3g

APPENDIX

Wood Smoking Flavor Table

FLAVOR	🐄	🐑	🐖	🐔	🦌	🐟	🦞	🍞	🥕
HICKORY	✓		✓	✓	✓			✓	✓
APPLE		✓	✓	✓				✓	✓
MESQUITE	✓			✓	✓	✓			
CHERRY	✓	✓	✓	✓				✓	✓
MAPLE	✓		✓			✓		✓	✓
PECAN	✓		✓	✓	✓			✓	✓
WHISKEY BARREL	✓				✓	✓	✓	✓	
ALDER	✓	✓	✓	✓		✓	✓	✓	✓
COMPETITION	✓	✓	✓	✓	✓	✓	✓	✓	✓
OAK	✓				✓	✓	✓	✓	
CHARCOAL	✓		✓	✓	✓				✓
CLASSIC	✓	✓	✓	✓	✓	✓			✓
FRUITWOOD		✓	✓	✓				✓	✓
TROPHY	✓		✓	✓	✓				

Internal Temperature Chart

DONENESS TEMPERATURE FOR MEAT, POULTRY AND FISH

INGREDIENT	STOP COOKING WHEN TEMPERATURE REACHES	FINAL SERVING TEMPERATURE
BEEF & LAMB		
Rare	115 - 120°F	120 - 125°F (after resting)
Medium-Rare	120 - 125°F	125 - 130°F (after resting)
Medium	130 - 135°F	135 - 140°F (after resting)
Medium-Well	140 - 145°F	145 - 150°F (after resting)
Well-Done	150 - 155°F	150 - 160°F (after resting)
PORK		
Medium	140 - 145°F	145 - 150°F (after resting)
Well-Done	150 - 155°F	155 - 160°F (after resting)
CHICKEN		
Whilte Meat	160°F	160°F
Dark Meat	175°F	175°F
FISH		
Rare	110°F (for tuna only)	110°F
Medium-Rare	125°F (for tuna or salmon)	125°F
Medium	140°F (for white-fleshed fish)	140°F

Conclusion

Some cooks argue that wood pellets are a more desirable option because they can be used in any manner of cooking. This is true, but there are some errors made by people who think that wood pellets won't have to be soaked first. In reality, soaking them will make the process much easier and ensure they heat properly.

While the initial investment may seem expensive, it's actually cheaper than propane or charcoal since it doesn't have to be replaced every few hours. This eliminates downtime for the cook and makes a stronger smoking product with less trash and less mess to clean up afterward.

It's important to make sure that the pellets are being soaked for a long enough period of time, as there will be a lengthy gap between when the product is created and when it will be used. The perfect amount of time to soak the wood pellets is 48 hours. This will make sure they're dry enough to use immediately and will also ensure they're completely saturated so they burn cleanly.

With proper planning and sufficient preparation, wood pellets are a fantastic alternative that can provide a similar level of taste without causing damage to the environment or putting people out in the cold. The best way to make sure you use wood pellet grills is to make sure they're clean and work properly.

If you have wood pellets that are three years old, it's a good idea to look at how they've been cared for.

Replacing the pellets can be done with simple tools, such as a shovel or even a rake. You'll want to take the time to scrape off any build up on the grill and smooth out any irregularities. When this has been done, you can replace them with new ones to ensure proper heating.

They can be used for cooking almost any type of meat or seafood, making it a great choice for you.

To ensure high-quality results from your wood pellet grill, start by selecting the right type of pellets. There are several types of pellets on the market that provide different types of flavoring and taste to food; however, unless you want to experiment with different food types, stick with the ones that are already known.

There are several kinds of pellets available and you should buy the ones that will work for your needs. If you don't want to experiment with different types, stick with what is known as smokeless pellets, also known as sawdust-based pellets. These are made from sawdust and dolomite powder. They typically have a long burn time and they produce much cooler flames than other kinds of wood pellet grills. Other types of pellets may be available on the market; however, these are not considered safe because they can burn too quickly for a beneficial result.

The temperature of the grill should be considered as well. While most grills can reach above 350 degrees Fahrenheit, that doesn't mean it's the best temperature for cooking.

The most important step in any wood pellet cooking process is the seasoning process. This will ensure that the pellets are soaked for long enough and it will help make sure they burn at a proper rate on the grill. For this reason alone, it's vital to follow instructions when it comes to soaking these pellets. You'll want to make sure they're dry enough to use immediately and that they don't leave a lot of residue behind when they're used. This is important for preserving the flavor as well. Moisture can affect how these pellets burn, so it's vital to keep this in mind.

Much like any type of pellet grill, you'll need to start with clean pellets. This can be done by simply removing the ash from the pellets and making sure they're not mildewed or damaged.

It's important that you understand how your grill works before trying to cook with wood pellets. Different types of grills will require a different amount of time for the pellets to burn at an effective rate. While some can burn as quickly as 15 minutes, others may require up to 45 minutes or more for them to reach temperatures at which they should be used.

Warming the grill up before you start is also a good idea. This will ensure that the temperature will be at an optimal level for cooking when you begin to cook. You should also wear pot holders or another type of thick glove as you work with your grill, especially if there is a lot of ash inside the grill.

When it comes to wood pellet grilling, there are two important steps and these are knowing how much pellets are needed and making sure they're ready to go before starting the process. This can be done by simply measuring the space available and then measuring your guests. You can figure out one pound of pellets per person for a meal, but if you're making food for more than three people, you may need to account for more than one pound of pellets per person. The second step is getting the wood pellets ready to use.

Pellet grills are very simple devices that you can use in your home to cook food or even just warm it up if it's cold outside. As long as you've got the right kind of grill, there's a lot that you can do with this type of grill. When it comes to wood pellet grills, you'll need the right kind of pellets as well. This is largely a personal preference. Some people will prefer different types of wood or pellets that smoke better than others. That's up to you and your personal preferences.

In my opinion, safety is a bit far down on the list for some people and, as I mentioned, it may not even be as important to you as other things. For most people, however, these things should be a top priority when it comes to cheap pellet grills so they can keep their families safe from harm and have themselves some nice grilling times if they want to go that route by spending a little more money on something that works well.

Most of the time, it's grilling for one or two people. I've got a couple that can grill for four, but it takes a bit of planning and preparation. That's why there's usually only one of us using the grill at any given time on a typical day when we own our home and probably 90% or more of the time when we don't feel like working outside.

Wood pellet smoker and grills are an excellent cooking option for anyone living in a small apartment. They use about as much electricity as your average lightbulb, so they're surprisingly energy efficient. Best of all, they don't emit any smoke or odors, so there's no need to worry about your neighbors!

You might opt for a smoker that uses electric or gas heat, but the flavor won't even be close to that generated from a wood pellet smoker.

How can you tell if you're getting the best wood pellet grill?

You'll want one with an easy to clean design. It needs to have aspects such as an ash pan and drip tray that are simple and easy to remove before cleaning. While it's recommended that you do clean your smoker at least once a week, that's not always possible with busy schedules. Having one with an easy to clean design will help you keep up with maintenance easier than ever before.

You'll want one with the right sized hopper as well. This will determine the amount of pellets you need to purchase as well as how often you burn wood. Buying too much will only make the heating process take longer and cost more. On the other hand, buying too little will make it harder for your smoker to generate heat.

You'll want a smoker that has a decent sized firebox. The firebox is the part that traps and burns the wood pellet. A badly designed one might not be able to keep up with your burning wood pellet supply, which can end up making it really hard to keep up with your cooking or grilling needs!

It should have great temperature control options as well as an easy-to-use ash catcher. If you're going to be using your smoker for smoking meats, then it's very important that you do not make it more difficult than it has to be. One thing is certain, a poorly designed pellet smoker can end up ruining your perfect meal.

Your wood pellet smoker should have an easy-to-use temperature gauge and an automatic ash catcher. With these features, making sure you don't burn the food becomes easier than ever before!

There are so many types of wood pellet smokers out there on the market that it can be a real chore trying to decide which one is right for you. This guide helps you find the best wood pellet smoker by showing you which ones are made from high-quality materials, and which ones boast amazing customer service.

While it's a good idea to shop around, it's important to do your research before you make any purchases. Descriptions can be deceiving! There are those that boast about how great they are, but when you get them home and try them out, you're left with a lot of disappointment.

It's also important to read reviews before making any purchases. As we stated earlier, descriptions can be deceiving! That's why it's important to find other people who have bought a smoker and ask them what they think of it.

If you have the money, then it makes sense to invest in one with as many features as possible.

When choosing your smoker, go for one that has high-quality construction and customer service that can help if something breaks or goes wrong.

Printed in Great Britain
by Amazon